SOCIAL Studies

United States History to 1865

HOUGHTON MIFFLIN HARCOURT
School Publishers

Series Authors

Dr. Michael J. Berson
Professor
Social Science Education
University of South Florida
Tampa, Florida

Dr. Tyrone C. Howard
Associate Professor
UCLA Graduate School of Education &
Information Studies
University of California Los Angeles
Los Angeles, California

Sara Shoob
Adjunct Instructor
George Mason University
Retired Social Studies Coordinator
Fairfax County Public Schools

Dr. Cinthia Salinas
Associate Professor
Department of Curriculum and
Instruction
College of Education
The University of Texas at Austin
Austin, Texas

Virginia Consultants and Reviewers

Aliceyn S. Applewhite
Teacher
Park View Elementary School
Portsmouth, VA

Becky W. Baskerville
Principal
Sutherland Elementary School
Sutherland, Virginia

Deanna Beacham
Weapemeoc
Virginia Indian History Consultant
Mechanicsville, Virginia

Lauren W. Berents
Teacher
Shady Grove Elementary School
Glen Allen, Virginia

Katherine R. Bohn
Teacher
Glen Forest Elementary School
Falls Church, Virginia

Kim Briggs
Teacher
Leesville Road Elementary School
Lynchburg, Virginia

Susan K. Dalton
Teacher
Woodstock Elementary School
Virginia Beach, Virginia

James J. Doran
Teacher
Olive Branch Elementary School
Portsmouth, Virginia

Agnes Dunn
Retired Coordinator for Social Studies
Stafford County Public Schools

Jeanie Hawks
Instructional Technology Specialist
Halifax County Public Schools

Sarah Duncan Hinds
Social Studies Instructional Specialist
Portsmouth Public Schools
Portsmouth, Virginia

Carter H. McIntyre
Teacher
Laurel Meadow Elementary School
Mechanicsville, Virginia

Rebecca Mills
Supervisor of Social Studies
Spotsylvania County Public Schools

Linda C. Owen
Supervisor of Elementary Instruction
Halifax County

Jaime Ratliff
Teacher
Stonewall Elementary School
Clearbrook, Virginia

Tanya Lee Siwik
Teacher
Kings Park Elementary School
Springfield, Virginia

Evelyn Soltes
Title 1 Specialist for School
Improvement
Richmond Public Schools
Richmond, Virginia

Andrea Nelson Tavenner
Teacher
Swift Creek Elementary School
Midlothian, Virginia

Kathryn Clawson Watkins
Retired Teacher
Chesterfield County

Cathy H. Whittecar
Teacher
Centerville Elementary School
Virginia Beach, Virginia

Karenne Wood
Monacan
Director
Virginia Indian Heritage Program
Kents Store, Virginia

Copyright © 2011 by Houghton Mifflin Harcourt Publishing Company

Printed in the U.S.A.

ISBN-13: 978-0-15-384352-5
ISBN-10: 0-15-384352-7

4 5 6 7 8   1421   14 13 12 11
4500311577

Planet Friendly Publishing
Made in the United States
Text printed on 100%
Recycled Paper
By using this paper,
Houghton Mifflin Harcourt
achieved the following
environmental benefits:

GREEN EDITION

- **Trees Saved: 79**
- **Air Emissions Eliminated: 18,446 pounds**
- **Water Saved: 15,237 gallons**
- **Solid Waste Eliminated: 5,447 pounds**

- *Learn more about our Planet Friendly Publishing efforts at greenedition.org*

- *Environmental impact estimates calculated using the Environmental Defense Fund Paper Calculator. For more information, visit www.papercalculator.org*

9

Using Your Interactive Textbook

Dear _____,

This year you will be using a different kind of textbook.
What makes it different? You can write in it! It's **interactive**.

 TextWork

As you read each lesson, look for the green TextWork boxes. Each
box has numbered questions and activities for you to complete.
You'll be asked to underline, circle, and draw in your book. And you
can write the answers right below the questions! So keep those
pencils sharp and markers ready.

EIP Explore!

Sometimes you'll see this symbol EIP in your book. It tells you that you or
your teacher can explore something in greater detail. You might study an
object more closely, take a virtual tour of a place, or watch a video about
an important event. These are just a few of the ways that you can explore
more online with Electronic Interactive Presentations (EIP).

Are you ready to use a new kind of textbook? Then let's get started!

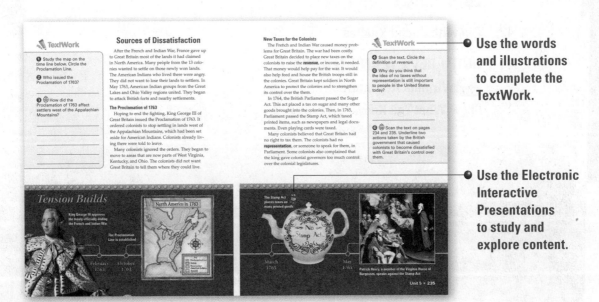

● Use the words
and illustrations
to complete the
TextWork.

● Use the Electronic
Interactive
Presentations
to study and
explore content.

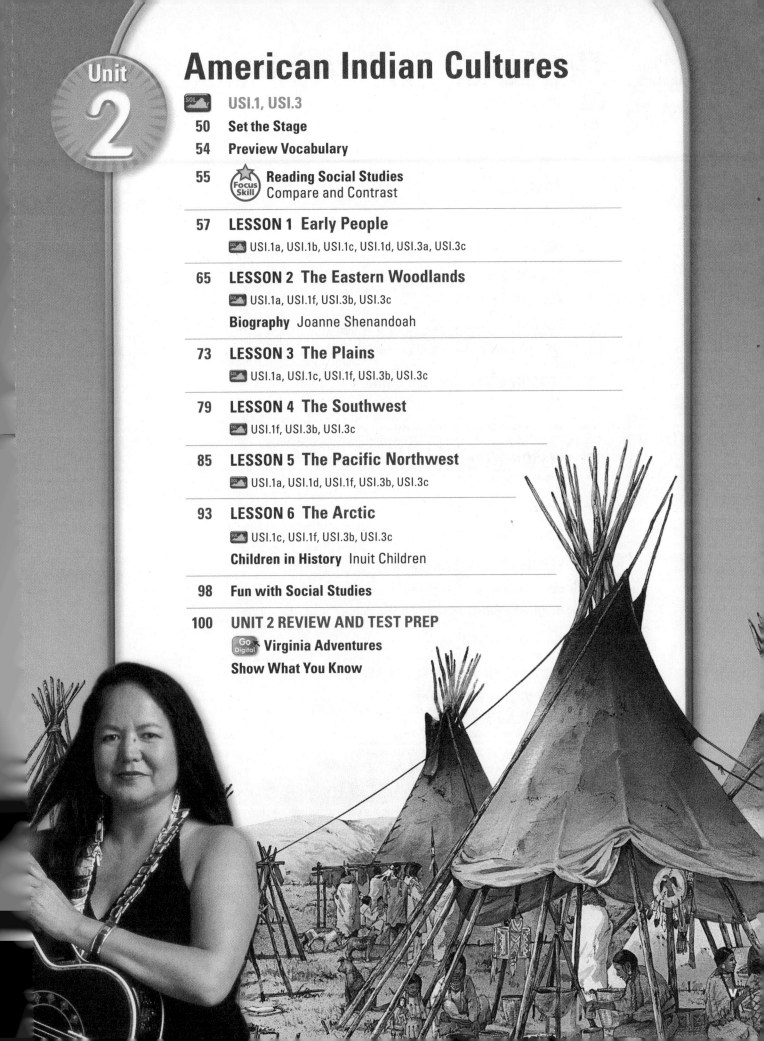

Unit 2

American Indian Cultures

USI.1, USI.3

v

Unit 3

The Age of Exploration

SOL USI.1, USI.4

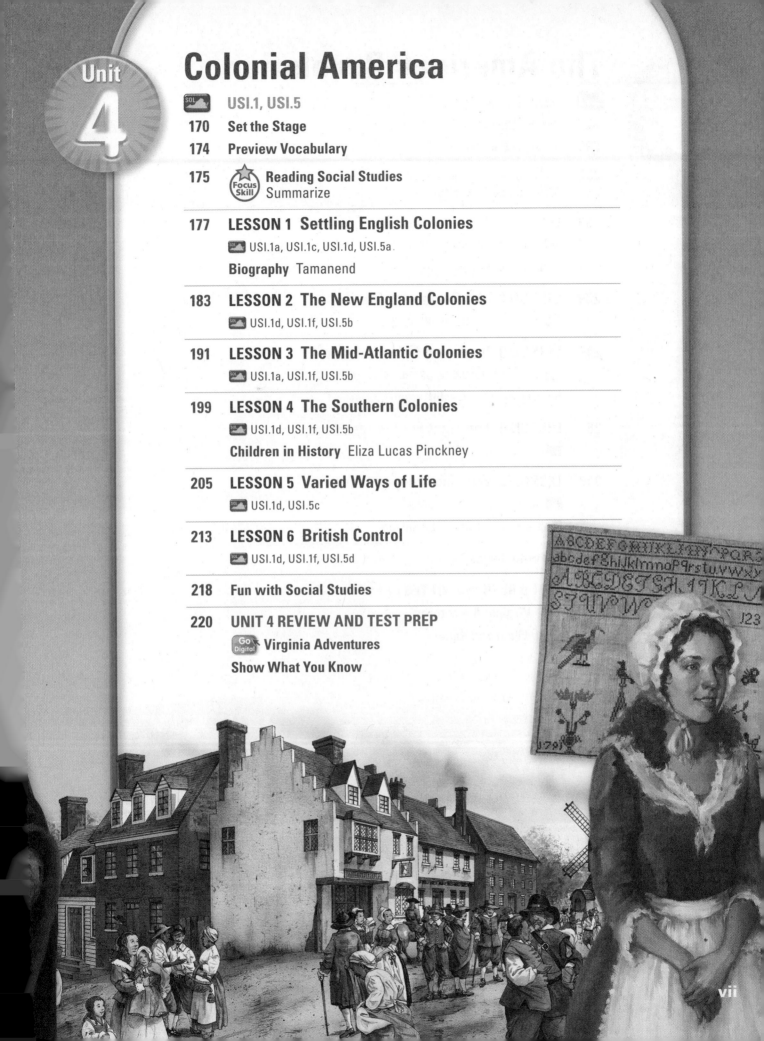

Unit 4

Colonial America

USI.1, USI.5

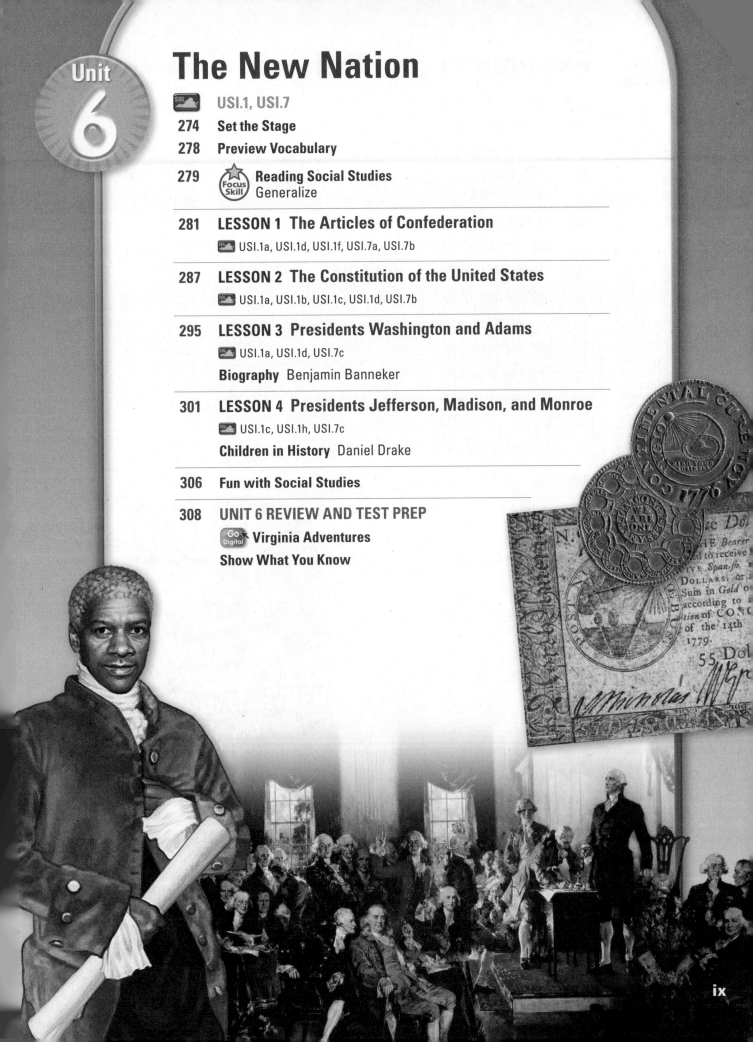

Unit 6

The New Nation

SOL USI.1, USI.7

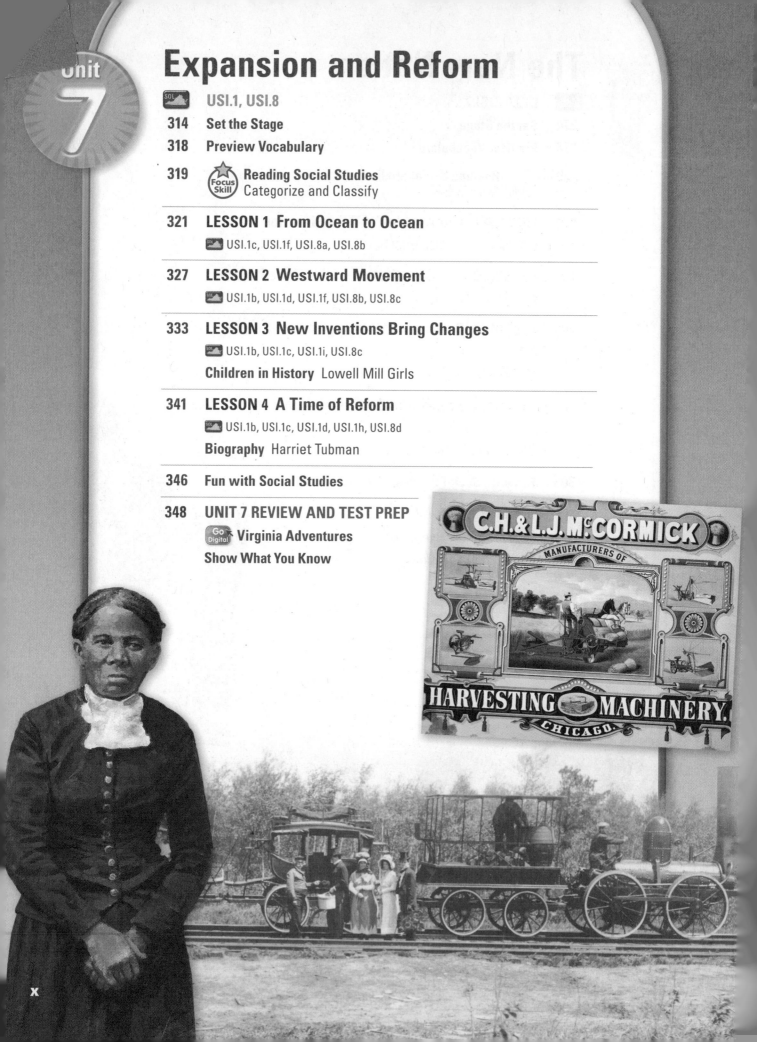

Unit 7

Expansion and Reform

SOL USI.1, USI.8

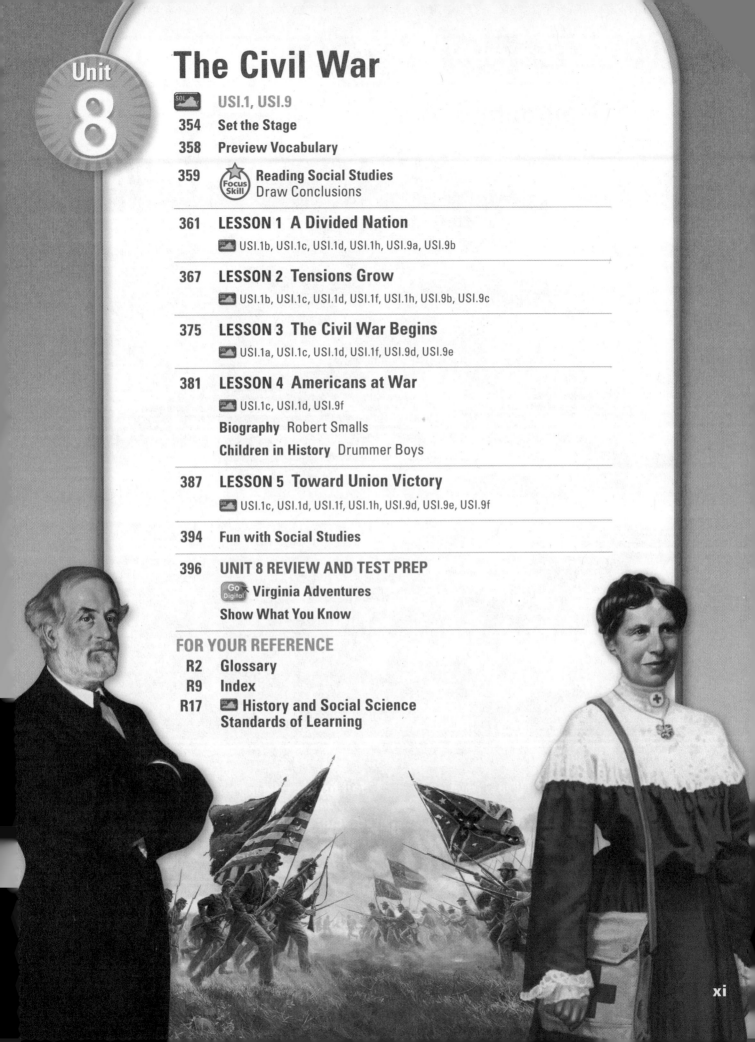

Unit 8

The Civil War

SOL USI.1, USI.9

Geography Terms

1 **basin** bowl-shaped area of land surrounded by higher land

2 **bay** an inlet of the sea or some other body of water, usually smaller than a gulf

3 **canyon** deep, narrow valley with steep sides

4 **cape** point of land that extends into water

5 **channel** deepest part of a body of water

6 **coastal plain** area of flat land along a sea or ocean

7 **delta** triangle-shaped area of land at the mouth of a river

8 **fall line** area along which rivers form waterfalls or rapids as the rivers drop to lower land

9 **glacier** large ice mass that moves slowly down a mountain or across land

10 **gulf** part of a sea or ocean extending into the land, usually larger than a bay

11 **inlet** any area of water extending into the land from a larger body of water

12 **isthmus** narrow strip of land connecting two larger areas of land

13 **marsh** lowland with moist soil and tall grasses

14 **mesa** flat-topped mountain with steep sides

15 **mountain pass** gap between mountains

16 **mountain range** row of mountains

17 **mouth of river** place where a river empties into another body of water

18 **peninsula** land that is almost completely surrounded by water

19 **plain** area of flat or gently rolling low land

20 **plateau** area of high, mostly flat land

21 **savanna** area of grassland and scattered trees

22 **sea level** the level of the surface of an ocean or a sea

23 **source of river** place where a river begins

24 **strait** narrow channel of water connecting two larger bodies of water

25 **swamp** area of low, wet land with trees

26 **tributary** stream or river that flows into a larger stream or river

27 **volcano** opening in Earth, often raised, through which lava, rock, ashes, and gases are forced out

Reading Maps

Maps give important information about the world around you. A map is a drawing that shows all or part of Earth on a flat surface. To help you read maps, mapmakers add certain features to their maps. These features often include a title, a map legend, a compass rose, a locator, and a map scale.

Mapmakers sometimes need to show certain places on a map in greater detail. Sometimes they must also show places that are located beyond the area shown on a map.

A **locator** is a small map or globe that shows where the place on the main map is located within a larger area.

An **inset map** is a smaller map within a larger one.

A **map legend**, or **map key**, explains the symbols used on a map. Symbols may be colors, patterns, lines, or other special marks.

A **map scale**, or **distance scale**, compares a distance on the map to a distance in the real world. It helps you find the real distance between places on a map.

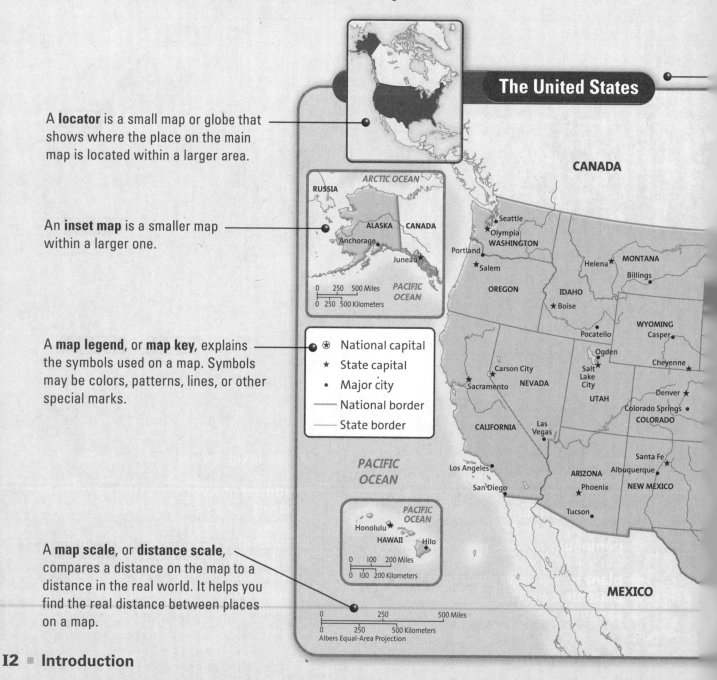

The United States

CANADA

ARCTIC OCEAN

RUSSIA

ALASKA   CANADA
Anchorage
Juneau ★

0   250   500 Miles
0   250   500 Kilometers

PACIFIC OCEAN

⊛ National capital
★ State capital
• Major city
── National border
── State border

Seattle
Olympia)
WASHINGTON
Portland
Salem ★

Helena ★   MONTANA
Billings •

OREGON   IDAHO
★ Boise

WYOMING
Pocatello •   Casper •
Ogden •
Carson City •   Salt Lake City ★   Cheyenne ★
Sacramento ★   NEVADA   UTAH
Denver ★
Colorado Springs •
COLORADO

CALIFORNIA   Las Vegas •

Santa Fe ★
Los Angeles •   Albuquerque •
ARIZONA   NEW MEXICO
San Diego •   Phoenix ★

PACIFIC OCEAN

Tucson •

PACIFIC OCEAN
Honolulu ★
HAWAII   Hilo •

0   100   200 Miles
0   100   200 Kilometers

MEXICO

0   250   500 Miles
0   250   500 Kilometers
Albers Equal-Area Projection

Find Alaska and Hawaii on the map below. These two states are a long distance from the 48 contiguous (kuhn•TIH•gyuh•wuhs) states. Each of the 48 contiguous states shares at least one border with another state. The United States covers a large area. To show very much detail for Alaska and Hawaii and the rest of the country, the map would have to be much larger. Instead, Alaska and Hawaii are each shown in a separate inset map, or a smaller map within a larger map.

A **map title** tells the subject of the map. It may also identify the kind of map.
- A **political map** shows cities, states, and countries.
- A **physical map** shows kinds of land and bodies of water.
- A **historical map** shows parts of the world as they were in the past.

A **compass rose**, or direction marker, shows directions.
- The **cardinal directions** are north, south, east, and west.
- The **intermediate directions**, or directions between the cardinal directions, are northeast, northwest, southeast, and southwest.

Finding Locations

Every place on Earth has its own location. To find the location of a place, you can use a map that has a grid system. A **grid system** is a set of lines the same distance apart that cross one another to form boxes.

The grid system on the map below shows rows and columns of boxes. The rows are labeled with letters, and the columns are labeled with numbers. You can give the location of a place by first naming the letter of the row it is in and then naming the letter of the column it is in. For example, the Great Dismal Swamp's location is in D-7.

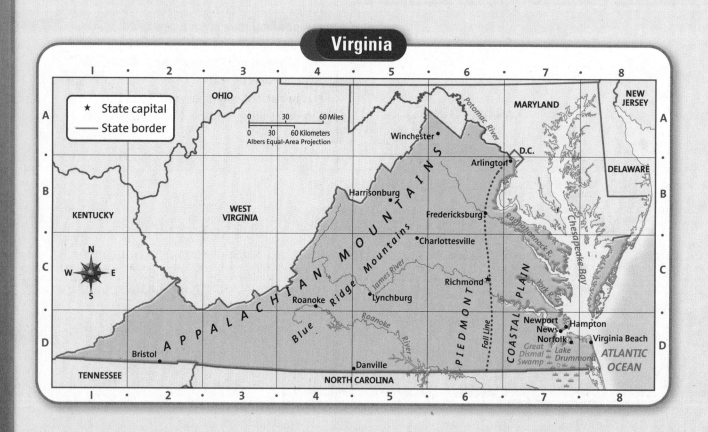

North America's Geography

Grand Teton National Park, in Wyoming

Spotlight on Standards

THE BIG IDEA People interact with their environment and are affected by it.

HISTORY AND SOCIAL SCIENCE SOL
USI.1a, USI.1c, USI.1f, USI.1g, USI.2a, USI.2b, USI.2c, USI.2d

Set the Stage

Study the map and the graphs. On the map, trace the longest river. Circle the name of the tallest mountain.

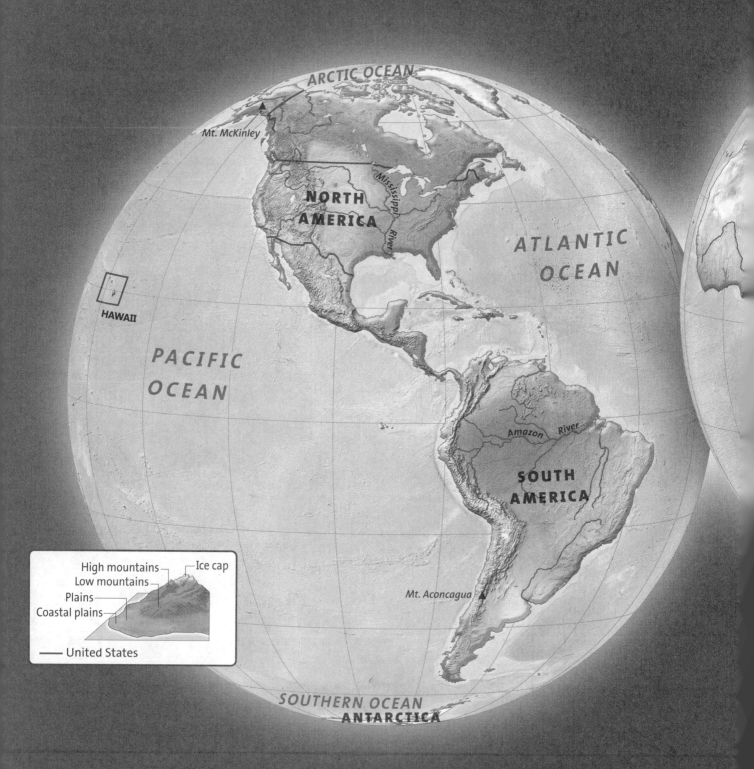

ARCTIC OCEAN

Mt. McKinley

NORTH AMERICA

Mississippi River

ATLANTIC OCEAN

HAWAII

PACIFIC OCEAN

Amazon River

SOUTH AMERICA

Mt. Aconcagua

High mountains — Ice cap
Low mountains
Plains
Coastal plains

—— United States

SOUTHERN OCEAN
ANTARCTICA

North America in the World

ARCTIC OCEAN

EUROPE

ASIA

Chang Jiang

Mt. Everest ▲

Nile River

AFRICA

▲ Mt. Kilimanjaro

INDIAN OCEAN

AUSTRALIA

SOUTHERN OCEAN
ANTARCTICA

Mountains of the World

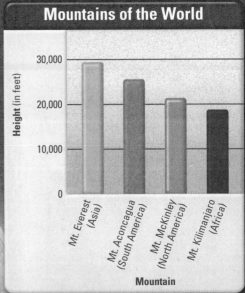

Height (in feet)

30,000

20,000

10,000

0

Mt. Everest (Asia) · Mt. Aconcagua (South America) · Mt. McKinley (North America) · Mt. Kilimanjaro (Africa)

Mountain

Rivers of the World

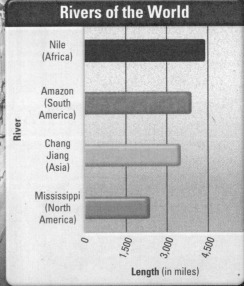

River

Nile (Africa)

Amazon (South America)

Chang Jiang (Asia)

Mississippi (North America)

0 · 1,500 · 3,000 · 4,500

Length (in miles)

The World's Population by Continent

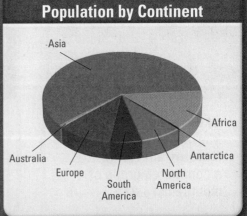

Asia

Africa

Antarctica

Australia

Europe

South America

North America

Preview Vocabulary

continent

The **continent** of Africa is one of Earth's seven largest land masses. It is almost completely surrounded by water. p. 7

tributary

The Yellowstone River is a **tributary** of the Missouri River. It flows into the Missouri River in North Dakota. p. 14

region

The Great Plains is a region of North America. A **region** is an area with distinctive characteristics that set it apart. p. 19

mountain range

Like most mountains, Maroon Bells is part of a **mountain range**, or a connected group of mountains. p. 22

natural resource

A **natural resource** is something in nature, such as soil and water, that people can use to meet their needs. p. 36

industry

The farming **industry** includes all the businesses and services that help grow crops and raise livestock. p. 38

Reading Social Studies

⭐ Main Idea and Details

LEARN

The **main idea** is the most important idea in what you read. **Details** give more information about the main idea. Each piece of writing has a main idea and details that support it. The main idea is often found at the beginning of the piece of writing. In long pieces of writing, each paragraph has its own main idea and supporting details.

Main Idea

The most important idea of a paragraph or passage

Details

| Facts about the main idea | Facts about the main idea | Facts about the main idea |

PRACTICE

Circle each paragraph's main idea, and underline its details. The first paragraph has been marked for you.

The United States and Canada share two large mountain ranges—the Rocky Mountains and the Appalachian Mountains. Both of these mountain ranges run north and south. The Rocky Mountains are much taller than the Appalachian Mountains.

> Main Idea
> Details

The land in the central part of the United States and Canada is mostly flat or rolling plains. The southern part of these plains has rich soil. Wheat and other crops grow well there. In the northern part of the plains, the soil is poor. The summer is too short for farming.

Read the article. Then complete the activities below.

Climates in North America

Because North America is so large, it has many different climates. A climate is the kind of weather a place has over time. Some parts of North America have desert climates. In other areas, the climate is freezing cold.

All deserts are arid, or dry. In most years, they receive little or no rainfall. Depending on their location and the time of year, deserts can be either hot or cold. Death Valley is a desert in southern California. It has some of the highest temperatures in the United States. However, on winter nights, the temperatures in Death Valley can be very low.

In the northernmost parts of Alaska and Canada, the climate is cold year-round. The land is mostly a large, flat area of frozen ground where trees cannot grow. During winter, it is very cold and dark. In summer, the top layer of soil melts, making the ground soggy. This area is windy and gets very little precipitation.

Because the ground is frozen for much of the year, there is not enough water for trees to grow. Only a few small plants—such as moss, lichen, and heath—can be found there. Animals that live in this region include reindeer, foxes, polar bears, and seals.

1. **Circle the main idea of the first paragraph.**

2. **Underline the details that support the idea that deserts can be either hot or cold.**

3. **What details support the idea that few plants and certain animals are found in the northernmost parts of Alaska and Canada?**

_____

_____

_____

Continents and Oceans

Earth's two largest geographic features are its continents and oceans. A **continent** is a large landmass that is mostly surrounded by water. An **ocean** is a large body of salt water. **Think about the names and locations of the continents and oceans.**

The world's largest globe, in Yarmouth, Maine

ESSENTIAL QUESTIONS
✓ What are the seven continents?
✓ What are the five oceans?

 HISTORY AND SOCIAL SCIENCE SOL
USI.1f, USI.1g, USI.2a

TextWork

1 Underline the names of Earth's seven continents. Which continent is the largest in land area?

_____

2 Study the center map below. Circle the equator and the prime meridian. Which line divides Earth into the Eastern and Western Hemispheres?

_____

3 Find North America on the map on page 9, and study the maps below. In which two hemispheres is North America located?

_____

The Seven Continents

If someone asked you to describe the location of the United States, what would you say? You could say that the United States is located in North America—one of Earth's seven continents. From largest to smallest in land area, the continents are Asia, Africa, North America, South America, Antarctica, Europe, and Australia.

Europe is usually considered a separate continent, even though it shares a long border with Asia. However, geographers sometimes group Europe and Asia together as one continent and call it Eurasia (yur•AY•zhuh).

Geographers use an imaginary line called the equator to divide Earth into the Northern Hemisphere and the Southern Hemisphere. The equator is located halfway between the North Pole and the South Pole. Another imaginary line, the prime meridian, runs from the North Pole to the South Pole. The prime meridian is often used to divide Earth into the Western Hemisphere and the Eastern Hemisphere.

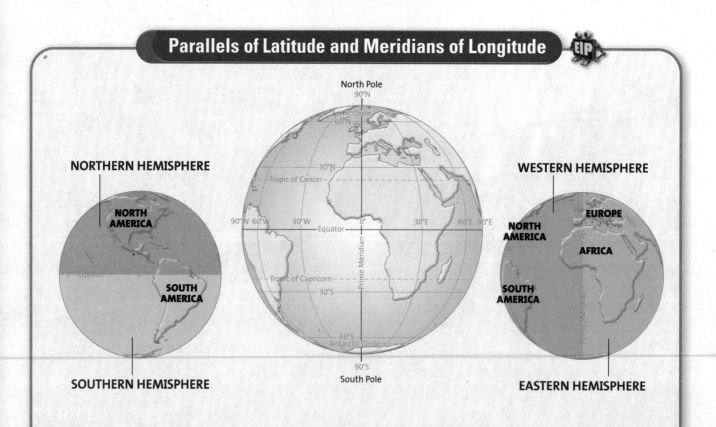

Parallels of Latitude and Meridians of Longitude

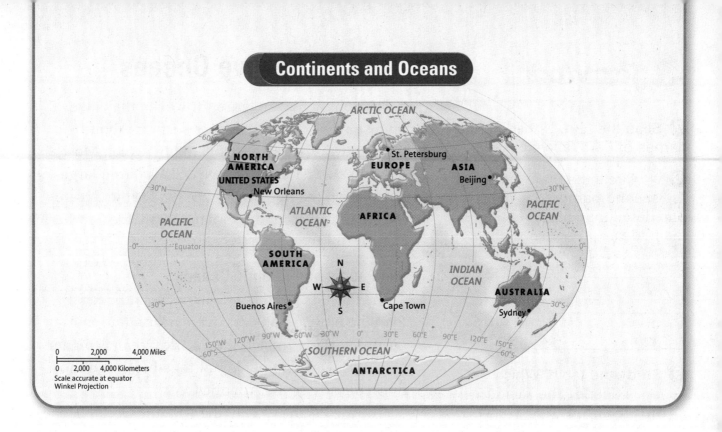

Continents and Oceans

Finding Locations

To help people find the absolute location, or exact location, of places on globes and maps, mapmakers add lines that intersect, or cross each other. These lines form a pattern of squares called a grid system.

The lines that run east to west are called **parallels of latitude**. These imaginary lines are measured in degrees north and south of the equator. The equator is labeled 0°, or zero degrees. Parallels north of the equator are marked N, for *north*. Parallels south of it are marked S, for *south*.

The lines that run north and south are called **meridians of longitude**. These imaginary lines are measured in degrees east and west of the prime meridian. The prime meridian is labeled 0°, or zero degrees. Meridians west of the prime meridian are marked W, for *west*. Meridians east of it are marked E, for *east*.

To describe a place's absolute location, give the parallel of latitude and the meridian of longitude closest to it. For example, the place at 60°N, 120°W is located where the lines 60°N and 120°W intersect through North America.

 TextWork

❹ Scan the text. Circle the paragraphs that describe parallels of latitude and meridians of longitude.

❺ Study the map. On which continent do the lines 30°N and 90°E intersect?

_____

❻ Study the map. Give the absolute location of the city of New Orleans by writing the closest parallel of latitude and meridian of longitude.

_____

TextWork

7 Scan the text. Underline the names of Earth's five oceans.

8 (Focus Skill) Circle the main idea of the second paragraph. Write one detail that supports the main idea.

_____

_____

_____

9 Study the table. Which ocean is deeper, the Atlantic or the Indian?

_____

Ocean Facts

OCEAN	AREA	GREATEST DEPTH
Pacific	64,185,629 square miles	35,837 feet
Atlantic	33,424,006 square miles	30,246 feet
Indian	28,351,484 square miles	24,460 feet
Southern	7,848,000 square miles	23,737 feet
Arctic	5,108,132 square miles	18,456 feet

The Five Oceans

The continents are large. However, they take up just a small part of Earth's surface. About three-fourths of Earth is covered by water. Most of Earth's water is in the five oceans. From largest to smallest, the five oceans are the Pacific Ocean, the Atlantic Ocean, the Indian Ocean, the Southern Ocean, and the Arctic Ocean.

The Pacific and Atlantic Oceans

The Pacific Ocean is much bigger and deeper than the other oceans. It covers nearly one-third of Earth's surface. In fact, the Pacific Ocean is bigger than all seven continents put together. It is almost twice the size of the Atlantic Ocean.

Like the Pacific Ocean, the Atlantic Ocean is one of the world's busiest transportation routes. For years, ships had to go around South America to get from the Atlantic Ocean to the Pacific Ocean. Since 1914, however, ships have been able to use the Panama Canal, which runs across the country of Panama in Central America. A **canal** is a human-made waterway dug across the land.

The Atlantic Ocean forms the eastern border of the United States.

Large icebergs frequently move through the icy waters of the Arctic Ocean.

The Indian Ocean

The Indian Ocean is the third-largest ocean. For many years, it has formed an important transportation route that links Africa, Asia, and Australia. Today, ships from Europe and the Americas can reach the Indian Ocean through the Mediterranean Sea by using the Suez (SOO•ez) Canal in Egypt.

The Arctic and Southern Oceans

The Arctic Ocean is the northernmost ocean. It is also the smallest and shallowest of the oceans. The Arctic Ocean is surrounded by North America, Europe, and Asia. It is located at the opposite end of Earth from the Southern Ocean.

The Southern Ocean is the southernmost ocean. It surrounds Antarctica and lies south of the 60°S parallel of latitude—or south of the southern parts of the Pacific, Atlantic, and Indian Oceans.

The Southern and Arctic Oceans are both covered with huge areas of packed ice. Because of the icy conditions, the Southern and Arctic Oceans are the least traveled oceans.

 **TextWork**

10 Underline the name of the ocean that forms an important transportation route linking Africa, Asia, and Australia.

11 What continent is surrounded by the Southern Ocean?

_____

12 How do the Arctic and Southern Oceans differ from the other oceans?

_____

_____

_____

1. **SUMMARIZE** What are the seven continents and the five oceans?

_____

_____

_____

_____

_____

2. Describe how a **parallel of latitude** is different from a **meridian of longitude**.

_____

_____

_____

_____

Circle the letter of the correct answer.

3. On which continent is the United States located?

   A Antarctica

   B Europe

   C North America

   D South America

4. The largest ocean is the—

   F Pacific Ocean

   G Atlantic Ocean

   H Indian Ocean

   J Southern Ocean

5. Which ocean surrounds Antarctica?

   A Pacific Ocean

   B Atlantic Ocean

   C Indian Ocean

   D Southern Ocean

Match the ocean's name on the left with a detail on the right.

6. Indian Ocean

7. Arctic Ocean

8. Atlantic Ocean

forms the eastern border of the United States

links Asia, Africa, and Australia

the northernmost ocean

activity

Draw a Map Draw a map of Earth's continents and oceans. Label each continent and ocean. Include on your map an outline of the United States.

Globe

Looking at Geographic Features

Geographers use different kinds of tools to study Earth. These tools help people recognize and understand the key geographic features of places. **Think about how key geographic features are shown on maps, globes, and diagrams and in pictures and photographs.**

The Grand Canyon, in Arizona

ESSENTIAL QUESTIONS
✓ What are some important categories of geographic features?
✓ What do these important geographic features look like when they appear on maps, globes, and diagrams?
✓ What do these important geographic features look like when they appear in pictures and photographs?

HISTORY AND SOCIAL SCIENCE SOL
USI.1f, USI.2d

1. What are two main categories of physical features shown on maps?

Physical features are water and land related features.

2. Underline the sentence that lists some important water-related features.

3. Study the map on this page. What color is used to show water-related features?

The color is blue.

Mapping Earth's Features

Geographers use different kinds of maps to show different kinds of information. However, most maps show certain key geographic features. Knowing how to recognize those features will help you better understand Earth's geography.

Several important categories of geographic features are shown on most maps. A category is a group of things that have something in common. Two main categories of physical features, or those found in nature, are water-related features and land-related features. Many maps also show human features, or those made by people, such as roads, bridges, and buildings.

Recognizing Water-Related Features

Mapmakers add colors, markings, and symbols to show different geographic features. Water-related features are often shown in blue on maps. Important water-related features include oceans, gulfs, bays, lakes, and rivers and their tributaries. A **tributary** (TRIH•byuh•tair•ee) is a river that flows into a larger river.

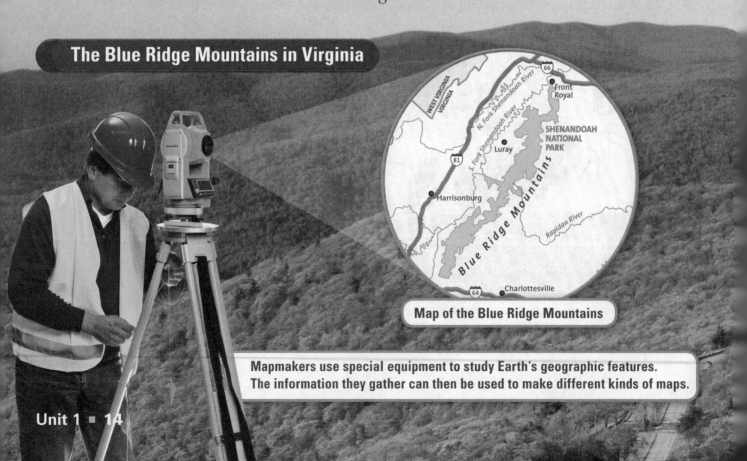

The Blue Ridge Mountains in Virginia

Map of the Blue Ridge Mountains

Mapmakers use special equipment to study Earth's geographic features. The information they gather can then be used to make different kinds of maps.

Recognizing Land-Related Features

Most land-related features on maps are usually shown by shades of green or brown. Green indicates areas where many grasses or trees grow, and brown indicates deserts or other dry areas. Areas covered by ice are often shown in white.

Important land-related features include mountains, hills, plains, plateaus, islands, and peninsulas. A **plain** is an area of mostly low, flat land. A **plateau** (pla•TOH) is an area of high, flat land. A **peninsula** is a piece of land bordered by water on three sides.

Some maps add symbols and other markings to show key geographic features. Black triangles are often used to indicate mountains. Red or black lines are used to mark the borders, or boundaries, of countries. Black lines are also used to indicate the borders of cities, counties, and states.

Some maps are made by using photographs taken from space by satellites or airplanes. A satellite is a vehicle or object that circles Earth or another body. Satellite photographs can show key geographic features from a distance. They are also used to track and forecast weather patterns.

TextWork

4 How does a plateau differ from a plain?

Plateaus differ from the plains in hight.

5 Underline the details that support the main idea in the second paragraph.

6 Study the map and satellite image on pages 14 and 15. What geographic features are visible in both?

I see mountains, rivers, roads, borders, and cities.

Satellite image of the Blue Ridge Mountains

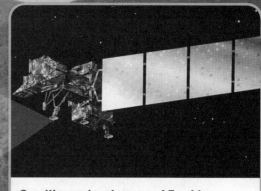
Satellites take pictures of Earth's geographic features from space. Images such as this one can help people see the physical and human features of places.

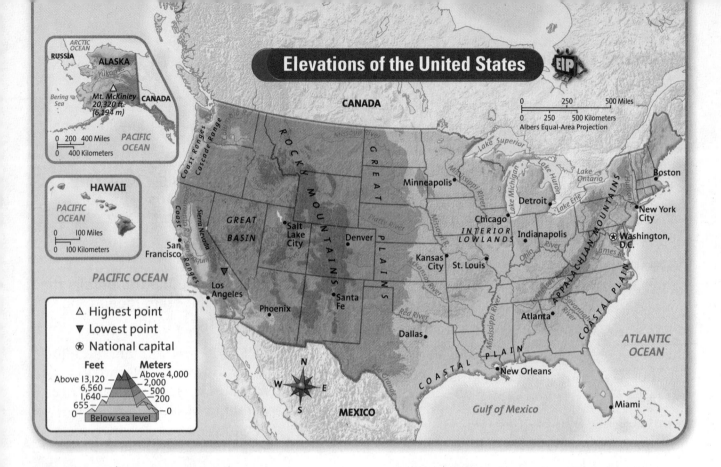

Elevations of the United States

TextWork

7 Study the map and map legend. What is the elevation of Santa Fe, New Mexico? Is the land higher or lower than the land near Boston, Massachusetts?

_____

_____

8 Study the map. In which direction does the Mississippi River flow? Explain.

_____

_____

_____

_____

Showing Elevation

Geographers use elevation maps to show whether a place has mountains or is lowland. **Elevation** (eh•luh•VAY•shuhn) is the height of the land above sea level, or the level of the ocean. The elevation of land at sea level is 0 feet.

Elevation maps use different colors to stand for an area's highest and lowest elevations and all of the elevations in between. The map legend tells you which colors are used to show different elevations.

Maps may also use shading to show **relief** (ruh•LEEF), or differences in elevation. Dark shading shows steep rises and drops in elevation. Light shading shows gentle rises and drops. Areas with no shading show land that is mostly flat.

Besides helping you find the elevation of an area, elevation maps can help you find out which way a river flows. Rivers can flow in any direction. However, they always flow from higher elevations to lower elevations.

Using Diagrams

Geographers also use diagrams to show elevation. An elevation profile is a diagram that shows a side view of Earth. Elevation profiles show changes in elevation from one point to another.

An elevation profile can provide more exact information about an area than an elevation map. Elevation maps use colors to show general ranges of elevation. An elevation profile shows the contour, or outline, of the land's surface. It also may include specific heights for some places.

In general, the elevation of the land in the United States rises gradually from the Atlantic coast to the Appalachian Mountains. Beyond the Appalachian Mountains, a large area of plains extends across the central part of the country. West of the Great Plains, the land rises at the Rocky Mountains and falls in the Great Basin area. It rises again at the Sierra Nevada and Cascade Mountains. It rises once more at the Coast Ranges before falling to sea level at the Pacific Ocean.

9 Elevation affects climate. In general, temperatures drop as elevation increases. Study the map on page 16 and the diagram below. Circle the area on the diagram that you think has the coldest yearly climate, the Rocky Mountains or the Appalachian Mountains. Explain why you think this.

_____

_____

_____

10 Study the diagram. Which coast—the Atlantic or the Pacific—generally has steeper land?

_____

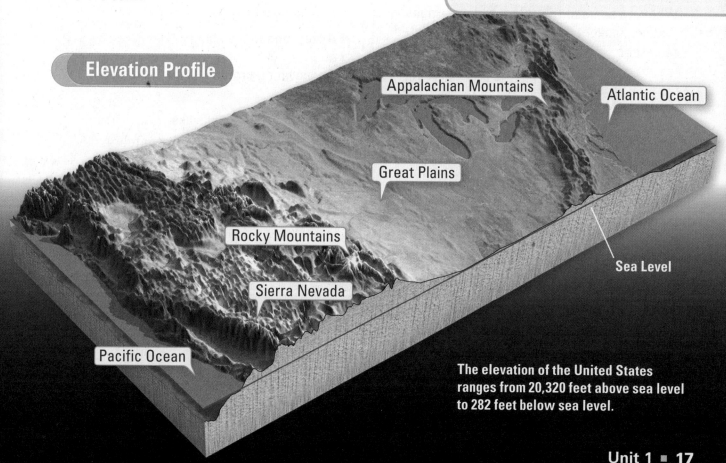

Elevation Profile

Appalachian Mountains

Atlantic Ocean

Great Plains

Rocky Mountains

Sea Level

Sierra Nevada

Pacific Ocean

The elevation of the United States ranges from 20,320 feet above sea level to 282 feet below sea level.

1. **SUMMARIZE** What are some of the key geographic features shown on maps, globes, and diagrams?

_____

_____

_____

_____

2. Use **relief** in a sentence describing **elevation**.

_____

_____

_____

_____

3. What are some of the colors and markings that mapmakers use to show key land-related features?

_____

_____

_____

Circle the letter of the correct answer.

4. Which of these can be grouped under the category of key land-related geographic features?

  A Gulf

  B Bay

  C Tributary

  D Plateau

5. A piece of land that is mostly surrounded by water is called a—

  F plateau

  G peninsula

  H tributary

  J plain

6. Rivers usually flow from—

  A north to south

  B east to west

  C high land to low land

  D low land to high land

7. An elevation profile is a diagram that shows—

  F what the land looks like from space

  G a side view of the land's contour

  H the borders of states and cities

  J where roads are located

activity

Make a Poster Make a poster to show three kinds of land-related geographic features and three kinds of water-related geographic features. Use pictures and a map to illustrate your poster.

Map

The Natural Bridge, in
Rockbridge County, Virginia

North America is a large continent with many different **regions**, or areas
of Earth with distinctive characteristics that make them different from other
areas. A geographic region is a region that has similar kinds of physical characteristics. **Think about how North America's geography differs from region to
region.**

ESSENTIAL QUESTIONS

✓ Where are the geographic regions of North America located?
✓ What are some physical characteristics of the geographic regions of
North America?

HISTORY AND SOCIAL SCIENCE SOL
USI.1f, USI.1g, USI.2b

Plains Regions

Three of the largest geographic regions in North America are plains—the Coastal Plain region, Interior Lowlands region, and Great Plains region.

The Coastal Plain

The Coastal Plain region stretches inland from the Atlantic Ocean between Massachusetts and Florida. From Florida, the Coastal Plain extends west along the Gulf Coast into eastern Mexico.

The land in the Coastal Plain region is mostly low and flat, and there are many pine forests. The coastline has many excellent harbors. A **harbor** is a protected area of water where ships can dock safely. Among the region's largest harbors are New York Bay, Chesapeake Bay, Tampa Bay, and Mobile Bay.

The Interior Lowlands

The Interior Lowlands region is located west of the Appalachian (a•puh•LAY•chee•uhn) Mountains and east of the Great Plains. Both the Interior Lowlands and Great Plains regions stretch across the middle of the United States and Canada.

The land in the Interior Lowlands is mostly flat, with some rolling hills. The region also has many rivers and broad valleys. There are more trees in the eastern part of the region, where rainfall is more plentiful. Farther west, the region is drier and mostly grassland.

The Great Plains

The Great Plains region is located west of the Interior Lowlands and east of the Rocky Mountains. The region is known for its vast grasslands and wheat fields. The Great Plains is mostly flat and dry, with few rivers and almost no trees.

Although the land is mostly flat, its elevation gradually increases westward toward the Rocky Mountains. In some places, such as the Black Hills of South Dakota, the land rises sharply.

Wheat farming on the Great Plains

Geographic Regions of North America

ARCTIC OCEAN

Brooks Range

Mt. McKinley
20,320 ft.

Alaska Range

Mt. Logan
19,550 ft.

Mackenzie Mts.

Coast Mountains

Hudson
Bay

C A N A D I A N   S H I E L D

R O C K Y

M O U N T A I N S

G R E A T

P L A I N S

Puget Sound Lowland

Willamette
Valley

Cascade Range

Coast Ranges

Sierra Nevada

GREAT
BASIN

Mt. Elbert
14,433 ft.

INTERIOR
LOWLANDS

Ozark
Plateau

APPALACHIAN MOUNTAINS

COASTAL PLAIN

PACIFIC
OCEAN

Central
Valley

Death
Valley
-282 ft.

ATLANTIC
OCEAN

COASTAL PLAIN

Baja California

Sierra Madre Occidental

Mexican Plateau

Sierra Madre Oriental

COASTAL PLAIN

Gulf of Mexico

Tropic of Cancer

Pico de Orizaba
18,855 ft.

Yucatán
Peninsula

Sierra Madre del Sur

Caribbean Sea

Legend

- Coastal Range
- Basin and Range
- Rocky Mountains
- Great Plains
- Interior Lowlands
- Canadian Shield
- Appalachian Highlands
- Coastal Plain
- Central America and the Caribbean

△ Highest point
▼ Lowest point
▲ Other mountain peak
⋯⋯ Continental Divide
— National border

N W E S

0   250   500 Miles
0   250   500 Kilometers
Lambert Azimuthal Equal-Area Projection

The Great Smoky Mountains in North Carolina get their name from the bluish-gray haze that covers their peaks.

Highlands and Mountains

The United States and Canada share two large mountain ranges—the Appalachian Mountains and the Rocky Mountains. A **mountain range** is a group of connected mountains.

The Appalachian Highlands

The Appalachian Highlands region is located west of the Coastal Plain and extends from western Alabama to eastern Canada. The region includes the tree-covered Appalachians, the oldest mountains in North America. Over time, their peaks have been worn down by wind, ice, and water. This gradual wearing away of Earth's surface is called **erosion**. Mount Mitchell in North Carolina is the highest peak in the Appalachians, at 6,684 feet.

The Appalachians are made up of many smaller mountain ranges, including the Allegheny Mountains, the Blue Ridge Mountains, and the Great Smoky Mountains. The rolling hills and valleys of the Piedmont (PEED•mahnt) lie on the eastern side of the Appalachians. The word *piedmont* means "at the foot of the mountain."

TextWork

5 Use clues from the text to complete these sentences:

The _____ Mountains cover much of the eastern United States.

The _____ Mountains cover much of the western United States.

6 Underline the sentences that describe the effects of erosion. What effect has erosion had on the Appalachian Mountains?

_____

_____

_____

The Rocky Mountains

The Rocky Mountains are located west of the Great Plains. The Rockies are North America's largest and longest mountain range. They extend from New Mexico through Canada and into Alaska.

The Rockies are much younger than the Appalachians. The peaks of the Rockies appear sharp and jagged because they have not been worn down for as long a time. At 14,433 feet, Mount Elbert in Colorado is the highest peak in the Rockies. Because the Rockies are so high, many of the peaks are covered with snow year round.

An imaginary line called the Continental Divide runs north and south along the peaks of the Rockies. As the name suggests, the Continental Divide divides North America into two parts. It also determines the directional flow of rivers. Water in rivers east of the divide eventually reaches the Atlantic Ocean. Rivers that begin west of the divide flow toward the Pacific Ocean.

TextWork

7 Scan the text. Circle the name of the mountain in the Rockies with the highest peak.

8 How do the Rocky Mountains differ from the Appalachian Mountains, and why is this so?

_____

_____

_____

_____

9 (Focus Skill) Underline the details that explain how the Continental Divide affects the flow of rivers.

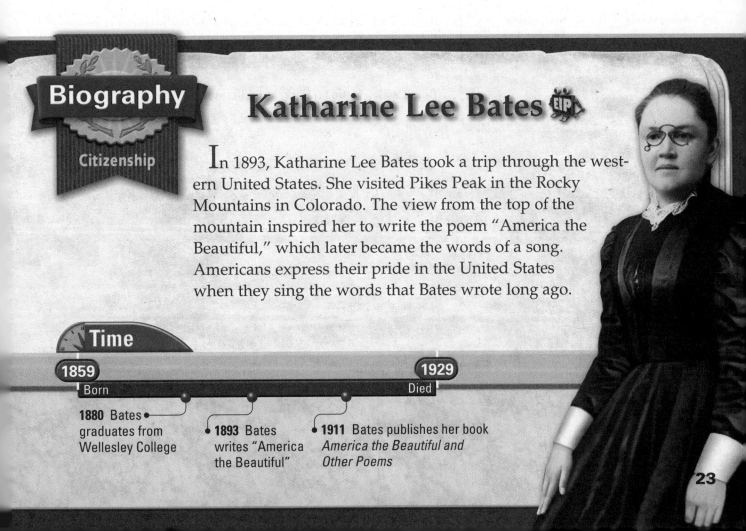

Biography

Citizenship

Katharine Lee Bates

In 1893, Katharine Lee Bates took a trip through the western United States. She visited Pikes Peak in the Rocky Mountains in Colorado. The view from the top of the mountain inspired her to write the poem "America the Beautiful," which later became the words of a song. Americans express their pride in the United States when they sing the words that Bates wrote long ago.

Time

1859 Born

1929 Died

1880 Bates graduates from Wellesley College

1893 Bates writes "America the Beautiful"

1911 Bates publishes her book *America the Beautiful and Other Poems*

23

TextWork

10 Scan the text on this page. Underline the names of three landforms found in the Basin and Range region.

11 Study the chart. What is the difference between the average winter temperature in the Canadian Shield and the highest recorded temperature in Death Valley?

Comparing Regions	
CANADIAN SHIELD	**DEATH VALLEY**
Highest Elevation 1,060 feet above sea level	**Lowest Elevation** 283 feet below sea level
Average Winter Temperature −9.4°F	**Highest Recorded Temperature** 134°F
Average Yearly Precipitation 12 inches	**Average Yearly Precipitation** 1.84 inches
Climate short cool summer, long cold winter	**Climate** dry, either hot or cold

The Basin and Range Region

The Basin and Range region lies between the Rockies and two other western mountain ranges—the Sierra Nevada and the Cascades. The Sierra Nevada (see•AIR•uh nuh•VAH•duh) extend north and south along California's eastern border. *Sierra Nevada* is Spanish for "snowy mountain range." The Cascades lie north of the Sierra Nevada, stretching into Washington and Oregon.

The Basin and Range region is an area of varying elevations and isolated mountain ranges. The Great Basin covers the middle part of the region. A **basin** is a low, bowl-shaped area with higher ground around it. Death Valley lies at the southwestern edge of the Great Basin. It is the lowest point in North America. Death Valley is one of the hottest and driest places in the United States. Only plants that need little water, such as cacti, can live there.

The Great Basin lies between the Columbia and Colorado Plateaus. The Grand Canyon stretches about 280 miles across the Colorado Plateau. It is one of the world's deepest and largest canyons.

Death Valley National Park, in California

The Coastal Range Region

The Coastal Range region is made up of rugged mountain ranges that extend west of the Basin and Range region, from California to Canada. Among these are the low mountains that give much of the Pacific Coast its rocky look. Large valleys lie east of these mountains. The soil in these valleys is **fertile**, or good for farming.

The Canadian Shield

The Canadian Shield is a rocky, horseshoe-shaped region that wraps around most of Hudson Bay in Canada. The region covers nearly half of Canada. The mountains of the Canadian Shield were eroded into low hills by slow-moving sheets of ice called **glaciers** (GLAY•sherz). In other places, glaciers carved out hundreds of lakes.

Today, evergreen trees grow in the southern part of the Canadian Shield. The northern part of the Canadian Shield is a **tundra**, or a cold, dry, treeless plain.

TextWork

12 Describe the location of the Coastal Range region.

_____

_____

_____

13 Underline the sentence that explains why valleys in the Coastal Range region are good for farming.

14 How did glaciers affect the Canadian Shield?

_____

_____

_____

The Coast Ranges, in California

Winter in the Canadian Shield

1. **SUMMARIZE** What are the eight major geographic regions found in North America?

_____

_____

_____

_____

_____

_____

_____

2. Use the term **mountain range** to describe the Appalachian Highlands region.

_____

_____

_____

Circle the letter of the correct answer.

3. Which region has many excellent harbors?
   A Coastal Plain
   B Appalachian Highlands
   C Great Plains
   D Rocky Mountains

4. The oldest mountains are found in the—
   F Coastal Range region
   G Appalachian Highlands region
   H Rocky Mountains region
   J Basin and Range region

5. What happens to water from rivers that begin east of the Continental Divide?
   A It flows to the Appalachian Mountains.
   B It eventually reaches the Atlantic Ocean.
   C It flows to the Rocky Mountains.
   D It eventually reaches the Pacific Ocean.

Match the region on the left with a geographic feature on the right.

6. Interior Lowlands   tundra

7. Basin and Range   grasslands

8. Canadian Shield   Death Valley

activity

> **Make Flash Cards** Use notecards to make flash cards. On one side of each card, write the name of a geographic region and draw a picture of it. On the other side of the card, write a description of the region.

A beach on the Coastal Plain

Bodies of Water

North America has numerous and varied waterways, or bodies of water that boats can use. People use these waterways for travel and to transport goods from place to place. These waterways help people **interact**, or affect one another. The waterways may also form borders and create connections, or links, between people in different regions and countries. **Think about how bodies of water help people interact and connect with others.**

Québec, on the St. Lawrence River, in Canada

ESSENTIAL QUESTIONS
✓ What are the major bodies of water in the United States?
✓ What are some ways bodies of water in the United States have supported interaction and created links to other regions?

 HISTORY AND SOCIAL SCIENCE SOL
USI.1a, USI.1c, USI.1f, USI.2c

Ocean Highways

① What two oceans are next to most of the United States?

Atlantic ocean,
pacific oceans

② Circle the paragraph that helps explain how the oceans linked the United States to other parts of the world.

③ Why do you think some explorers considered the Pacific Ocean a destination?

To use the oceans
to explore the of
the North America.

Most of the United States lies between the Atlantic and Pacific Oceans. This location has allowed Americans to use both oceans to access other parts of the world.

Before the invention of the airplane, the oceans served as highways on which explorers, settlers, and immigrants traveled to North America. An **immigrant** is a person who comes into a country to make a new life.

In the 1500s and 1600s, Europeans used the oceans to explore the coasts of North America and South America. For some explorers, the Pacific Ocean was itself a destination, or a place they wanted to reach.

Over time, early settlers established towns in coastal areas with deep harbors. Some of these coastal towns grew into busy ports. A **port** is a place where ships are loaded and unloaded. In the 1800s and 1900s, the port cities along the Atlantic coast attracted millions of immigrants. Most immigrants arrived at Ellis Island in New York Harbor.

Ships traveling across the Atlantic Ocean must pass by the Statue of Liberty as they enter or leave New York Harbor.

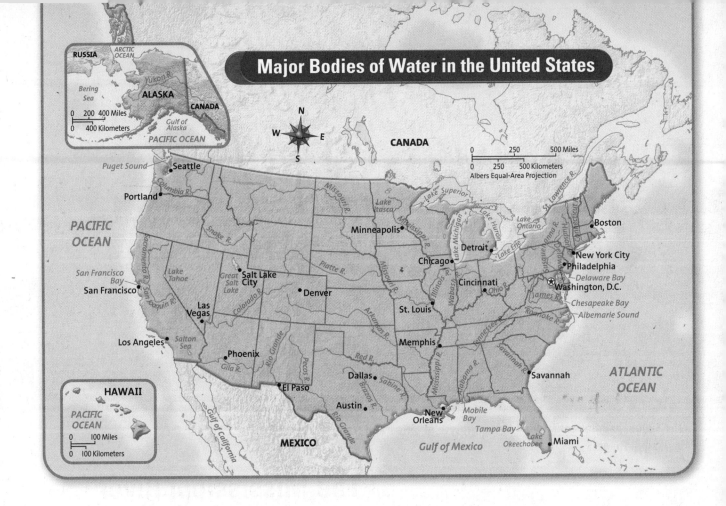

Major Bodies of Water in the United States

Gulfs and Bays

Hundreds of inlets are found along the coastline of the United States. An **inlet** is an area of water extending into the land from a larger body of water. The country's two largest inlets are the Gulf of Mexico and the Gulf of Alaska. The largest bay in the eastern United States is Chesapeake Bay.

The Gulf of Mexico borders the southeastern United States and parts of Mexico and Cuba. The Gulf of Alaska is located south of Alaska along the Pacific coast. In the past, Spanish and French explorers sailed on the Gulf of Mexico to reach Mexico and the southern parts of what became the United States.

Several important rivers, including the Mississippi River, flow into the Gulf of Mexico. The rivers connect the gulf to inland areas and are used for travel and trade. Some of the country's largest inlets border the Gulf of Mexico.

 **TextWork**

❹ Use the word *inlet* to describe the Chesapeake Bay.

The largest bay in eastern united states of America is chesapeake bay.

❺ Study the map. Underline the name of the body of water that was important to early Spanish explorers.

❻ Study the map. What river connects the middle part of the United States to the Gulf of Mexico?

mississippi River.

In the 1800s, paddleboats added to the growth of cities and trade along the Mississippi River.

The Mississippi River

Hundreds of rivers flow through the United States. The Mississippi River is one of the country's longest. It extends for 2,340 miles through the central part of the country. The Mississippi flows from its source, or beginning, at Lake Itasca in Minnesota to its mouth, or end, at the Gulf of Mexico.

The Mississippi River is joined by many tributaries. A river and its tributaries make up a **river system**. A river system drains, or carries water away from, the land around it. The Mississippi River and its tributaries form the largest river system in the United States. This river system drains most of the land between the Appalachian Mountains and the Rocky Mountains.

The longest tributary of the Mississippi River is the Missouri River. The Missouri River joins with the Mississippi to form an important transportation route through the country's interior. For years, farmers and traders have used this route to transport crops and other goods to port cities along the Gulf of Mexico and then to other parts of the world.

TextWork

7 Study the map on page 29. Find the Mississippi River. Circle the source of the river. Place an *X* at its mouth.

8 Scan the text on this page. Underline the name of the longest tributary of the Mississippi River.

9 How does the Mississippi River system link farmers and cities?

To bring the goods to the cites and towns.

Other Major Rivers

The Ohio River is another important tributary of the Mississippi River. It flows almost 1,000 miles southwest from Pittsburgh, Pennsylvania, to Cairo, Illinois. Early settlers used the Ohio River as a **gateway** to the western United States. A gateway is a path that connects to distant lands.

Two of the longest rivers in the western United States are the Columbia and Colorado Rivers. The Columbia River crosses into Washington from Canada and empties into the Pacific Ocean. In 1805, Meriwether Lewis and William Clark explored the Columbia and followed it to the Pacific Ocean. The Colorado River flows from the Rocky Mountains, through the Grand Canyon, and into Mexico. The Spanish first explored the river in the 1600s.

Two other major rivers form national borders. The Rio Grande forms part of the border between the United States and Mexico. The St. Lawrence River forms part of the United States's northeastern border with Canada.

 **TextWork**

10 Why is the Ohio River described as a gateway?

A gateway is a path that connects to distant lands.

11 (Focus Skill) List two details that support the main idea stated below.

Main Idea: Two rivers form parts of national borders.

Detail: *Rio Grande and The St. Lawrence river.*

Detail: *The Rio Grande is border of mexico.*

Children IN HISTORY

Mark Twain

When Samuel Langhorne Clemens, better known as Mark Twain, was four years old, his family moved to Hannibal, Missouri. Hannibal is located on the banks of the Mississippi River. As a boy, Twain watched steamboats on the Mississippi River and dreamed of becoming a steamboat pilot.

After Twain grew up, he earned his steamboat pilot's license. When the Civil War shut down steamboat traffic on the Mississippi, Twain traveled the country and began writing stories that made him a famous author.

Make It Relevant How might where people live affect the kind of work they do?

Lakes

The largest chain of lakes in the United States is known as the Great Lakes. The five Great Lakes are Superior, Michigan, Huron, Erie, and Ontario. Lake Michigan is the only one of the Great Lakes that lies totally within the United States. The other Great Lakes form part of the border between the United States and Canada.

Many rivers flow into the Great Lakes. These rivers connect the lakes to one another or to inland areas. Early settlers built ports on the Great Lakes or along the rivers. Farmers and traders carried goods on boats and rafts to those inland ports. The goods were then transported by wagon, boat, and railroad to other parts of the country.

Today, the inland port cities of Chicago, Illinois, and Cleveland, Ohio, are two of the largest cities on the Great Lakes. Chicago is on Lake Michigan. Cleveland is on Lake Erie. Other inland port cities on the Great Lakes include Duluth, Minnesota, and Milwaukee, Wisconsin.

12 The word *HOMES* can help you remember the names of the Great Lakes. Complete the list below by filling in the name of the lake that starts with each letter provided.

H Hurn

O ontario

M michgain

E Erie

S superior

13 Underline the paragraph that describes how the Great Lakes have supported interaction between inland areas.

The city of Chicago, Illinois, lies on the shore of Lake Michigan.

Connecting the Great Lakes

In the past, large ships could not pass all the way from the Great Lakes to the Atlantic Ocean. Only one river, the St. Lawrence River, connects the Great Lakes to the Atlantic coast. However, the river contains dangerous rapids, and some parts of it are too shallow or narrow for ships to use.

Ships also could not pass from one end of the Great Lakes to the other. Along the way, the water at Niagara Falls drops about 167 feet. Niagara Falls is part of the Niagara River, which links Lake Erie and Lake Ontario.

In 1825, the state of New York completed a canal that connected Lake Erie to the Hudson River. It linked Buffalo, New York, on Lake Erie, to Troy, on the Hudson River. From Troy, ships traveled down the Hudson to New York City and the Atlantic.

Today, ships travel between the Great Lakes and the Atlantic Ocean on the St. Lawrence Seaway. This waterway, which was completed in 1959, links Lake Erie to Montreal, on the St. Lawrence River.

14 Underline the name of the river that connects the Great Lakes to the Atlantic Ocean.

15 The time line below is a vertical time line. It is read from top to bottom. Place the letter from these two events in the proper sequence on the time line.

A. The Erie Canal is completed.

B. The St. Lawrence Seaway is completed.

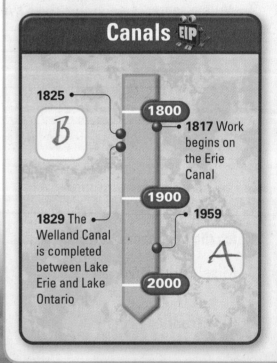

Canals EIP

1825 — B

1800

1817 Work begins on the Erie Canal

1900

1829 The Welland Canal is completed between Lake Erie and Lake Ontario

1959 — A

2000

1. **SUMMARIZE** What are the different kinds of bodies of water found in the United States?

_____

_____

_____

_____

2. Write a sentence defining a **river system**.

_____

_____

_____

_____

Circle the letter of the correct answer.

3. Which is a tributary of the Mississippi River?

   A Gulf of Mexico

   B St. Lawrence River

   C Rio Grande

   D Missouri River

4. Which river was considered to be a gateway to the western United States?

   F St. Lawrence River

   G Ohio River

   H Colorado River

   J Mississippi River

5. Which body of water connects the Great Lakes and the Atlantic Ocean?

   A St. Lawrence River

   B Rio Grande

   C Ohio River

   D Arctic Ocean

Match the river name on the left with the information on the right.

6. Mississippi River

   part of the border between Mexico and the United States

7. Rio Grande

   flows into the Gulf of Mexico

8. St. Lawrence River

   part of the border between Canada and the United States

writing

Write a Paragraph Write a paragraph describing how bodies of water can create links between people of different regions or countries.

A lighthouse in Virginia

Geographic Features and History

Land and water features have always influenced, or affected, United States history. People's actions are influenced by their **environment**, or surroundings. In turn, people have changed their environments to meet their needs, travel, and do their jobs. **Think about how geography has affected people's actions.**

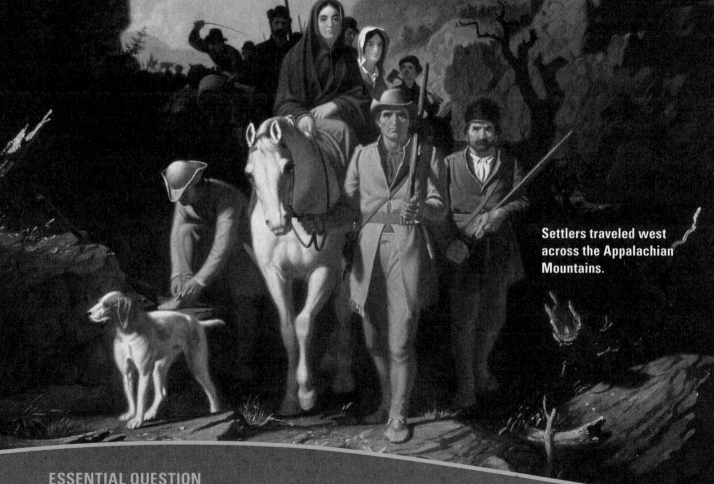

Settlers traveled west across the Appalachian Mountains.

ESSENTIAL QUESTION

✓ Why are geographic features important in United States history?

 HISTORY AND SOCIAL SCIENCE SOL
USI.1f, USI.2d

St. Louis, in Missouri, is one of many cities built along the Mississippi River. This picture shows St. Louis in 1859.

TextWork

1 Scan the text on this page. Underline the names of geographic features that have made settlement easier.

2 Circle the sentences that describe geographic features that have made settlement more difficult.

3 Why were cities often located near transportation routes?

_____

_____

_____

_____

Locations of Cities and Towns

Geographic features—such as landforms, bodies of water, climate, and natural resources—have affected the locations of many cities and towns. A **natural resource** is something in nature that people can use to meet their needs.

In the past, most people settled in plains regions, where the ground was mostly flat or rolling and the soil was good for farming. Other natural resources, such as trees for building and metals for trading, have also influenced settlement. Fewer people settled in desert or mountainous regions. In such areas, it was difficult to build shelters, find food and water, and travel.

Until the late 1920s, most people lived in **rural**, or country, areas. Today, most Americans live and work in **urban**, or city, areas. Cities are often found near waterways or other transportation routes, such as railroads or highways. Those transportation routes make it easier for people to travel and ship goods.

Westward Movement

In the late 1700s and early 1800s, settlers in the United States moved west of the frontier, across the Appalachian Mountains. The **frontier** was the land just beyond the areas already settled by Europeans.

Some geographic features encouraged westward movement. For example, the flat or rolling lands of the Coastal Plain and the Interior Lowlands made it easier for people there to build roads and railroads. Wide rivers in the regions also made it easier for settlers to travel and transport goods.

Other geographic features were barriers that blocked westward movement. At the Fall Line, the land drops sharply and rivers form waterfalls and rapids, which prevented travel inland by boat. Mountains were also barriers to travel.

To overcome these geographic barriers, people modified, or changed, the environment. They cleared mountain paths and built bridges over waterways, valleys, and rivers. People also built roads, canals, and railroads to reduce travel times.

TextWork

❹ Write a sentence that describes the location of the frontier in the late 1700s and early 1800s.

_____

_____

_____

_____

❺ (Focus Skill) Underline the details that support the main idea that some geographic features were barriers to westward movement.

❻ Study the map. By what year was all of Illinois settled?

_____

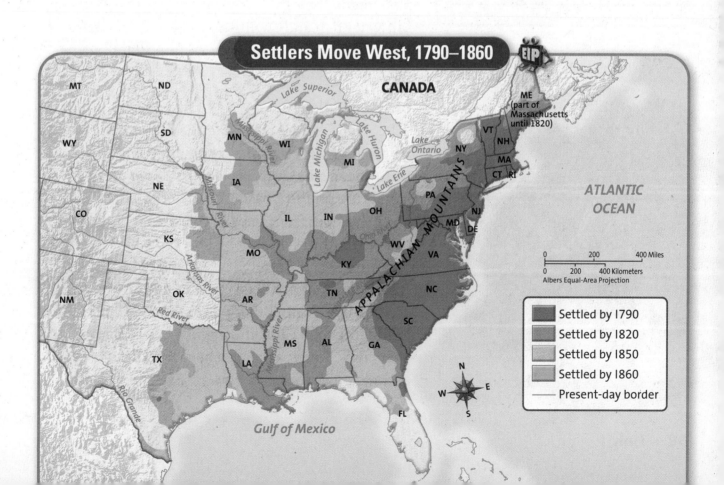

Settlers Move West, 1790–1860

Legend:
- Settled by 1790
- Settled by 1820
- Settled by 1850
- Settled by 1860
- Present-day border

Fishers pull in the catch.

Geography and Industry

Geographic features have affected industries in the United States. An **industry** is all the businesses that make one kind of product or provide one kind of service. The diverse geography of the country has also led to different kinds of land use. **Land use** is the way most of the land in a place is used.

The Agriculture Industry

In the past, most land in the United States was used for agriculture, or farming. Most farming took place on the Coastal Plain, on the Interior Lowlands, and in valleys in the West. In those regions, the land is generally fertile, and there is usually enough water for crops to grow. In grazing areas, where the land is too dry or poor to grow many crops, farmers and ranchers have raised livestock.

The Fishing Industry

Many people along waterways have worked in fishing and shipping businesses. For years, people have made their living by catching many kinds of saltwater fish and shellfish off the ocean coasts. Freshwater fishing has been an important business near the Great Lakes.

Other Land Uses

People in the United States have used large amounts of land for forestry, mining, and manufacturing, or making goods. Most large areas of forests are on the Coastal Plain and in mountainous areas. Lumber from trees has been used to make buildings, ships, and many wood products, such as furniture.

Most mining has been done in mountainous areas, as well as in other places where minerals are found. Much manufacturing has taken place in or near cities. Cities have also been important centers of trade and transportation.

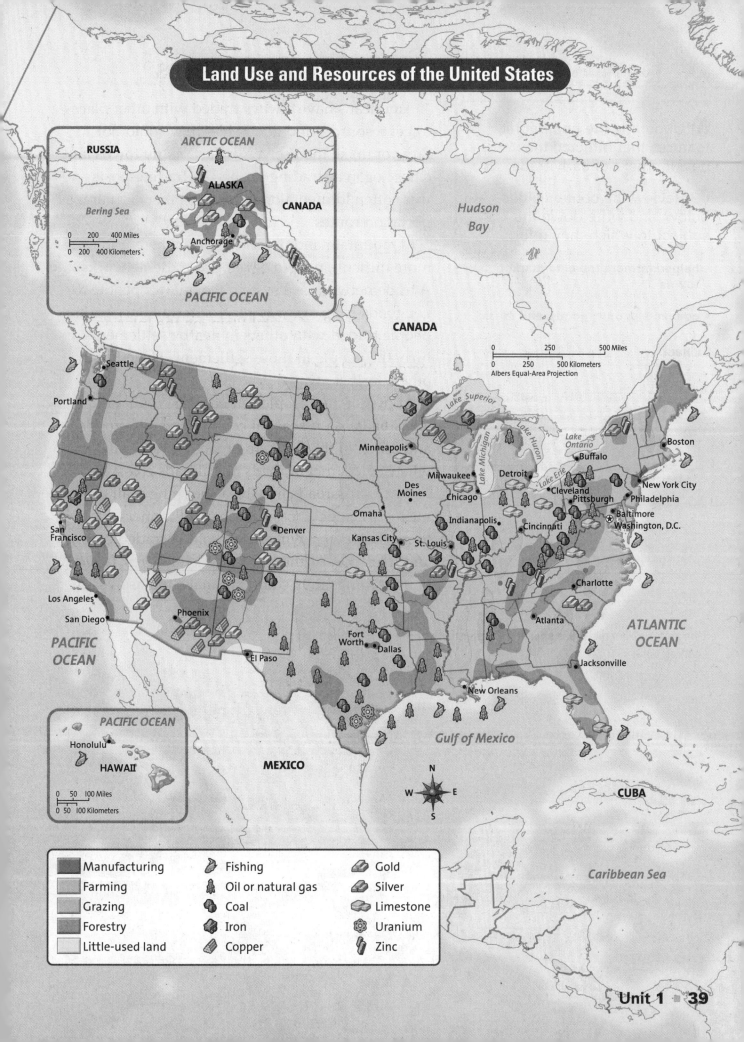

Land Use and Resources of the United States

RUSSIA

ARCTIC OCEAN

ALASKA

CANADA

Bering Sea

0   200   400 Miles
0   200   400 Kilometers

Anchorage

PACIFIC OCEAN

Hudson Bay

CANADA

0   250   500 Miles
0   250   500 Kilometers
Albers Equal-Area Projection

Seattle

Portland

Lake Superior

Lake Michigan

Lake Huron

Minneapolis

Lake Ontario

Boston

Milwaukee

Detroit

Buffalo

Lake Erie

Des Moines

Chicago

Cleveland

New York City

Pittsburgh

Philadelphia

San Francisco

Omaha

Denver

Indianapolis

Cincinnati

Baltimore
Washington, D.C.

Kansas City

St. Louis

Los Angeles

San Diego

Phoenix

Charlotte

PACIFIC OCEAN

Atlanta

ATLANTIC OCEAN

El Paso

Fort Worth

Dallas

Jacksonville

New Orleans

Gulf of Mexico

MEXICO

N
W   E
S

CUBA

PACIFIC OCEAN

Honolulu

HAWAII

0   50   100 Miles
0   50   100 Kilometers

Caribbean Sea

Symbol	Land Use / Resource
	Manufacturing
	Farming
	Grazing
	Forestry
	Little-used land
	Fishing
	Oil or natural gas
	Coal
	Iron
	Copper
	Gold
	Silver
	Limestone
	Uranium
	Zinc

Trade Patterns

⓫ Underline the geographic features that affected the development of early trade.

⓬ Review the context clues below, and write down the subject to which they refer.

• helped farmers travel to market towns

• connects people, goods, and ideas

Subject: _____

_____

_____

Americans have always traded with other places to get resources and goods that they could not grow or make themselves. In fact, many towns and cities began as trading posts. The trading posts were often located along rivers or other early transportation routes.

In mountain and desert regions, where trade was more difficult, people developed trade networks. A trade network is a system that allows people to get goods from faraway places. In trade networks, people traded with others in nearby settlements. In turn, the people in those settlements traded with others farther away.

At first, many people settled near crossroads. A **crossroads** is a place that connects people, goods, and ideas. In the past, crossroads were located where rivers met or roads or railroads crossed. Today, a crossroads may be a shopping mall or business center. Crossroads helped farmers travel to market towns, where they sold or traded crops and livestock. At the towns' general stores, farmers bought things they could not make themselves.

This picture from the 1860s shows a frontier town built along railroad lines heading west.

1. **SUMMARIZE** In what ways has geography influenced United States history?

_____

_____

_____

2. What is the difference between an **urban** area and a **rural** area?

_____

_____

_____

_____

_____

3. What are some geographic features that encouraged westward movement?

_____

_____

_____

_____

Circle the letter of the correct answer.

4. Cities are often located—

   A in mountainous areas

   B along waterways

   C in deserts

   D in rural areas

5. Which geographic feature made it difficult to travel west of the Coastal Plain by boat?

   F Fall Line

   G Atlantic Ocean

   H Appalachian Mountains

   J Great Plains

6. In the past, most land in the United States was used for—

   A farming

   B trade

   C fishing

   D mining

7. Many people work in the fishing industry—

   F near the Great Basin

   G in the Great Lakes region

   H in the Great Plains region

   J in the Rockies

activity

Make a Chart Make a chart listing the geographic features that have affected one of the following: locations of cities and towns, westward movement, industry, or trade.

A farmer on the frontier

Fun With Social Studies

GRAND CANYON

APPALACHIAN MOUNTAINS

Terrific Travels

On her trip across the United States, Emmy sent postcards. Complete each message by naming the geographic region or landform she is describing. Write the message number on the correct postcard.

Atlantic Coast Beaches

ROCKY MOUNTAINS

1

Dear Uncle Albert,
The mountain peaks here in the
_____
are sharp and jagged. Erosion has not worn them down for as long as other ranges. What will they look like millions of years from now?

2

Hi, Marco!
Florida is fantastic! We went sailing today. We docked our boat in a harbor. My mom said that the
_____
region has wide, flat beaches like this one all the way from here to Massachusetts.

3

Dear Ms. Brown,
Remember when we talked in class about how canyons are formed? Today, in the _____ region, I walked down into one of the world's largest canyons. Walking back to the top was the hard part!

4

Dear Grandma,
The mountainsides covered with trees are so pretty! The park ranger said the _____ are the oldest mountains in the United States. Do you think they are older than Grandpa?

Miss Information

Miss Information is guiding visitors through the natural history museum. Unfortunately, one of her facts is wrong. Circle the incorrect fact. Then rewrite it so that it is correct.

_____

_____

_____

The equator divides Earth into the Southern and Northern Hemispheres.

The Pacific Ocean is almost twice the size of the Atlantic Ocean.

Asia is the largest continent.

Earth's two largest geographic features are its continents and oceans.

The prime meridian runs from the North Pole to the South Pole.

About three-fourths of Earth is covered by land.

Picture This

abc VOCABULARY

Can you figure out the words shown? Match each puzzle to one of the definitions on the right.

env + 🔺 + 🍬

fron + 👁

in + 🧹 + 🌳

✗ + 🌉

con + 🗑 + 🐜

A place that connects people, goods, and ideas

All the businesses that make one kind of product or provide one kind of service

The land just beyond settled areas

One of Earth's largest land areas

People's surroundings

Unit 1

Review and Test Prep

The Big Idea

People interact with their environment and are affected by it.

Summarize the Unit

Main Idea and Details Complete the organizer to show that you know how to identify a main idea based on some supporting details about the geography of the United States.

Main Idea

_____

_____

Details

Land in plains regions is mostly flat or rolling.	The United States has several large mountain ranges.	Bodies of water have shaped the land.

Use Vocabulary

Fill in the missing word in each sentence, using the correct word from the Word Bank.

1. Each geographic _____ of North America has distinctive characteristics that make it different from other areas.

2. A _____ is surrounded on at least three sides by water.

3. Over time, _____ has worn down the peaks of the Appalachian Mountains.

4. Today, most Americans live in _____ areas.

5. Some geographers group Europe and Asia as one _____ .

Word Bank

continent p. 7

peninsula p. 15

region p. 19

erosion p. 22

urban p. 36

rural p. 36

Think About It

Circle the letter of the correct answer.

6.

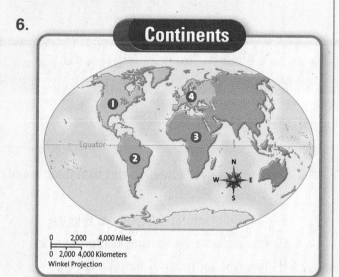

Continents

Which continent is Africa?

A 1

B 2

C 3

D 4

7.

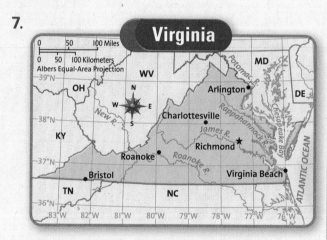

Virginia

Which best describes the location of Arlington?

F 37°N, 82°W

G 38°N, 79°W

H 39°N, 77°W

J 37°N, 77°W

8. Which ocean is almost twice the size of the Atlantic Ocean?

A Pacific Ocean

B Southern Ocean

C Indian Ocean

D Arctic Ocean

9. Mapmakers use relief to show—

F parallels of latitude

G differences in elevation

H locations of resources

J bodies of water

10.

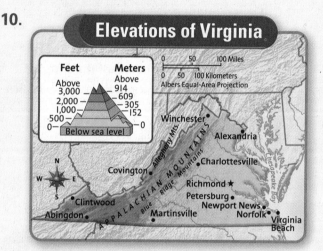

Elevations of Virginia

What is the elevation of the land around Richmond?

A Above 3,000 feet

B Between 2,000 and 3,000 feet

C Between 1,000 and 2,000 feet

D Below 500 feet

11. The Coastal Plain may be described as—

F rocky land along the Atlantic Ocean

G a range of mountains along the Atlantic Ocean

H flat, mostly low land along the Atlantic Ocean

J an area of hills and valleys along the Atlantic Ocean

12.

What geographic region is shaded on the map?

A Great Plains

B Rocky Mountains

C Coastal Range

D Basin and Range

13. Why does the eastern part of the Interior Lowlands have more trees than the western part?

F It gets more rainfall.

G It has more rivers.

H It is farther from the ocean.

J It is part of a basin.

14.

This picture BEST represents a—

A coastal region in the United States

B mountain region in the United States

C plains region in the United States

D desert region in the United States

15.

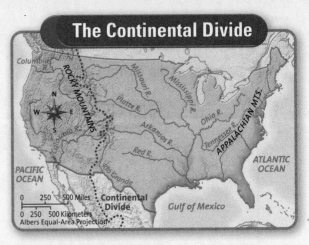

Which two rivers have water that eventually reaches the Pacific Ocean?

F The Colorado and Columbia Rivers

G The Colorado and Mississippi Rivers

H The Missouri and Columbia Rivers

J The Platte and Arkansas Rivers

16.

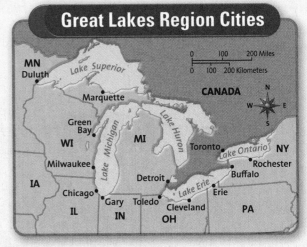

Near what body of water was the city of Chicago built?

A Lake Huron

B Lake Superior

C Lake Michigan

D Lake Erie

17.

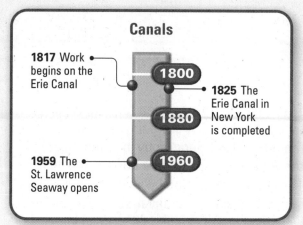

Canals

1817 Work begins on the Erie Canal — 1800

1825 The Erie Canal in New York is completed — 1880

1959 The St. Lawrence Seaway opens — 1960

How many years after the Erie Canal was completed did the St. Lawrence Seaway open?

F 7

G 30

H 97

J 134

18. In the past, most people settled in—

A desert regions

B mountainous areas

C plains regions

D urban areas

19. In which area does the fishing industry provide jobs for many people?

F Near the Interior Lowlands

G Along the Great Lakes

H Along the Fall Line

J Near the Great Basin

Answer these questions.

20. How does the Rocky Mountains region compare to and contrast with the Appalachian Highlands region?

_____

_____

_____

21. How have the Mississippi and Missouri Rivers supported interaction among different regions?

_____

_____

_____

22. What geographic features encouraged settlers to move west of the frontier?

_____

_____

_____

Hall of Geograp

I just saw something move inside that exhibit!

HMH

The Time Museum is open for field trips today. You and Eco are going to check out the new Hall of Geography, but you'd better not expect this to be a normal museum. These exhibits can pull you in and show you geography as you've never seen it. Find the key stand in the exhibit hall to unlock the secret! Play the game now online.

Show What You Know

✏ Writing Write a Short Story

Imagine you are traveling on a boat from the Great Lakes to the Gulf of Mexico. Write a short story about your journey. Name in order the waterways on which you travel to reach your destination. Describe the land that you see along the way. Also describe the different activities that you see happening on the waterways.

🖌 Activity Make an Atlas

Make at least three maps to include in an atlas of the United States. Use your textbook and other resources to make maps that show different kinds of information about the United States, such as landforms, elevation, bodies of water, climate, population, and land use and resources. Include labels on your maps, and make a map legend to explain the symbols that you use.

American Indian Cultures

An American Indian gathering, in Charlotte, North Carolina

Spotlight on Standards

THE BIG IDEA People use the different resources in their environment to meet their basic needs for food, shelter, and clothing.

HISTORY AND SOCIAL SCIENCE SOL
USI.1a, USI.1b, USI.1c, USI.1d, USI.1f, USI.3a, USI.3b, USI.3c

49

Set the Stage

Study the map. Circle the name of an early American Indian group that lived in what is now Virginia. On what major landform did that group live?

_____

HOPI Name of American Indian tribe

ASIA

INUIT

ARCTIC OCEAN

Bering Sea

Brooks Range

INU

Yukon River

Aleutian Islands

INUIT

Alaska Range

ATHAPASCAN

Great Bear Lake

ALEUT

HAN

Gulf of Alaska

Mackenzie River

Great Sla Lake

ROCKY

TLINGIT

KASKA

HAIDA

BELLA COOLA

Vancouver Island

KWAKIUTL

NOOTKA

KOOTENAI

MAKAH

CHINOOK

BLAC

M O U N T A

NEZ PERCÉ

COAST RANGES

CASCADE RANGE

Columbia

PACIFIC OCEAN

Great Salt Lake

PAIUTE

GREAT SHOSHONE

POMO

COAST RANGES

SIERRA NEVADA

BASIN

PAIUTE

YOKUTS

Grand Canyon

Colorado

CHUMASH

Mojave Desert

NA ZI

Sonoran Desert

Gulf of California

Baja California

COCHIMI

YAQUI

American Indians of the Southwest

N

W E

S

HU

0   250   500 Miles

0   250   500 Kilometers

Lambert Azimuthal Equal-Area Projection

Greenland

INUIT

INUIT INUIT

INUIT

INUIT

**ATLANTIC
OCEAN**

Hudson
Bay

CHIPEWYAN

NASKAPI

Newfoundland

CREE

CREE

BEOTHUK

CREE

CANADIAN SHIELD

Lake
Winnipeg

MICMAC

CHIPPEWA

CHIPPEWA

ALGONKIN

PENOBSCOT

Lake Superior

OTTAWA

MANDAN

HURON

Lake
Ontario

IROQUOIS

MASSACHUSET

LAKOTA

Mississippi River

SAC
FOX

Lake Michigan

Lake Huron

Lake Erie

ERIE

**American Indians of the
Eastern Woodlands**

MIAMI

MOUNTAINS

INTERIOR LOWLANDS

IOWAY

LENNI LENAPE

ARAPAHO

River

ILLINOIS

Central
Plains

POWHATAN

KAW

MISSOURI

Arkansas River

OSAGE

Ohio River

KIOWA

QUAPAW

YUCHI

TUSCARORA

APPALACHIAN

CHEROKEE

CHICKASAW

Red

CADDO

River

COMANCHE

CHOCTAW

COASTAL PLAIN

**American Indians of
the Plains**

NATCHEZ

COASTAL PLAIN

TIMUCUA

CALUSA

Rio Grande

Gulf of
Mexico

SIERRA MADRE ORIENTAL

COAHUILTEC

CIBONEY

TAINO

Cuba

TAINO

ARAWAK

ARAWAK

CIBONEY

Hispaniola

TOLTEC

MAYA

AZTEC

Yucatán
Peninsula

Caribbean Sea

MIXTEC

OLMEC

ZAPOTEC

Set the Stage

1 Circle the name of the American Indian group that hunted buffalo for food.

2 How were the early peoples of the Arctic and the Pacific Northwest similar?

_____

A Pueblo Family

People of the Southwest

- Lived mostly in the desert areas of what is now the southwestern United States and northern Mexico
- Built their houses in sides of cliffs and mesas
- Used a variety of natural resources to build their houses

Pacific Northwest People

- Lived in what is now western Canada and the present-day states of Washington and Oregon
- Skilled fishers and whalers
- Traveled long distances to trade

A Kwakiutl Family

A Lakota Family

An Iroquois Family

Plains People

- Lived in a wide area from what is now Texas to what is now Canada
- Main food source was buffalo

Eastern Woodlands People

- Lived mostly in areas east of the Mississippi River in what is now the United States
- Used wood to make shelters, tools, and canoes
- Main crops were corn, beans, and squash

Arctic People

- Lived in an area that covered much of what is now northern Canada and northern Alaska
- Skilled fishers and seal hunters

An Inuit Family

Preview Vocabulary

artifact

Scientists study **artifacts** to learn about past ways of life. Those artifacts include any object made or used by people. p. 58

wampum

Some American Indians used **wampum**, or beads cut from seashells, to trade for other goods. p. 70

confederation

The Iroquois formed a **confederation**. This loose group of governments worked together to settle disputes. p. 70

irrigation

People in desert areas dug ditches to bring water to their crops. This method is called **irrigation**. p. 81

economy

Trade was an important part of the **economy**, or the way that people use resources to meet their needs. p. 90

kayak

Arctic fishers were able to paddle through icy waters in small one-person canoes called **kayaks**. p. 94

Reading Social Studies

Compare and Contrast

LEARN

When you **compare**, you tell how two or more things are alike, or similar. When you **contrast**, you tell how they are different. Some words that are used to compare are *like, both, all, also, too, similar,* and *same.* Some words that are used to contrast are *but, instead, unlike, however, different,* and *differ.*

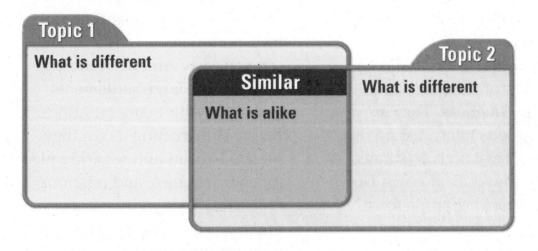

Topic 1 — What is different

Similar — What is alike

Topic 2 — What is different

PRACTICE

Circle the sentences that describe how people in the past and people today are similar. Underline the sentences that describe how the people are different. The first paragraph has been done for you.

People in some desert areas have had to adapt to living in extreme heat. Early American Indian groups constructed homes with thick walls to help stay cool. Many modern homes in desert areas are built the same way. However, homes today have air-conditioning systems. Homes long ago did not.

Similar

Different

The small amount of rain in desert regions makes it difficult to grow crops there. Early American Indians collected rainwater and dug ditches to direct water to their crops. Today, people living in the desert still dig water channels. But unlike early people, they have electric pumps to move water.

Read the article. Then complete the activities below.

Links to the Past

People today practice some ways of life that are similar to those of early American Indian groups. Much has changed in the centuries since people first settled the Americas. But some ways of life have stayed the same.

Centuries ago, beans and corn were important foods in many parts of the Americas. They are important foods today, too. In fact, those foods have been on dinner tables for thousands of years. Do you enjoy snacking on popcorn? Many early American Indian groups ate popcorn, too.

Many early American Indians paddled down rivers and across lakes in canoes. Today, many people still travel in canoes. However, most people use them for enjoyment and not for transportation.

Some early American Indian groups built large settlements and cities with many buildings. Before constructing a city, they planned ahead and set aside places for shops, homes, and religious buildings. Today, city planners organize cities and neighborhoods in much the same way.

1. **In the second paragraph, circle the sentences that tell that the foods early American Indians ate are similar to the foods people eat today.**

2. **How do people today use canoes differently from early American Indians?**

_____

_____

_____

3. **How is the way Americans today plan cities similar to the way early American Indians planned cities?**

_____

_____

_____

Early People

Scientists do not agree about when and how people arrived in the Western Hemisphere. However, early people likely lived in the region thousands of years ago. Those people were the ancestors, or early family members, of present-day American Indians. **Think about how the environment may have affected early people.**

Early people hunted woolly mammoths and other large animals.

ESSENTIAL QUESTIONS

✓ Why is archaeology important?

✓ Where is one of the oldest archaeological sites in the United States located?

✓ How did geography and climate affect the way American Indian groups met their basic needs?

✓ How did the American Indians use natural, capital, and human resources?

 HISTORY AND SOCIAL SCIENCE SOL
USI.1a, USI.1b, USI.1c, USI.1d, USI.3a, USI.3c

CACTUS HILL

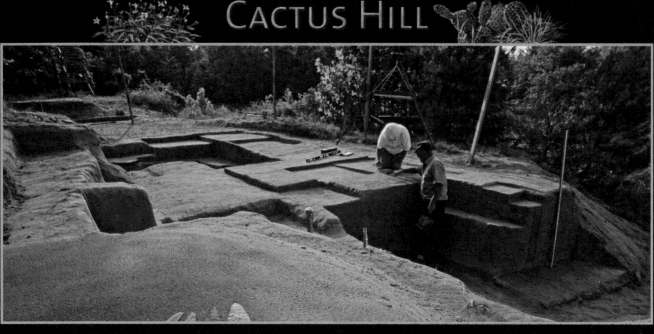

Archaeologists uncover artifacts at Cactus Hill.

TextWork

1 Write a sentence that uses the word *culture* to explain the meaning of archaeology.

I S Like people
Seacrh a old
artfact in the ground

2 Why do archaeologists study artifacts?

_____

_____

_____

3 Underline the sentence that describes what archaeologists can learn by comparing artifacts from different times.

Learning About Early People

The earliest people of North America left no recorded history of how they lived. Much of what we know about them comes from the artifacts they left behind. An **artifact** is any object made or used by people in the past.

Artifacts can provide important evidence about past **cultures**, or ways of life. The study of past cultures is called **archaeology** (ar•kee•AH•luh•jee). To study human behavior and to learn about past cultures, archaeologists recover buried artifacts. From artifacts such as spear points, archaeologists can figure out how people hunted or fought. Hoes, needles, or other tools provide scientists with clues about how people grew food or made products.

When removing artifacts from an archaeological site, archaeologists generally dig in layers. Artifacts discovered nearest to the surface belonged to people who lived at the site more recently. Older objects are found in deeper layers. By comparing artifacts from different times, archaeologists can see how cultures have changed or remained the same.

The artifacts found in each layer at the Cactus Hill site provided archaeologists with clues about the lives of the different groups who lived there.

Cactus Hill

Cactus Hill is one of the oldest sites where early people lived in North America. It is located on the banks of the Nottoway (NAH•tuh•way) River, in southeastern Virginia.

In the uppermost layers of the Cactus Hill site, archaeologists discovered artifacts that are more than 10,000 years old. These artifacts include spear points that were sharpened with a piece of stone or a bone. The spear points were hollowed out at one end. Archaeologists think this was done so the points could be attached to a wooden shaft. Such evidence tells archaeologists that Cactus Hill was probably a campsite for early hunters.

Discoveries made by archaeologists can sometimes change people's **historical perspectives**, or how they look at the past. At the lowest layer of the Cactus Hill site, archaeologists found artifacts that may be at least 15,000 years old. Because of the age of these artifacts, most archaeologists now believe that people inhabited North America earlier than previously thought.

TextWork

❹ Circle the name of one of the oldest sites where early people lived in North America.

❺ Study the illustration. Place an *X* over the artifact you think is the oldest. What clues led you to conclude this?

_____

_____

_____

❻ Underline the sentence that explains how discoveries at Cactus Hill have changed the historical perspectives of most archaeologists.

The Earliest Americans

7 (Focus Skill) How did the climate of the Ice Ages differ from today's climate?

_____

_____

_____

8 Circle the different views that archaeologists have about how early people may have arrived in North America.

9 What perspective do many American Indians have about their ancestors' history?

_____

_____

_____

_____

Thousands of years ago, Earth's climate was much different from that of today. There were several periods of freezing cold, known as Ice Ages. During these Ice Ages, much of Earth's water was frozen in glaciers. As a result, the water level of the oceans dropped. At times, a "bridge" of dry land surfaced between Asia and North America.

For years, archaeologists believed that people first arrived in North America by crossing that land bridge about 12,000 years ago. However, discoveries at Cactus Hill suggest that people already inhabited North America long before other groups crossed the land bridge during the last Ice Age.

Today, archaeologists have more evidence. However, they still disagree about when and how people first arrived in North America. Some early groups may have followed coastal land routes. Others groups may have traveled by boat, crossing from island to island over many hundreds of years.

Many American Indians have a different perspective about their ancestors' history. They believe their people have always lived in the Americas.

Early people moved from place to place, following the animals they hunted. Over thousands of years, people slowly moved across North America and South America.

Early Ways of Life

Early people likely traveled in bands, or small family groups that lived and worked together. They hunted woolly mammoths, mastodons, and other large animals. They also gathered wild foods, such as nuts and berries. For this reason, archaeologists call them hunters and gatherers.

About 10,000 years ago, the last Ice Age ended. When the climate became warmer, many large animals became extinct, or died out. People adapted by fishing and by hunting smaller animals. They made new hunting tools, such as bows and arrows.

By about 5,000 years ago, some people began to plant and harvest crops. This meant that they no longer had to hunt and gather all their food. Having a steady supply of food allowed people to stay in one place and build permanent shelters. In time, more groups built permanent settlements.

Some groups formed what are now called tribes. These are groups of American Indians who share the same traditional language, land, and leaders. Each tribe developed its own culture, which made it different from other tribes.

TextWork

10 How did the end of the last Ice Age affect the lives of early people?

_____

_____

_____

11 Which of these events happened first? Circle the letter of the correct entry.

A. Early people began to grow food instead of gathering it.

B. Early people built permanent settlements.

C. Early people fished and also hunted smaller animals, using tools such as bows and arrows.

TextWork

12 Scan the text on these pages. Circle the three types of resources that American Indians used to produce goods.

13 Circle the paragraph that describes the ways that American Indians used natural resources in their environment to meet their basic needs.

14 Study the illustration. What natural resources are used to make farming tools?

_____

_____

Using Resources

Both geography and climate affected how American Indian groups met their basic needs for food, shelter, and clothing. Because American Indians lived in different environments, they had different resources available to them. These resources influenced what products were produced and how they were produced.

Natural Resources

In the past, American Indians depended on the natural resources in their environment to meet their basic needs. For food, they gathered plants, nuts, and berries, and they hunted animals and fished in rivers. Some American Indians also grew crops for food. They made clothing and tools from animal skins and bones. They built shelters from wood, stones, sod, clay, or animal skins.

Some natural resources and goods were used for trade. People traded to get things they could not make or grow. Among some tribes, clay pottery was used to store and transport food and other goods.

Early people used digging sticks and other tools made of wood and stone to grow crops such as corn (left) and squash.

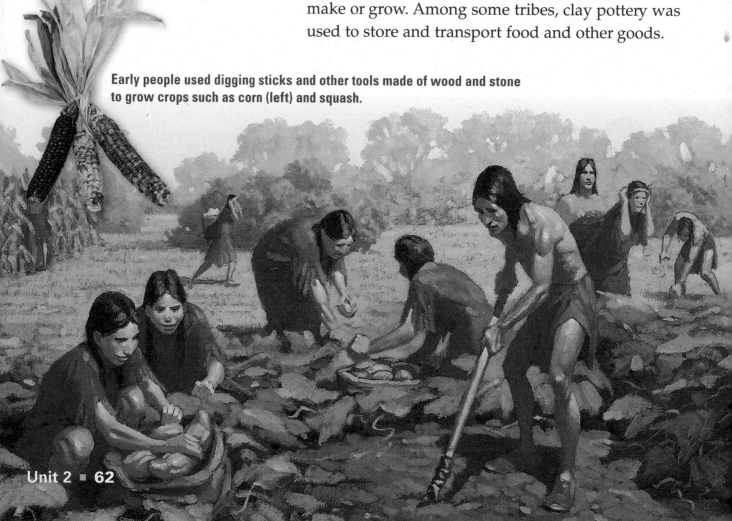

Fish were an important natural resource. Catching them for food required both capital and human resources.

Human Resources

Human resources are the workers who produce goods or provide services. Early American Indians who fished, made clothing, hunted animals, and did other tasks for a tribe were human resources. Some workers gathered natural resources such as wood or water. Others transported goods and resources to other tribes for trade. By working together as a group, members of a tribe could make better use of their resources.

Capital Resources

Capital resources are goods that are produced to make other goods or to provide services. Tools, canoes, bows, spears, and weirs were examples of early capital resources. A weir is a fence-like barrier used to trap fish. Many of these early capital resources were made from wood, stone, or animal parts. Spear points were made from flint, a kind of stone. Bones and antlers were sharpened into tools. Other animal parts were used to make thread and containers.

TextWork

15 Study the illustration above. Place an *X* above the human resources working to catch fish.

16 In the illustration above, draw a circle around the capital resources working to make a canoe.

17 What capital resources shown in the illustration above were used to catch fish?

_____

_____

_____

_____

1. **SUMMARIZE** Why is archaeology important in learning about early people?

_____

_____

_____

_____

2. Write a sentence describing the difference between a **capital resource** and a **human resource**.

_____

_____

_____

_____

_____

Circle the letter of the correct answer.

3. Archaeologists found some of the earliest artifacts in North America at—

   A Richmond

   B Cactus Hill

   C Norfolk

   D Arlington

4. When did early American Indians begin to harvest crops?

   F About 15,000 years ago

   G About 12,000 years ago

   H About 5,000 years ago

   J About 3,000 years ago

5. Which is a natural resource used by early people to build shelters?

   A Stone

   B Steel

   C Iron

   D Glass

Match the kind of resource on the left with the information on the right.

6. human resource   a weir used to trap fish

7. capital resource   a fisher who uses a weir

8. natural resource   wood used to make a weir

writing

✏ **Write a Story** Write a story describing how American Indians living thousands of years ago related to the environment in their daily life.

Early spear points

The Eastern Woodlands

Before the first Europeans arrived in North America, many American Indian tribes already lived there. In fact, American Indians lived in all areas of North America. Each tribe was different. However, the tribes that lived within the same area often had similar ways of life. They were affected by the same geography and climate, and they depended on the same kinds of natural resources. **Think about the kinds of natural resources that Eastern Woodlands tribes might have used to meet their basic needs in the past.**

A recreated Eastern Woodlands settlement, in Connecticut

ESSENTIAL QUESTIONS

- In which areas did the American Indians live?
- Where do American Indians live today?
- How did geography and climate affect the way American Indian groups met their basic needs?
- How did the American Indians use natural, capital, and human resources?

 HISTORY AND SOCIAL SCIENCE SOL
USI.1a, USI.1f, USI.3b, USI.3c

TextWork

❶ (Focus Skill) **What natural resource did all people in the Eastern Woodlands use?**

_____

_____

❷ How did people in the Eastern Woodlands use wood from trees?

_____

_____

_____

❸ Scan the text. Circle the sentences that describe how Eastern Woodlands people got their food.

Eastern Woodlands Tribes

The Eastern Woodlands region stretched from the Mississippi River valley to the Atlantic Ocean. The region's name comes from the thick forests that once covered the land. American Indians who lived in the region built their settlements along the many rivers and streams that flowed through the forests.

Many different tribes lived in the Eastern Woodlands. However, they all depended on an important natural resource—trees. People in the Eastern Woodlands used wood from the trees to build shelters and canoes and to make tools and weapons. They also gathered fruits and nuts from trees. Some produced maple syrup from tree sap.

The Eastern Woodlands people were farmers as well as hunters and gatherers. In the northeastern part of the Eastern Woodlands, however, the soil is mostly rocky. People there did more hunting and gathering than farming. They also fished in the area's many lakes and rivers. In the southern part of the Eastern Woodlands, the soil and climate were better for growing crops.

The forests of the Eastern Woodlands provided people with wood that was used to make homes, canoes, weapons, and tools.

Eastern Woodlands

ALGONKIN ABENAKI
WYANDOT
WINNEBAGO
FOX
POTAWATOMI ERIE IROQUOIS
PEQUOT
MIAMI SUSQUEHANNOCK
ILLINOIS DELAWARE
SHAWNEE POWHATAN
CHEROKEE
TUSCARORA
CHICKASAW CATAWBA
TUSKEGEE
CADDO CREEK
CHOCTAW
ATAKAPA
TIMUCUA
CALUSA
--- Present-day border

The Algonquian, Siouan, and Iroquoian

The Eastern Woodlands people are generally divided into three main language groups—the Algonquian (al•GAHN•kwee•uhn), the Siouan (SOO•uhn), and the Iroquoian (ir•uh•KWOY•uhn). Among the Algonquian-speaking groups were the Powhatan, Ottawa, Chippewa, and Miami. Most Algonquian groups lived on the Coastal Plain.

The Siouan-speaking tribes included the Monacan, Saponi (suh•poh•NEE), and the Catawba (kuh•TAW•buh). These tribes lived mostly in the Piedmont, in what are now Virginia, North Carolina, and South Carolina.

The homelands of the Iroquoian-speaking tribes included the southern Appalachians and the northeastern part of North America. The five largest Iroquoian tribes were the Cayuga (kay•YOO•guh), Mohawk, Oneida (oh•NY•duh), Onandaga (ah•nuhn•DAW•guh), and Seneca. Together, they were known as the Iroquois, or the Five Nations. These tribes lived in what is now New York and Pennsylvania and along Lake Ontario in Canada.

 TextWork

❹ What were the three main language groups in the Eastern Woodlands?

_____

_____

_____

❺ Study the map. Find and circle the name of an Algonquian-speaking group.

❻ Underline the name on the map of a tribe that lived in what is now Virginia. To which language group did the tribe belong?

_____

_____

TextWork

7 Circle the paragraph that describes how a longhouse was built.

8 Study the illustration. Place an *X* over three examples of people using wood.

9 What other natural resources, besides wood, are people in the illustration using?

_____

_____

_____

Iroquois Settlements

The Iroquois usually built their settlements on high ground near water. To protect against enemies, they surrounded their towns with tall palisades. A **palisade** is a wall made of tall wooden poles.

People of the Longhouse

The Iroquois call themselves the Haudenosaunee (hoh•deh•noh•SHOH•nee), or "People of the Longhouse." A longhouse was a rectangular-shaped shelter with a curved roof. The frame was made of poles cut from young trees, which were then bent and covered with bark. Holes in the roof let out smoke from a central fire.

Most towns had eight or ten longhouses. Several related Iroquois families lived in one longhouse. Family members slept on wooden platforms built along the inside walls and covered with woven mats and animal furs. Goods were usually stored under the platforms or on shelves above them, while other goods were hung from the walls.

An Iroquois Settlement

The palisade could be as high as 20 feet.

The Iroquois were skilled hunters.

Working Together

Iroquois families divided work to make it easier to meet the needs of the settlement. The men used bows and arrows to hunt deer and other animals. They used spears, nets, and weirs to fish. Women raised crops and prepared the food. They also made clothing and pottery and wove baskets, rope, and mats.

Like most Eastern Woodlands groups, the Iroquois grew corn, beans, and squash. They called these crops the Three Sisters because all three were planted in the same field and grew well together. After a field was farmed for a few years, it became less fertile. The Iroquois then cleared another field and began farming there. They preserved some of the food they grew and stored it for later use.

The Iroquois used animal skins to make clothing and moccasins. They wore leggings, skirts, capes, and winter coats made of animal skins. They sharpened antlers and bones to make sewing utensils, and they dried and stretched certain parts of animals such as deer to make thread.

TextWork

10 Scan the first paragraph. Underline three examples of capital resources.

11 Study the illustration. List three activities that required human resources.

_____

_____

_____

Baskets were woven from reeds.

Animal hides were used to make clothing.

Trade and Travel

⑫ What caused Iroquois tribes to trade with each other?

_____

_____

⑬ Write a sentence describing wampum.

_____

_____

_____

⑭ Study the wampum belt. What does each symbol on the belt represent?

_____

_____

Like other American Indians, the Iroquois traded to get resources and goods that they could not produce or find themselves. The Iroquois transported goods in canoes to trade with other towns. They also laid out trading trails that connected towns.

Iroquois canoes were usually covered with elm or spruce bark. The canoes were light enough to carry over land between rivers. However, they were sturdy enough to transport heavy goods.

Like other Eastern Woodlands groups, the Iroquois traded shell beads called **wampum** for goods. The Iroquois often made wampum out of quahog clam shells, which are purple and white. The beads were strung into belts with complex designs. The belts were used to record important events and to mark agreements between tribes.

About 1570, the Iroquois League of Peace was formed. It acted as a **confederation**, or a loose group of governments working together. The league's goal was to peacefully settle disputes among the various Iroquois tribes.

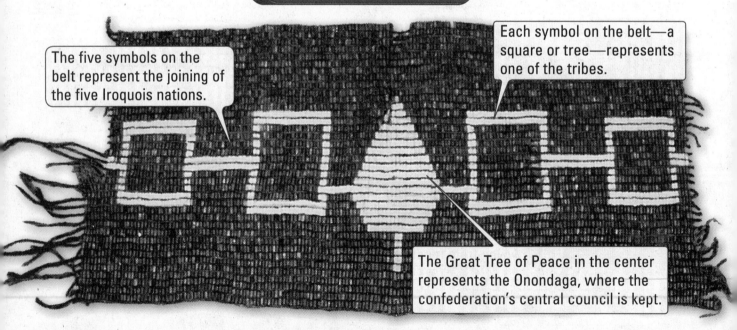

Iroquois Wampum Belt

The five symbols on the belt represent the joining of the five Iroquois nations.

Each symbol on the belt—a square or tree—represents one of the tribes.

The Great Tree of Peace in the center represents the Onondaga, where the confederation's central council is kept.

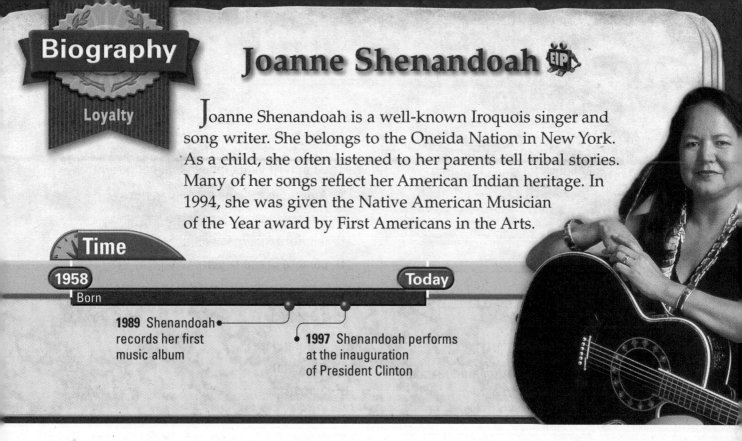

Joanne Shenandoah

Joanne Shenandoah is a well-known Iroquois singer and song writer. She belongs to the Oneida Nation in New York. As a child, she often listened to her parents tell tribal stories. Many of her songs reflect her American Indian heritage. In 1994, she was given the Native American Musician of the Year award by First Americans in the Arts.

Time

1958 Born — **Today**

1989 Shenandoah records her first music album

1997 Shenandoah performs at the inauguration of President Clinton

The Iroquois Today

Today, the Iroquois are among the ten largest American Indian groups in the United States. Like other American Indians, the Iroquois live in all parts of the United States. Some Iroquois still live in their homelands in New York and Canada. Many live in large cities and towns.

The Iroquois are employed in all kinds of jobs. However, they are perhaps best known as steelworkers. Steelworkers from the Mohawk tribe are called "skywalkers" because of their skill in building very tall structures. They have been building skyscrapers and bridges in New York City and other cities for years.

Like other American Indians, the Iroquois work hard to keep their traditions alive. A **tradition** is an idea, a belief, or a way of doing things that has been handed down from the past. Iroquois groups often gather to celebrate their culture. At these gatherings, people wear traditional clothing, dance to traditional music and songs, and share stories. Some gatherings are held in traditional longhouses.

TextWork

15 Where do many Iroquois live today?

_____

_____

16 Underline the sentences that describe a kind of job Iroquois people are known for today.

17 What are some of the ways that the Iroquois work to keep their culture alive? Why is this important?

_____

_____

_____

_____

Unit 2 ■ 71

1. **SUMMARIZE** How did geography and climate affect the way American Indians in the Eastern Woodlands related to their environment?

_____

_____

_____

_____

2. Use **confederation** in a sentence about the Iroquois League.

_____

_____

_____

_____

Circle the letter of the correct answer.

3. The Eastern Woodlands is named after the—

   A American Indians who lived there

   B forests that once covered the land

   C landforms in the region

   D climate in the region

4. What language group lived mostly on the Coastal Plain?

   F Algonquian

   G Iroquoian

   H Siouan

   J Mohawk

5. What capital resource did the Iroquois use to transport goods in the past?

   A Weirs

   B Canoes

   C Carts

   D Sailboats

Match the resource on the left with a product on the right.

6. wood   wampum

7. clam shells   longhouse

8. animal skins   clothing

activity

Draw a Scene Draw a scene of an early Eastern Woodlands settlement. Show how people used natural resources of the forests to meet their basic needs. Include a caption that describes the scene and lists the natural, human, and capital resources shown.

A recreated Iroquois longhouse in Victor, New York

The Plains

The Lakota and other Plains tribes lived on the vast grasslands between the Mississippi River and the Rocky Mountains. Millions of buffalo, or American bison, once roamed the plains, feeding off the grasslands. **Think about some of the ways that Plains people might have used buffalo to meet their basic needs.**

The Black Hills, in North Dakota

ESSENTIAL QUESTIONS

✓ In which areas did the American Indians live?
✓ Where do American Indians live today?
✓ How did geography and climate affect the way American Indian groups met their basic needs?
✓ How did the American Indians use natural, capital, and human resources?

 HISTORY AND SOCIAL SCIENCE SOL
USI.1a, USI.1c, USI.1f, USI.3b, USI.3c

Life on the Plains

TextWork

❶ Scan the text. Underline the sentences that describe the items that American Indians made from buffalo. Then use the information to complete the diagram on this page.

❷ Number these events in their correct sequence.

_____ Hunters travel longer distances to hunt buffalo.

_____ Buffalo hunters capture wild horses and learn to ride them.

_____ Spanish explorers bring horses to the Americas.

❸ Circle the paragraph that describes the different ways buffalo meat was prepared.

The Plains people depended on the buffalo for most of their basic needs. They ate buffalo meat and made products from almost every part of the animal. From the horns, they made cups and spoons. From the skin, they made clothing, moccasins, blankets, shields, drums, and shelters. From the bones, they made tools, arrowheads, and pipes.

For many years, American Indians hunted buffalo on foot. Some buffalo hunters wore animal skins as disguises in order to sneak up on a herd undetected. Later, after Spanish explorers first brought horses to the Americas in the 1500s, buffalo hunters captured wild horses and learned to ride them. On horseback, hunters could travel long distances to hunt buffalo.

After a hunt, the buffalo were skinned and the various parts were prepared for use. Some of the meat was eaten right away, while the rest was dried and stored for use during the cold winter months. Dried meat was mixed with fat and berries to make a food called pemmican (PEM•i•kuhn).

American Indian Uses of the Buffalo EIP

Skin
_____
_____
_____

Horns
_____
_____
_____

Bones
_____
_____
_____

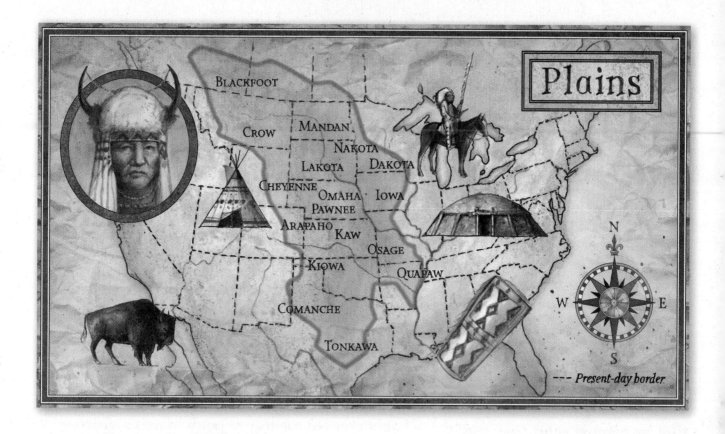

Plains

--- Present-day border

People of the Eastern Plains

Some Plains Indians, such as the Iowa and the Nakota, lived on the Interior Lowlands west of the Mississippi River and east of the Great Plains. These people were farmers as well as hunters and gatherers. They grew crops in the fertile valleys of the Missouri and Platte Rivers. They fished in the rivers and hunted deer and elk in the forests.

The eastern Plains groups lived in communities made up of large round earthen shelters called lodges. Twice a year, they left their communities to hunt buffalo.

People of the Great Plains

Other Plains Indians, such as the Lakota, the Cheyenne (shy•AN), and the Kiowa (KY•uh•wuh), lived on the Great Plains. The dry soil there was not good for growing crops. The people who lived on the Great Plains did not farm or live in permanent, or long-lasting, settlements. Most of them led a nomadic way of life, following herds of buffalo. A nomadic group moves from place to place.

TextWork

❹ Study the map. Which tribe lived farther north, the Lakota or the Kiowa?

_____

❺ (Focus Skill) How did the eastern Plains groups live differently from the Great Plains groups?

_____

_____

❻ What caused the people of the Great Plains to lead a nomadic way of life?

_____

_____

TextWork

7 Scan the text. Circle three materials used to make a teepee.

8 Use the word *scarce* to explain why the Lakota reused teepee poles to make travois.

_____

_____

_____

9 Study the illustration on page 77. Place an *X* over the human resources preparing buffalo hides for use.

10 Use context clues from the text to identify the subject of the following descriptions.

• was a way to record history

• had spiral patterns

Subject: _____

_____

11 Study the calendar robe on page 77. Why do you think it was important for the Lakota to record their history on calendar robes?

_____

_____

_____

_____

_____

The Lakota

The Lakota were one of the largest American Indian groups on the Great Plains. They lived mostly in what are now the states of North Dakota and South Dakota.

Using Scarce Resources

In the past, the Lakota lived in shelters called teepees (TEE•peez). These cone-shaped tents were easy to take apart and move. A teepee was made with wooden poles placed in a circle and tied together at the top with cord. The poles were covered with buffalo skins. Teepees were big enough to fit a family.

The wooden teepee poles were highly valued because wood was **scarce**, or in short supply. Few trees grow on the Great Plains, so the Lakota often had to travel long distances to get them. The Lakota reused the teepee poles to make a carrier, which the French called a **travois** (truh•VOY). A travois was made up of two poles tied together at one end and fastened to a harness on a dog or horse.

Because wood was scarce, the Lakota often had to use other sources of fuel for fires. Some people burned dried buffalo droppings, called chips.

The Lakota used the resources around them in other ways, too. Water was carried in bags made of buffalo stomachs. Buffalo hair was used to make cords and insect swatters, and buffalo hooves were used to make a kind of glue. Porcupine quills and later colored beads were used to decorate clothing, moccasins, and other products. Headdresses were sometimes decorated with eagle feathers.

Recording History

Like many Plains groups, the Lakota recorded their history on painted buffalo hides. Each year, tribal leaders decided what event should be represented on these hides, called calendar robes or winter counts. The drawings were often painted in a spiral pattern using dyes made from plants.

The Lakota

In hot weather, teepee flaps were opened to let air in.

Eagle-feathered headpiece

Porcupine quills

Beadwork and fringes

Laced leggings

Moccasins

The pictures and symbols on this calendar robe represent important events in a tribe's history.

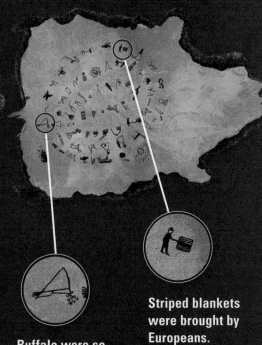

Buffalo were so plentiful that their tracks came close to teepees.

Striped blankets were brought by Europeans.

The Lakota Today

Daniel Garneaux is a Lakota dancer who lives in Norfolk, Virginia.

Today, many Lakota live in their traditional homelands in North Dakota, South Dakota, Minnesota, and parts of Canada. Many Lakota also live in other areas of North America.

Like other American Indians, the Lakota work in all kinds of jobs. They are business owners, teachers, doctors, and lawyers. Some work as farmers or ranchers. Others are trying to develop new sources of electricity, such as wind power, on their homelands in the Black Hills.

The Lakota work hard to keep their history and culture alive. Every year, they hold powwows or other ceremonies. These gatherings help build a strong sense of unity among the Lakota.

Lesson 3 Review

1. **SUMMARIZE** How did geography and climate affect the way the Plains people met their needs?

   _____

   _____

2. Use the word **travois** to describe the Lakota's nomadic way of life.

   _____

   _____

3. Write a sentence comparing a lodge and a teepee.

   _____

   _____

4. Where do many Lakota live today?

   _____

   _____

writing

✎ **Write Instructions** Write step-by-step instructions for building a teepee. Include a list of materials.

Teepee

The Southwest

The Pueblo peoples and other American Indian groups in the Southwest lived mostly in what is now Arizona and New Mexico. The Southwest region differed from other parts of North America. Its rough and rocky landscape includes deserts, mountains, cliffs, and canyons. The Southwest has intense summer heat, bitter winter cold, and little rainfall or snow. **Think about some of the ways that people's lives are affected by a desert environment.**

Taos Pueblo, in New Mexico

ESSENTIAL QUESTIONS

- ✓ In which areas did the American Indians live?
- ✓ Where do American Indians live today?
- ✓ How did geography and climate affect the ways American Indian groups met their basic needs?
- ✓ How did the American Indians use natural, capital, and human resources?

HISTORY AND SOCIAL SCIENCE SOL
USI.1f, USI.3b, USI.3c

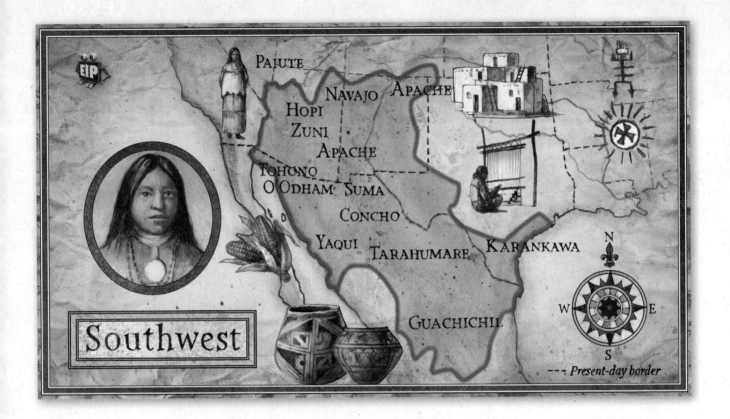

Southwest

Present-day border

Life in the Southwest

In the past, two of the American Indian tribes in the Southwest were the Hopi (HOH•pee) and the Zuni (ZOO•nee). The Hopi settled in what is now Arizona. The Zuni lived southeast of there, mostly in what is now New Mexico. The Hopi, the Zuni, and most other tribes in the Southwest became known as Pueblo peoples.

Some Pueblo tribes built settlements on steep canyon walls or on mesas. A mesa is a flat-topped mountain. When Spanish explorers later arrived in the area, they called those towns pueblos. The word *pueblo* means "town" in Spanish.

The geography and climate of the Southwest affected how the Pueblo peoples and other groups in the region lived and met their basic needs. The Pueblo Indians lived in mostly desert areas, where few trees grew. As a result, water and wood were often scarce. In order to survive, tribes in the Southwest had to find ways to relate to life in their harsh environment.

 TextWork

❶ Study the map. Circle the Hopi and Zuni, two of the tribes that became known as Pueblo peoples.

❷ How did geography affect where Pueblo tribes built settlements?

_____

_____

_____

❸ Why was wood scarce in the Southwest?

_____

_____

_____

Relating to Desert Life

Since wood was scarce, most Pueblo Indians lived in shelters made of mud, stone, or adobe (uh•DOH•bee). **Adobe** is a brick made of sun-dried earth and straw. Some people in the Southwest still use adobe building materials today.

To grow crops in dry areas, Pueblo Indians collected rainwater and dug irrigation canals through the desert. **Irrigation** is the use of canals, ditches, or pipes to move water from one place to another.

Like many American Indians, Pueblo peoples grew corn, beans, and squash. The corn was ground into cornmeal, using smooth, flat stones. Most Pueblo tribes harvested a **surplus**, or extra amount, of crops to survive in times of drought. Pueblo Indians also harvested cotton, which they used to make clothing and weave beautiful textiles such as carpets and blankets.

Pueblo peoples traded surplus cornmeal, colorful textiles, pottery, and baskets for goods they could not produce or find themselves. They established large trade networks throughout the Southwest. These networks allowed Pueblo Indians to get goods from faraway tribes.

Ancient Pueblo pottery

 TextWork

4 ⭐ How did Pueblo houses differ from Lakota houses?

_____

_____

5 Use the word *irrigation* in a sentence about farming in the Southwest.

_____

_____

6 Underline a reason why people in the Southwest established trade networks.

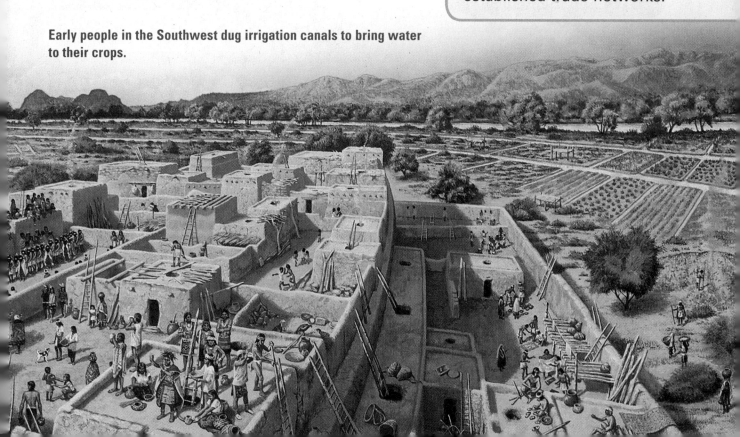

Early people in the Southwest dug irrigation canals to bring water to their crops.

TextWork

7 Why do you think Pueblo shelters had more than one level?

_____

_____

_____

_____

8 Scan the text. Underline the natural resources the Pueblo Indians used to build shelters.

9 Study the illustration. Circle a capital resource used to make cloth.

Pueblo Settlements

In Pueblo settlements, shelters were often built next to or on top of one another, much like apartments today. Some settlements had as many as five levels. Ladders were used to enter shelters or to reach other levels. In case of attack, the Pueblo peoples pulled up the ladders.

The thick walls of Pueblo shelters kept the rooms inside cool in summer and warm in winter. The walls were usually made with mud, stones, adobe, and wood from pine and juniper trees. Pueblo Indians sometimes had to travel to distant forests to get the wood.

Pueblo women often worked outdoors on flat rooftop terraces. In addition to grinding corn and making pottery, Pueblo women made baskets for storing food. The men harvested the crops. They also wove cotton cloth, working on upright wooden looms.

A Pueblo Settlement

Looms were used for weaving cloth.

Pueblo Arts and Crafts

Pueblo women often painted geometric designs and pictures of desert animals on pots and bowls. They also painted scenes on pueblo walls. They made paints and cloth dyes from plants.

Men carved and painted masks worn in religious ceremonies. The masks represented important spirits called *kachinas* (kuh•CHEE•nuhz). Pueblo families made kachina dolls to help their children learn about the spirits.

Pueblo dancers wore painted masks and dressed like kachinas during traditional gatherings. During the gatherings, held in large outdoor places, Pueblo groups honored important spirits of the sun, rain, and earth.

Pueblo peoples also held smaller ceremonies in underground kivas (KEE•vuhz). A *kiva* was a room used for ceremonies. Each settlement had several kivas.

TextWork

10 What natural resource was used to make paints and dyes?

_____

_____

11 Underline the sentence that tells why families made kachinas.

12 Study the illustration. What kinds of products are being made outdoors?

_____

_____

_____

Clay pottery was used to store food and water.

Corn was ground up to make meal.

Clay ovens were used for cooking food.

The Pueblo Peoples Today

Most Pueblo peoples still live in their homelands in the Southwest region. Many still practice their traditional arts. They perform kachina dances and continue to make beautiful pottery, blankets, baskets, and jewelry. Pueblo artists are known for making jewelry from silver and turqouise stones.

Many Pueblo families still make wooden kachina dolls. These dolls are not toys. Instead, they are learning tools. The doll is decorated in a special way and represents an important value, such as kindness, discipline, or respect for elders. Through the kachina dolls, children learn the importance of practicing these values in their own lives.

A Hopi weaver

Lesson 4 Review

1. **SUMMARIZE** How did the geography and climate affect the ways American Indians in the Southwest met their basic needs?

   _____

   _____

2. Write a sentence describing the materials used to make **adobe**.

   _____

   _____

3. Describe two examples of how the Pueblo peoples related to the desert environment.

   _____

   _____

4. Where do most Pueblo peoples live today?

   _____

   _____

Pueblo jewelry

writing

Write a Letter Imagine you have just visited a Pueblo community long ago. Write a letter to a friend to describe daily life in the community.

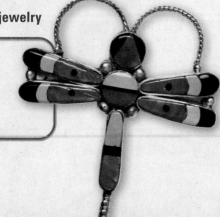

The Pacific Northwest

Cool ocean breezes often bring heavy rains to the Pacific Northwest, causing tall trees to grow in the thick forests. The forests were once filled with animals, and the rivers that ran through those forests were filled with fish. **Think about how people's lives might be affected by this kind of geography and climate.**

Stanley Park,
in Vancouver,
British Columbia

ESSENTIAL QUESTIONS

✓ In which areas did the American Indians live?

✓ Where do American Indians live today?

✓ How did geography and climate affect the ways American Indian groups met their basic needs?

✓ How did the American Indians use natural, capital, and human resources?

 HISTORY AND SOCIAL SCIENCE SOL
USI.1a, USI.1d, USI.1f, USI.3b, USI.3c

Life in the Pacific Northwest

The Pacific Northwest region includes parts of what are now Washington and Oregon in the United States and British Columbia in Canada. The region, which extends inland from the Pacific Ocean, has a mild, rainy climate.

Many American Indian groups lived in the Pacific Northwest region. One of the largest groups was the Kwakiutl (kwah•kee•YOO•tuhl). Most Kwakiutl lived on what is now Vancouver Island, along the western coast of British Columbia. The Makah (MAH•kah) lived to the south of the Kwakiutl, in what is now the state of Washington. The Chinook (shuh•NUK) lived in what is now Oregon, along the Columbia River.

Because their climate was mostly cool and damp, people along the Pacific Northwest coast did not farm. Instead, they met their food needs by fishing, hunting, and gathering. Much of their food came from coastal waters and rivers. Salmon was a **staple**, or main, food. They also ate halibut, shellfish, sea grass, and berries. Most of their meat came from whales, seals, elk, and deer.

TextWork

1 Why do you think American Indians settled in the Pacific Northwest area?

Beacuse they need food to Live.

2 Study the map. Find the Kwakiutl and circle the name on the map. Then underline the name of the northernmost tribe.

3 Scan the text. Circle the name of the main food staple in the Pacific Northwest.

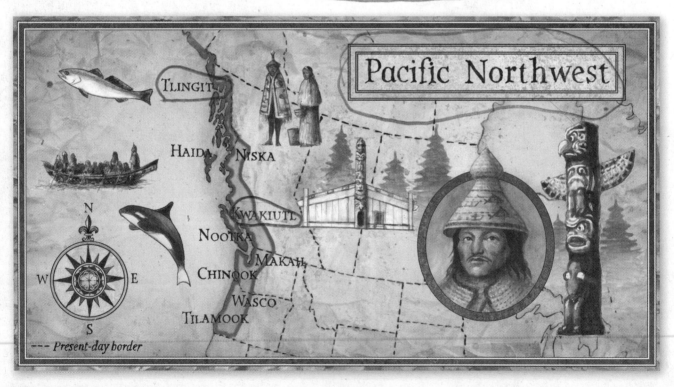

Pacific Northwest

TLINGIT
HAIDA   NISKA
KWAKIUTL
NOOTKA
MAKAH
CHINOOK
WASCO
TILAMOOK

N W E S

--- Present-day border

The chief harpooner in a whale hunt showed his respect for the whale by singing a special song.

Hunting Whales

Traditionally, some tribes in the Pacific Northwest, such as the Kwakiutl, captured whales that were stranded on the shore. Other tribes, such as the Makah, hunted whales at sea with harpoons. A harpoon is a long spear with a sharp point.

Whale hunts often lasted several days. Whale hunters paddled out to sea in large dugout canoes, which could carry up to 60 people. People of the Pacific Northwest made dugout canoes by hollowing out large logs.

To hunt such large animals, whale hunters often worked in groups. They tried to hit each whale with many harpoons. Hunters tied sealskin floats to the harpoons, which made it difficult for the whale to get away. Once the whale died, the hunters towed it back to shore.

The Pacific Northwest people used many parts of the whale. Whales supplied meat and fat. The fat could be melted into oil to burn in lamps. Tools were made from whalebones. Other parts of the whale were used to make ropes and bags.

TextWork

4 ⭐(Focus Skill) How were the whale-hunting methods of the Kwakiutl different from those of the Makah?

The difference was kwakiutl hunted form shores, makah use canoes.

5 Study the illustration. Place an X over one example of a human resource. Circle one example of a capital resource that is being used.

6 Scan the text. Underline the products made from whale parts.

Kwakiutl Settlements

7 Why was wood an important natural resource to the Kwakiutl?

Beacuse use the wood for tools, house, boats,

8 (Focus Skill) How was a Kwakiutl house similar to an Iroquois house?

They both had long houses.

9 Study the illustration. Circle a capital resource made from wood.

The Kwakiutl lived in settlements near the Pacific Ocean or other waterways in the region. They often arranged their shelters in rows facing the water. The Kwakiutl and other Pacific Northwest tribes used wood from the trees that grew in the forests to make houses, boats, and tools. Trees grow very tall in the region's rainy climate.

The Kwakiutl lived in long rectangular shelters. The shelters were made of long wooden planks, or boards, and had no windows. The floors and roofs were also covered with wide wooden planks. The wood usually came from tall cedar trees. Some houses were about 60 feet in length.

The Kwakiutl painted clan symbols around the entrances of the largest homes. All the members of a **clan**, or extended family, lived together in one house. An extended family included grandparents, parents, aunts, uncles, and children. Each person in a clan had a specific rank. Clans made important decisions about community life. They also taught children songs, stories, and woodcarving skills.

A Kwakiutl Settlement

Dugout canoes were used for fishing.

Kwakiutl cut the planks that they used to make their homes.

Kwakiutl Arts

Kwakiutl artists carved clan symbols, animal shapes, and human figures into tall wooden posts called totem poles. The totem poles stood in front of many shelters. The carvings on the totem poles were used to tell stories related to a group's history. Some Kwakiutl artists still carve totem poles today.

The Kwakiutl were among the best wood-carvers in the Pacific Northwest. They produced many objects from wood, including furniture, utensils, tools, hats, boxes, toy rattles, wooden masks, and dugout canoes. Many of those objects were also painted with colorful patterns and figures.

Most of the wood-carvers among the Kwakiutl were men. The women wove hats, baskets, and blankets. They made waterproof hats and baskets from long, thin strips of wood. Some of the spring and summer clothing that the Kwakiutl wore was made of cedar bark. To keep warm in winter, the Kwakiutl wore garments made from animal skins and fur. They fashioned jewelry out of seashells.

TextWork

10 Scan the text. Circle the jobs that Kwakiutl men did. Underline the jobs that Kwakiutl women did.

11 (Focus Skill) How was the Kwakiutl's winter clothing different from the clothing they wore in the spring and summer?

In the winter K indians wore animal skins.

Totem poles stood in front of many homes.

Some clothing was made of cedar bark.

Salmon were dried for food.

Baskets were made with long, thin strips of wood.

TextWork

12 Circle the name of a trading center in the Pacific Northwest. Why was its location important to trade?

Was located on the columbia River.

13 Use the word *barter* in a sentence about trading goods.

When People barter they exchange goods without using money.

14 Study the artifacts and images on page 91. How did potlatches reflect the Kwakiutl's views of gift-giving and owning property?

_____

_____

_____

_____

_____

A Kwakiutl hat

Trade

Trade was an important part of the Pacific Northwest's economy. An **economy** is the way people use their resources to meet their needs. Many groups in the Pacific Northwest became wealthy by trading goods and natural resources.

The Kwakiutl traded mostly with the Nootka, a neighboring group. However, traders often traveled long distances over the region's waterways in dugout canoes. The Dalles (DALZ) was one of the busiest trading centers in the Pacific Northwest. It is located on the Columbia River, about 200 miles inland from the Pacific Ocean.

The Chinook were among the Pacific Northwest's best-known traders at the Dalles. They developed a special language for trade. The language allowed them to barter goods on behalf of groups that spoke different languages. When people **barter**, they exchange goods without using money.

The Potlatch

To show off the property they owned, the people of the Pacific Northwest held potlatches frequently. A **potlatch** was a special gathering that was meant to express the host's good fortune and to divide property among the people.

Potlatch also means "to give." During a potlatch, clan leaders gave away valuable gifts. These gifts might include food, blankets, canoes, and ornamental metal plates made from copper. Gift-giving was one of the most important cultural values in Pacific Northwest society.

Potlatches were usually held in the winter, after the fishing and hunting season. A potlatch involved a large feast, in which people ate surplus salmon, whale, and seal. Potlatches also featured ceremonial dancing and singing. The dancers acted out stories about important events in the lives of clan members. The potlatch was also a time to celebrate important events in their tribe's history.

A Kwakiutl Potlatch

Ceremonial dancers wore painted masks carved into the shapes of clan animals and human figures.

A ceremonial ladle shaped like a bird

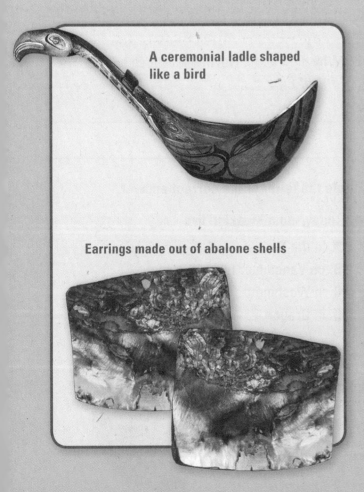

Earrings made out of abalone shells

Chiefs wore traditional outfits made from cedar bark.

Copper plates were highly valued.

The Kwakiutl Today

Today, most Kwakiutl still live on Vancouver Island, along the Pacific coast of western Canada. They earn their livings doing a variety of jobs. Many of them work in fishing and whaling businesses. Others earn their livings in the logging and forestry industries. Others work in stores or offices.

The Kwakiutl today keep their culture alive by continuing to participate in potlatches and other traditional gatherings. At the potlatches, people wear traditional clothing, share stories, and perform traditional dances. At schools in Kwakiutl communities, children learn the traditional arts of woodcarving and textile weaving. They also learn the Kwakiutl language.

These Kwakiutl fishers from Vancouver Island are catching salmon.

Lesson 5 Review

1. **SUMMARIZE** How did geography and climate affect Pacific Northwest groups?

   _____

   _____

   _____

2. Write a sentence describing what happens at a **potlatch**.

   _____

   _____

3. Why did Pacific Northwest tribes hunt whales?

   _____

   _____

Circle the letter of the correct answer.

4. Today, most Kwakiutl live—

   A in the Dalles

   B on Vancouver Island

   C in Washington

   D in Oregon

Kwakiutl rattle

writing

✎ **Write a Diary Entry** Imagine you are a Kwakiutl trader. Write a diary entry describing your experiences in exchanging goods and natural resources with another group.

The Arctic region extends from Alaska across northern Canada to Greenland. The temperatures in the Arctic region are below freezing much of the year. Much of the land is tundra, a cold, dry region where trees cannot grow. **Think about how limited resources in the Arctic might affect the way people live there.**

Dogsledding across northern Alaska

ESSENTIAL QUESTIONS

✓ In which areas did the American Indians live?

✓ Where do American Indians live today?

✓ How did geography and climate affect the way American Indian groups met their basic needs?

✓ How did the American Indians use natural, capital, and human resources?

 HISTORY AND SOCIAL SCIENCE SOL

USI.1c, USI.1f, USI.3b, USI.3c

TextWork

1 Study the map. How did location affect life in the Arctic?

They had a tobule life

2 Circle the sentence that explains how a kayak was made.

3 Underline the sentence that explains how fur was used. Why would this be important to people in the Arctic?

Life in the Arctic

Two main groups of people inhabited the Arctic region—the Aleut (a•lee•OOT) and the Inuit (IH•noo•wuht). The Aleut lived along the coast of the Aleutian (uh•LOO•shuhn) Islands. The Inuit lived in what is now Alaska, the northernmost parts of Canada, and the island of Greenland.

Because of the freezing cold climate of the Arctic, the Aleut and Inuit could not harvest crops. In the past, they mostly fished and hunted for food, or got it through gathering. They also used harpoons and kayaks (KY•aks) to hunt seals, walruses, and whales. A **kayak** is a one-person canoe made of waterproof skins stretched over bone or wood.

The Arctic people made full use of their scarce resources. They hunted seals and caribou not only for their meat, but also for their skins. Animal skins were made into clothing and tents. The fur was used to line parkas and shoes. Arctic people made tools and art objects out of animal bones, antlers, horns, and teeth. They burned whale oil to heat and light shelters.

--- *Present day border*

Arctic

Inuit people worked together and learned the skills they needed to survive.

Arctic Shelters

For much of the year, the Aleut lived together in large sod huts. The walls and roofs of the huts were strengthened with beams made of whalebones. Inuit families lived in tents made of driftwood and caribou hides.

During hunting season, the Inuit often built temporary houses called igloos (IH•glooz). The Inuit constructed igloos by stacking ice blocks into a dome shape. The builders left a hole in the top of the igloo to let out smoke from the camp fire. Clear ice blocks served as windows.

Transportation

The Arctic people often had to travel great distances to find animals to hunt. They raced over the snow and ice on large sleds pulled by packs of dogs. Occasionally on the barren land, people built stone landmarks called inukshuk (in•OOK•shook). The inukshuk may have been markers that guided travelers or pointed out hunting and fishing areas.

 TextWork

❹ Study the illustration. Circle the capital resources being used.

❺ What kind of shelters did the Aleut live in for much of the year?

for much of the year.

❻ (Focus Skill) How was an igloo similar to a teepee?

They buided it same like people buiding.

TextWork

7 Why did Inuit groups have to share food to survive?

_____

_____

_____

_____

_____

_____

8 Scan the text. Underline two traditional games that the Inuit played.

9 Circle the sentence that describes the effect of playing some games.

Inuit Settlements

The Inuit usually lived in loosely formed bands of 60 to 300 people. These bands were made up of several extended families. The families came together to make important choices for the good of the settlement.

The Inuit hunted and traveled in groups, and they often shared food in order to survive in their harsh environment. To pass the time, the Inuit played games and sports. Some of the games were developed to improve people's strength and skills.

The Inuit game of "tugging" was like a tug-of-war contest. Two people sat on the ground, facing each other. The object of tugging was to pull the other person up off the ground. In the game of "blanket toss," players were tossed into the air on a blanket made from seal or walrus skin. The player who was tossed the highest won the game.

The game of blanket toss was usually played at special ceremonies and other gatherings. At these gatherings, families shared stories, danced, and played music.

Children IN HISTORY

Inuit Children

Inuit children in the past had less time to play than most children today. Boys hunted and fished with their fathers, while girls helped their mothers cook and prepare meals. Inuit children did have toys, and they played many games. These games included kickball, blanket toss, and tugging. Teenage boys learned to play a game that was similar to the game of soccer played today. The game was played on ice. Players used a ball made of caribou or moose hide.

Make It Relevant **What kind of games do you like to play?**

The Inuit Today

Many Inuit still live in their homelands in Alaska, northern Canada, and Greenland. Some Inuit still work as hunters, but most have other kinds of jobs. Many make a living from tourism. Tourism is the selling of goods and services to visitors.

The Inuit take tourists on dogsled trips to watch polar bears and other Arctic wildlife. Inuit art is also an important part of the tourism business. Skilled artists carve detailed designs into objects made from whalebone and walrus tusks.

Every two years, the Inuit host the Arctic Winter Games. These games include dog mushing, snowshoeing, and other traditional cold-weather sports. The games also provide Arctic groups with an opportunity to share their culture with others.

The Inuit still play games such as blanket toss at special gatherings.

Lesson 6 Review

1. **SUMMARIZE** How did the geography and climate affect the ways people in the Arctic met their basic needs?

   _____

   _____

2. Write a sentence describing how an **igloo** was made.

   _____

3. What American Indian group lived in what is now northernmost Canada and Alaska? Does the group still live there today?

   _____

4. How did Inuit houses differ from those of the Aleut?

   _____

   _____

writing

✎ **Write a Poem** Write a poem celebrating the ways the Inuit made use of scarce resources in the Arctic to meet their basic needs.

Model of an Inuit boat

Fun With Social Studies

" This city was built and settled by <u>nomadic people</u>. "

_____

Dig It Right

Professor Prattle is good at digging up artifacts, but he's not very good at drawing conclusions about them. Change the underlined word or words in each statement to make it correct.

" This wampum was made by the <u>Inuit</u>. "

_____

" This spear was used to <u>paddle a dugout canoe</u>. "

_____

Tricky T-Shirts

Match who should wear each T-shirt.

Eastern Woodlands Indians

Plains Indians

Pacific Northwest Indians

Arctic Indians

Family Secrets

abc VOCABULARY

The words that match the clues are hiding in the family members' names. Can you find the words? The right letters are in order reading from left to right, but there may be other letters in between.

UNCLE ANDY

An extended family

_____

Bricks made of sun-dried earth and straw

AUNT DORA BELLE

_____

BIG SIS LOULOU

A temporary shelter made of ice

_____

To exchange goods without using money

_____

BABY BROTHER

A wall made of tall wooden poles

_____

OUR PAL IS ARDEN

Picture This!

Write the letters to match the American Indian groups to the region.

Plains

Pacific Northwest

Southwest

A. Kwakiutl
B. Hopi
C. Lakota
D. Makah
E. Kiowa
F. Zuni

_____   _____

Review and Test Prep

The Big Idea

People use the different resources in their environment to meet their basic needs for food, shelter, and clothing.

Summarize the Unit

Focus Skill **Compare and Contrast** Complete the graphic organizer to compare and contrast some American Indian groups that lived in different regions of North America.

Topic 1

The Iroquois

_____

_____

Similar

_____

_____

Topic 2

The Kwakiutl

_____

_____

_____

Use Vocabulary

Fill in the missing term in each sentence, using the correct vocabulary word from the Word Bank.

1. _____ members included grandparents, parents, aunts, uncles, and children.

2. The Lakota used a _____ to carry goods.

3. Pueblo shelters were usually made of mud, clay, or _____.

4. Stone tools, canoes, and spears are examples of _____.

5. Some Iroquois built wooden _____ around their villages.

Word Bank

artifacts p. 58

palisades p. 68

wampum p. 70

travois p. 76

adobe p. 81

clan p. 88

Think About It

Circle the letter of the correct answer.

6. Scientists who dig up buried artifacts to study the cultures of people who lived long ago are called—

   A descendants

   B archaeologists

   C gatherers

   D ancestors

7.
   First

   During the Ice Ages, much of Earth's water was frozen in glaciers.

   ↓

   Next

   ?

   ↓

   Last

   A "bridge" of dry land appeared between Asia and North America.

   ↓

   What event is missing from the sequence?

   F The temperature of the water rose.

   G The water level of the oceans dropped.

   H The glaciers made the soil fertile.

   J The number of glaciers decreased.

8. Archaeologists discovered some of the earliest American Indian artifacts in Virginia at—

   A Richmond

   B Cactus Hill

   C Dismal Swamp

   D Arlington

9.

What does this artifact tell archaeologists about the people who made it?

   F They likely obtained food by harvesting crops.

   G They were probably hunters.

   H They likely built forts and settlements.

   J They probably formed confederations to settle disputes.

10. Which of these is a capital resource used by American Indians in the past?

    A Maize

    B Arrowhead

    C Irrigation

    D Fisher

11. Which of these groups lived in the Eastern Woodlands?

    F Iroquois

    G Lakota

    H Inuit

    J Hopi

12. Which feature in the environment most affected the lives of Iroquois groups?

    A Grassy plains

    B Hot, dry climate

    C Forests

    D Cold climate

13. In what two regions did American Indians live in rectangular shelters made of wood?

   F Eastern Woodlands and Plains

   G Pacific Northwest and Southwest

   H Southwest and Arctic

   J Eastern Woodlands and Pacific Northwest

14.

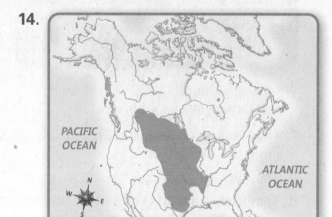

Which American Indian group lived in the highlighted region?

   A Iroquois

   B Pueblo

   C Lakota

   D Inuit

15. Which natural resource did the Lakota rely on the most to meet their needs?

   F Whales

   G Salmon

   H Buffalo

   J Trees

16. In the past, what did American Indians in the Plains, Arctic, and Pacific Northwest regions have in common?

   A They depended on farming.

   B They depended on whales and salmon.

   C They depended on hunting.

   D They depended on ice to build shelters.

17.

Who made this shelter?

   F Plains Indians

   G Eastern Woodlands Indians

   H Pacific Northwest Indians

   J Arctic Indians

18. Which group lived in desert areas bordering cliffs and mountains?

   A Pueblo

   B Kwakiutl

   C Lakota

   D Iroquois

19.

How were Pueblo shelters similar to apartments today?

   F They were built of wood.

   G They were often built next to or on top of one another.

   H They had elevators to help people go up or down.

   J They had air conditioning.

20.

In what region are these people hunting?

A Pacific Northwest

B Southwest

C Eastern Woodlands

D Arctic

21. What material did the Inuit use to build temporary shelters?

F Wood planks

G Adobe

H Ice blocks

J Sod

22. Today, many Inuit live in—

A the Great Plains

B Alaska and Canada

C New Mexico and Arizona

D the Pacific Northwest

Answer these questions.

23. How have recent discoveries at Cactus Hill changed archaeologists' perspectives about when people began living in the Western Hemisphere?

_____

_____

_____

24. How did the geography and climate of the Pacific Northwest affect how the Kwakiutl met their basic needs?

_____

_____

_____

25. How did American Indians use natural, capital, and human resources to meet their basic needs?

_____

_____

Brr. Be careful. That polar bear looks mad.

A burglar has struck at the Time Museum. You and Eco must head back into the strange halls of the museum to try to solve the mystery. Watch out for the Time Tunnel—it will take you and Eco back in time to North America more than 600 years ago! Just imagine the people you might meet along the way. Play the game now online.

Show What You Know

Writing Write a Report

Choose two American Indian groups discussed in this unit. Compare and contrast the environments that affected their ways of life. Describe their shelters and their sources of food, clothing, and tools.

Activity Create an American Indian Book

Write and illustrate a book about the American Indian groups discussed in this unit. Describe the ways they used natural, human, and capital resources to meet their basic needs. Include drawings, charts, and maps in your book. On at least one map, show where members of each group lived in the past and where they live today.

The Age of Exploration

European explorers, in
North America, in 1492

Spotlight on Standards

THE BIG IDEA Competition for land and
resources can lead to both cooperation and conflict
among different groups of people.

 HISTORY AND SOCIAL SCIENCE SOL

USI.1a, USI.1d, USI.1f, USI.1g, USI.4a, USI.4b, USI.4c

Set the Stage

Study the map. Circle the names of the rivers that Coronado crossed.

The French explored the Mississippi River.

The Spanish looked for gold in North America.

NORTH AMERICA

Lake Superior

MARQUETTE & JOLIET, 1673

Mississippi R.

Lake Huron

Lake Michigan

Lake Ontario

St. Lawrence R.

CHAMPLAIN, 1603

Newfou

Missouri R.

LA SALLE, 1678

Lake Erie

Hudson R.

CABOT, 1497

Colorado R.

CORONADO, 1539

Arkansas R.

Ohio R.

Cape Cod

40°N

Rio Grande

Tennessee R.

Chesapeake Bay

Cape Hatteras

ATLANTIC OCEAN

Gulf of California

CORONADO, 1539

Gulf of Mexico

Bahamas

COLUMBUS, 1492

CORTÉS, 1519

Yucatán Peninsula

Cuba

COLUMBUS, 1492

CORTÉS, 1519

Hispaniola

Puerto Rico

20°N

110°W

Caribbean Sea

70°W

60°W

10°N

PACIFIC OCEAN

SOUTH AMERICA

80°W

90°W

Equator

0°

60°N

Early Voyages of Exploration

CABOT, 1497

Ireland

THE NETHERLANDS

ENGLAND
London
Amsterdar

50°N

CHAMPLAIN, 1603

Paris

EUROPE

FRANCE

ATLANTIC OCEAN

SPAIN
Madrid

40°N

Lisbon
Sagres

Mediterranean
Sea

N
W   E
S

COLUMBUS, 1492

30°N

AFRICA

20°N

Great empires controlled trade
in West Africa.

10°N

← Sent by England
← Sent by France
← Sent by Spain
— Present-day border

0   250   500 Miles
0   250   500 Kilometers
Miller Cylindrical Projection

Equator   0°

40°W   30°W   20°W   10°W   0°

Set the Stage

1 Draw an *X* on the time line where this event would appear:

1507 North America and South America appear on a map of the world for the first time.

2 Circle the name of the person who spoke out against the cruel treatment of American Indians.

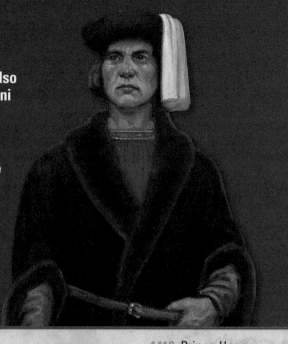

1450?–1499?
- Italian explorer also known as Giovanni Caboto
- Explored Newfoundland, in Canada, for the English

The Age of Exploration

1275 Marco Polo reaches China, p. 114

1418 Prince Henry of Portugal opens a school for sailing, p. 128

1200   **1300**   **1400**

At the Same Time

1215 King John of England signs the Magna Carta

1325 The Aztecs build their capital, Tenochtitlán, in Mexico

Bartolomé de Las Casas

1484–1566
- Catholic priest who spoke out against the cruel treatment of American Indians
- Wrote a book called *Tears of the Indians*

Estevanico

1503?–1539
- Enslaved African who took part in several Spanish explorations
- Learned to speak several American Indian languages

Queen Isabella

1451–1504

- Queen of Spain, who with King Ferdinand, paid for Christopher Columbus's voyages
- Wanted to spread the Catholic religion to new lands

Christopher Columbus

1451–1506

- Italian sailor who explored the Americas for Spain
- Made four journeys to the Americas

1492 Christopher Columbus claims land in the Americas for Spain, p. 134

1673 Jacques Marquette and Louis Joliet explore the Mississippi River, p. 145

1682 Robert La Salle explores the mouth of the Mississippi River, p. 145

1500

1600

1700

1508 Michelangelo begins painting the ceiling of the Sistine Chapel, in Rome

1607 The Jamestown settlement is started in Virginia

1620 English settlers land at Plymouth, in Massachusetts

Francisco Vásquez de Coronado

1510–1554

- Spanish explorer
- Led an expedition in southwestern North America in search of the Seven Cities of Gold

Samuel de Champlain

1567–1635

- French mapmaker who explored and mapped areas in what is now southeastern Canada
- Set up a trading post that became the city of Québec

Preview Vocabulary

empire

By the 1300s, Mali had become a large **empire**. It ruled the lands in West Africa that it had conquered. p. 116

monarch

Countries in Europe were led by **monarchs**. These kings and queens competed with each other for land and resources. p. 122

navigation

At Prince Henry's school of **navigation**, sailors learned how to plan and control the course of a ship. p. 128

expedition

The Spanish made many **expeditions**. The purpose of these trips was to explore for gold and other riches. p. 130

colony

Québec was part of the **colony** of New France. New France was ruled by another country, France. p. 137

mission

At religious settlements called **missions**, priests taught American Indians about Christianity. p. 157

Reading Social Studies

 **Sequence**

LEARN

Sequence is the order in which events happen. Noticing the sequence of historical events can help you better understand what you read, and it can help you see important relationships between events. Dates help show sequence. So do certain clue words, such as *first, second, third, next, then, last, finally, later,* and *after.*

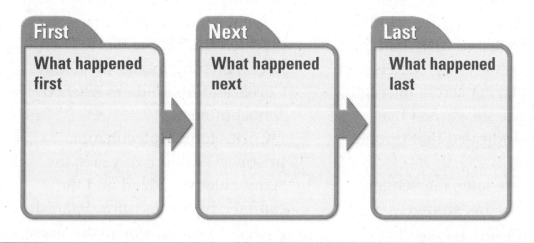

First	**Next**	**Last**
What happened first	What happened next	What happened last

PRACTICE

Underline the sequence clues in the paragraphs. The first paragraph has been marked for you.

On his first journey across the Atlantic Ocean in 1492, Christopher Columbus landed on an island in the Caribbean Sea. He named the island San Salvador. A short time later, Columbus encountered a group of people from the Taino (TY•noh) Indian tribe. After that, Columbus and his crew explored the coast of what is now Cuba. Finally, they landed on the island of Hispaniola.

Sequence

Columbus made three more voyages to North America, from 1493 to 1504. On his second voyage, Columbus returned to Hispaniola. On his third, he sailed to what is now Trinidad and Venezuela. On his fourth and final trip, he sailed to lands that are now Mexico, Honduras, Panama, and Jamaica.

Read the article. Then complete the activities below.

Americans and Europeans Meet

The year was 1519. The ruler of the Aztec people, Motecuhzoma (moh•tay•kwah•SOH•mah), was worried. Several strange events had recently occurred. First, the ground had shaken violently. Then, the capital city, Tenochtitlán (tay•nawch•teet•LAHN), had flooded. Most recently, comets had been seen blazing across the night sky. Aztec priests warned that these signs indicated that trouble was coming.

A short time later, messengers brought news that strangers were marching toward Tenochtitlán. Could the Aztec god Quetzalcoatl (ket•sahl•KOH•a•tahl) be returning, as he had promised?

The person the Aztecs thought might be Quetzalcoatl was actually the Spanish explorer Hernando Cortés (er•NAHN•doh kawr•TES). In the spring of 1519, Cortés and his army landed on the east coast of what is now Mexico. First, he defeated the people there. Then, after marching inland for 83 days, Cortés and his soldiers reached Tenochtitlán.

Cortés took Motecuhzoma prisoner. Within two years, the Aztec ruler was dead and the capital city was in ruins. Spanish weapons and European diseases had nearly destroyed the Aztec army. By 1521, Cortés had conquered, or defeated, the Aztecs.

1. In the first paragraph, circle the clue words that show sequence.

2. Circle the sentence that tells when Cortés landed in Mexico. Underline the sentences that tell what happened after he landed.

3. How long did it take for Cortés to defeat the Aztec people? Explain how you reached your answer.

_____

_____

_____

World Trade and Travel

For years, Europeans knew nothing about the Americas—North America and South America—and very little about Asia and Africa. That all started to change, however, as European nations began to explore unknown regions beyond Europe. **Think about why people might be interested in exploring faraway places.**

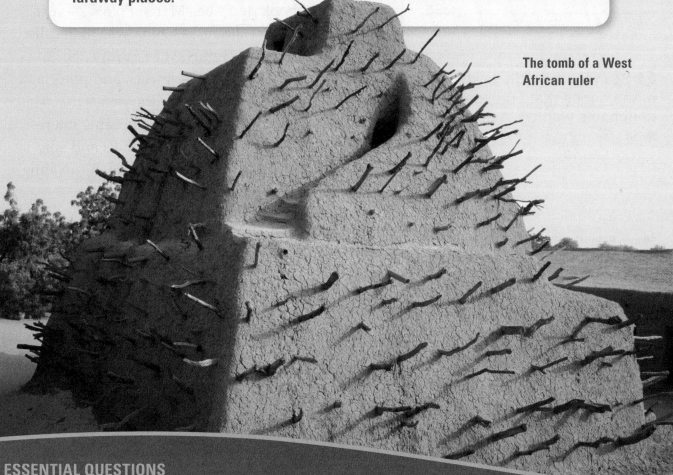

The tomb of a West African ruler

ESSENTIAL QUESTIONS

✔ What was the importance of Ghana, Mali, and Songhai?
✔ Where were the empires of Ghana, Mali, and Songhai located?
✔ When did the empires of Ghana, Mali, and Songhai exist in Africa?
✔ How did West African empires impact European trade?

HISTORY AND SOCIAL SCIENCE SOL
USI.1d, USI.1f, USI.1g, USI.4c

Marco Polo's Travels

TextWork

1 Underline the name of the new age of learning that lasted from about 1400 to 1600.

2 How did Marco Polo's book affect European perspectives, or views, about trading with people in Asia?

_____

_____

_____

3 Scan the text. Circle some of the goods that European merchants wanted to get from Asia.

In the 1400s, a new age of learning and discovery began in Europe. This time of new ideas is known as the Renaissance (REH•nuh•sahns), which means "rebirth." The Renaissance started in Italy and then spread across the European continent. It lasted from about 1400 to 1600.

Johannes Gutenberg helped with the spread of ideas by developing a new printing press in the 1450s. This press made it easier to print books, so more books were produced. One of the most popular books published during the Renaissance was *The Travels of Marco Polo*. Written almost 200 years earlier, the book describes Marco Polo's 24-year journey through Cathay, as China was then called.

When Marco Polo returned to Europe, he brought back Chinese silks, jewels, and porcelain. Europeans were fascinated by the riches that Marco Polo described in his book. They became interested in buying Chinese goods such as silks and spices. Soon, many European merchants began traveling the long, difficult land routes to Asia.

Marco Polo (right) wrote about visiting the palace of Kublai Khan, China's ruler, (below) in *The Travels of Marco Polo*.

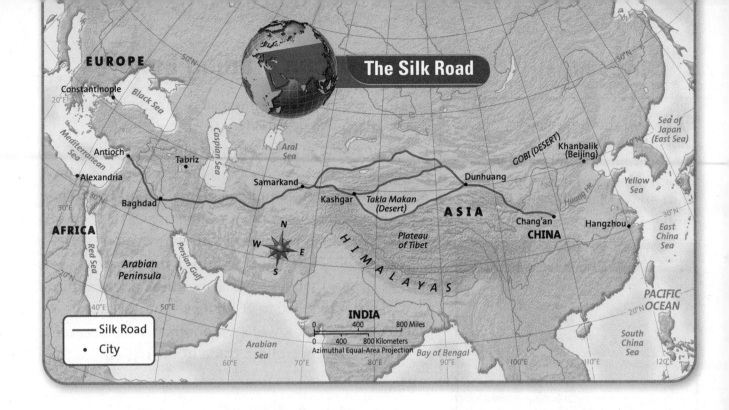

The Silk Road

Before the 1500s, no Europeans had traveled to Asia by sea. To reach China, Europeans had to travel by horse or camel along a series of land routes that became known as the Silk Road. The Silk Road stretched nearly 4,000 miles through the deserts and high plains of central Asia.

Some European merchants became wealthy from the money they earned in trade along the Silk Road. However, travel on the Silk Road was difficult and slow. Sometimes it was dangerous because thieves often robbed merchants of their money. To better protect themselves, the merchants generally traveled in **caravans**, or groups of travelers.

Because of the many dangers they faced, most European merchants traveled only part of the way along the Silk Road. Europeans traded for Asian goods in cities along the Mediterranean coast of northern Africa and southwestern Asia. The cities they visited included Alexandria in northern Africa and Antioch (AN•tee•ahk), Constantinople (kahn•stan•tuh•NOH•puhl), and Baghdad (BAG•dad) in southwestern Asia.

TextWork

4 Use the word *caravan* in a sentence about traveling on the Silk Road.

_____

_____

_____

5 Study the map. Circle the name of the desert that made travel in the cental part of the Silk Road difficult.

6 Study the map. Use parallels of latitude and meridians of longitude to give the absolute location of Hangzhou.

_____

 **TextWork**

African Trading Empires

Europeans became interested in traveling to Africa as well as Asia. In Africa, they traded with merchants from three wealthy empires—Ghana (GAH•nuh), Mali (MAH•lee), and Songhai (SAWNG•hy). An **empire** is made up of lands ruled by the nation that conquered them.

All three empires were located in western Africa, near the Niger River and south of the Sahara, a huge desert that stretches across the northern third of Africa. From 300 to 1600, these empires dominated West Africa, one after another. They became powerful by controlling trade in the region.

Ghana

The Ghana Empire developed around 750. Ghana's capital, Kumbi-Saleh (koom•BY sah•LAY), was a walled city with palaces and busy markets. It was located in what is now the country of Senegal.

Gold was Ghana's main source of wealth. Merchants from northern Africa traveled across the Sahara to trade salt for West Africa's gold.

7 ⭐(Focus Skill) On the time line below, mark the time period when the three empires dominated West Africa. Mark the beginning date with an *X*. Mark the end date with a dot.

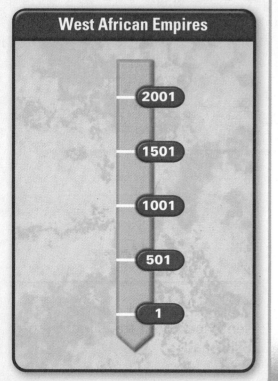

West African Empires

- 2001
- 1501
- 1001
- 501
- 1

The Mali city of Jenné, about 1000

Muslim scholars used new tools for studying astronomy.

Mali

In the 1100s, the Mali Empire formed and took control of Ghana. By the 1300s, the Mali Empire had grown to about twice the size of the Ghana Empire. Much of this growth came during the time of Mansa Musa, who ruled Mali from 1312 to 1337.

During Mansa Musa's rule, the city of Timbuktu (tim•buhk•TOO) became known as a center of learning as well as trade. Mansa Musa invited Muslim scholars to come teach at a new university in Timbuktu. Muslims follow the religion of Islam. The Muslim scholars at Timbuktu taught astronomy, geography, mathematics, law, and medicine.

Songhai

By the 1400s, much of the Mali Empire had become part of the new Songhai Empire. A traveler from north Africa named Leo Africanus visited Songhai in the early 1500s. He found "rich merchants who travel constantly about the region with their wares [goods]." In the city of Gao (GOW), people traded gold for goods that came from Europe, Asia, and northern Africa.

 **TextWork**

8 What valuable metal found in West Africa was important to the growth of West African trade?

_____

9 Scan this page. Underline the name of the Mali city that became a center of learning as well as trade.

10 (Focus Skill) Which was established first, the Mali Empire or the Songhai Empire?

_____

WEST AFRICAN TRADING EMPIRES

African people and African goods played an important role in increasing European interest in world trade and travel.

West Africans sold gold, ivory, cloth, and fish.

Tripol

Sahara

Salt merchants traveled across the desert in caravans.

Africa

Timbuktu

Gao

Kumbi-Saleh

Jenné

Niger River

People purchased gold jewelry in trade centers such as Timbuktu.

Atlantic Ocean

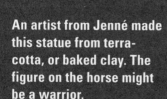

West African metal workers made jewelry and other objects from gold. Medallions like this were worn in the Ghana Empire.

An artist from Jenné made this statue from terra-cotta, or baked clay. The figure on the horse might be a warrior.

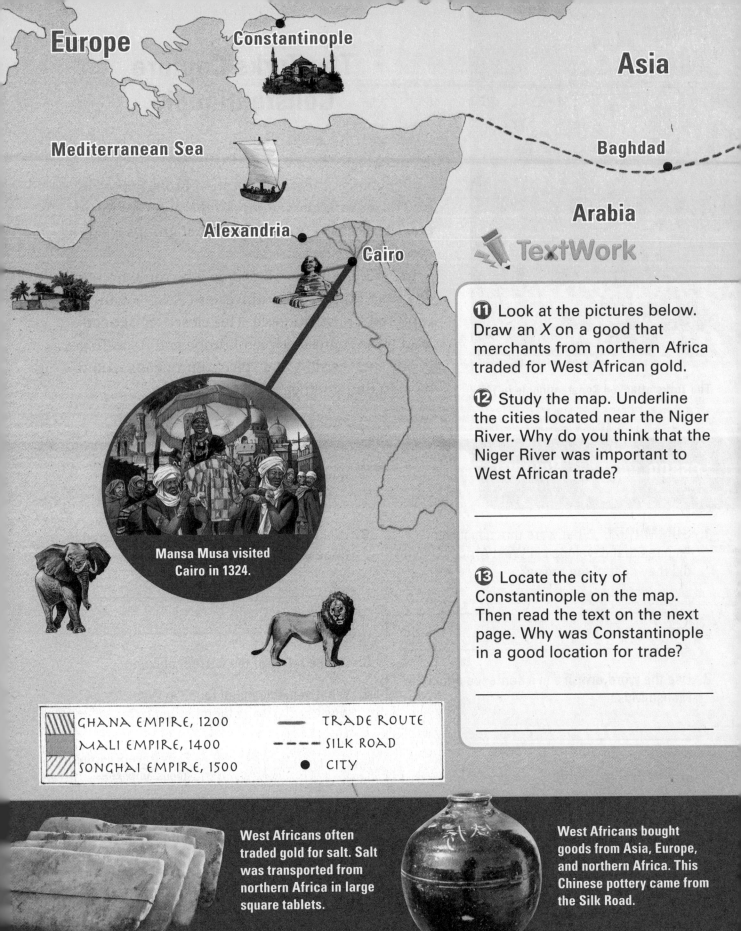

Europe

Constantinople

Asia

Mediterranean Sea

Baghdad

Arabia

Alexandria

Cairo

Mansa Musa visited Cairo in 1324.

11 Look at the pictures below. Draw an *X* on a good that merchants from northern Africa traded for West African gold.

12 Study the map. Underline the cities located near the Niger River. Why do you think that the Niger River was important to West African trade?

_____

_____

13 Locate the city of Constantinople on the map. Then read the text on the next page. Why was Constantinople in a good location for trade?

_____

_____

GHANA EMPIRE, 1200   TRADE ROUTE
MALI EMPIRE, 1400   SILK ROAD
SONGHAI EMPIRE, 1500   ● CITY

West Africans often traded gold for salt. Salt was transported from northern Africa in large square tablets.

West Africans bought goods from Asia, Europe, and northern Africa. This Chinese pottery came from the Silk Road.

The Turks Capture Constantinople

The city of Constantinople was an important crossroads that connected Asian and African trade routes. Constantinople's location brought the city great wealth, so it was a frequent target for invaders. For almost 1,000 years, several groups tried to conquer the city.

In 1453, the Turks—a people who came from the Ottoman Empire in southwestern Asia—finally captured Constantinople. This closed most overland trade routes between Europe and Asia. To get goods such as silks and spices, Europeans would have to find another route to Asia.

The Turks attacked Constantinople in 1453.

Lesson 1 Review

1. **SUMMARIZE** What were three important empires that developed in West Africa? When did they control the region?

   _____

   _____

2. Use the word **empire** in a sentence about Mansa Musa.

   _____

   _____

3. What led Europeans to become interested in trade with Africa?

   _____

   _____

Circle the letter of the correct answer.

4. What valuable metal found in West Africa was used to trade for other goods?

   A Silk

   B Gold

   C Salt

   D Spices

Early traders carried goods on camels.

writing

✏ **Write a Journal Entry** Imagine you are an early trader on a caravan traveling across West Africa. Write a journal entry that describes the characteristics of one of the empires you encounter. Tell how African people and goods have impacted European trade.

Background to Exploration

Lesson 2

After the Turks captured Constantinople in 1453, most of the land routes to Asia became unsafe for Europeans to use. European countries began to search for a new and faster water route to Asia. **Think about what could make countries want to explore unknown places.**

Explorers carefully planned early voyages.

ESSENTIAL QUESTIONS

✓ Why did European countries compete for power?
✓ What were the obstacles faced by the explorers?

HISTORY AND SOCIAL SCIENCE SOL
USI.1a, USI.1d, USI.4a

Henry IV was crowned King of England in 1399.

Motivating Forces for Exploration

During the Renaissance, Europe experienced important political, economic, and religious changes. Many of these changes helped **motivate**, or provide a reason for, European rulers to support the exploration of faraway places.

Political Motivations

In the past, most of Europe was divided into many small land areas, each controlled by a different noble. The nobles were too busy fighting each other to spend their resources on exploration.

Over time, some of these separate land areas were joined to form countries. By the 1400s, Portugal, Spain, France, and England had developed strong central governments. Those governments were ruled by powerful **monarchs**, or kings and queens.

Europe's monarchs were strong leaders who believed that their own cultures were superior to, or better than, others. They began to compete with each other for land and resources in order to gain more power to build great empires.

Economic Motivations

To increase their power, countries needed more economic resources, or resources related to wealth and trade. After the Turks captured Constantinople in 1453, Europeans began to search for new trade routes to Asian markets. Later, European monarchs wanted to **claim**, or declare they owned, the lands they explored. They hoped that these new lands would provide them great riches in gold and silver, as well as other valuable natural resources. They also wanted to find new markets where they could sell European goods.

Religious Motivations

In the 1400s, all of Europe's monarchs belonged to the Catholic Church. At this time, however, some people began to question the Church's power. They called for **reforms**, or changes, in the Church.

To gain new followers for the Church and to help spread Christianity to faraway places, the Catholic Church sent **missionaries**, or religious teachers, to the lands claimed by European countries. Catholic leaders wanted to keep their power, and like the monarchs, share in the wealth of those new lands.

TextWork

4 (Focus Skill) Place these events in order.

___1___ Constantinople is captured.

___3___ European monarchs claim the lands they explore.

___2___ Europeans begin to search for new trade routes to Asian markets.

5 Why did the Catholic Church send missionaries to other lands?

They wanted to spread Christianity and gain more power wealth.

Cathedrals were the most important buildings in Europe's largest cities. Some explorers placed stone crosses (right) to mark the lands they claimed.

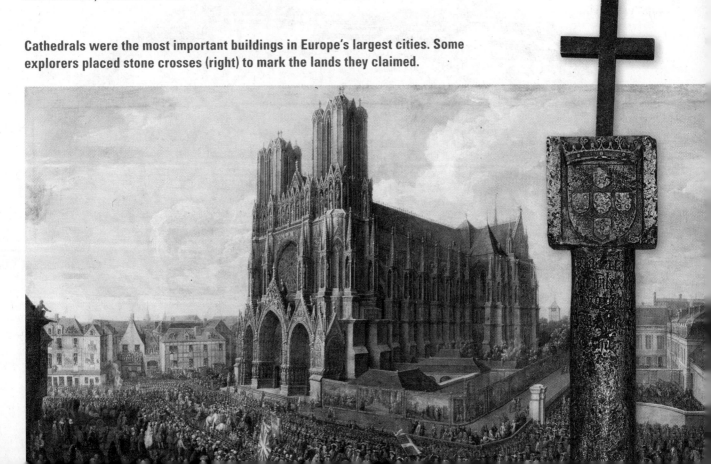

6 Scan the text on this page. Underline the main obstacles to exploration.

7 Study the map. What continents do you see? How was this map different from world maps today?

I see three continents Europe, Asia, Africa. Today we have 7 continents, North and South America, Australia, antarctica

This map from 1489 only shows Europe, Asia, and Africa. Many Europeans believed that the only land west of Europe was Asia.

Obstacles to Exploration

Before Europeans could make long ocean voyages and explore faraway places, they had to solve a number of **obstacles**, or things that stood in the way. These obstacles included slow ships, poor tools and maps, a lack of adequate supplies, disease, and fear of the unknown.

Slow Ships and Poor Tools and Maps

Until the late 1400s, Europeans used square-sailed ships that could sail only with the wind. These ships were built primarily to sail in the calm waters of the Mediterranean Sea. However, they were slow and hard to steer in rough ocean waters.

Sailors lacked the instruments they needed to find accurate directions. They had not yet developed ways of using both parallels of latitude and meridians of longitude to measure their exact location. Most maps at that time were not accurate. They did not reflect Earth's true size, and they showed only Europe, Asia, and Africa. Mapmakers did not even know that the Americas existed.

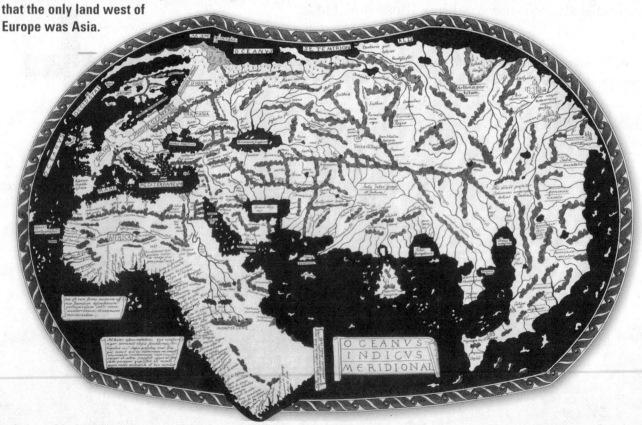

European paintings and maps often showed sea serpents and other sea monsters. These pictures reinforced people's fears of unknown places.

A Lack of Supplies

Explorers needed a large amount of money to build and supply ships. However, there were many risks in exploration. For example, a ship could sink or sail off course, or an explorer might find nothing of value. Explorers often had trouble persuading supporters that the risks were worth the amount of money they needed to pay for voyages.

Disease and Starvation

Many sailors died from diseases and starvation. In the 1300s and 1400s, diseases such as influenza and smallpox were common in European cities. Because of unsanitary conditions aboard cramped ships, food and water supplies quickly spoiled.

Fear of the Unknown

Many Europeans did not want to venture into places they did not know about. They believed that the world outside the places where they lived was dangerous. Many sailors believed stories about horrible sea monsters waiting beneath the ocean to swallow ships whole. Some also thought that if they traveled too far south, near the equator, the sun would be so hot that the sea would boil.

TextWork

8 Scan the text. Underline the main idea of each of the three paragraphs.

9 Circle the sentences that explain why many Europeans long ago did not want to venture into places they did not know about.

10 Why did some people believe it was dangerous to travel close to the equator?

Beacuse they thought that sun was so hot that sea boil.

1. **SUMMARIZE** Why did European nations compete with each other for land and resources?

   _____

   _____

   _____

2. Why were **missionaries** sent to faraway places?

   _____

   _____

   _____

3. Why did explorers have trouble persuading monarchs to pay for voyages of exploration?

   _____

   _____

   _____

Circle the letter of the correct answer.

4. Which was a motivation for European exploration in the 1400s?

   A To reform the Catholic church

   B To divide land among European nobles

   C To claim new land

   D To find the equator

5. Until the late 1400s, most world maps—

   F included North America

   G reflected the Earth's true size

   H showed only Europe, Asia, and Africa

   F showed only Europe

6. Which was an obstacle for European exploration in the 1400s?

   A The invention of the compass

   B The formation of countries

   C Fear of the unknown

   D Competition amongst countries for power

writing

✏️ **Write a Speech** Imagine that you are a European monarch in the 1400s. Write a speech to give to your country's people about why you want to explore and claim new lands. Explain how you will overcome obstacles to exploration.

Queen Isabella of Spain

Portugal Leads the Way

In the 1400s, explorers from Portugal began to search for a sea route to Asia's trading centers. To help achieve that goal, Portuguese explorers learned to sail faster ships and use improved tools for locating places. This new technology helped make long ocean voyages possible. **Technology** is the use of scientific knowledge or tools to make or do something. **Think about ways in which new technology may affect travel.**

Explorers from Portugal sailed around Africa's Cape of Good Hope in 1488.

ESSENTIAL QUESTIONS

✔ What were the obstacles faced by the explorers?
✔ What were the accomplishments of the explorations?
✔ What regions were explored by Portugal?
✔ How did West African empires impact European trade?

HISTORY AND SOCIAL SCIENCE SOL
USI.1a, USI.1f, USI.4a, USI.4c

New Tools for Discovery

In 1419, King John I of Portugal asked his son, Prince Henry, to direct his country's search for a water route to Asia. Prince Henry opened a school of navigation (na•vuh•GAY•shuhn) at the town of Sagres (SAH•gresh), on the Portuguese coast. **Navigation** is the skill of planning and controlling the course of a ship. The aim of the school was to develop better ships, maps, and navigational tools.

Improved Ships

In the early 1400s, Portuguese explorers began to use a new kind of ship, called a caravel. A caravel used two or three triangle-shaped sails. This kind of sail, which came from Arabia, allowed the caravel to travel long distances swiftly.

Caravels were smaller and lighter than other ships of the time, which made them easier to control in rough seas. They were also sturdy enough to withstand ocean travel. Over time, the Portuguese built larger caravels to carry enough cargo, crew, and supplies for long voyages.

Portuguese caravels

Prince Henry

More Accurate Maps

Mapmakers at Prince Henry's school read the journals of early explorers. Using new information from these journals, they were able to draw more accurate maps. Portuguese mapmakers were also among the first to add parallels of latitude and meridians of longitude to maps, which helped explorers find locations.

Better Tools for Navigation

Prince Henry hired scientists to make sure explorers had the newest navigational tools. In the 1400s, explorers used two tools to help determine their direction and location at sea—the compass and the astrolabe (AS•truh•layb).

European sailors learned about the magnetic compass from China. A magnetic compass always points north, so sailors could use it to help them know in which direction they were traveling. The astrolabe, which came from North Africa, was used to determine the positions of the sun, moon, and stars. By using an astrolabe, sailors could figure out their location.

TextWork

❹ Why did explorers need more accurate maps?

_____

_____

_____

_____

_____

❺ Scan the text. Circle the names of two navigational instruments used in the 1400s.

❻ Look at the compass and the astrolabe. Mark an X on the navigation tool that was used to figure out the positions of the sun, moon, and stars.

Navigational Tools EIP

COMPASS

ASTROLABE

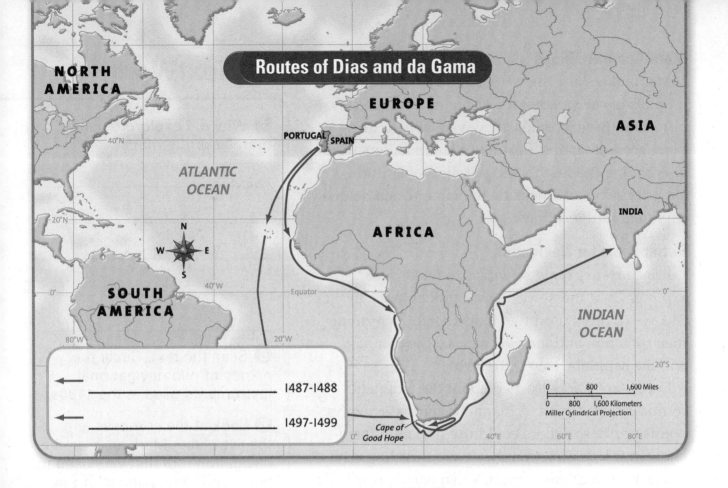

Routes of Dias and da Gama

NORTH AMERICA

EUROPE

ASIA

PORTUGAL SPAIN

ATLANTIC OCEAN

40°N

20°N

AFRICA

INDIA

SOUTH AMERICA

0°

40°W

Equator

INDIAN OCEAN

80°W

20°W

_____ 1487-1488

_____ 1497-1499

Cape of Good Hope

0°

40°E

60°E

80°E

20°S

0   800   1,600 Miles

0   800   1,600 Kilometers

Miller Cylindrical Projection

Exploring West Africa

Prince Henry believed that the most direct way to reach Asia by sea would be to travel around the southern part of Africa and then sail east across the Indian Ocean. He sent dozens of expeditions in search of the best route. An **expedition** is a trip whose purpose is exploration.

As the Portuguese made voyages of discovery along the western coast of Africa, they set up trading stations that were heavily armed, almost like forts. Catholic priests were sent to these trading stations to teach Africans about Christianity.

The Portuguese traded European goods, such as metals, cloth, and other manufactured products, for gold, ivory, and spices. They also traded for enslaved Africans who had been kidnapped and forced into slavery. **Slavery** is the practice of holding people against their will and making them work. Enslaved Africans were shipped to Europe, where they were sold as workers and servants.

TextWork

7 Scan the text. Circle the names of goods that the Portuguese traded for in West Africa.

8 Underline the sentence that defines the word *slavery*. What was a consequence of this practice?

_____

_____

_____

Reaching India

For years after Prince Henry's death, the Portuguese continued to search for a sea route to Asia. The rough ocean waters along the southern coast of Africa had prevented Portuguese explorers from reaching the Indian Ocean.

Finally, in 1488, Bartholomeu Dias (DEE•ahsh) became the first European to successfully reach the southern tip of Africa. The Portuguese later called this area the Cape of Good Hope. However, the stormy weather around the Cape forced Dias and his crew to return home.

Ten years later, Vasco da Gama (dah GA•muh) became the first European to sail all the way from Portugal, around the Cape of Good Hope, to India. In 1499, da Gama returned to Portugal with ships full of spices and jewels. However, many of his crew did not survive the long voyage.

Da Gama's expedition led to regular voyages between Europe and India. In time, Portugal became one of the most important trading powers in the Indian Ocean.

TextWork

9 Study the map on page 130. Use what you have read to complete the map's legend.

10 (Focus Skill) At the correct location on the time line, write the letter of each event described below.

A. 1488: Bartholomeu Dias reaches the southern coast of Africa

B. 1498: Vasco da Gama reaches India

11 (Focus Skill) Study your completed time line. From the time Prince Henry opened his navigation school, how long was it until Portuguese explorers reached India?

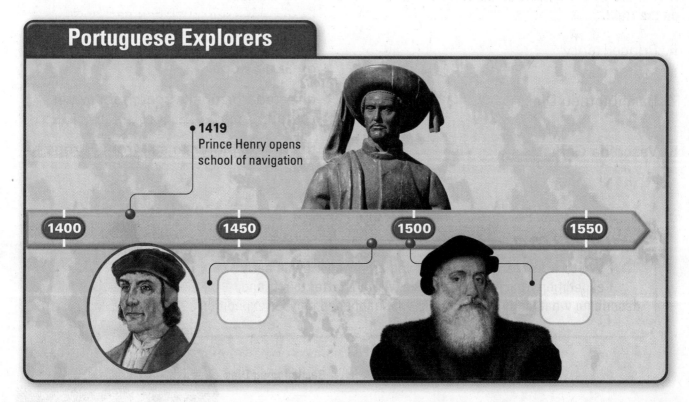

Portuguese Explorers

1419
Prince Henry opens school of navigation

1400   1450   1500   1550

1. **SUMMARIZE** What were the accomplishments of Portuguese explorers?

   _____

   _____

   _____

   _____

2. Explain how **technology** helped improve **navigation**.

   _____

   _____

   _____

   _____

   _____

Circle the letter of the correct answer.

3. Prince Henry of Portugal is known for—

   A sailing from Portugal to India

   B setting up a school of navigation

   C inventing new navigation tools

   D sailing around the southern tip of Africa

4. Portuguese explorers sailed around Africa to find a quicker route to—

   F South America

   G West Africa

   H Asia

   J Sagres

5. In West Africa, Portuguese explorers—

   A manufactured products

   B traded for enslaved Africans

   C learned to use compasses and astrolabes

   D built caravels

Match the person's name on the left with the person's accomplishment on the right.

6. Prince Henry   the first European to sail around Cape of Good Hope

7. Bartholomeu Dias   directed Portugal's search for water route to Asia

8. Vasco da Gama   the first explorer to sail from Europe to Asia

writing

✎ **Write a Letter** Imagine that you are a sailor on an early expedition from Portugal to Asia. Write a letter to a friend, describing what lands you saw and what happened on your expedition.

Bartholomeu Dias

The Spanish Explore

In 1492, an Italian sailor named Christopher Columbus persuaded the king and queen of Spain to sponsor, or pay for, an expedition across the Atlantic Ocean. Columbus believed that he could reach Asia from Europe by sailing west across the Atlantic Ocean. He thought this route would be shorter and faster than sailing around Africa. **Think about why people would risk exploring unknown routes and places.**

Spanish explorers, in what is now the southeastern United States

ESSENTIAL QUESTIONS

✓ Why did European countries compete for power in North America?
✓ What were the obstacles faced by the explorers?
✓ What were the accomplishments of the explorations?
✓ What regions of North America were explored and settled by Spain?

 HISTORY AND SOCIAL SCIENCE SOL
USI.1f, USI.4a

To commemorate his voyage to North America, the Spanish government built replicas of the three ships used by Christopher Columbus.

 **TextWork**

❶ Which European explorer sailed west across the Atlantic Ocean in 1492?

_____

❷ Underline the sentences that describe some of the obstacles that Columbus and his crew faced on their voyage.

❸ Why did Columbus call the people he saw on San Salvador *Indians*?

_____

_____

_____

Columbus Sails West

On August 3, 1492, Christopher Columbus and his crew of 90 sailors set sail from the port of Palos, Spain, on three ships. The ships were called the *Niña*, the *Pinta*, and the *Santa María*.

Columbus and his crew sailed west across the Atlantic Ocean for more than two months, and they faced many obstacles. Frequent storms damaged their ships. Sometimes there was no wind to fill the sails, and the ships just drifted for days. As the voyage dragged on, the sailors grew restless. Finally, in the early morning hours of October 12, they saw land. The ships anchored off an island in the Caribbean sea. Columbus named the island San Salvador and claimed it for Spain.

Because Columbus believed he had reached the Indies, in Asia, he called the people he met on the island *Indians*. Columbus did not find any silk or spices. However, he explored nearby islands and collected a few gold items and some of the islands' plants and animals. He also captured several American Indians and took them back to Spain.

Columbus Returns to Europe

When Columbus and his crew returned to Spain, they were treated like heroes. King Ferdinand and Queen Isabella of Spain saw the gold, animals, and plants Columbus returned with, and they were eager to sponsor more voyages. Columbus made three more trips to what he thought were the Indies. Columbus never found great riches, but he claimed more land for Spain. He also showed that it was possible to sail across the Atlantic Ocean.

Not everyone believed that Columbus had found Asia. In 1499, Amerigo Vespucci (veh•SPOO•chee) of Italy sailed to a place just south of where Columbus landed. Vespucci did not see anything that fit descriptions of Asia. He began to believe that Columbus had reached a continent unknown to Europeans.

In 1507, a German mapmaker named Martin Waldseemüller (VAHLT•zay•mool•er) drew a world map that showed lands between Europe and Asia. He named the lands for Amerigo Vespucci. This was the first time *America* appeared on a map.

TextWork

❹ Scan the text. Circle the sentence that describes how King Ferdinand and Queen Isabella reacted to Columbus's discoveries.

❺ For whom was America named?

_____

❻ How did Amerigo Vespucci's voyage change the way Europeans viewed the world?

_____

_____

_____

Children IN HISTORY

Diego Bermúdez

Some of the sailors on Columbus's ships were as young as 12 years old. That was the age of Diego Bermúdez when he sailed with Columbus in 1492. Diego was a page, which was the lowest rank on a ship. Pages did the jobs that most sailors did not want to do, such as cooking, cleaning, and keeping track of the time. Diego kept track of the time by using an hourglass. When the sand had all fallen to the bottom of the hourglass, Diego rang a bell and called out a short prayer. His actions let everyone know what time it was.

Make It Relevant **What jobs do you have to do at home or at school?**

Spanish Explorers in North America

Legend:
- ← Columbus, 1492
- ← Ponce de León, 1513
- ← Cortés, 1519
- ← De Niza, 1539
- ← De Soto, 1539–1542
- ← Coronado, 1540–1542
- ← De Avilés, 1565
- ▦ Aztec Empire
- — Present-day border

Quivira • Cíbola • Culiacán • NORTH AMERICA • NEW SPAIN • Compostela • Tenochtitlán (Mexico City) • Veracruz • Yucatán Peninsula

PACIFIC OCEAN • Gulf of California • Río Grande • Colorado River • Arkansas River • Missouri R. • Ohio River • Tennessee River • Mississippi R.

Gulf of Mexico • Tampa Bay • Havana • Cuba • Bahamas • Jamaica • Hispaniola • Puerto Rico • Caribbean Sea • ATLANTIC OCEAN

250 500 Miles
0 250 500 Kilometers
Miller Cylindrical Projection

40°N · 20°N · 110°W · 80°W · 70°W

The Spanish Explore Florida

The king of Spain offered large sums of money, called **grants**, to encourage explorers to lead more voyages to the Americas. These Spanish explorers became known as conquistadors (kahn•KEES•tah•dawrz), or "conquerors." Some of them dreamed of discovering gold and other riches, while others wanted to win national glory and bring Christianity to North America.

In 1513, one of the conquistadors, Juan Ponce de León, landed in what is now the state of Florida. He was the first Spanish explorer to set foot on land that would become part of the United States. Ponce de León was searching for the so-called Fountain of Youth. Its waters supposedly made old people young again.

Ponce de León returned to Florida in 1521 to start a settlement. This led to conflict with the Calusa, an American Indian tribe in the region. The Calusa defended their lands against the Spanish. Ponce de León was wounded in the fighting and later died, never having found the Fountain of Youth.

TextWork

7 Use the word *grant* in a sentence about Spanish exploration.

_____

_____

_____

8 Circle the sentence that describes the motivations of the conquistadors.

9 Study the map. Which three conquistadors explored the Florida peninsula?

_____

_____

_____

New Spain

In 1519, Spain sent another conquistador, named Hernando Cortés (kawr•TES), to search for gold and to claim lands in what is now Mexico. These lands were controlled by the Aztec Empire, which included as many as 5 million people.

Cortés landed in Mexico with about 640 soldiers. He marched inland and captured Motecuhzoma (moy•tay•kwah•SOH•mah), the Aztec ruler, and by 1521, he and his soldiers had conquered the Aztec people. The Aztec were strong fighters. However, they did not have horses or guns as the Spanish did. Many Aztec died in battles and from diseases unknowingly brought by the Spanish.

In 1535, Spain founded the colony of New Spain. A **colony** is a land ruled by another country. Much of New Spain's lands were in what is now Mexico, and Mexico City became the capital of New Spain. The Spanish built Mexico City on the site of the former Aztec capital, Tenochtitlán (tay•nawch•teet•LAHN).

TextWork

10 Underline the sentence that describes what Hernando Cortés was searching for in the Americas.

11 How did the Spanish explorers affect the lives of the Aztec people?

_____

_____

12 Study the illustration. Why do you think the harquebus gave the Spanish an advantage in fighting the Aztec?

_____

_____

_____

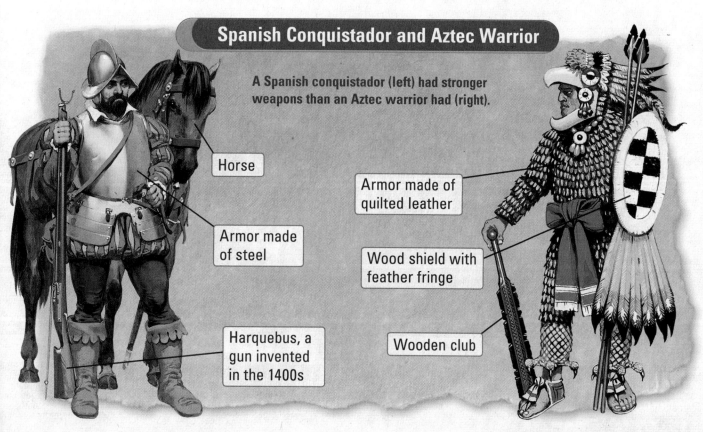

Spanish Conquistador and Aztec Warrior

A Spanish conquistador (left) had stronger weapons than an Aztec warrior had (right).

Horse

Armor made of steel

Harquebus, a gun invented in the 1400s

Armor made of quilted leather

Wood shield with feather fringe

Wooden club

TextWork

⑬ Why did Coronado explore what is now the southwestern United States?

_____

_____

_____

⑭ (Focus Skill) Study the time line. When did Spain start the colony of New Spain? Did this happen before or after Coronado's expedition?

_____

_____

Coronado's Expedition

After Cortés found some gold among the Aztec, the Spanish searched for more riches. Spanish leaders in Mexico City had heard stories about the existence of the Seven Cities of Gold. They sent a priest named Marcos de Niza (day NEE•sah) on an expedition to find those golden cities.

De Niza took along an enslaved African named Estevanico (es•tay•vahn•EE•koh), who knew about the region. Estevanico was killed during the expedition. However, De Niza returned and said he had seen a golden city.

In 1540, Francisco Vásquez de Coronado (kawr•oh•NAH•doh) heard De Niza's story. Coronado set out on another expedition to find the Seven Cities of Gold. He explored and claimed the lands in what is now the southwestern United States. Members of his expedition may have been among the first Europeans to see the Grand Canyon. Coronado never found any gold. However, he claimed more lands for New Spain.

Spanish Explorers, 1490–1570

1490	1510	1530
1492 Columbus lands in North America	**1521** Cortés conquers the Aztec Empire	**1535** Spain starts the colony of New Spain

Other Expeditions

From 1539 to 1542, another conquistador, named Hernando de Soto (day•SOHT•oh), explored what is now the southeastern United States. He and 600 men traveled through Florida and parts of Georgia, South Carolina, North Carolina, Tennessee, Alabama, Arkansas, and Louisiana. They were the first Europeans to see the Mississippi River.

De Soto and his soldiers encountered many American Indians during their expedition. Those meetings often ended in bloody battles. One of the worst battles took place against the Mobile tribe in what is now the state of Alabama. Like other conquistadors, De Soto claimed the lands he explored, even though American Indians already lived there.

In 1565, Pedro Menendez de Avilés (may•NAYN•days day ah•vee•LAYS) and about 1,500 soldiers, sailors, and settlers sailed from Spain. That same year, they settled St. Augustine, in Florida. It was the first permanent European settlement built in what is now the United States.

TextWork

15 Who led the first European expedition to see the Mississippi River?

_____

16 Scan the text. Underline the names of the lands that De Soto claimed.

17 What was the first permanent European settlement in what is today the United States?

_____

Coronado's expedition included soldiers, priests, farmers, and American Indian scouts.

1550

1570

1540 Coronado searches for gold

1565 The Spanish found St. Augustine

1. **SUMMARIZE** What motivated the Spanish to explore North America?

_____

_____

_____

2. Use the word **colony** in a sentence about New Spain.

_____

_____

_____

_____

3. What did Christopher Columbus hope to accomplish by sailing westward across the Atlantic Ocean?

_____

_____

_____

_____

_____

Circle the letter of the correct answer.

4. Juan Ponce de León was searching for the—

   A Northwest Passage

   B Fountain of Youth

   C Seven Cities of Gold

   D Indies

5. The capital of New Spain was located at—

   F San Salvador

   G Mexico City

   H St. Augustine

   J Mobile

6. Which explorer led an expedition through the southwestern part of what is now the United States?

   A Hernando Cortés

   B Juan Ponce de León

   C Francisco Vásquez de Coronado

   D Hernando de Soto

7. What did Coronado achieve on his expedition?

   F He found the Seven Cities of Gold.

   G He claimed new lands for New Spain.

   H He conquered the Aztecs.

   J He passed through the Northwest Passage.

activity

Make a Time Line Do additional research on one of the Spanish explorers in this lesson. Make a time line showing some of the other important accomplishments of that explorer. Illustrate your time line with pictures or photographs.

Conquistador's helmet

The French in North America

By the early 1500s, France had joined the competition among European countries to claim land in North America. The French believed that if they could find a western trade route to Asia, they might share in the riches to be found there. They thought that Asia could be reached by sailing through or around North America. This belief led explorers to search for a route they called the Northwest Passage. **Think about how knowledge gained by early explorers might have changed the motivations and views of later explorers.**

Jacques Marquette on the banks of the Mississippi River, in 1673

ESSENTIAL QUESTIONS

✓ Why did European countries compete for power in North America?
✓ What were obstacles faced by the explorers?
✓ What were the accomplishments of the explorations?
✓ What regions of North America were settled and explored by France?

HISTORY AND SOCIAL SCIENCE SOL
USI.1f, USI.4a

TextWork

1 Read the quotation from Giovanni da Verrazano. Why do you think he seemed disappointed about what he found?

_____

_____

_____

2 Study the map. On which waterway did both Cartier and Champlain travel?

_____

_____

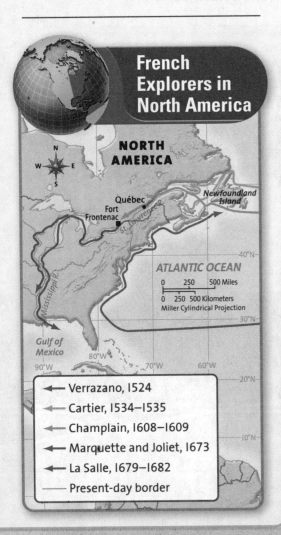

French Explorers in North America

NORTH AMERICA

Québec
Fort Frontenac

Newfoundland Island

St. Lawrence R.

Mississippi R.

40°N

ATLANTIC OCEAN

0   250   500 Miles

0   250   500 Kilometers
Miller Cylindrical Projection

30°N

Gulf of Mexico

80°W

90°W   70°W   60°W

20°N

← Verrazano, 1524
← Cartier, 1534–1535
← Champlain, 1608–1609
← Marquette and Joliet, 1673
← La Salle, 1679–1682
— Present-day border

10°N

Early French Voyages

In 1524, King Francis I of France sent an Italian explorer named Giovanni da Verrazano (vair•uh•ZAH•noh) to find the Northwest Passage. Verrazano landed on the coast of what is now North Carolina. He then sailed northeast along the Atlantic coast as far north as Canada.

Along the route, Verrazano explored several large bays and rivers, including what is now called New York Bay. He claimed the land along the waterways for France and continued north to Newfoundland Island in present-day Canada. Along the way, Verrazano encountered different American Indian tribes. He wrote that some tribes were friendly, while others were not.

Although Verrazano made two more voyages to the Americas, he could not find the Northwest Passage. In his journal, Verrazano wrote,

> **"My intention [aim] on this voyage was to reach Cathay [China] ... but I did not expect to find such an obstacle of new land as I have found."**

Jacques Cartier on the St. Lawrence River

Cartier Explores Canada

In 1534, King Francis I sent Jacques Cartier (ZHAHK kar•TYAY) on another voyage to search for the Northwest Passage. He also told Cartier to look for gold. Cartier made three voyages to North America between 1534 and 1541.

On the first voyage, Cartier reached the mouth of the St. Lawrence River and claimed all the land surrounding it for France. On his second voyage, Cartier sailed up the St. Lawrence River to what is now Montreal, Canada. His ships could not pass the shallow, rough rapids there, so he turned back.

In 1541, Cartier visited the St. Lawrence River again, but he was never able to find the Northwest Passage. When Cartier returned to France, he brought back some corn that a group of Iroquois had given him. Many Europeans had never seen corn before.

❸ Why was Jacques Cartier sent to North America?

_____

_____

_____

_____

❹ What obstacle did Cartier encounter on his second voyage?

_____

_____

_____

_____

✳ French Explorers in North America ✳

1524 Giovanni da Verrazano lands in what is now North Carolina

A

✓

1608 Samuel de Champlain builds a settlement at Québec

1524   1534   1608

5 (Focus Skill) Complete the timeline by writing the letter of each entry below at the correct location.

A. Jacques Cartier reaches the St. Lawrence River.

B. Jacques Marquette and Louis Joliet explore the Mississippi River.

How many years passed between entries A and B?

139 years

6 What usually happens to the price of a product when the supply of it is low but the demand for it is high?

The product's price goes up in price.

New France

In 1603, a group of merchants hired Samuel de Champlain (sham•PLAYN) to find a good location along the St. Lawrence River for a settlement. By then, Spain and England had already established North American colonies. The French king wanted to protect his country's claims to lands in what is now Canada and the northeastern United States. The French called this region New France.

Champlain built a settlement at Québec (kwih•BEK) along the St. Lawrence River in 1608. He also entered into a trading **alliance**, or formal partnership, with the Huron people. The Huron took beaver and other animal furs to Québec to exchange for European goods.

The **demand**, or desire, for beaver fur was high in Europe. However, the supply of beaver fur was low. The **supply** is the amount of a product that is offered for sale. When the demand for a product is high and the supply is low, the price of the product usually goes up. The French made lots of money shipping furs from North America to Europe.

1682 Robert de La Salle reaches the mouth of the Mississippi River

B

1673

1682

Exploring the Mississippi

The king of France later sent explorers southwest of Québec to explore the Mississippi River. The French hoped the Mississippi River would prove to be the Northwest Passage. With the help of American Indians, Jacques Marquette (mar•KET) and Louis Joliet (zhohl•YAY) explored parts of the Mississippi River in 1673.

Marquette was a French missionary who was sent to teach American Indians about the Catholic religion. Because the Mississippi River flows south, Marquette and Joliet knew it was not the Northwest Passage. However, their expedition opened new areas to French settlement and trade.

In 1682, Robert de La Salle traveled to the mouth of the Mississippi River. La Salle claimed all of the Mississippi Valley for France. This area extends from the Appalachian Mountains to the Rocky Mountains and from the Gulf of Mexico to the Great Lakes. He named the area Louisiana in honor of King Louis XIV. In 1722, the town of New Orleans became Louisiana's capital.

 **TextWork**

❼ Scan the text. Underline the sentence that explains why France sent explorers to search the Mississippi River.

❽ How did Marquette and Joliet know the Mississippi River could not be the Northwest Passage?

Because Missisippi River flows south.

❾ For whom was Louisiana named?

King Louis XIV

1. **SUMMARIZE** Where in North America did the French explore and build settlements?

_____

_____

_____

_____

_____

2. Why did the French enter into an **alliance** with the Huron?

_____

_____

_____

_____

_____

Circle the letter of the correct answer.

3. What waterway did Samuel de Champlain use to explore Canada?

   A Mississippi River

   B St. Lawrence River

   C Lake Erie

   D New York Bay

4. Among the things Jacques Marquette sought to accomplish in New France was to—

   F find the Seven Cities of Gold

   G teach Christianity to American Indians

   H establish a trade alliance with Mexico

   J conquer the Aztec people

5. The area that Robert de La Salle named as Louisiana included the—

   A settlement at Québec

   B area north of the St. Lawrence River

   C Great Lakes region

   D Mississippi River valley

Match the name of the explorer to his accomplishment.

6. Samuel de Champlain   explored the Mississippi River in 1673

7. Jacques Marquette and Louis Joliet   established a settlement at Québec

8. Robert de La Salle   claimed Louisiana for France

writing

✎ **Write a Report** Research and write a report on the motivations and accomplishments of one of the explorers discussed in this lesson. Include a map and illustrations in your report.

Jacques Cartier

The English in North America

Most of the early English explorers who sailed to North America were first attracted by the valuable fishing resources found along the eastern coast of what is now Canada. Like other European countries, England competed for power in North America and claimed large areas of land there. **Think about why English explorers might have been interested in fish and other natural resources.**

A statue of explorer John Cabot, in Newfoundland, Canada

ESSENTIAL QUESTIONS

✓ What regions of North America were settled and explored by England?

✓ What were the accomplishments of the explorations?

HISTORY AND SOCIAL SCIENCE SOL
USI.1a, USI.1d, USI.1f, USI.4a

❶ Scan the text. Underline the name of the first explorer to claim North American lands for England.

❷ Why do you think John Cabot believed he had landed in China?

Because John Cabot had very long, slow voyage.

England Begins to Explore

The English began to explore North America just a few years after learning about Columbus's voyages for Spain. In 1497, King Henry VII of England sponsored a voyage led by an Italian sailor named Giovanni Caboto (kah•BOH•toh). The English called him John Cabot. In May 1497, Cabot and a crew of 18 set sail on a course north of Columbus's original route.

Cabot Lands in North America

Cabot and his crew reached land on June 24, 1497, after a long, slow voyage. Cabot claimed the land for England, and then sailed southeast along the coast before returning to England.

Like Columbus, Cabot believed he had reached China—even though he did not find gold, spices, or other riches from the Indies. Many people today believe Cabot actually reached the coast of what is now a part of Canada—Newfoundland and Labrador.

John Cabot places the English flag on what is now Canada.

Investigating the Past

Cabot and his crew did not leave any written record of their voyage. The only primary sources describing Cabot's voyage come from other people from the time. A **primary source** is a record with a direct link to the past. It is made by people who saw or took part in an event or who lived during the time the event took place. Examples of primary sources include letters, journals, and maps.

When Cabot returned to England, he described to others a place with amazing natural resources. In December 1497, a merchant named John Day wrote to Christopher Columbus that Cabot had "found tall trees of the kind masts are made, and other smaller trees, and the country is rich in grass."

Over the years, many other accounts of Cabot's voyage have been written. These are secondary sources. A **secondary source** is a record made by someone who does not have a direct link to an event. Examples of secondary sources include textbooks and encyclopedia articles.

TextWork

3 Write a sentence describing how a primary source differs from a secondary source.

The difference in beetween primary Secondary source is direct and indirect link to it.

4 Is the excerpt from John Day's letter a primary or a secondary source? Explain.

It is a primary source because it is a letter.

Letter from John Day, December 1497

❝ *All along the coast they found many fish like those which in Iceland are dried in the open and sold in England and other countries, and these fish are called in English 'stockfish'; and ... it seemed to them that there were fields where they thought might also be villages, and they saw a forest whose foliage looked beautiful.* ❞

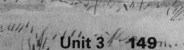

Fishing Resources

5 What kinds of fish did Cabot find off Newfoundland's coast?

John cabot, found Cod, and haddock, and other fish.

6 Scan the text. Circle the names of the two European groups that built fishing stations off the southeast coast of what is now Canada.

7 Why were Europeans attracted to cod fishing?

Because Europeans made made pofit out off cod fishing.

When Cabot returned to England, he reported that the fishing was so good that a person could simply lower baskets into the water and draw them up filled with fish. Cabot had found large amounts of cod, haddock, and other fish in the waters off Newfoundland's southeast coast. This area became known as the Grand Banks.

In the early 1500s, the fishing resources of the Grand Banks attracted many Europeans. By the late 1500s, both the English and the French had built small fishing stations off the southeast coast of Newfoundland Island and the eastern coast of what is now Nova Scotia, also in Canada. These stations were regular stopping places for food, fuel, and other needed supplies.

At many fishing stations, workers processed cod. The cod were dried and preserved on platforms and in temporary sheds built near the shore. The dried cod were then shipped to Europe and sold for profit. A **profit** is the money left after all costs have been paid.

A cod fishing station, in Newfoundland, in the 1700s

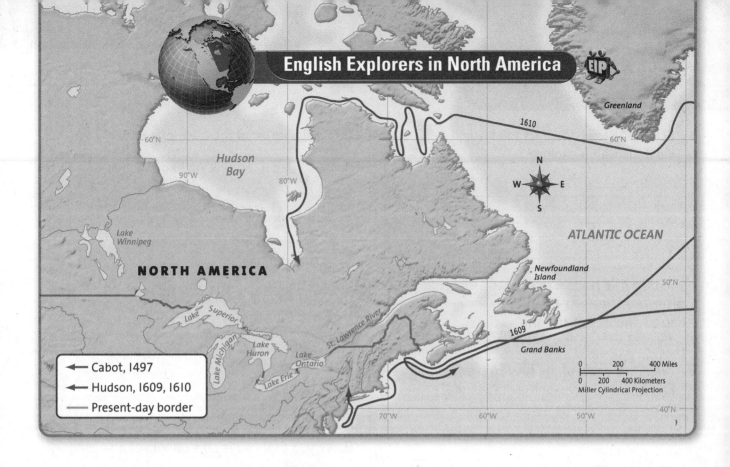

English Explorers in North America

Greenland

1610

60°N

Hudson
Bay

90°W   80°W

N
W   E
S

ATLANTIC OCEAN

Lake
Winnipeg

NORTH AMERICA

Newfoundland
Island

50°N

Lake Superior

St. Lawrence River

1609

Lake Michigan

Lake
Huron

Lake
Ontario

Grand Banks

Lake Erie

Cabot, 1497
Hudson, 1609, 1610
Present-day border

0   200   400 Miles
0   200   400 Kilometers
Miller Cylindrical Projection

70°W   60°W   50°W   40°N

Other Voyages

By the 1600s, European monarchs were no longer the only ones sponsoring explorations. European trading companies also began to send explorers to claim lands and search for the Northwest Passage. These companies got permission to trade in raw materials such as wood and fur. A **raw material** is any resource that can be used to make a product.

In the early 1600s, an English explorer named Henry Hudson led four voyages in search of the Northwest Passage. An English trading company sponsored the first two voyages. In 1608, Hudson reached an island east of Greenland. On the second voyage, he sailed farther north into the Arctic Ocean. The Dutch East India Company paid for his third voyage, to what is now New York Bay.

In 1610, an English company paid for Hudson's last voyage. Hudson sailed along the northern coast of North America to the bay that became known by his name—Hudson Bay. He claimed the land around the bay for England.

TextWork

8 On the map, circle the name of a waterway that was named after Henry Hudson.

9 (Focus Skill) Number these events in the correct sequence.

_____ Henry Hudson claims land around what is now Hudson Bay for England.

_____ Henry Hudson reaches an island east of Greenland.

_____ The Dutch East India Company hires Hudson to explore what is now New York Bay.

1. **SUMMARIZE** What areas of North America did John Cabot explore?

_____

_____

_____

_____

_____

2. What are some of the **raw materials** the English discovered in North America?

_____

_____

_____

_____

3. Why is John Day's letter about John Cabot's discovery a primary source?

_____

_____

_____

_____

Circle the letter of the correct answer.

4. John Cabot thought he had reached—

   A Asia

   B the Northwest Passage

   C Mexico

   D Newfoundland

5. What natural resource first attracted Europeans to Newfoundland?

   F Gold

   G Beaver furs

   H Lumber

   J Fish

6. Which of these is an example of a secondary source?

   A A map used by John Cabot

   B The log from John Cabot's expedition

   C An encyclopedia article about John Cabot

   D A document signed by John Cabot

7. Henry Hudson led four voyages in search of—

   F written records of John Cabot's voyage

   G fishing stations

   H the Northwest Passage

   J the Grand Banks

activity

Make a Table of Explorers Make a table listing the major accomplishments of each of the explorers discussed in this lesson. Include the area each person explored.

Henry Hudson

Two Worlds Meet

The Age of Exploration led to economic and cultural interactions between Europeans and American Indians. In an **economic interaction**, people share or exchange goods and resources to meet their needs. In a **cultural interaction**, people share or exchange ideas and ways of living. These interactions sometimes resulted in cooperation. Sometimes they resulted in conflict. **Think about how interactions among groups from different cultures might affect how people live.**

Europeans frequently interacted with American Indians.

ESSENTIAL QUESTIONS

✓ What were the accomplishments of the explorations?
✓ How did American Indians and Europeans interact with each other?

 HISTORY AND SOCIAL SCIENCE SOL
USI.1a, USI.1d, USI.1f, USI.4a, USI.4b

TextWork

❶ Scan the text. Underline three accomplishments made by European explorers.

❷ Study the compass below. How did the compass help make long ocean voyages possible?

The copmass heips Them to where to go,

❸ Study the map on page 155. Which two countries claimed land along the Gulf of Mexico?

Spanish

❹ Scan the text. Circle the name of the country that made voyages of discovery along the west coast of Africa.

A compass from about 1570

The Accomplishments of Early European Explorers

By the 1600s, European explorers had accomplished many important things. They had shared goods and ideas with people in other parts of the world. They had developed faster ships and better navigational tools. They had claimed large areas of land. All of these accomplishments brought together the cultures of Europe, Asia, Africa, and the Americas. They also caused important changes.

Sharing Goods and Ideas

As European merchants began to travel to Asia and Africa, they shared many goods and ideas. From the Chinese, Europeans learned about the magnetic compass. From North Africans, they learned about the astrolabe. From Arabians, they learned about triangle-shaped sails, which allowed sailors to steer against the wind.

Developing Faster Ships and Navigational Tools

Improved ships and navigational tools helped make long ocean voyages possible. Portugal led the way in using a new type of ship called the caravel. Portuguese sailors also began to use compasses and astrolabes to find their location at sea.

Claiming Lands

In time, Spanish, French, and English explorers claimed large areas of land in different parts of North America. The Spanish claimed lands that included what are today Mexico, the southwestern United States, and Florida. France claimed lands in what is now Canada and the lands that make up the entire Mississippi River valley. England claimed parts of what is now Canada and the lands along the eastern coast of what is now the United States. Portugal made voyages of discovery along the west coast of Africa and later claimed lands in South America.

EARLY EUROPEAN LAND CLAIMS

Québec, in Canada

Jamestown, in Virginia

Atlantic Ocean

Gulf
of
Mexico

St. Augustine, in Florida

☐ British

☐ French

☐ Spanish

Pacific Ocean

TextWork

5 Why did the Spanish enslave many of the peoples they conquered?

european exploration
brought spansih
French English
Aifcan and American
Inaids Cultures

6 Use the word *mission* in a sentence about cultural interactions between the Spanish and American Indians.

The Spansih have
complet themission

Cultural Interactions

European exploration brought Spanish, French, English, African, and American Indian cultures together. Explorers and early settlers interacted with American Indians in many different ways. These cultural interactions changed people's lives.

Conquering and Enslaving American Indians

The Spanish explorers conquered many of the American Indians they encountered during their expeditions. Many American Indians were strong warriors. However, they did not have guns, metal armor, or horses like the Spanish. Many American Indians died in battles with the Spanish, but even more died of diseases carried by the soldiers.

To protect their land claims, the Spanish established the colony of New Spain. The Spanish needed many workers to grow crops and to mine silver. They forced many of the American Indians they had conquered into slavery. Later, the Spanish also brought enslaved Africans to work in the colonies.

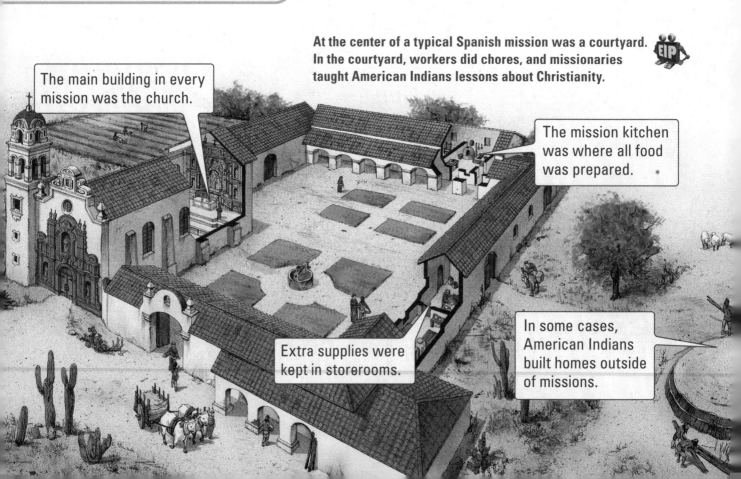

At the center of a typical Spanish mission was a courtyard. In the courtyard, workers did chores, and missionaries taught American Indians lessons about Christianity.

The main building in every mission was the church.

The mission kitchen was where all food was prepared.

Extra supplies were kept in storerooms.

In some cases, American Indians built homes outside of missions.

An early French trading post in North America

Establishing Missions

Both Spain and France set up **missions**, or small religious settlements, to spread Christianity. The American Indians who lived near missions were often forced to work at the missions. They also had to learn Spanish or French and to change the way they lived and worshipped.

Establishing Trading Posts

In 1608, the French built the first of many trading posts at Québec, along the St. Lawrence River. Québec became the center of the French fur trade in North America. The French often entered into agreements with different American Indian groups in the region. Those **allies**, or partners, served as agents for the French in the fur trade.

French traders carried beaver furs in birchbark canoes. American Indians taught their French allies how to build and use those canoes. In time, some French traders began to live in American Indian settlements. Many of them adopted American Indian languages and ways of life.

TextWork

7 Study the illustration. Circle the European goods that the American Indians wanted.

8 What skill did French traders learn from American Indians?

Tradeing Knives Guns and Fur.

Tisquantum (right) taught English settlers in the Plymouth Colony in Massachusetts new methods of growing crops such as corn, beans, and squash.

⚔ TextWork

❾ Scan the text. Circle the sentences that describe how American Indians helped the English.

❿ How did Europeans' perspectives about land differ from those of American Indians?

_____

_____

_____

_____

_____

_____

Different Ideas About Land

In time, the Spanish, French, and English established settlements in different parts of North America. In the early 1600s, the English built their first permanent settlements in what are now Virginia and Massachusetts. Europeans often settled on or near areas where American Indians already lived and hunted.

At first, some American Indians helped the settlers. In Virginia, Powhatan allowed his people to trade food to the settlers. In Massachusetts, Tisquantum, or Squanto as the English called him, showed the English where to fish and how to grow crops, such as corn. He helped the settlers trade for furs and other products with neighboring tribes.

Europeans believed that once they claimed an area, they owned the land. It was theirs to live on and use. When American Indians "sold" land to settlers, they thought they were agreeing to share it. Many American Indians believed that no one person could own land. The disagreement over land led to many conflicts.

Cooperation in Economic Interactions

Competition for scarce resources often led to economic cooperation. The Europeans traded plants, animals, and manufactured products with American Indians in exchange for food, furs, and other goods.

Europeans exchanged weapons, metal farm tools, and other manufactured goods for beaver furs, pottery, and cloth. European products, such as metal sewing needles and tools, wool yarn, and iron knives, became part of the lives of American Indians. American Indians made copper kettles into necklaces and cutting tools. They turned iron knives and ax heads into other kinds of tools.

Europeans brought to the Americas many crops that American Indians had never seen, including lettuce, onions, and oranges. They also brought animals such as pigs, cattle, horses, and chickens. Explorers returned to Europe with plants and animals from the Americas.

TextWork

11 Scan the text. Circle an example of an economic interaction that involved cooperation.

12 Study the illustration. What do you think life in North America would be like today if Europeans had not brought items such as iron, horses, and bees?

_____

_____

_____

_____

_____

Exchanging Goods and Ideas

Pigs   Cows
Sheep   Goats
Horses Bees
Chickens Iron

East to West

NORTH AMERICA

EUROPE

AFRICA

West to East

Potatoes Turkeys
Cotton   Peas
Corn   Cocoa
Squash   Tomatoes

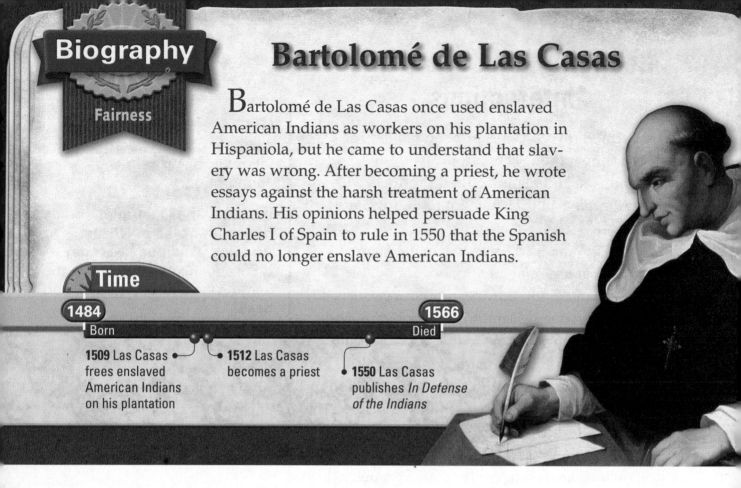

Biography

Fairness

Bartolomé de Las Casas

Bartolomé de Las Casas once used enslaved American Indians as workers on his plantation in Hispaniola, but he came to understand that slavery was wrong. After becoming a priest, he wrote essays against the harsh treatment of American Indians. His opinions helped persuade King Charles I of Spain to rule in 1550 that the Spanish could no longer enslave American Indians.

Time

1484
Born

1566
Died

1509 Las Casas frees enslaved American Indians on his plantation

1512 Las Casas becomes a priest

1550 Las Casas publishes *In Defense of the Indians*

TextWork

13 Scan the text on pages 160 and 161. Underline five areas of conflict among Europeans and American Indians.

14 List some ways that American Indians were affected by conflict over land and trade.

_____

_____

_____

_____

Areas of Conflict

Interactions between Europeans and American Indians sometimes led to conflict. There were several reasons for the conflicts.

Conflict Over Land and Trade

Fighting often broke out over land and resources. Some tribes were nearly wiped out in battles with Europeans. Many others were forced to give up their lands. Competition over trade was another source of conflict. In 1609, for example, Samuel de Champlain led the Huron in the first of many battles against the Iroquois for control of the fur trade.

Europeans often enslaved American Indians they had defeated in battle. Some American Indians tried to escape from slavery. However, many were killed or forced to return to work. A few European colonists, such as Bartolomé de Las Casas, a Spanish missionary, began to speak out against the cruel treatment of enslaved American Indians.

Cultural Conflicts and Diseases

Language and cultural differences also caused conflicts between Europeans and American Indians. American Indians who lived near missions were often forced to learn English, Spanish, or French and change the way they lived and worshipped. Some tried hard to hold onto their language and culture. Others fought back against the missionaries, tearing down churches and other mission buildings.

One of the most serious threats to American Indians at missions was disease. Europeans unknowingly brought diseases such as smallpox, measles, and influenza to North America. The Indians did not have protection against these diseases, and their bodies often could not fight them. Thousands of American Indians died.

 TextWork

15 (Focus Skill) Place these events in order.

_____ Many American Indians at the missions die of disease.

_____ Europeans unknowingly bring diseases to North America.

_____ Many American Indians are made to live at missions.

Lesson 7 Review

1. **SUMMARIZE** What were the results of the interactions between American Indians and Europeans?

_____

_____

_____

_____

2. Describe an **economic interaction** between Europeans and American Indians.

_____

_____

3. List a cause of conflict between Europeans and American Indians.

_____

_____

writing

Write a Paragraph Write a paragraph describing the interactions between Europeans and American Indians. Include two examples of cooperation and two examples of conflict.

Squash is native to the Americas.

Fun with Social Studies

Head West to Asia

Champlain says he found a new way to the Indies

Top School for Sailors

Queen Isabella hopes new school will make Portugal a sea power

---

What's Going On?

In the 1400s and 1500s, reports from Europe brought big news. Edit these reports to make them correct.

The Mississippi: No Northwest Passage

Cortés and Motecuhzoma bring disappointing news

Treasure Terms

abc VOCABULARY

Match the clues on the map to the correct vocabulary terms. The underlined letters in the correct terms will complete the name of a famous ship that reached North America long ago.

CARAVAN   EMPIRE
EXPEDITION   CLAIM
MISSIONARY

_ A N _ _   _ A _ _ A

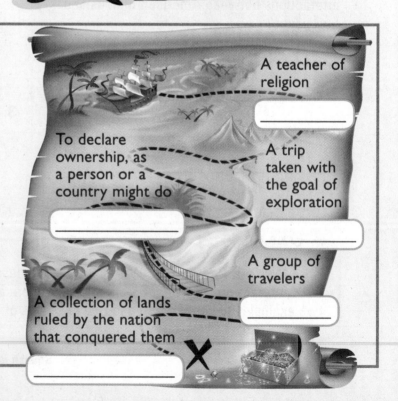

A teacher of religion

_____

To declare ownership, as a person or a country might do

_____

A trip taken with the goal of exploration

_____

A group of travelers

_____

A collection of lands ruled by the nation that conquered them

_____

Musical History

Match the song title to the historical "artist" who may have written it.

Name	Artist
Rollin' on the Mississippi	Champlain, S.
I Fought the Aztecs and the Aztecs Lost	La Salle, R.
You Say Kebec, I Say Québec	Polo, M.
Looking for Gold in All the Wrong Places	Coronado, F.
I'm a Traveling Man in Asia	Cortés, H.

Museum Mix Up

Circle the item that does not belong in the Museum of Early Exploration.

Compass

Map

Spanish conquistador helmet

Submarine

Review and Test Prep

The Big Idea

Competition for land and resources can lead to both cooperation and conflict among different groups of people.

Summarize the Unit

Focus Skill Sequence Complete the graphic organizer to place events from the Age of Exploration in their correct sequence.

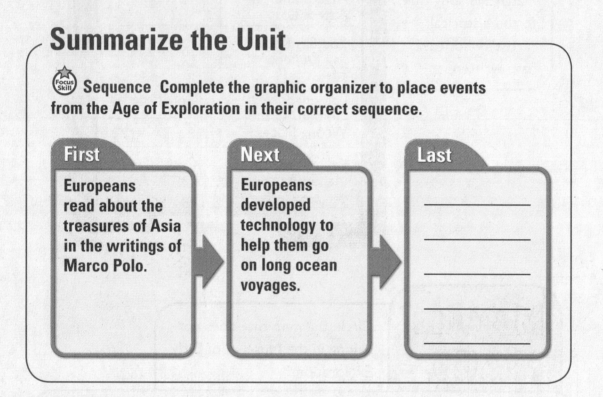

First

Europeans read about the treasures of Asia in the writings of Marco Polo.

Next

Europeans developed technology to help them go on long ocean voyages.

Last

_____

_____

_____

_____

_____

Use Vocabulary

Fill in each missing term, using the correct vocabulary term from the Word Bank.

1. The _____ for beaver fur was high in Europe in the 1600s.

2. At _____, the Spanish taught Christianity to American Indians.

3. Trading fur for metal tools is an example of _____ among Europeans and American Indians.

4. Merchants often traveled in _____ along the Silk Road.

5. Prince Henry of Portugal sent dozens of _____ to the west coast of Africa.

Word Bank

caravans p. 115

claim p. 123

expeditions p. 130

demand p. 144

economic interaction p. 153

missions p. 157

Circle the letter of the correct answer.

6.
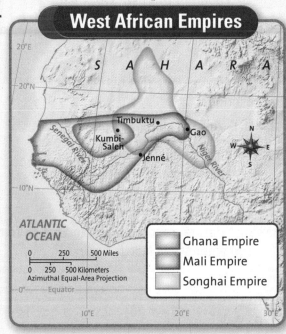

West African Empires

The Ghana Empire was located—

A between 20°N and 30°N

B between 10°N and 20°N

C between 10°E and 30°E

D between 20°E and 30°E

7. How did Ghana, Mali, and Songhai become powerful empires?

F By manufacturing goods

G By farming the land

H By controlling trade

J By capturing enemies

8. What motivated Europeans to begin exploring parts of the world that were unknown to them?

A Competition for power

B Limited food supplies

C Years of war

D Crowded living conditions

9. Which was an obstacle for explorers?

F Competition among nations for power

G Poor navigational tools

H The invention of the caravel

J Increasing interest in world resources

10.
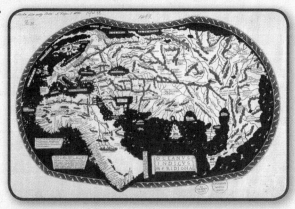

Which continent is not included on this early world map?

A Asia

B Africa

C North America

D Europe

11. What did Prince Henry accomplish?

F He drew a new map of the world.

G He built larger sailing ships.

H He started a school for training sailors.

J He invented the astrolabe.

12. The Portuguese traded European goods in West Africa for—

A gold

B silk

C spices

D codfish

13.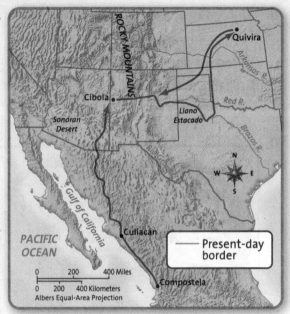

Which explorer took the route shown on this map across the Rocky Mountains and the Rio Grande?

F Robert de La Salle

G Samuel de Champlain

H Francisco de Coronado

J John Cabot

14. Francisco de Coronado explored parts of North America in search of the—

A Northwest Passage

B mouth of the Mississippi River

C Fountain of Youth

D Seven Cities of Gold

15. What did Samuel de Champlain accomplish?

F He explored the Mississippi River valley.

G He made voyages to West Africa.

H He established the settlement of Québec.

J He claimed lands for Spain.

16. Robert de La Salle explored to find the—

A Northwest Passage

B mouth of the Mississippi River

C Fountain of Youth

D Seven Cities of Gold

17.

> "They found many fish like those which in Iceland are dried in the open and sold in England and other countries, and these fish are called in English 'stockfish.'"
>
> —John Day

What place does this quote from 1497 describe?

F Newfoundland and Labrador

G The Fountain of Youth

H Mississippi and Ohio River valleys

J The Pacific Ocean

18. What natural resource did the English find in large amounts in North America?

A Salt

B Oil

C Gold

D Codfish

19.

> 1. European settlers trade weapons and metal farm tools.
> 2. American Indians exchange crops for manufactured goods.
> 3. Europeans and American Indians compete for control of the fur trade.
> 4. American Indians teach farming techniques to European settlers.

Which of these areas of economic interaction did NOT lead to cooperation between Europeans and American Indians?

F 1

G 2

H 3

J 4

20. What did Tisquantum teach to the English?

   A How to grow crops

   B How to protect themselves against diseases

   C How to build their own birchbark canoe

   D How to irrigate fields

21. What was brought to Europe as a result of exploration in North America?

   F Horses

   G Iron

   H Potatoes

   J Silk

22.

This person came to North America to—

   A protect European settlers

   B teach European Christianity to American Indians

   C teach American Indian culture to the Europeans

   D bring wealth to European monarchs

Answer these questions.

23. What motivated Europeans to explore faraway places?

_____

_____

_____

24. Why did John Cabot think that he had reached China?

_____

_____

_____

25. How did European ideas about land differ from those of American Indians?

_____

_____

_____

_____

The treasure must be hidden inside the wall of St. Augustine!

Eco is sailing to North America on board the Time Ship. The plan is to cross the Atlantic Ocean and then visit the new Spanish, French, and English colonies. You'd better stay on the lookout, because this could be a dangerous crossing. Who knows what lives out there in the ocean? Play the game now online.

Show What You Know

Writing Write a Report
In a report, discuss how competition for land and resources in North America led to cooperation and conflict among different groups of people. Write from the perspectives of the American Indians, the Portuguese, the Spanish, the French, and the English.

Activity Make a Museum of Exploration
Make museum exhibits about the exploration of North America. Decide which people, places, and events to include and how you will present the information about them. Prepare brief reports, journal entries, drawings, maps, and models to include in your exhibits.

Colonial America

These English settlers arrived in North America in 1620.

 Spotlight on Standards

THE BIG IDEA People in different regions often depend on each other for goods and natural resources.

SOL **HISTORY AND SOCIAL SCIENCE SOL**
USI.1a, USI.1c, USI.1d, USI.1f, USI.5a, USI.5b, USI.5c, USI.5d

Set the Stage

Study the map. Circle the mountain range that lies between New France and the New England, Mid-Atlantic, and Southern colonies.

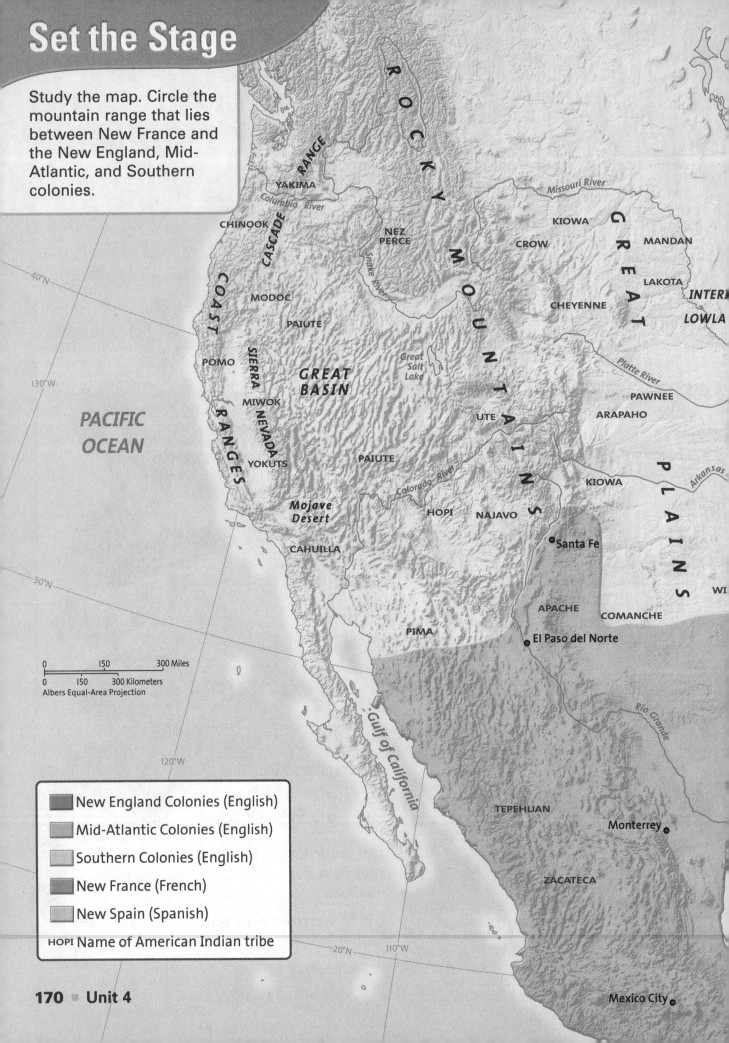

ROCKY MOUNTAINS

RANGE

CASCADE

COAST RANGES

SIERRA NEVADA

GREAT BASIN

GREAT PLAINS

PACIFIC OCEAN

YAKIMA

Columbia River

CHINOOK

NEZ PERCE

Snake River

MODOC

PAIUTE

POMO

MIWOK

YOKUTS

Great Salt Lake

UTE

PAIUTE

Colorado River

Mojave Desert

CAHUILLA

HOPI

NAJAVO

PIMA

Missouri River

KIOWA

CROW

MANDAN

CHEYENNE

LAKOTA

INTER

LOWLA

Platte River

PAWNEE

ARAPAHO

KIOWA

Arkansas

Santa Fe

APACHE

COMANCHE

WI

El Paso del Norte

Rio Grande

Gulf of California

TEPEHUAN

Monterrey

ZACATECA

Mexico City

40°N

130°W

30°N

120°W

20°N

110°W

0   150   300 Miles
0   150   300 Kilometers
Albers Equal-Area Projection

New England Colonies (English)

Mid-Atlantic Colonies (English)

Southern Colonies (English)

New France (French)

New Spain (Spanish)

HOPI Name of American Indian tribe

Colonial America, 1740

Québec

ABENAKI
(part of MA)

Montreal

Lake Superior

OTTAWA

ALGONKIN

Lake Huron

OTTAWA

Lake Michigan

FOX

HURON

Lake Ontario

IROQUOIS

(claimed by
NY and NH)

NEW
HAMPSHIRE

Boston

MASSACHUSETTS

SAC

Detroit

Lake Erie

NEW
YORK

Providence
RI

KICKAPOO

DELAWARE

CONNECTICUT

MIAMI

WYANDOT

PENNSYLVANIA

New York City

ILLINOIS

Philadelphia

NEW
JERSEY

MISSOURI

SHAWNEE

Baltimore

DELAWARE

MARYLAND

Vincennes

Ohio River

VIRGINIA

St. Louis

Richmond

OSAGE

Tennessee River

Williamsburg

APPALACHIAN MOUNTAINS

Roanoke River

NORTH
CAROLINA

New
Bern

CHEROKEE

Wilmington

CHICKASAW

SOUTH
CAROLINA

CADDO

CREEK

Savannah River

Charles
Town

NATCHEZ

GEORGIA

Savannah

CHOCTAW

St. Augustine

ATLANTIC
OCEAN

New Orleans

SEMINOLE

N
W E
S

Gulf of Mexico

60°W

40°N

0°N

90°W

80°W

Shipbuilding, in Mystic
Seaport, Connecticut

Trade, in New York
Harbor, New York

Farming, in Virginia

Set the Stage

❶ How many years after the first settlers arrived at Plymouth was the Massachusetts Bay Colony founded?

_____

❷ Circle the name of the person who started a colony for religious reasons.

John Smith

1580–1631
- English sailor who traveled to many parts of the world
- Served as a leader of the Jamestown settlement

Colonial America

1585 The first colonists arrive at Roanoke, p. 178

1607 The Jamestown settlement is started, p.178

1620 The *Mayflower* lands at Plymouth, p. 179

1630 The Massachusetts Bay Colony is founded, p. 180

1550   **1600**   **1650**

At the Same Time

1632 Work on the Taj Mahal begins in India

1636 The Dutch set up trading posts on the coast of Taiwa

James Oglethorpe

1696–1785
- Founded the Georgia Colony
- Wanted to give poor people in England a chance to start a new life in the Americas

Benjamin Franklin

1706–1790
- Pennsylvania leader and famous inventor
- Published *Poor Richard's Almanack*

Anne Hutchinson

1591–1643

- Puritan settler who began preaching in her home
- Started a colony in Rhode Island for religious reasons

Tamanend

1628?–1701?

- Lenni Lenape chief who sold land to Pennsylvania settlers
- His name means "affable," or friendly

1681 William Penn founds the Pennsylvania Colony, p. 181

1733 James Oglethorpe founds the Georgia Colony, p. 182

1753 The French and Indian War begins, p. 216

1700

1750

1800

1707 The Act of Union unites England and Scotland as Great Britain

1742 The Incas fight against Spanish rule in Peru

1770 Captain James Cook claims Australia for Great Britain

Eliza Lucas Pinckney

1722–1793

- Daughter of a South Carolina plantation owner
- Experimented with crops such as indigo

Olaudah Equiano

1745?–1797

- Enslaved African American who later purchased his freedom
- Spoke out against slavery in his writings and speeches

Preview Vocabulary

separatist

The Pilgrims were **separatists**. They wanted to break away from the Church of England. p. 179

specialization

The work of blacksmiths was an example of **specialization**, or focusing on making one or more products. p. 186

diverse
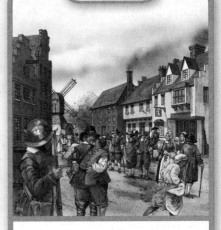
The Mid-Atlantic region was **diverse**. The people there had many different backgrounds and ways of life. p. 191

plantation

Some colonial familes lived on **plantations**. They grew tobacco, rice, or indigo on these large farms. p. 199

apprentice

Many workers started as **apprentices**. They lived and trained with a master craftworker for several years. p. 208

tax

The British made colonists pay fees on some goods. These **taxes** were used to pay for government services. p. 215

Reading Social Studies

 **Summarize**

LEARN

When you **summarize**, you state in your own words a shortened version of what you have read. A summary includes only the most important ideas and facts.

Key Facts

Important idea from the reading

Important idea from the reading

Summary

A shortened version of what you read

PRACTICE

Write a sentence to summarize the second paragraph. The first paragraph has been summarized for you.

Most people in the English colonies in North America worked as farmers. Farms in the Southern colonies, such as Virginia, were often much larger than farms in the Mid-Atlantic and New England colonies. In time, the economy of the Southern colonies was based mostly on those large farms.

Key Facts

Summary: Farming was the most important industry in the Southern colonies.

Summary

All of England's colonies in North America once allowed slavery. In the Southern colonies, most enslaved people worked on large farms. In the other English colonies, however, most enslaved people worked in homes and shops.

Summary: _____

_____

Read the paragraphs. Then complete the activities below.

Young Colonists at Work

Children were important in doing work in the colonies. Children as young as four might spin yarn, fetch water, help to plant crops, or take care of farm animals. At seven, a child was considered old enough to participate fully in the work of the household.

Between the ages of 10 and 14, a boy might become an apprentice to a skilled worker, or master worker, such as a blacksmith or a printer. Apprentices usually spent about seven years learning a trade. Often the master worker also saw to it that the apprentice learned to read and write. Eventually, the apprentices were ready to work on their own.

Some children came to the English colonies as indentured servants. A company would often pay for the children's trip from Europe to the colonies. In return, the children would work without pay for a period of time, usually about seven years. After the children completed their time of service, they would receive some basic supplies, some food, and their freedom.

Life as an indentured servant was hard. However, it was often the only choice for many poor children and adults. If they could survive their period of service, they would have a fresh start in a new land.

1. Underline the sentence that best summarizes the first paragraph.

2. Circle the key facts about apprentices learning new skills.

3. Write a sentence that summarizes the third paragraph.

_____

_____

_____

Settling English Colonies

England's leaders saw that Spain had grown rich from its colonies. They wanted to establish colonies of their own. In time, England had 13 different colonies along the eastern coast of what is now the United States. These colonies were established for both religious and economic reasons. **Think about why England might have wanted colonies and why people might have wanted to establish settlements in North America.**

Jamestown, in
Virginia

ESSENTIAL QUESTION
✓ Why did Europeans establish colonies in North America?

HISTORY AND SOCIAL SCIENCE SOL
USI.1a, USI.1c, USI.1d, USI.5a

TextWork

1 Scan the text. Circle a sentence that describes why the first two English colonies were established.

2 Which colony was founded first, Jamestown or Roanoke Island?

Roanoke Island

3 Study the illustration. Circle a raw material or natural resources that the Roanoke Island colony might provide.

The First English Colonies

The first English colonies were established as economic ventures. Wealthy leaders risked money to start the colonies. In return, they hoped to profit from raw materials the colonies would provide.

Roanoke Island and Jamestown Settlement

In 1585, English colonists tried to settle Roanoke Island, in what is now North Carolina. The first group of colonists at Roanoke Island ran low on food, and returned to England in 1586. The second group of colonists had disappeared from Roanoke Island by 1587. What happened to the Lost Colony, as it became known, is still a mystery.

In the early 1600s, merchants set up the Virginia Company to try to establish another colony. To raise money, the merchants sold **stock**, or shares of ownership, in the company. Those who bought stock would share in the colony's profits.

In 1607, the Virginia Company settled Jamestown in what is now Virginia. It was the first permanent English settlement in what became the United States. Jamestown might have failed without the leadership of Captain John Smith, who made the colonists work for their food and established trade with American Indians.

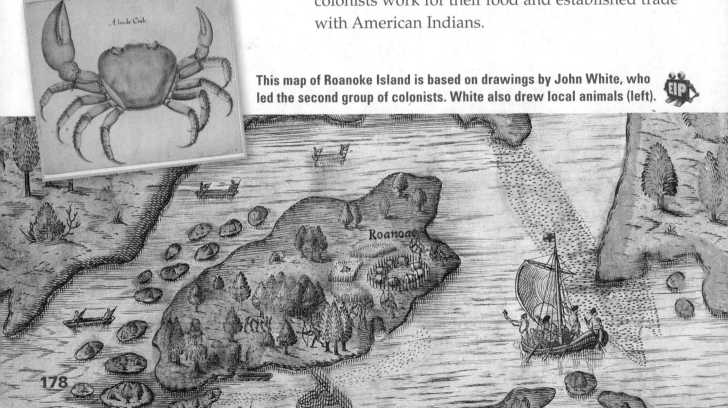

This map of Roanoke Island is based on drawings by John White, who led the second group of colonists. White also drew local animals (left).

A lande Crab.

Roanoac

Plymouth Colony settlers gather to hear a sermon.

The Plymouth Colony

In September 1620, a religious group that became known as Pilgrims set sail for Virginia on a ship called the *Mayflower*. A pilgrim is a person who makes a journey for religious reasons. The Pilgrims were **separatists**, or people who wanted to break away from the Church of England.

Everyone in England had to be a member of or had to attend the Church of England. Those who chose not to attend suffered religious persecution, or punishment. The Pilgrims wanted to establish a colony where they could freely follow their religious beliefs.

The Virginia Company agreed to pay for the Pilgrims' trip to North America. In return, the Pilgrims would repay the company with lumber and furs from their new land.

During the voyage to Virginia, storms blew the *Mayflower* off course. The ship landed at Cape Cod, in what is now Massachusetts. The Pilgrims chose a site, which they called Plymouth, to start a settlement. Plymouth Colony was located on a deep harbor. The area had fresh water and good land for growing crops.

TextWork

4 Use the word *separatist* in a sentence about the Pilgrims.

The pilgrims wanted to be separatists to be free from England.

5 Why did the Pilgrims want to establish Plymouth colony?

So they get there own corps and Religon.

6 Scan the text. Underline the reasons why the Virginia Company agreed to pay for the Pilgrims' passage.

Massachusetts Bay Colony

7 Write a sentence that summarizes the reasons why the Puritans established the Massachusetts Bay Colony.

They named this cony Boston and the putrains named it from the town of Enbnd.

8 How was John Winthrop's perspective about starting a colony different from that of the leaders of the Virginia Company?

_____

_____

_____

_____

In 1628, another group of colonists established a settlement at what is now Salem, Massachusetts. Like the Pilgrims, the settlers at Salem came to North America to avoid religious persecution and to practice their religious beliefs freely. They also came to start farms and businesses.

Unlike the Pilgrims, though, the new settlers did not want to break away from the Church of England. They wanted to change some of the church's religious practices to make it more "pure." For this reason, they were known as Puritans.

In 1630, a second group of Puritans, led by John Winthrop, settled in what became known as the Massachusetts Bay Colony. Winthrop's group of Puritans built their settlement south of Salem, near the mouth of the Charles River. They named their settlement Boston, after a town in England.

Winthrop hoped that the Puritan settlement at Boston would become an example of Christian living. In a sermon, he said,

❝We shall be as a city upon a hill. The eyes of all people are upon us.❞

Puritan ministers such as John Winthrop (right) delivered sermons at churches like this one in Hingham, Massachusetts.

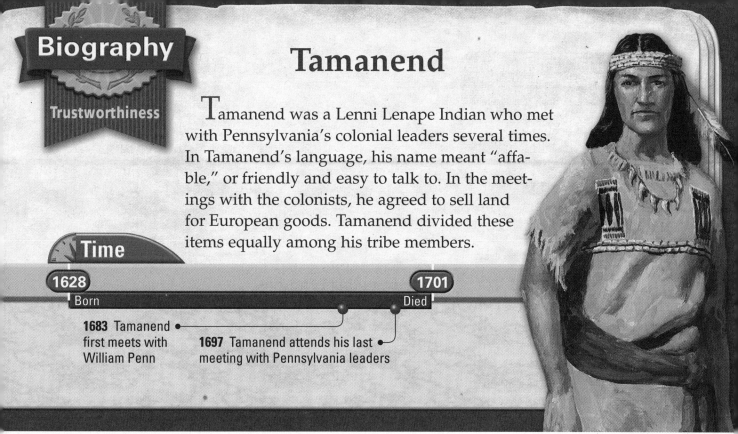

Tamanend

Tamanend was a Lenni Lenape Indian who met with Pennsylvania's colonial leaders several times. In Tamanend's language, his name meant "affable," or friendly and easy to talk to. In the meetings with the colonists, he agreed to sell land for European goods. Tamanend divided these items equally among his tribe members.

Time

1628
Born

1701
Died

1683 Tamanend first meets with William Penn

1697 Tamanend attends his last meeting with Pennsylvania leaders

Pennsylvania

In 1681, King Charles II gave William Penn, a member of a religious group called the Quakers, permission to start a colony. The Quakers believed that all people are equal. They refused to fight in wars or to swear loyalty to any king or country. Like the Pilgrims and the Puritans, the Quakers wanted to establish a settlement where they could practice their faith without interference.

King Charles II owed money to Penn's father. Instead of paying back the money, the king made Penn the **proprietor** (pruh•PRY•uh•ter), or owner, of a new colony. Penn named the colony Pennsylvania, which means "Penn's woods." He wanted all people living in the colony—Quakers and non-Quakers alike—to live together peacefully.

Penn also wanted American Indians to be treated fairly. He met Tamanend (TAM•uh•nend) and other leaders of the Lenni Lenape tribe. Penn paid them for most of the land King Charles II had given him and built a long-lasting peace with the Indians.

TextWork

9 Scan the text. Circle the sentence that tells why the Quakers wanted to establish a settlement in Pennsylvania.

10 Why do you think William Penn wanted American Indians to be treated fairly?

Because they want to be eqabural.

11 Study the table on page 182. Circle the names of the colonies that were started for religious reasons.

Founding of the 13 Colonies

COLONY	DATE	REASONS SETTLED
Virginia	1607	Economic venture
Massachusetts	1630	Religious freedom
Maryland	1632	Religious freedom
Connecticut	1636	Religious freedom
Delaware	1638	Trade; religious freedom
Rhode Island	1647	Religious freedom
North Carolina	1663	Trade and agriculture
New Jersey	1664	Trade; religious freedom
New York	1664	Trade
New Hampshire	1680	Fishing and trade
Pennsylvania	1681	Religious freedom
South Carolina	1712	Trade and agriculture
Georgia	1733	Refuge for debtors

Georgia

In 1733, King George II gave James Oglethorpe permission to start a colony named Georgia, in honor of the king. Oglethorpe was a wealthy English leader. He had an idea to send **debtors**, or people who had been put in prison for owing money, to settle the new colony. The debtors would get a chance to experience economic freedom and start a new life. They would also defend the land against other countries.

By that time, England, France, and Spain all claimed the area to the south of South Carolina. King George II knew that to gain control of that area, he had to send colonists there. The first group to arrive in the Georgia Colony established the settlement of Savannah.

Lesson 1 Review

1. **SUMMARIZE** Name three reasons why the English established North American colonies.

   Bearse they wanted to be wealthy and Have Power.

2. Use the word **debtor** in a sentence about the settlement of Georgia.

   The Debotors were not like by King George II,

Circle the letter of the correct answer.

3. Why did the Pilgrims and Puritans want to establish colonies?

   A They wanted religious freedom.
   B They wanted to find gold and silver.
   C They wanted to find a place for debtors.
   D They wanted to profit from fur and lumber.

Queen Elizabeth I

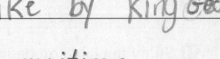

Write a Speech Write a persuasive speech to Queen Elizabeth I asking permission to start a colony in North America. Tell why you want to start a colony.

The 13 English colonies could be divided into three different regions—the New England, Mid-Atlantic, and Southern colonies. The geographic features, climate, and resources of each region affected how the colonists lived and worked. **Think about how the geographic features, climate, and resources of New England affected the way people lived and worked there.**

Plymouth Colony was settled in 1620.

ESSENTIAL QUESTIONS

- How did climate and geographic features and other available resources distinguish the three regions from each other?
- How did people use the natural resources of their region to earn a living?
- What are the benefits of specialization and trade?
- How did political and social life evolve in each of the three regions?

HISTORY AND SOCIAL SCIENCE SOL
USI 1d, USI 1f, USI 5b

TextWork

1 Why were Roger Williams and Anne Hutchinson forced to leave the Massachusetts Bay Colony?

_____

_____

2 Why did David Thomson settle Portsmouth?

_____

_____

3 Study the map. Circle the settlement that is located on the Connecticut River. Who established the settlement?

_____

Settling New England

In 1630, the Puritans established the Massachusetts Bay Colony in New England. The Puritan leaders tried to keep strict control over the colony. They did not welcome people whose beliefs were different from their own.

Some colonists—such as Roger Williams, a minister from Salem, and Anne Hutchinson, from Boston—began to disagree with the Puritan leaders. They tried to reform, or change, the church. Williams and Hutchinson were forced to leave Massachusetts. They both started settlements in what became the Rhode Island Colony.

Thomas Hooker, another Puritan minister and religious reformer, left the Massachusetts Bay Colony and established a settlement at Hartford. In 1636, Hartford joined nearby settlements to form the Connecticut Colony.

Other colonists moved north for economic opportunities. In 1623, a Scottish settler named David Thomson started a fishing settlement called Portsmouth. In 1629, the settlement joined others in the area to form the New Hampshire Colony.

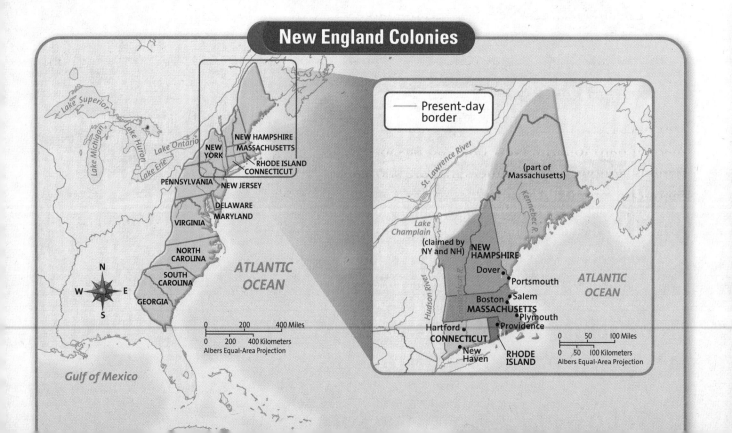

New England Colonies

Reenactors show what daily life was like in the Plymouth Colony.

New England's Geographic Features

Most of New England's earliest settlements were built along the Atlantic coast. The region's jagged, or uneven, coastline has many bays and deep harbors. The Boston settlement was built on one of New England's largest harbors. Because large ships could sail into Boston's deep harbor, the settlement developed into a busy trade center.

New England's hard, rocky soil and thick forests made farming difficult. Farmers had to clear rocks and trees from the land. The region's climate also made it hard to farm. New England has long, cold winters, followed by summers that are short and moderate, or mild. As a result, the growing season, or the time during which the weather is warm enough for plants to grow, is short in New England.

The land to the west of the Coastal Plain includes rolling hills, broad valleys, and low mountain ranges. These mountain ranges are part of the Appalachian Mountains, which extended across parts of the 13 English colonies.

 TextWork

❹ Scan the text. Underline the words for two water-related geographic features in the text. How did those geographic features affect settlement?

_____

_____

❺ How did New England's climate affect farming?

_____

_____

❻ What geographic feature extended across parts of the 13 colonies?

_____

_____

Whalers often had to go on long journeys in dangerous seas to find whales.

TextWork

7 Scan the text. Circle the names of three industries in which New England colonists specialized.

8 Underline two examples of naval stores.

9 List two examples of products manufactured from New England's thick forests.

_____

_____

New England Resources

The New England colonies had many different natural, capital, and human resources. Specialization allowed the colonists to make the best use of those resources. **Specialization** is focusing on making one or more products. As a result of specialization, the colonists became skilled at certain industries, such as fishing, shipbuilding, and making naval stores. **Naval stores** are products or supplies, such as turpentine and tar, used to build ships.

Many colonists in coastal areas made a living by catching fish such as cod, herring, and mackerel. Surplus fish were dried, packed in barrels, and sent to markets in other English colonies or in Europe. New Englanders also hunted whales along the coast. The whales' blubber, or fat, was boiled to get oil, which was used as fuel for lamps.

In New England's thick forests, loggers cut down trees for lumber. The lumber was used to build houses and ships. Shipbuilding was a leading industry in New England. As a result of shipbuilding, trading became an important part of New England's economy.

Trade and Interdependence

The New England colonies traded to get raw materials and products from other places. This trade led to **interdependence** (in•ter•dih•PEN•duhnts), or two or more people or places depending on one another for goods and services.

Specialization made the colonies interdependent. Through trade, the colonies could get goods and services they could not produce for themselves. The New England colonies depended on the Mid-Atlantic colonies for grains and livestock. They also depended on the Southern colonies for raw materials such as cotton. In turn, the Mid-Atlantic and Southern colonies depended on the New England colonies for fish, lumber, and whale oil.

Some colonial trading ships followed what became known as **triangular trade routes**. These routes connected England, the English colonies, and Africa. On a map, these routes formed large triangles across the Atlantic Ocean.

TextWork

10 Write a sentence defining the word *interdependence* in your own words.

_____

_____

_____

11 Study the map and scan the text. What products did the New England colonies get from the Mid-Atlantic colonies?

_____

_____

_____

_____

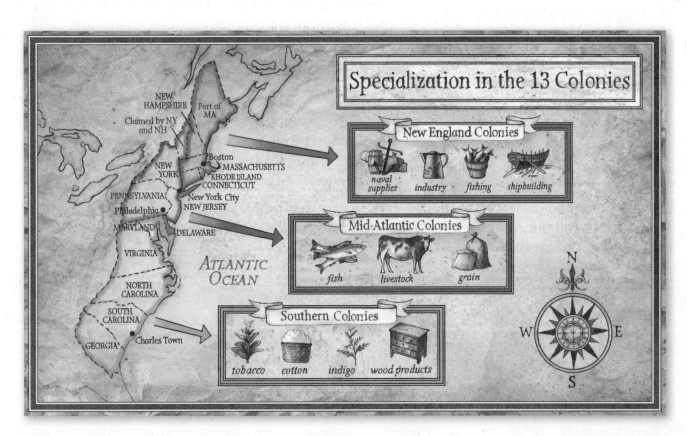

Specialization in the 13 Colonies

New England Colonies

naval supplies   industry   fishing   shipbuilding

Mid-Atlantic Colonies

fish   livestock   grain

Southern Colonies

tobacco   cotton   indigo   wood products

NEW HAMPSHIRE   Part of MA
Claimed by NY and NH
NEW YORK   Boston   MASSACHUSETTS   RHODE ISLAND   CONNECTICUT
PENNSYLVANIA   New York City   NEW JERSEY
Philadelphia   DELAWARE
MARYLAND
VIRGINIA   ATLANTIC OCEAN
NORTH CAROLINA
SOUTH CAROLINA
GEORGIA   Charles Town

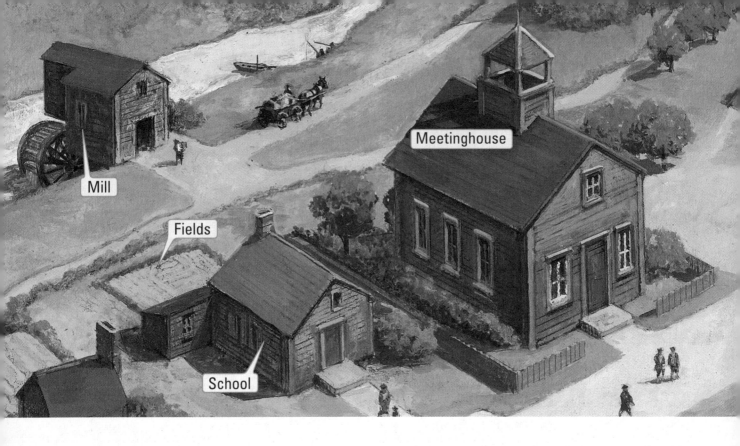

Mill

Fields

School

Meetinghouse

New England Towns

Most people in New England lived in small towns or on farms. At the center of each town was a **common**, a grassy area shared by the town's people. It was used for grazing sheep, cattle, and other livestock.

The colonists built their homes, shops, and other buildings around the common. Many towns had a general store, a sawmill, and a blacksmith shop, where skilled craftspeople and shopkeepers worked. Many towns also had a school. However, the meetinghouse, or town church, was the most important building.

The town and the church were the center of life in the New England colonies. On Sunday, every person had to attend church services at the meetinghouse. Schools were also important to the Puritans because they believed that everyone should be able to read the Bible. New England schools usually had only one room and one teacher. Most children left school at an early age because their families needed them to work at home.

TextWork

⓬ Study the illustration. Circle the building that was the center of town life. Why do you think it was so important?

_____

_____

_____

⓭ (Focus Skill) Write a sentence that summarizes the information in the last two paragraphs.

_____

_____

_____

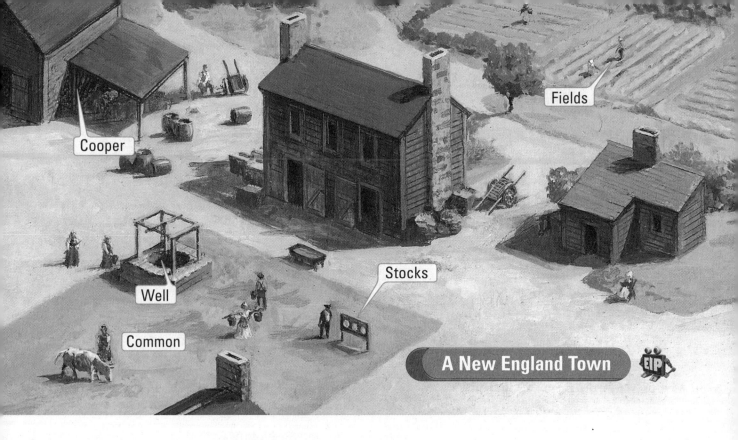

Cooper

Fields

Well

Stocks

Common

A New England Town

Political Life

Even before they arrived at Plymouth Colony, the men aboard the *Mayflower* signed a compact, or agreement. This document became known as the Mayflower Compact. It gave the colonists who signed it the right to govern themselves. At a time when monarchs ruled, self-government was a very new idea. The Mayflower Compact also included the idea of **majority rule**. If more than half the people agreed to a law or decision, everyone had to follow it.

At least once a year, New England colonists in each town gathered at the meetinghouse for a town meeting. At a **town meeting**, people voted on laws and elected town leaders. Anyone could attend, but only free white men who owned property could vote. Other workers, women, and enslaved people could not vote in any of the colonies.

The colonists also voted for leaders to represent them in the colony's legislature, or the lawmaking branch of its government. Each colony had its own legislature, which made laws for the whole colony.

TextWork

14 Scan the text. Underline the right that the Mayflower Compact gave to the Plymouth colonists.

15 How did New England colonists participate in their government?

_____

_____

_____

_____

1. **SUMMARIZE** How did the New England economy depend on fish and lumber?

_____

_____

_____

_____

_____

2. Write a sentence describing the importance of **specialization**.

_____

_____

_____

_____

Circle the letter of the correct answer.

3. The New England colonists used whale blubber to make—

   A lamp oil

   B tar

   C turpentine

   D naval stores

4. What goods did the New England colonies get from the Mid-Atlantic colonies?

   F Grains and fish

   G Grains and livestock

   H Lumber and livestock

   J Lumber and fish

5. A town meeting was where Puritans—

   A listened to sermons all day

   B voted on laws and elected leaders

   C raised their livestock

   D taught their children how to read the Bible

Match the leader's name on the left with the colony's name on the right.

6. Thomas Hooker   Connecticut Colony

7. Anne Hutchinson   New Hampshire Colony

8. David Thomson   Rhode Island Colony

A cooper made barrels.

writing

✎ **Write a Report** Write a report describing New England's trade with other colonies. Then use the information to explain the interdependence of the New England, Mid-Atlantic, and Southern colonies.

The Mid-Atlantic Colonies

The Mid-Atlantic colonies included what are today the states of New York, New Jersey, Delaware, and Pennsylvania. People in the region came from **diverse**, or many different, places and backgrounds. They brought different cultures with them. They also brought different languages and different religious beliefs. **Think about how people from diverse backgrounds might affect a region's culture and economy.**

New York City, in the late 1600s

ESSENTIAL QUESTIONS

✓ How did climate and geographic features and other available resources distinguish the three regions from each other?

✓ How did people use the natural resources of their region to earn a living?

✓ What are the benefits of specialization and trade?

✓ How did political and social life evolve in each of the three regions?

HISTORY AND SOCIAL SCIENCE SOL
USI.1a, USI.1f, USI.5b

Settling the Mid-Atlantic

The Dutch established the first permanent European colony in the Mid-Atlantic region—the New Netherland Colony—in 1625. The English did not settle in the region until 1664, when they sent warships to the city of New Amsterdam and took over the Dutch colony of New Netherland.

New Netherland was split into two new colonies—New York and New Jersey. The city of New Amsterdam was renamed New York City. Many of the early settlers who came to New Jersey were Quakers. A few years later, in 1681, William Penn established the Pennsylvania Colony. The next year, he also became the owner of what is now Delaware.

Penn planned his home settlement of Philadelphia in Pennsylvania very carefully. The name *Philadelphia* means "brotherly love" in Greek. Like all of Pennsylvania, the settlement of Philadelphia was founded on the idea that people of different backgrounds could live peacefully together.

TextWork

❶ When did the English begin to establish settlements in the Mid-Atlantic region?

_____

❷ Study the map. Circle the English colonies that were established on lands that once belonged to the Dutch.

❸ Scan the text. Circle the reasons why settlers from Europe might have been attracted to the Pennsylvania Colony.

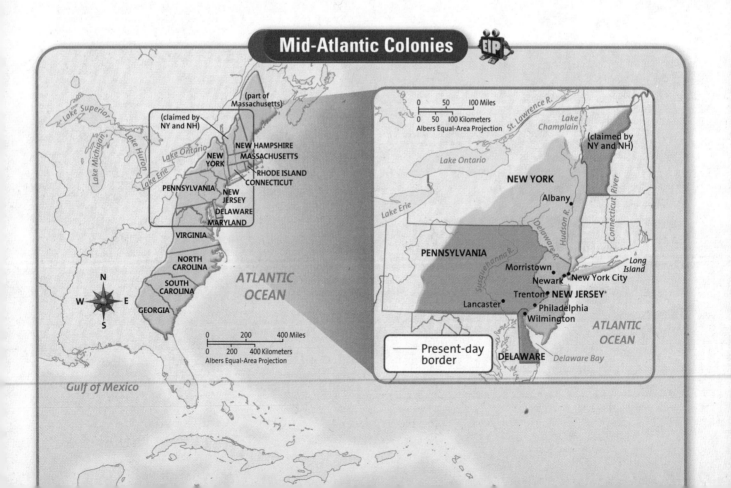

Mid-Atlantic Colonies

Most Mid-Atlantic farms had a variety of animals, such as cows, horses, chickens, hogs, sheep, and goats.

Geography and Climate

Unlike New England, the Mid-Atlantic region had plenty of rich farmland. The Mid-Atlantic's coastal lowlands, grassy meadows, and rolling hills were good for farming and raising livestock. The region also had thick forests with plenty of wildlife. The colonists hunted and trapped animals such as deer and beavers in the forests.

The mild winters and moderate climate were also good for farming. The region received the right amount of rain each year for growing crops such as wheat, corn, and rye. Because the Mid-Atlantic colonies harvested crops used in making bread, they became known as the "breadbasket" colonies.

In addition to its fertile land, the Mid-Atlantic region had several large bays and harbors along the Atlantic Ocean. These harbors were connected to wide and deep rivers, such as the Hudson River and the Delaware River. These rivers were deep enough to let large ships travel inland, making trade with other colonists easier.

TextWork

4 How did the Mid-Atlantic region's land differ from that of New England?

_____

_____

5 Scan the text. Underline the sentence that explains why the Mid-Atlantic colonies were known as the breadbasket colonies.

6 Trace the Hudson and Delaware Rivers on the map on page 192. How did water-related features affect trade in the Mid-Atlantic colonies?

_____

_____

Market Towns

7 (Focus Skill) Write a sentence that summarizes the kinds of activities that occurred at a market town.

_____

_____

_____

8 Scan the text. Circle four kinds of craftworkers.

9 Study the illustration. Why do you think market towns in the Mid-Atlantic colonies usually had a gristmill?

_____

_____

_____

Most people in the Mid-Atlantic region were farmers who specialized in harvesting wheat or other grains, raising livestock, and fishing. Farm families often traveled to market towns or villages to sell or trade their surplus crops and livestock for goods and services. A **market** is a place where goods are bought and sold.

Every market town had a gristmill, which ground grain into flour. Most market towns also had a lumber mill. Families bought goods from skilled craftworkers and from the general store.

Most craftworkers made products from raw materials. Blacksmiths used iron to form horseshoes, nails, or hinges. Coopers made barrels out of wood. Carpenters used wood to build houses and ships. Tanners turned animal skins into leather, which cobblers used to make and repair shoes.

General stores sold manufactured goods, including iron tools, shoes, paint, and buttons, which were shipped into the colonies from England. Many of these goods were products that the colonists could not make themselves.

Farmers grow grain.

Towns and Cities

After farmers and traders dropped off their crops at market towns, these goods were transported to port cities along rivers and harbors. The goods were then loaded onto ships and transported to other colonies or to England.

Philadelphia and New York City were the two busiest ports in the English colonies. Farmers, merchants, and traders throughout the Mid-Atlantic colonies depended on trade in those cities. Many people specialized in sea-related work, such as fishing and shipping industries. Other skilled and unskilled workers moved to Mid-Atlantic ports to find jobs or to make and sell goods.

As in New England, specialization and interdependence affected the production of goods and services. The Mid-Atlantic colonies traded their grain, livestock, and fish with the New England and Southern colonies, as well as with England, for goods they did not produce themselves.

TextWork

10 Underline a sentence that tells why Philadelphia and New York City were important ports.

11 Study the graph. How much more was the value of the goods New York shipped to England than the value of the goods that New England shipped to England?

_____

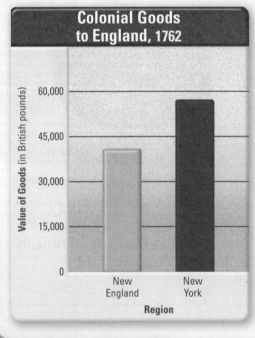

Colonial Goods to England, 1762

Value of Goods (in British pounds)

60,000 · 45,000 · 30,000 · 15,000 · 0

New England | New York

Region

A Gristmill

Millstones grind the grain into flour.

Flour is taken to market.

Farmers take the grain to the mill.

TextWork

⑫ Study the graph. List the three largest ethnic groups in the Mid-Atlantic colonies.

_____

_____

_____

Population of the Mid-Atlantic Colonies by Ethnicity, 1776

English
German
Other
African
American Indian
Scottish
French, Swedish
Scotch-Irish
Irish
Dutch

⑬ Scan the text and study the artifacts on page 197. What is one way that Benjamin Franklin improved Philadelphia?

_____

_____

_____

⑭ Use the term *religious toleration* in a sentence about the diverse religious beliefs in the Mid-Atlantic colonies.

_____

_____

_____

A Mix of People and Religions

Settlers in the Mid-Atlantic colonies came from many different places and backgrounds. Some of these settlers left their home countries to escape war or to find religious freedom. Others wanted better economic opportunities. Those from Africa arrived as enslaved people.

The varied and diverse groups of people in the Mid-Atlantic colonies could be seen in Philadelphia. By 1770, it had more than 28,000 people, a large number for the time. People in Philadelphia had diverse ways of life. They spoke many languages and ate many kinds of foods.

Philadelphia's most famous resident was Benjamin Franklin. He was a printer, a writer, a scientist, and an inventor. He also became a government leader. Franklin improved Philadelphia in many ways. For example, he organized a trained firefighting company, raised money to build the city's first hospital, and established Pennsylvania's first college and first public library.

Diverse Religions

When William Penn set up the Pennsylvania Colony's government in 1682, he gave the citizens freedom of religion. Unlike the New England colonies, the Mid-Atlantic colonies became home to people of many different religious groups. The greater diversity of religious beliefs led to greater **religious toleration**, or acceptance of religious differences, in the region.

Towns and cities such as Philadelphia often had many different places of worship. A Presbyterian church might be only a block away from a Quaker meetinghouse. The first Jewish synagogue in the Mid-Atlantic colonies was built in New York City in 1730. Religion was a major part of social life in the Mid-Atlantic colonies. After religious services, people talked and exchanged news.

Benjamin Franklin's
Contributions

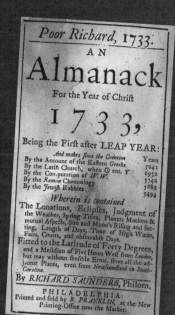

Poor Richard, 1733.
AN
Almanack
For the Year of Christ
1733,

Franklin set up the first trained firefighting company in the English colonies.

Franklin published *Poor Richard's Almanack* for 20 years.

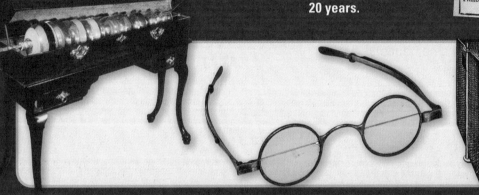

Benjamin Franklin invented a musical instrument called an armonica (left), the first bifocals (center), and the Franklin stove (right).

Franklin conducted experiments with electricity.

1. **SUMMARIZE** How did geographic features, climate, and natural resources affect the economy of the Mid-Atlantic colonies?

_____

_____

_____

_____

2. Use the word **diverse** in a sentence about the Mid-Atlantic colonies.

_____

_____

_____

3. Why were the Mid-Atlantic colonies known as the breadbasket colonies?

_____

_____

_____

_____

Circle the letter of the correct answer.

4. Which of these was NOT important to the economy of the Mid-Atlantic colonies?

   A Fertile soil

   B Long rivers

   C Hot, humid climate

   D Deep harbors

5. Most people in the Mid-Atlantic colonies earned a living by—

   F making naval stores

   G farming

   H fishing

   J building ships

6. Farmers traveled to market towns to—

   A meet with British leaders

   B sell furs to European merchants and traders

   C trade farm products for goods and services

   D purchase naval stores

7. Which city in the Mid-Atlantic colonies became a busy port?

   F Boston

   G Philadelphia

   H Plymouth

   J Jamestown

A colonial advertisement

writing

Write an Advertisement Imagine that you live in a Mid-Atlantic colony. You are seeking a skilled craftworker to work in your shop. Write an advertisement describing what skills the person must have, what jobs he or she will perform, and what you will offer him or her in return.

The Southern Colonies

The Southern colonies succeeded by growing **cash crops**, or crops that people harvested to sell rather than to use themselves. Cash crops, such as tobacco, rice, and indigo, were harvested on large farms called **plantations**. Plantations depended on large numbers of workers. Many of these were enslaved Africans. They helped the Southern colonies grow and prosper. **Think about why the Southern colonies were able to grow large amounts of cash crops.**

Shirley Plantation, in Virginia

ESSENTIAL QUESTIONS

✓ How did climate and geographic features and other available resources distinguish the three regions from each other?

✓ How did people use the natural resources of their region to earn a living?

✓ What are the benefits of specialization and trade?

✓ How did political and social life evolve in each of the three regions?

HISTORY AND SOCIAL SCIENCE SOL
USI.1d, USI.1f, USI.5b

TextWork

1 Why did the Calverts want to establish a colony in what is now Maryland?

Safe, Place.

---

2 Scan the text. Underline the geographic features that made the Southern colonies good for farming.

3 Study the map. Circle the towns in North Carolina. How do you think these towns were affected by their location?

Fish and farming.

Settling the Southern Colonies

The Southern colonies were Virginia, Maryland, North Carolina, South Carolina, and Georgia. The Maryland Colony was established in 1632 by the Calverts, a wealthy Catholic family. The Calverts hoped to start a colony that would be a safe place for Catholics.

In 1663, King Charles II gave a group of wealthy men permission to start a colony south of Virginia. They named the new colony Carolina, for King Charles. In 1712, Carolina's leaders divided the colony into North Carolina and South Carolina.

At first, many Southern colonists settled on the Atlantic Coastal Plain. In time, other colonists settled the Piedmont region, which lies between the Coastal Plain and the Appalachian Mountains.

The Southern colonies offered settlers many important natural resources. The region has many good harbors and broad rivers. The land was generally fertile, and the region's humid climate—with its hot summers and mild winters—was good for farming.

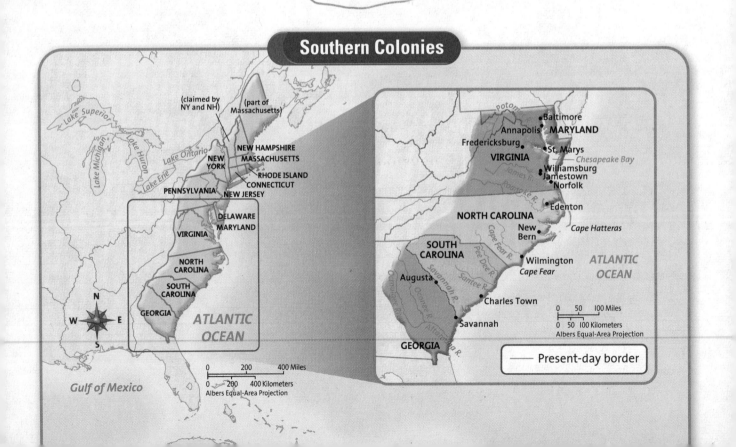

Southern Colonies

Present-day border

Gulf of Mexico

Eliza Lucas Pinckney

Eliza Lucas Pinckney moved to South Carolina with her parents in 1738. When she was 16 years old, Eliza started experimenting with growing indigo plants. After three years, Eliza was able to grow an indigo plant that produced an excellent dye. She gave some of her seeds to neighbors and friends. Within a few years, South Carolina planters were selling one million pounds of indigo a year to clothmakers in Europe.

Make It Relevant **Why is it important to work hard at whatever task you have?**

Cash Crops

The Southern colonies specialized in harvesting cash crops. In Maryland, Virginia, and North Carolina, the main cash crop was tobacco. In South Carolina and Georgia, the climate was too warm and wet for tobacco. Farmers there grew rice instead. On drier land, farmers grew indigo, a blue dye used to color clothing. Some farmers tried to grow cotton. However, it was difficult to remove the seeds from cotton by hand.

Although cash crops were the most important part of the Southern economy, forests were also important. They supplied natural resources for manufacturing wood products. Wilmington, North Carolina, became an important shipping center for forest goods and naval stores.

The Southern colonies depended on the New England colonies for many manufactured goods. These included tools and equipment. They also bought grain from the Mid-Atlantic colonies. In turn, the New England and Mid-Atlantic colonies bought cash crops from the Southern colonies.

TextWork

4 (Focus Skill) Write a sentence summarizing the information on the cash crops harvested in the Southern colonies.

_____

_____

_____

5 How did geographic features and climate affect farmers in South Carolina and Georgia?

_____

_____

_____

6 Underline the city that was an important shipping center for forest goods.

Plantation Economy

The economy of the Southern colonies was based mostly on large plantations. Plantations depended on the labor of enslaved people. The cash crops produced by enslaved workers made some **planters**, or plantation owners, the richest people in the Southern colonies.

Not all planters were alike. A few planters started as indentured servants. An **indentured servant** was someone who agreed to work for a time without pay for a person who paid for their trip to the colonies. Other planters were wealthy English settlers who were given huge pieces of land.

As planters grew richer, the amount of land they owned grew. In fact, some plantations looked like small communities. The planter's house was the main building. Many other buildings, including workshops where enslaved workers produced items used on plantations, were scattered around the planter's house.

Cities and County Seats

Plantations were often built far from one another, and the Southern colonies had fewer cities than the New England and Mid-Atlantic colonies. By the mid-1700s, some towns along the Atlantic coast, such as Norfolk, Baltimore, and Savannah, had grown into large cities. These cities became busy ports by shipping cash crops.

Some of the largest towns were the county seats. A **county seat** was the town where the county government was located. Most county seats had a general store, a courthouse, and a jail. The counties were large and included many plantations and smaller farms.

Several times a year, plantation families would travel to the county seat to attend church services, hold dances, and trade crops for goods. Many planters belonged to the Church of England. Church services at the county seat were important social gatherings. Some planters bought and sold enslaved African Americans at the county seat.

Baltimore was founded in 1729. It grew quickly into a busy port.

TextWork

9 Why were county seats important to people living on Southern plantations and farms?

_____

_____

_____

10 Complete the chart on this page. Use information from previous lessons in this unit to add details about the colonies.

Comparing the Colonies

	GEOGRAPHY AND CLIMATE	RESOURCES	SOCIAL AND POLITICAL LIFE
New England Colonies	hilly land, rocky soil, rocky coastline, cold winters, mild summers	_____ _____	village and church at center of life, religious reformers and separatists, town meetings
Mid-Atlantic Colonies	_____ _____	rich farmland, rivers, grain, fish	villages and cities, varied and diverse cultures, diverse religions, market towns
Southern Colonies	flat coastal plain, wide and deep rivers, good harbors and bays, humid climate with mild winter and hot summers	rich farmland, rivers, tobacco, cotton, indigo, wood products	plantations, slavery, indentured servants, few cities, few schools, Church of England, counties

1. **SUMMARIZE** How did the geography and climate of the Southern colonies affect the way colonists earned a living?

   Dry Land and dry cash corp.

2. Write a sentence describing why **cash crops** were important to the Southern colonies.

   So a cash corp is like a corp is from a plater

Circle the letter of the correct answer.

3. In which industries did the Southern colonies specialize?

   A Tobacco, rice, indigo, wood products
   B Fishing, wheat, naval stores
   C Tobacco, wheat, fish
   D Livestock, grain, shipbuilding

4. A person who agreed to work for a time without pay for someone who paid for their trip to the colonies was—

   F a planter
   G an overseer
   H an indentured servant
   J a minister

5. Which of these was a large city and busy port in the Southern colonies?

   A Philadelphia
   B Boston
   C Baltimore
   D Portsmouth

Match the colony on the left with the information on the right.

6. Maryland   established by a Catholic family

7. Virginia   grew tobacco as a cash crop

8. South Carolina   grew indigo as a cash crop

Indigo plant

activity

Make a Table Make a two-column table. List the Southern colonies in the first column and the crops grown in each colony in the second column.

Varied Ways of Life

What would it be like to live in colonial times? What kind of work would you do? What kind of education would you get? What kind of house would you live in? The answers would depend on your social position. The lives of farmers, large landowners, artisans, indentured servants, women, enslaved African Americans, and free African Americans were very different. **Think about how the social position of a person in the colonies affected his or her life.**

A wealthy colonial family

ESSENTIAL QUESTION

✓ How did people's lives vary among the different social groups in colonial America?

HISTORY AND SOCIAL SCIENCE SOL
USI.I.d, USI.5.c

 **TextWork**

❶ Where in the colonies did most large landholders live?

In large Houses. ✓

❷ Circle the sentences that describe how the children of planters were educated.

❸ Study the illustration. Why do you think that planters lived in large houses?

To take care of their clidren and the slaves. ✓

Large Landholders

Most large landholders lived on Southern plantations. These planters had a rich social culture. They often lived in large houses filled with fine furniture, china, and silverware. They wore elegant clothes and held dances and balls. Some planters served as judges or as members of the colonial assembly.

Southern planters were among the best-educated people in the colonies. Some planters set up their own schools for their children and hired teachers from Europe. Later, the planters' sons might go to Europe to complete their education. Girls went to school only until the age of 12 or 13. Planters' daughters were expected to learn only basic skills—"to read and sew with their needle."

For the labor needed to run large plantations, planters relied on enslaved African Americans or on indentured servants. A planter and his wife were responsible for taking care of the many people who lived on the plantation. They had to clothe, feed, and provide medical care for their family members and workers.

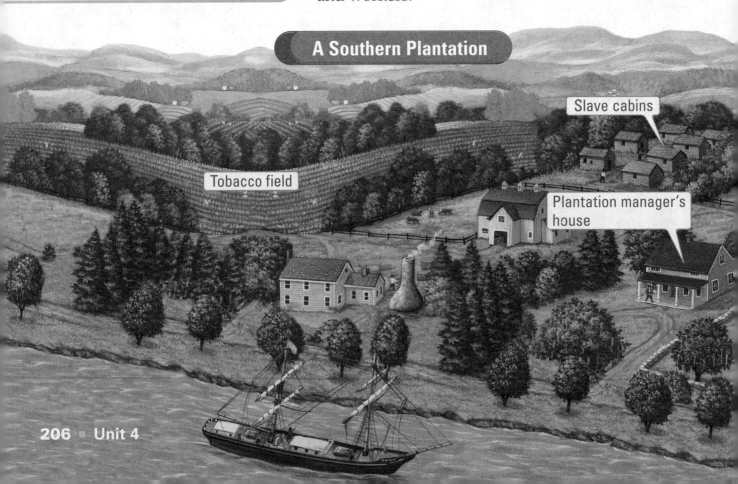

A Southern Plantation

Tobacco field

Slave cabins

Plantation manager's house

Farmers

John M.

Few people in the colonies owned large plantations. In fact, most colonists lived and worked on small farms. They generally raised the grains, vegetables, fruits, or other crops that grew best in their region. They lived mostly on what they raised. If they had anything left over, they sold it at local markets. The money the farmers earned at the market was used to buy any goods they could not make for themselves.

Most owners of small farms relied on family members for labor. Together, the family members did all the work. They chopped down trees, built barns, plowed fields, planted crops, and raised animals. A few farmers could afford to have enslaved workers or indentured servants.

Unlike planters, few farmers grew rich. Colonial farmhouses usually had only two or three rooms and a loft. Most also had a large fireplace that provided heat and a place to cook. Farm families owned only a few items of furniture.

 TextWork

4 Write a sentence that describes the work of small farmers in the colonies.

The small farmers relied on the family and Labor.

5 In general, how were the homes of the owners of small farms different from those of planters?

The owners house is much bigger than the mangers house.

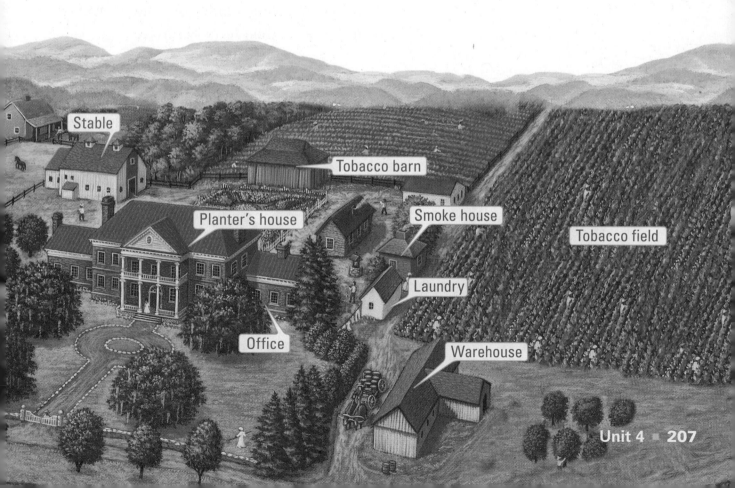

Stable

Tobacco barn

Planter's house

Smoke house

Tobacco field

Laundry

Office

Warehouse

Artisans and Indentured Servants

Plantations as well as cities and towns were often the workplaces of **artisans**, or skilled craftworkers. In the colonies, the air was filled with sounds of the work of carpenters, blacksmiths, silversmiths, and brickmakers. Bakers, butchers, flour millers, and soapmakers had their own shops as well. There were printers, shoemakers, and clockmakers, too.

The skills needed by artisans were not taught in schools. Instead, young people learned these skills by becoming apprentices. An **apprentice** lived and trained with a master craftworker for several years. Boys became apprentices by the age of 14. Girls generally did not become apprentices.

Apprentices usually worked for a master craftworker for about seven years. Then they were ready to work on their own. Some artisans relied on the work of indentured servants. Life as an indentured servant was hard. Indentured servants had to work without pay for four to seven years. They had few rights and could not vote. However, they were free after their term of service.

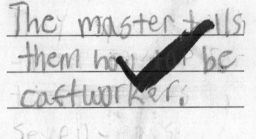

TextWork

6 Use the word *artisan* to describe a job in the colonies.

The Artisan makes crafts

7 (Focus Skill) Write a sentence summarizing how an apprentice was trained.

They master tells them how to be craftworkers seven years!

This reenactor is shaving a wooden board using the same kinds of tools colonists used.

Colonial women did much of the work in the home.

Women

Women in colonial times were often married by the age of 14. They were not allowed to own property or businesses. In most cases, when a woman got married, her husband became the owner of everything she had.

Women and girls had fewer chances to work outside the home than men and boys. Most women worked as homemakers, caretakers, and housekeepers. They cooked vegetables and fruits and preserved them in jars for winter. They churned milk into butter and cheese and made candles and soap. They sewed, spun yarn, and knitted clothing.

Women also cared for children. Colonial families were often very large. One visitor to the colonies noted, "There's not a cabin but has 10 or 12 young children in it." With few doctors in the colonies, women also took care of their children when they were hurt or sick.

Women could not vote, and they had few opportunities to attend school. Only New England girls and planters' daughters generally learned to read.

⑨ The women should not marry someone at 14 yrs.
② They could not own property.

8 Circle the paragraph that describes the kind of work that women and girls did in the home.

9 List two rights that women have today that they did not have in colonial times.

They should to be married by 15 not 14. The other thing is that they should have more outside work the inside.

An embroidered sampler

During the Middle Passage, ships were so crowded that captives had almost no room to move.

African Americans

For hundreds of years, slave traders brought Africans to the colonies. These Africans had been kidnapped in Africa and then sold to the traders. The enslaved African Americans were then placed on ships that took them across the Atlantic Ocean to the colonies and sold into slavery.

The voyage across the sea, called the **Middle Passage**, was terrible. Slave traders jammed the captives into ships and chained them. They gave them little food or water. During the rough voyage, thousands of them became sick and died.

Enslaved African Americans

Enslaved African Americans faced many hardships in the colonies. They were owned as property for life and had no rights. By law, they were not allowed to learn to read and write. Some enslaved workers were insulted, beaten, and whipped by their owners. "No day ever dawns for the slave, nor is it looked for," one enslaved person wrote. "For the slave it is all night—all night, forever."

TextWork

10 Study the graph. By how much did the enslaved population in the colonies increase from 1760 to 1770?

100 to 2,0000

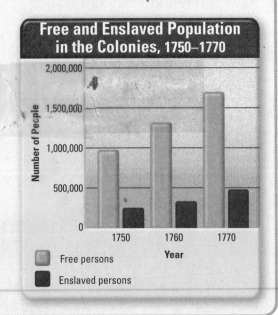

Free and Enslaved Population in the Colonies, 1750–1770

Free persons

Enslaved persons

One way that enslaved people tried to deal with their hardships was by keeping their culture alive. They told stories and sang songs about Africa.

Most enslaved African Americans worked on southern plantations. Some enslaved African Americans also worked in the homes of the planters. Many enslaved people worked in skilled trades, such as blacksmithing and carpentry.

Children of enslaved African Americans were born into slavery. By the age of 10, enslaved children were working along with the adults.

Free African Americans

A few enslaved people, such as Olaudah Equiano (oh•LOW•duh ek•wee•AHN•oh), were able to buy their freedom. A few owners freed their enslaved workers.

Free African Americans had more economic freedom than enslaved people. They could work for pay and decide how to spend their money. They could own land. They could not, however, vote or hold public office.

TextWork

⓫ Where in the colonies did most enslaved African Americans live?

The most enslaved African Americans are in southern Plantions.

⓬ List some ways that the lives of enslaved African Americans were different from the lives of free African Americans.

The African Americans had not a lot of money or food or water.

Enslaved African Americans worked long days. Olaudah Equiano (inset) later wrote about his life as an enslaved person.

1. **SUMMARIZE** How were the lives of most colonial people different from planters' lives?

   The Platers house is much bigger than the people Houses in the plantion.

2. Write a sentence describing the training that an **apprentice** received.

   They speeid alot of years with their master than they do the work by ther self.

3. How were children of planters educated?

   Their clidren go to get teach by a eurpore teacher.

4. How were indentured servants and enslaved African Americans alike? How were they different?

   Because the Enslaved people had more work in the plantion.

Circle the letter of the correct answer.

5. To run large plantations, planters relied on the work of—

   A free African Americans

   B enslaved African Americans

   C apprentices

   D artisans

6. An artisan likely learned his skills—

   F by going to school in Europe

   G by becoming an apprentice

   H from apprentices

   J from indentured servants

7. Which is true about most colonial women?

   A They went to Europe to complete their education.

   B They worked as apprentices.

   C They could vote or own land.

   D They could not vote or own land.

8. How did some enslaved African Americans gain their freedom?

   F They declared their freedom.

   G They bought their freedom.

   H They voted to be free.

   J They traded jobs with indentured servants.

writing

✎ **Write a Diary Entry** Write a diary entry from the perspective of one of the groups of colonial people described in this lesson. Give details about one full day in that person's life. Describe how that person likely felt about his or her life.

A child playing a colonial game

British Control

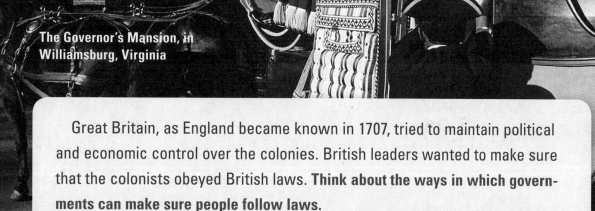

The Governor's Mansion, in Williamsburg, Virginia

Great Britain, as England became known in 1707, tried to maintain political and economic control over the colonies. British leaders wanted to make sure that the colonists obeyed British laws. **Think about the ways in which governments can make sure people follow laws.**

ESSENTIAL QUESTION

How did Great Britain impose its political and economic control over the colonies?

 HISTORY AND SOCIAL SCIENCE SOL
USI.Id , USI.If , USI.5d

Political Relationships

The Parliament in London was the lawmaking branch of Great Britain's government. It passed laws for all British people, including the colonists. However, Parliament allowed the colonies to set up legislatures to make some of the laws that affected them. For example, Virginia's House of Burgesses (BER•juhs•iz) was the first legislature set up in the British colonies. It was established in 1619.

Each colony also had its own governor. Although the colonial legislatures made laws for each colony, the governors kept a careful watch on the legislatures. All laws passed by a legislature had to be approved by the governor. The governors monitored colonial legislatures to make sure that they were making laws that the British government would approve of. They also made sure the colonists were obeying laws passed by the British Parliament and monarch.

In some of the colonies, the governor was appointed by the king or queen. Those colonies were known as royal colonies. In the other colonies, the governor was named by the colony's proprietor.

❶ Who appointed colonial governors?

_____

_____

_____

_____

❷ How did colonial governors help Great Britain impose political control over the colonies?

_____

_____

_____

_____

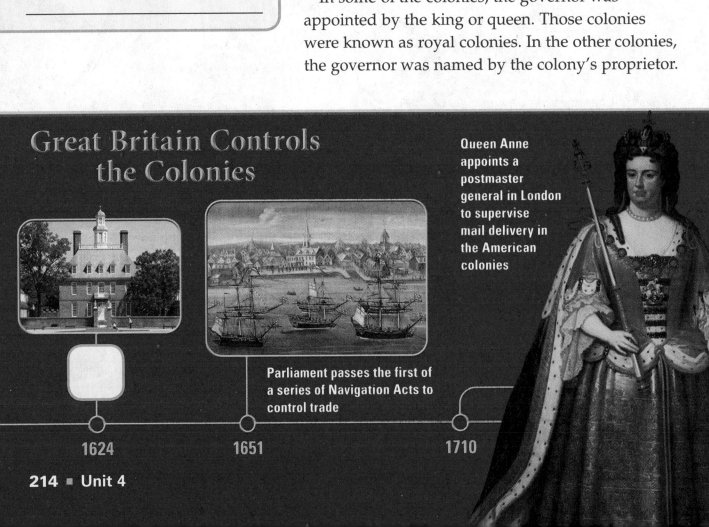

Great Britain Controls the Colonies

Queen Anne appoints a postmaster general in London to supervise mail delivery in the American colonies

Parliament passes the first of a series of Navigation Acts to control trade

1624   1651   1710

Economic Relationships

Beginning in 1651, Great Britain passed the first in a series of laws to control trade in the colonies. These laws are known as the Navigation Acts. Through these laws, the British government imposed strict rules on colonial trade.

Colonial merchants could only send their **exports**, or goods leaving a country, to Great Britain or to other British colonies. The British government also said that the colonists could buy only British-made **imports**, or goods brought into a country to be sold. The colonies depended on trading raw materials for goods. However, the colonists could not trade with other countries, even if they offered better prices.

Great Britain also tried to control the economy of the colonies by placing taxes on the goods traded in the colonies. A **tax** is money collected by a government to pay for government services. For example, Parliament placed taxes on tobacco, molasses, sugar, tea, and even paper documents to help pay the costs of fighting wars in North America in the 1750s and 1760s.

TextWork

3 Use the words *exports* and *imports* in a sentence about the Navigation Acts.

_____

_____

_____

4 Study the time line. Use the letters to place these events correctly on the timeline.

A. 1624: Parliament declares Virginia is a royal colony.

B. 1765: Parliament passes the Stamp Act, which placed a tax on many paper goods.

King George III sends British troops to the colonies to fight against the French

Parliament passes a tax on sugar and molasses

1755

1764

1765

The French and Indian War

❺ Underline the sentence that explains why the Ohio Valley was important to the British. Circle the sentence that explains why it was important to the French.

❻ (Focus Skill) Study the map and text on page 217. What lands did France give up as a result of the French and Indian War?

_____

_____

_____

_____

_____

Spain, France, and Great Britain tried hard to keep control of their lands in North America. Both the French and the British claimed the Ohio Valley, a region that stretches along the Ohio River from the Appalachians to the Mississippi River. Each side believed it had a claim to the land because of earlier exploration and settlement. To the French, the Ohio Valley was an important link between France's holdings in Canada and Louisiana. The British saw the Ohio Valley as an area for trade and growth.

By 1750, British settlers had moved west into the Ohio Valley. The French built new forts there to protect their land. They also sent soldiers to drive the British out of the region. The British viewed this as an act of war.

In 1754, the British sent 150 soldiers from Virginia to take the Ohio Valley from the French. They were led by a young officer named George Washington. Fighting soon broke out, which led to a war between Great Britain and France.

British soldiers wore red uniform jackets, which made them easy targets.

Britain Wins Control

American Indians fought for both sides in the war, but mainly for the French. For this reason, the war was called the French and Indian War. At first, the British troops did poorly. They were used to fighting in open fields. They were surprised to find that the French and their American Indian allies fought from behind trees and large rocks.

Great Britain sent more troops and supplies to the colonies, and the war slowly turned in its favor. In time, the British captured many French forts and then seized Québec and Montreal. The French surrendered in 1763. France gave most of Canada and its lands east of the Mississippi to Great Britain. France gave its land west of the Mississippi to Spain. Spain gave Florida to Great Britain.

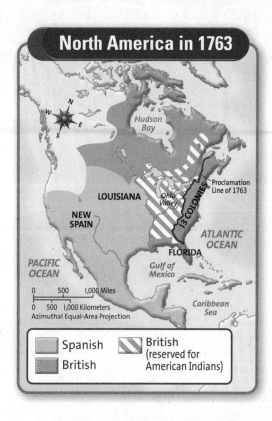

North America in 1763

Spanish
British
British (reserved for American Indians)

Lesson 6 Review

1. **SUMMARIZE** How did Great Britain maintain control over the colonies?

   _____

   _____

2. Explain how governments raise money through **taxes**.

   _____

   _____

   _____

Circle the letter of the correct answer.

3. The British government fought the French and Indian War because it was—

   A competing for world power

   B fighting with the Indians

   C competing for trade

   D fighting over taxes

This ring was used to mark a wax seal on letters and documents.

Write a Letter Imagine that you are the British king. Write a letter to a colonial governor. Tell exactly how and why the governor should control the colony's government and trade.

Fun With Social Studies

Bound for the Colonies

Can you guess from the songs which colonists are going to Georgia? to Massachusetts? to Pennsylvania? Write your answers on the blanks.

The winters are cold,
But that's okay. We can worship and live in our Puritan way.

_____

Long for peace?
We can show it.
We're Quakers and proud that you know it!

_____

Couldn't pay what I owe.
Woe is me!
Had a chance to get out.
Now I'm free! Gonna start a new life cross the sea!

_____

What's Under There?

VOCABULARY

Write the letters that belong in the yellow squares and you'll know.

□□□□□□ A grassy area shared by the town's people

□□□□□□ A product brought into a country

□□□□□□ A place where goods are bought and sold

□□□□□□□□□ An owner

□□□□□□□□□ A worker who lived and trained with a master craftworker

□□□□□ Shares of ownership

□□□□□ A person who was put in prison for owing money

_____

Help Wanted

Who would apply for the following jobs? Write your answer on the blank below each ad.

Mapping Mishaps

The mapmaker has made some mistakes on the map. Circle the names of the colonies that he has gotten wrong. Then write in the correct name of the colony that he has wrong in each region.

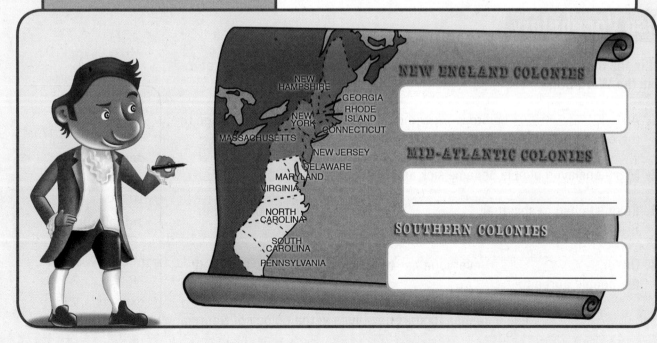

NEW ENGLAND COLONIES

MID-ATLANTIC COLONIES

SOUTHERN COLONIES

Review and Test Prep

The Big Idea

People in different regions often depend on each other for goods and natural resources.

Summarize the Unit

Focus Skill **Summarize** Complete the graphic organizer to summarize information about colonial America.

Key Facts

_____

_____

_____

_____

Summary

The colonies were made up of different groups of people whose lives varied depending on their social position.

Use Vocabulary

Fill in the missing term in each sentence, using the correct vocabulary term from the Word Bank.

1. An _____ had to work without pay in exchange for a voyage to the colonies.

2. Many enslaved people became sick and died during the _____.

3. Colonists had to ship their _____ to Great Britain or to other British colonies.

4. Under _____, everyone has to follow a law if more than half the people agree to it.

5. _____ had a chance to start new lives in the colony of Georgia.

> **Word Bank**
>
> **separatists** p. 179
>
> **debtors** p. 182
>
> **majority rule** p. 189
>
> **indentured servant** p. 202
>
> **Middle Passage** p. 210
>
> **exports** p. 215

Circle the letter of the correct answer.

6.

The Virginia Colony

1584 1585 1586 1587

1584 Queen Elizabeth I gives Sir Walter Raleigh permission to start a colony in Virginia

?

1587 Settlers on Roanoke Island are missing

What event is missing from the time line?

A The Virginia Company decides to start a colony in Virginia.

B The first English settlers arrive on Roanoke Island.

C The Virginia Company builds a settlement at Jamestown.

D The first settlers on Roanoke Island return to England.

7. Settlements at Roanoke Island and Jamestown were established—

F as economic ventures

G for religious freedom

H for military protection

J to help debtors

8. Both Plymouth Colony and Massachusetts Bay Colony were established by settlers who wanted to—

A find wealth

B trade with American Indians

C have freedom of religion

D own more land

9. The Puritans left England to—

F separate from the Church of England

G change some religious practices of the Church of England

H live under the King of England's rule

J develop New England's whaling industry

10.

"By such a Colony, many families, who would otherwise starve, will be provided for, and made masters of houses and lands."
—James Oglethorpe

Which colony was Oglethorpe referring to in this description?

A Pennsylvania

B Georgia

C New Jersey

D North Carolina

11. The New England colonies specialized in—

F fishing and naval supplies

G livestock and dairy products

H tobacco and wood products

J cotton and indigo

12. Which of these is something New England colonists did at town meetings?

A They elected leaders.

B They sold crops.

C They taught their children.

D They met with American Indians.

13. How did specialization and trade affect the colonies?

F Specialization and trade made them more interdependent.

G Specialization and trade allowed the colonies to make everything they needed.

H Specialization and trade made them less dependent on other colonies.

J Specialization and trade made them less interdependent.

14. Which of these geographical features helped the Middle Colonies become known as the "breadbasket" colonies?

A Fertile land and a good climate for growing grain

B Deep harbors

C Long rivers

D Fertile land and a hot, humid climate

15.

Goods from Mid-Atlantic Colonies	Goods from Southern Colonies
Grain Livestock	Tobacco Cotton Indigo

This exchange between the Mid-Atlantic and Southern colonies BEST shows economic—

F interdependence

G choice

H scarcity

J specialization

16. What was the main cash crop grown in the northern areas of the Southern colonies?

A Indigo

B Wheat

C Tobacco

D Rice

17. Most enslaved people in the Southern colonies worked—

F in port cities

G on plantations

H in market towns

J on fishing ships

18. Which is an example of an artisan?

A Silversmith

B Fisher

C Whaler

D Farmer

19. Who would most likely have gone to school?

F Daughters of a small-farm owner

G Daughters of a planter

H Daughters of an enslaved worker

J Daughters of an artisan

20.

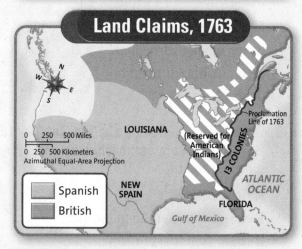

In general, how did European land claims in North America change after the French and Indian War?

A France lost land.

B Great Britain lost land.

C France gained land.

D Spain lost land.

21. Great Britain tried to control colonial trade by—

F limiting the number of ships that could transport goods

G allowing colonists to export goods only to Great Britain and other British colonies

H stopping colonists from selling goods to American Indians

J allowing only plantation owners to sell goods

22. What did the British government do to help pay the expenses of the French and Indian War?

A It printed more colonial money.

B It forced the colonists to buy more goods from Great Britain.

C It passed new tax laws for the colonies.

D It sold western lands to settlers.

Answer these questions.

23. How was the Puritans' religious perspective different from that of the Pilgrims?

_____

_____

_____

_____

24. What are some of the reasons why people from varied backgrounds settled in the Mid-Atlantic colonies?

_____

_____

_____

_____

25. How and why did Great Britain try to establish political and economic control over the colonies?

_____

_____

_____

_____

Wow, those pigs are pretty speedy.

Eco has a new business helping settlers in the English colonies. Your first job is in the New England colonies, where a prize pig has escaped. First, you must find a way to catch the pig! Nobody knows what other problems you and Eco could face in the Mid-Atlantic and Southern colonies. Play the game now online.

Show What You Know

Writing Write a Narrative

Imagine that you are a new settler in Jamestown. Write a story about life in your colony. Tell why your colony was started. Then explain the role of trade and government in your society. Also explain how people in your colony make a living.

Activity Plan a Colonial Fair

For a colonial fair, plan a display about daily life in one of the New England, Mid-Atlantic, or Southern colonies. Decide how your display will show what life was like there. Your display should focus on how people lived, worshipped, worked, and were governed. Also show how people in the colony interacted with people in other colonies.

Colonial Fair

The American Revolution

Battle of Princeton, in New Jersey, in 1777

Spotlight on Standards

THE BIG IDEA People are willing to face many dangers to win their freedom.

 HISTORY AND SOCIAL SCIENCE SOL

USI.1a, USI.1b, USI.1c, USI.1d, USI.1f, USI.1h, USI.6a, USI.6b, USI.6c, USI.6d

Set the Stage

Study the map. Circle the names of the 13 British Colonies.

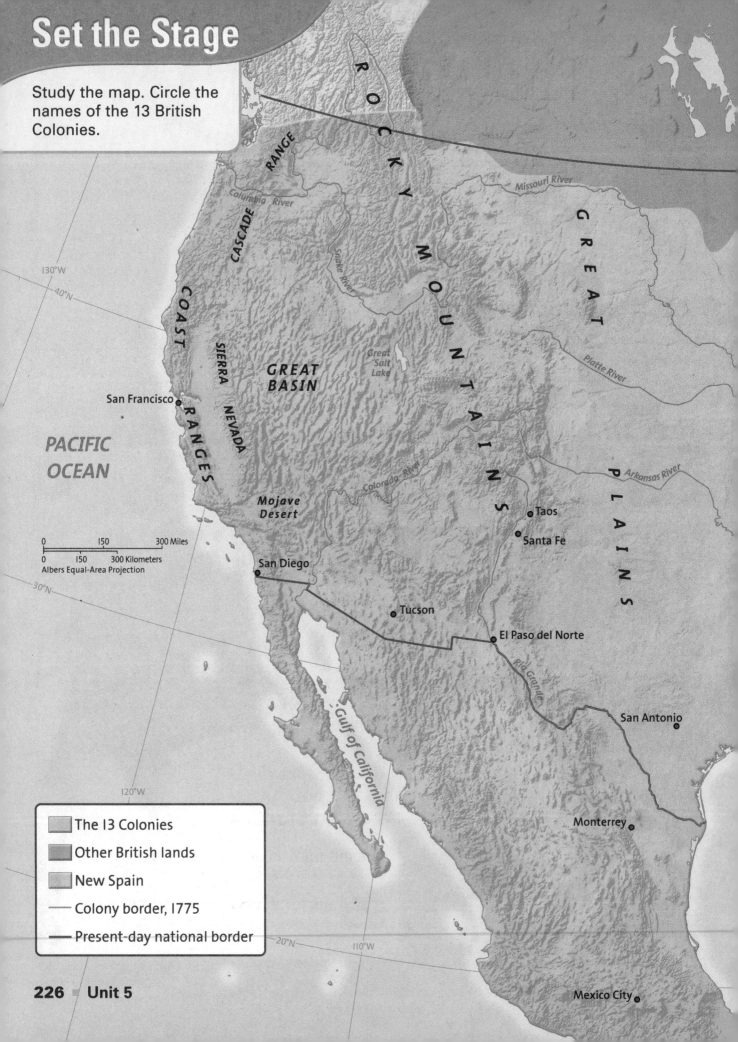

130°W
40°N

ROCKY RANGE

CASCADE RANGE

Columbia River

Missouri River

R O C K Y   M O U N T A I N S

G R E A T

Snake River

COAST RANGES

SIERRA NEVADA

GREAT BASIN

Great Salt Lake

Platte River

PACIFIC OCEAN

San Francisco

Mojave Desert

Colorado River

Arkansas River

P L A I N S

Taos

Santa Fe

0   150   300 Miles
0   150   300 Kilometers
Albers Equal-Area Projection

San Diego

30°N

Tucson

El Paso del Norte

Rio Grande

San Antonio

Gulf of California

120°W

The 13 Colonies

Other British lands

New Spain

Colony border, 1775

Present-day national border

Monterrey

20°N

110°W

Mexico City

Colonial America, 1775

Lake Superior

Lake Michigan

Lake Huron

Lake Erie

Lake Ontario

St. Lawrence

Mississippi River

Ohio River

Tennessee River

Savannah River

Roanoke River

Potomac R.

APPALACHIAN MOUNTAINS

Québec
(claimed by NY and NH)

(part of MA)

Montreal

St. Louis

New Orleans

St. Augustine

NEW HAMPSHIRE

Portsmouth

Albany

NEW YORK

Boston

MASSACHUSETTS

Providence

Newport

Hartford

RHODE ISLAND

CONNECTICUT

PENNSYLVANIA

Philadelphia

New York City

NEW JERSEY

Baltimore

DE

MARYLAND

VIRGINIA

Richmond

Williamsburg

NORTH CAROLINA

Wilmington

SOUTH CAROLINA

Charles Town

GEORGIA

Savannah

ATLANTIC OCEAN

Gulf of Mexico

60°W

30°N

20°N

90°W

80°W

70°W

N E S W

Old North Church, in Boston

Pennsylvania State House, in Philadelphia

Virginia Capitol, in Williamsburg

Set the Stage

❶ Draw an *X* on the time line to show where this event would appear:

   1775 The American Revolution begins

❷ Circle the name of the person who wrote plays protesting British rule.

Crispus Attucks

1725?—1770
- Killed by a British soldier at the Boston Massacre
- Often called the first person to be killed in the struggle for American freedom

The American Revolution

1765 The Stamp Act is passed, p. 235

1770 The Boston Tea Party takes place, p. 240

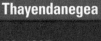

1760

1770

At the Same Time

1762 Catherine the Great becomes ruler of Russia

1769 English inventor James Watt builds a steam engine

1770 James Cook explores Australia

Patrick Henry

1736–1799
- Member of the Virginia House of Burgesses
- Spoke out against British rule and taxes

Thayendanegea

1742–1807
- Mohawk leader who later took the name Joseph Brant
- Helped the British during the American Revolution

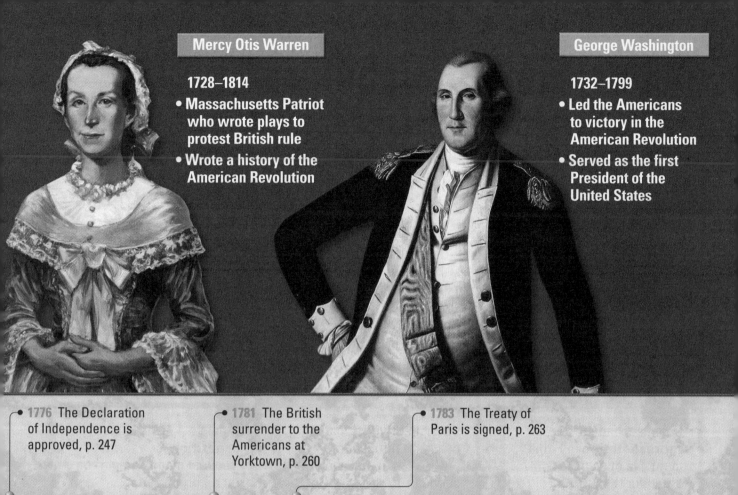

Mercy Otis Warren

1728–1814

- Massachusetts Patriot who wrote plays to protest British rule
- Wrote a history of the American Revolution

George Washington

1732–1799

- Led the Americans to victory in the American Revolution
- Served as the first President of the United States

1776 The Declaration of Independence is approved, p. 247

1781 The British surrender to the Americans at Yorktown, p. 260

1783 The Treaty of Paris is signed, p. 263

1780

1790

1784 Great Britain takes control of lands in India

1789 The French Revolution begins

Bernardo de Gálvez

1746–1786

- Governor of Spanish Louisiana
- Helped the Americans during the American Revolution

Phillis Wheatley

1753–1784

- Began writing poetry as a teenager
- First African American woman in the colonies to have a book published

229

Preview Vocabulary

representation

Colonists had no **representation** in Parliament. No one spoke or acted for them. p. 235

boycott

During a **boycott**, many colonists refused to buy British goods and services. p. 236

petition

Some colonists signed a **petition**, or a formal request made to a person or an organization. p. 241

revolution

The colonists wanted a **revolution**. They felt that a sudden change in government was needed. p. 242

independence

Americans are free to govern themselves. This **independence** began with the signing of a declaration. p. 245

turning point

In war, there is often a **turning point**, or an event that causes an important change. p. 254

Reading Social Studies

Cause and Effect

LEARN

Understanding cause and effect can help you see why events happen. A **cause** is an event or an action that makes something else happen. An **effect** is what happens because of that event or action. Certain words and phrases, such as *because, since, so, for these reasons,* and *as a result,* are hints that can help you see cause-and-effect relationships. In some paragraphs, the effect or effects may be stated before the cause.

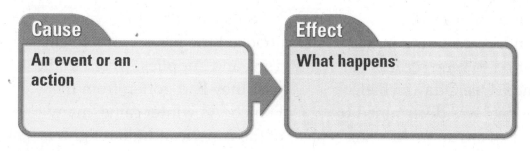

Cause

An event or an action

Effect

What happens

PRACTICE

Circle the cause in each paragraph. Then underline the effect or effects of that cause. The first paragraph has been marked for you.

Unlike Great Britain, France did not send many settlers to North America. To the French, trade was more important than settlement. Many French fur trappers were friendly with American Indians and lived among them. As a result, most American Indian groups were allies of the French during the French and Indian War.

Cause

Effect

Other American Indian groups, including the Mohawk and the Iroquois, traded with the British. These groups had formed close ties with Great Britain. For these reasons, the Mohawk and the Iroquois became allies of Great Britain.

Read the article. Then complete the activities below.

Chief Pontiac

After the French and Indian War, lands between the Appalachian Mountains and the Mississippi River came under British control. As a result, many colonists began to settle there. However, those lands were already home to several American Indian groups.

American Indians living in the region wanted to keep settlers out of their lands. One Ottawa chief, named Pontiac, was determined to stop the loss of any more hunting grounds. So he and other leaders united American Indians in the Great Lakes and Ohio Valley regions to fight the settlers.

In May 1763, Pontiac and his followers began attacking British forts in what is now western Pennsylvania, Ohio, Michigan, and Indiana. Most of the forts were captured and destroyed. Because there were no soldiers to protect the settlements near the forts, Pontiac also destroyed many of those towns.

Pontiac and his followers attacked the British forts to get guns and supplies, which in the past they had gotten from the French. As winter came, many of the American Indian fighters signed peace treaties with the British and began to return to their homes. Pontiac did not have enough supplies or fighters to continue. For these reasons, Pontiac had to give up control of the British forts.

1. **In the first paragraph, circle the sentence that explains why many colonists began to settle the lands between the Appalachian Mountains and the Mississippi River.**

2. **Underline the words that explain why Pontiac was able to destroy many towns.**

3. **What was the effect of Pontiac's not having enough supplies or fighters?**

_____

_____

_____

Growing Unrest

Great Britain's desire to remain a world power had resulted in the French and Indian War. Great Britain had fought hard to keep control of its colonies and remain a world power. Now it was in debt. Great Britain's plan to pay the costs of the war made colonists even more unhappy with their rulers across the Atlantic Ocean. **Think about how people might feel when they do not have a voice in their government.**

Tax protesters, in Portsmouth, New Hampshire

NO STAMPS

ESSENTIAL QUESTIONS
✓ What steps did Great Britain take to increase control over its colonies?
✓ Why did many colonists become dissatisfied with Great Britain's control over the colonies?
✓ Who were some of the key individuals in the Revolutionary War?
✓ What role did key individuals play in the Revolutionary War?
✓ What were some of the key events that occurred during the Revolutionary War period?

 HISTORY AND SOCIAL SCIENCE SOL
USI.1a, USI.1b, USI.1c, USI.1d, USI.6a, USI.6c

TextWork

1 Study the map on the time line below. Circle the Proclamation Line.

2 Who issued the Proclamation of 1763?

King George III

3 (Focus Skill) How did the Proclamation of 1763 affect settlers west of the Appalachian Mountains?

That they don't want Great brain to were they live.

Sources of Dissatisfaction

After the French and Indian War, France gave up to Great Britain most of the lands it had claimed in North America. Many people from the 13 colonies wanted to settle on those newly won lands. The American Indians who lived there were angry. They did not want to lose their lands to settlers. In May 1763, American Indian groups from the Great Lakes and Ohio Valley regions united. They began to attack British forts and nearby settlements.

The Proclamation of 1763

Hoping to end the fighting, King George III of Great Britain issued the Proclamation of 1763. It ordered colonists to stop settling in lands west of the Appalachian Mountains, which had been set aside for American Indians. Colonists already living there were told to leave.

Many colonists ignored the orders. They began to move to areas that are now parts of West Virginia, Kentucky, and Ohio. The colonists did not want Great Britain to tell them where they could live.

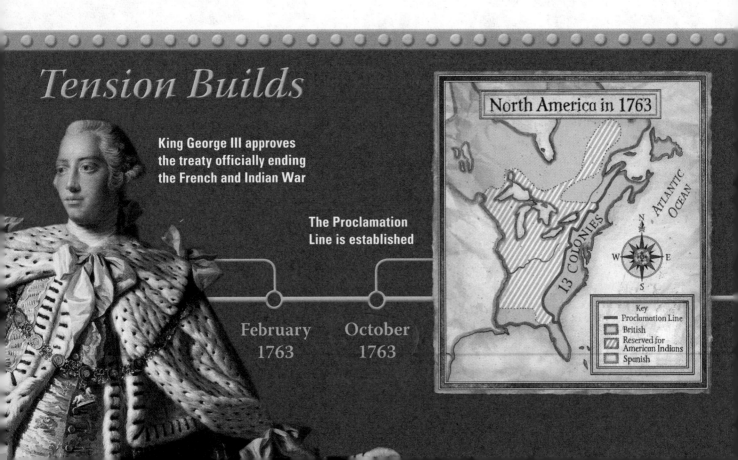

Tension Builds

King George III approves the treaty officially ending the French and Indian War

The Proclamation Line is established

February 1763

October 1763

North America in 1763

13 COLONIES

ATLANTIC OCEAN

N
W E
S

Key
Proclamation Line
British
Reserved for American Indians
Spanish

New Taxes for the Colonists

The French and Indian War caused money problems for Great Britain. The war had been costly. Great Britain decided to place new taxes on the colonists to raise the **revenue**, or income, it needed. That money would help pay for the war. It would also help feed and house the British troops still in the colonies. Great Britain kept soldiers in North America to protect the colonies and to strengthen its control over them.

In 1764, the British Parliament passed the Sugar Act. This act placed a tax on sugar and many other goods brought into the colonies. Then, in 1765, Parliament passed the Stamp Act, which taxed printed items, such as newspapers and legal documents. Even playing cards were taxed.

Many colonists believed that Great Britain had no right to tax them. The colonists had no **representation**, or someone to speak for them, in Parliament. Some colonists also complained that the king gave colonial governors too much control over the colonial legislatures.

TextWork

4 Scan the text. Circle the definition of *revenue*.

5 Why do you think that the idea of no taxes without representation is still important to people in the United States today?

They can't devinc theirsreves

6 (Focus Skill) Scan the text on pages 234 and 235. Underline two actions taken by the British government that caused colonists to become dissatisfied with Great Britain's control over them.

The Stamp Act places taxes on many printed goods

EIP

March 1765

May 1765

Patrick Henry, a member of the Virginia House of Burgesses, speaks against the Stamp Act

Children IN HISTORY

Supporting the Boycott

To support the boycott against British goods, sewing groups sprang up all over the colonies. Much of the spinning, weaving, and sewing was done by girls. Fifteen-year-old Charity Clark spun wool in her home in New York City. In a letter to her cousin in Great Britain, she wrote, "Heroines may not distinguish themselves at the head of an Army, but freedom [will] also be won by a fighting army of [women] . . . armed with spinning wheels."

Make It Relevant **What would you have done to support the colonial boycott? Explain.**

TextWork

7 Circle the words that give the meaning of protest.

8 Study the graph. How did the value of colonial imports from Great Britain change between 1764 and 1766?

3,5000,000

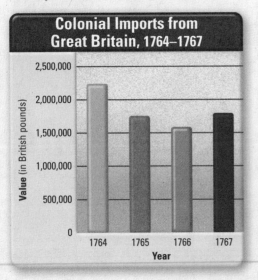

Colonial Imports from Great Britain, 1764–1767

(bar graph showing Value in British pounds by Year: 1764 ≈ 2,250,000; 1765 ≈ 1,750,000; 1766 ≈ 1,550,000; 1767 ≈ 1,800,000)

Colonists Speak Out

As Great Britain took steps to expand its control over the colonies, many colonists became upset. Angry colonists soon began to **protest**, or work against, the Stamp Act. Some colonists chose not to pay the tax. Others signed letters asking the king to do away with the Stamp Act. Many colonists chose to **boycott**, or refuse to buy, British goods. A group called the Daughters of Liberty supported the boycott by weaving their own cloth.

Another group, called the Sons of Liberty, held protest marches against the Stamp Act. The Sons of Liberty attacked the homes of tax collectors and other British officials. They also captured some tax collectors and chased them from their towns.

So many colonists stopped buying British goods that the boycotts hurt businesses in Great Britain. After much discussion, Parliament voted in 1766 to **repeal**, or cancel, the Stamp Act. However, new taxes were placed on goods such as glass, paint, and tea. Once again, the colonists protested. All the new taxes were repealed, except the one on tea.

The Boston Massacre

As protests grew, Parliament sent more British soldiers to the colonies. Most of them were stationed in cities along the Atlantic coast. About 4,000 of the soldiers were sent to Boston.

Many colonists did not want the soldiers in their towns. They often shouted insults at the soldiers. They called them "redcoats," to make fun of their bright red uniforms. Some British soldiers responded by destroying the colonists' property.

On the night of March 5, 1770, an angry crowd gathered near the Massachusetts State House in Boston. The crowd shouted at a group of British soldiers and threw rocks and snowballs at them. As the crowd moved forward, the soldiers fired their guns. Five colonists died. Crispus Attucks (A•tuhks), an African American sailor, was the first person killed. The event soon became known as the Boston Massacre (MA•sih•ker), even though the shooting was not really a massacre. A *massacre* is the killing of many people who cannot defend themselves.

This picture by Paul Revere shows his view of the Boston Massacre. Crispus Attucks (right) was the first person killed.

happyBoston! fee thy Sons deplore,   If fealding drops fromRage from AnguifhWrung,But knowFate fummons to that awful Goal.

TextWork

11 🎯 **How do you think the Boston Massacre affected the colonists' view of British soldiers?**

_____

_____

_____

_____

_____

After the Boston Massacre

The soldiers who fired at the colonists in Boston were charged with murder. The British government asked John Adams, a Boston lawyer, to defend the soldiers. Adams argued that the soldiers had fired their guns in self-defense. Six of the soldiers were found not guilty, while two others were found guilty of a less serious crime.

To show his support for the protesters, Paul Revere made a colorful picture titled *The Bloody Massacre.* Revere was a well-known silversmith and artist. His picture shows the soldiers shooting at the colonists, with some colonists lying dead on the ground. The picture was used on posters that stirred up more anger against the British.

Lesson 1 Review

1. **SUMMARIZE** What actions and events led to unrest in the colonies?

_____

_____

2. Why was **representation** in the British Parliament important to the colonists?

_____

_____

_____

3. Who was Crispus Attucks, and what role did he play in the colonists' fight for freedom?

_____

_____

Circle the letter of the correct answer.

4. Colonists worked against the new British tax laws by—

   A paying taxes

   B boycotting British goods

   C working harder

   D pledging loyalty to the king

writing

✎ **Write a Letter to the Editor** Imagine that you are living in Virginia during the late 1700s. Write a letter to your newspaper's editor to express your opinion about the new British tax laws.

Tax stamps

The Colonies Unite

Statue of Paul Revere, near the Old North Church, in Boston

In the years following the Boston Massacre, the British Parliament again angered the colonists by passing more tax laws. **Think about what might make leaders decide to go to war with another country.**

ESSENTIAL QUESTIONS

✓ What steps did Great Britain take to increase control over its colonies?

✓ Why did many colonists become dissatisfied with Great Britain's control over the colonies?

✓ Who were some of the key individuals in the Revolutionary War?

✓ What role did key individuals play in the Revolutionary War?

✓ What were some of the key events that occurred during the Revolutionary War period?

 HISTORY AND SOCIAL SCIENCE SOL
USI.1a, USI.1d, USI.1f, USI.1h, USI.6a, USI.6c

TextWork

① (Focus Skill) What was the cause of the Boston Tea Party?

The conlonsit were trowing 300 boxs of tea.

② Scan the text. Underline three ways that Parliament reacted to the Boston Tea Party.

③ Circle the sentence that describes many colonists' view of Parliament's reaction to the Boston Tea Party.

The colonists who took part in the Boston Tea Party refused to pay for the tea they had destroyed.

Colonists Speak Out

In 1773, Parliament passed the Tea Act. This new law said that only the East India Company of Great Britain could sell tea to the colonies. The colonists could buy the tea—and pay the tax on it—or else not drink tea. Many boycotted tea.

On the night of December 16, 1773, about 150 members of the Sons of Liberty dressed as American Indians and marched to Boston Harbor. The group, led by Samuel Adams and Paul Revere, boarded three British ships. The colonists threw more than 300 chests of tea overboard. This angry protest became known as the Boston Tea Party.

In March 1774, Parliament passed a set of laws to punish the colonists after the Boston Tea Party. One law closed the port of Boston until the colonists paid for the destroyed tea. Another law stopped the Massachusetts government from meeting. Parliament also ordered the colonists to **quarter**, or give food and housing to, British soldiers. Many colonists said that the new laws were intolerable, or unacceptable. They became known as the Intolerable Acts.

The First Continental Congress

In September 1774, leaders from all the colonies except Georgia met in Philadelphia. The meeting was later called the First Continental Congress. A **congress** is a formal meeting of delegates, or representatives.

Delegates hoped for a peaceful solution to their problems with Great Britain. The Congress sent a **petition**, or a signed request, to King George III. The petition reminded the king of the colonists' basic rights as British citizens. Congress voted to stop most trade with Great Britain. It also asked the colonies to form **militias**, or armies of citizens.

"Give Me Liberty or Give Me Death!"

Some colonial leaders in Virginia suggested that the colonists begin preparing for war. In a speech, Patrick Henry, an outspoken member of the Virginia House of Burgesses, said, "I know not what course others may take, but as for me, give me liberty or give me death!" These words inspired other colonists and soon became a favorite **patriotic slogan**. A patriotic slogan is a saying that people repeat to express pride in their country.

TextWork

4 Use the word *petition* in a sentence about how the colonists hoped to solve their problems with Great Britain peacefully.

They trying to petition the brisith Armys to be peaceful.

5 How do you think Patrick Henry's slogan inspired colonial patriotism, or love for one's country?

Because He is trying to say the people that colonines has right to gave them new-Laws.

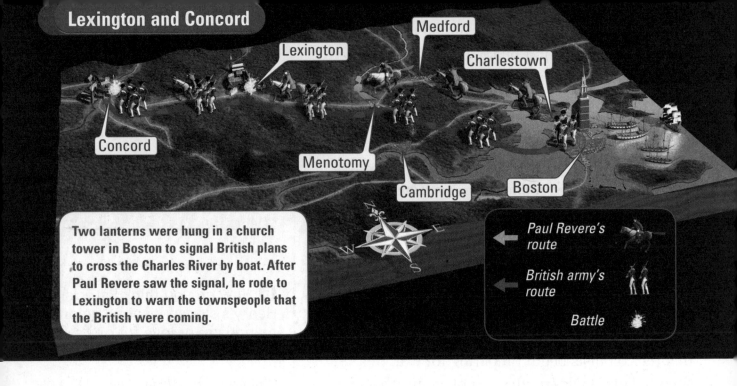

Lexington and Concord

Two lanterns were hung in a church tower in Boston to signal British plans to cross the Charles River by boat. After Paul Revere saw the signal, he rode to Lexington to warn the townspeople that the British were coming.

Paul Revere's route

British army's route

Battle

 TextWork

6 Study the map. Circle the town in which Paul Revere's route began. Why did Paul Revere ride to Lexington?

Becouse the bristsh Armys gonna Arsseted them hiding guns, gunpowder, other supplies

7 What do you think the poet Ralph Waldo Emerson meant in 1837 when he called the first shot fired at Lexington "the shot heard 'round the world"? Are his words an example of a primary source or a secondary source?

Because they their mad at the bristish Armys donig supid dumb things.

Lexington and Concord

In April 1775, British soldiers marched toward the towns of Lexington and Concord in Massachusetts. They planned to arrest two leaders of the Sons of Liberty and capture the group's weapons. The British wanted their plan to be a secret, but Paul Revere found out about it. He rode to Lexington to warn the townspeople.

Members of Massachusetts's militia, called Minutemen, were waiting for the British in Lexington. Their leader shouted, "Don't fire unless fired upon, but if they mean to have war, let it begin here." No one knows which side fired first, but shots rang out. Eight Minutemen were killed, and several others were injured.

The British moved on to Concord, where they faced the Minutemen again. After much fighting, the British retreated, or fell back, to Boston. The fighting at Lexington and Concord turned out to be the first armed conflict in a long war called the American Revolution. A **revolution** is a sudden, complete change of government.

The Road to War

News of the fighting at Lexington and Concord spread through the colonies. Hoping to avoid more fighting, colonial leaders called for the Second Continental Congress to meet in Philadelphia on May 10, 1775. The delegates expressed their desire for a peaceful end to the fighting. By June, however, the delegates agreed that the colonies should prepare for war with Great Britain.

The first step was for Congress to form an army. It was called the Continental Army. Unlike the part-time militias that each of the 13 colonies already had, the Continental Army was made up of full-time soldiers.

Congress chose George Washington of Virginia as the commander of the Continental Army. Washington's skills as a leader were well known in the colonies. Phillis Wheatley, a former enslaved African American, honored George Washington in a poem. Wheatley wrote many poems and plays supporting American independence.

TextWork

8 Study the excerpt from Phillis Wheatley's poem. How do you think it reflects how Wheatley felt about Washington?

She like George Washtion as the commder of the contanital Army. And makeing proms about him.

9 Scan the text on the next page. Circle the sentence that tells how the Battle of Bunker Hill changed Great Britain's view of fighting with the colonies.

Phillis Wheatley was the first African American woman in the colonies to have her writings published.

PHILLIS WHEATLEY

CA 1753-1784

BORN IN WEST AFRICA AND SOLD AS A SLAVE FROM THE SHIP *PHILLIS* IN COLONIAL BOSTON, SHE WAS A LITERARY PRODIGY WHOSE 1773 VOLUME *POEMS ON VARIOUS SUBJECTS, RELIGIOUS AND MORAL* WAS THE FIRST BOOK PUBLISHED BY AN AFRICAN WRITER IN AMERICA.

"A crown, a mansion, and a throne that shine,

With gold unfading, WASHINGTON! be thine."

From a poem by Phillis Wheatley about George Washington

Bunker Hill

The first major battle of the American Revolution was fought on June 17, 1775, on Breed's Hill, near Boston. The battle was wrongly named for nearby Bunker Hill. The fighting was much tougher than the British had expected. Twice, the British were forced back. In Boston, people watched in horror as the nearby city of Charlestown was hit and set on fire by cannons shot from British ships in the harbor.

The British eventually won the battle. However, they suffered heavy losses. More than 1,000 British soldiers were killed or wounded. About 350 colonists had been killed or wounded. The British learned that fighting the Americans would not be as easy as they had thought.

At the Battle of Bunker Hill, the colonists fired on the British from behind earthworks on top of Breed's Hill.

Lesson 2 Review

✓1. SUMMARIZE What did the colonists do to protest British rule?

They don't flowing their suiPuid rule.

✓2. In your own words, write a definition for the word **revolution**.

The revolution is that you want Inpecapedce from somebody.

activity

🖌 **Make a Poster** Imagine you are living in the colonies in 1775. Make a poster using a patriotic slogan that will inspire colonists to join the fight for freedom from Great Britain.

Circle the letter of the correct answer.

3. What was the first major battle of the American Revolution?

A. Battle of Yorktown
B. Boston Massacre
C. Battle of Lexington and Concord
(D) Battle of Bunker Hill

Patrick Henry

Declaring Independence

After the Battle of Bunker Hill, more colonists started to think that their problems with Great Britain could not be settled. Some colonists began to call for **independence**, or the freedom to govern themselves. **Think about the meaning and importance of independence.**

Independence Hall, in Philadelphia, Pennsylvania

ESSENTIAL QUESTIONS

✓ What ideas about government were expressed in the Declaration of Independence?

✓ Who were some of the key individuals in the Revolutionary War?

✓ What role did key individuals play in the Revolutionary War?

✓ What were some of the key events that occurred during the Revolutionary War period?

HISTORY AND SOCIAL SCIENCE SOL
USI.1a, USI.1b, USI.1c, USI.1d, USI.1h, USI.6b, USI.6c

George Mason and the other delegates at the Virginia Convention met in the capitol in Williamsburg (left) to approve the Virginia Declaration of Rights (right).

TextWork

1 (Focus Skill) Scan the text. Underline the sentences that tell the points of view of some European thinkers about government. How did these ideas affect the colonists?

_____

_____

_____

2 Who wrote the Virginia Declaration of Rights?

George Mason

3 Circle the names of two rights included in the Virginia Declaration of Rights.

Debating Independence

New ideas about government were reaching the colonies from Europe. Some European philosophers, or thinkers, believed that government was an agreement between people and their rulers. Leaders had the responsibility to rule justly, and people had the right to replace unjust rulers.

Virginia Takes the Lead

These new ideas were on the minds of the delegates meeting at the Virginia Convention in Williamsburg in 1776. In May of that year, they approved a **resolution** in support of independence. A resolution is a statement of a group's beliefs. The delegates at the Virginia Convention also approved the Virginia Declaration of Rights. This **declaration**, or official statement, was written by George Mason. It listed the rights guaranteed to all Virginians—including freedom of religion and freedom of speech. The Virginia Declaration of Rights became a model for the United States Declaration of Independence.

The Second Continental Congress

On June 7, 1776, Richard Henry Lee presented the Virginia Convention's resolution to the Second Continental Congress, which was meeting in Philadelphia. The resolution stated that "these united colonies are, and of right ought to be, free and Independent States."

The Congress formed a committee to write a declaration explaining the reasons for independence. All the members, including Benjamin Franklin and John Adams, offered their ideas. However, 33-year-old Thomas Jefferson of Virginia wrote most of it. He included many of the key ideas about government expressed by European philosophers.

On July 4, 1776, the Congress voted to approve the Declaration of Independence. Throughout the colonies, people celebrated. John Adams, who had championed the cause of independence, wrote to Abigail Adams, his wife, that Independence Day should be celebrated "from this time forward." Ever since, Americans have celebrated the Fourth of July as a national holiday.

TextWork

4 Scan the text. Circle the name of the person who was the main writer of the Declaration of Independence. Underline the names of two other committee members.

5 Number these events in the correct sequence.

_2_ The Declaration of Independence is written.

_1_ The Virginia Declaration of Rights is written.

_3_ The Congress votes to approve the Declaration of Independence.

6 Underline how Americans today celebrate the vote to approve the Declaration of Independence.

Biography

Citizenship

Thomas Jefferson

Thomas Jefferson is best known as the main writer of the Declaration of Independence and the third President of the United States. However, he accomplished much more. He studied law and government. He designed his own house, which is called Monticello. Jefferson also started the University of Virginia.

Time

1743 Born

1826 Died

1776 Jefferson is the main writer of the Declaration of Independence

1801 Jefferson becomes President of the United States

The Declaration of Independence

The Declaration of Independence begins with a preamble, or introduction. The preamble states why the Declaration was needed. In the preamble, Jefferson explained that sometimes a group of people has no choice but to form a new nation.

The second part of the Declaration describes the colonists' main ideas about government. Jefferson stated that people have certain "unalienable" (uhn•AYL•yuh•nuh•buhl) rights, including life, liberty, and the pursuit of happiness. These rights cannot be taken away by government.

The second part of the Declaration explains that a government gets its power from the people. In fact, people set up governments to protect their rights. In turn, people have a right and a duty to change a government if it violates their rights.

In the third and longest part of the Declaration, Jefferson listed the colonists' grievances, or complaints, against King George III. He also listed the ways in which the colonists had tried to peacefully settle their differences with the king.

In the last part of the Declaration, Jefferson included a statement declaring that the 13 colonies were no longer part of Great Britain. He said the colonies were now free and independent states.

Signing the Declaration

On August 2, 1776, some of the members of the Second Continental Congress began to sign the Declaration. John Hancock, the president of the Congress, was the first to sign the document. He wrote his name very large, supposedly so that King George III could read it without his glasses.

Signing the document was a dangerous act. If the colonies lost the war, the signers would be charged with treason, or the act of working against the government. Treason was punishable by death.

THE DECLARATION OF INDEPENDENCE

★ ★ ★ ★ ★ ★ ★ ★ ★ ★ ★ ★ ★ ★ ★ ★ ★ ★ ★

Thomas Jefferson used this desk when he wrote the Declaration

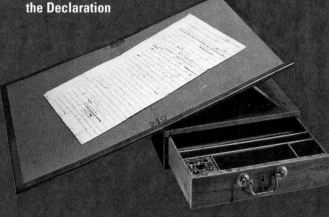

The draft of the Declaration is presented to the Second Continental Congress

"We hold these truths to be self-evident, that all men are created equal, that they are endowed [provided] by their Creator with certain unalienable Rights, that among these are Life, Liberty, and the pursuit of Happiness."

Delegates used this inkstand to sign the Declaration

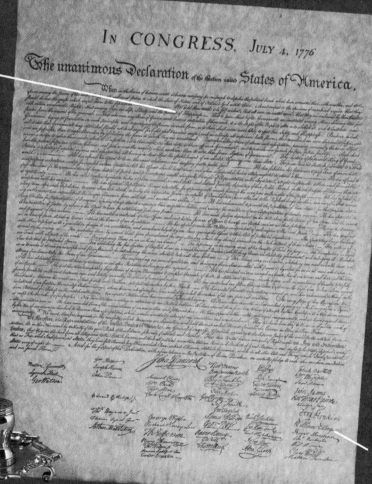

Signers

1. **SUMMARIZE** What ideas about government are expressed in the Declaration of Independence?

   was that the cosonlsqt were mad at the bristish Laws.

2. Why is **independence** important to Americans?

   so that get their wishs to have a war.

3. How was the Virginia Declaration of Rights important to the Declaration of Independence?

   Beacause the Rights are the thing they want to happen.

4. What rights are described in the Declaration of Independence as "unalienable"?

   The Declaration Independence is a Imopant thing in History.

Match each person to his role in declaring independence.

5. John Hancock   wrote the Virginia Declaration of Rights

6. George Mason   wrote the Declaration of Independence

7. Thomas Jefferson   first to sign the Declaration of Independence

writing

✎ **Write a Newspaper Article** Imagine that you are a newspaper reporter living in Philadelphia at the time of the Second Continental Congress. Write a newspaper article describing the events that are taking place.

John Hancock

Lesson 4

The Fight for Independence

The American Revolution was a time of hardships for nearly everyone in the colonies. Both **Patriots**, those who supported independence, and **Loyalists**, people who remained loyal to the king, faced low supplies, economic problems, and danger. The soldiers who fought the war faced the worst hardships of all. **Think about the different people who fought in the war and how they were affected by the war.**

Yorktown Battlefield, in Virginia

ESSENTIAL QUESTIONS

- ✓ Who were some of the key individuals in the Revolutionary War?
- ✓ What role did key individuals play in the Revolutionary War?
- ✓ What were some of the key events that occurred during the Revolutionary War period?

SOL **HISTORY AND SOCIAL SCIENCE SOL**

USI.1c, USI.1d, USI.6c

Heroes of the Revolution

Many individuals—including women, African Americans, and American Indians—played important roles in shaping the events of the American Revolution. Some were close to the fighting. Others helped the war effort at home.

Mercy Otis Warren

Sybil Ludington

EIP

TextWork

1 (Focus Skill) Underline the sentences that describe how the British navy caused economic hardships for colonists.

2 Why do you think prices rose as the shortage of goods grew worse?

_____

_____

_____

3 List three different ways in which women helped in the American Revolution.

_____

_____

_____

Americans and the Revolution

The war affected the lives of many people. The British attacked and burned many colonial towns. There was also a shortage of goods in the colonies because British warships stopped trading ships from unloading goods at American ports. As the shortage of goods grew worse, prices rose.

Women and the War

Women in the colonies took on new roles during the war. Some ran farms and businesses. Others raised money for the war and collected clothing for the soldiers. In army camps, women nursed soldiers, cooked food, and washed clothes.

Other women and girls joined the men in battle. Deborah Sampson dressed in men's clothes so that she could fight. One night in 1777, 16-year-old Sybil Ludington rode on horseback to tell American soldiers of a British attack.

Other women used their talents to support the Patriot cause. Mercy Otis Warren wrote patriotic poems about people fighting for freedom.

Peter Salem

James Armistead

Thayendanegea

African Americans and the War

African Americans—both free and enslaved—took part in the war, too. For example, Peter Salem, a free African American, fought in the Battle of Bunker Hill. About 5,000 enslaved African Americans fought for the Continental Army. Many were promised their freedom as a reward for their service. James Armistead, an enslaved man from Virginia, served as a spy for George Washington.

People in the West

At first, most American Indians and settlers in the western lands remained **neutral**. They did not choose sides. However, American Indians became divided. Many sided with the British. The Mohawk leader Thayendanegea (thay•en•da•NEG•ah), known as Joseph Brant, hoped to stop more settlers from moving west. Other groups, such as the Oneida and Tuscarora, fought for the Patriots.

The perspectives of many western settlers also changed. Many did not support the Patriot cause. However, they wanted to help drive the British out of their lands.

 TextWork

❹ Why did some African Americans decide to fight in the American Revolution?

_____

_____

❺ Underline two sentences that summarize the views of most American Indians and western settlers about the war.

❻ (Focus Skill) What caused western settlers to change their perspectives about the war?

_____

_____

_____

Struggles and Triumphs

❼ How long after the Battle of Trenton was the Battle of Saratoga?

_____

❽ Describe in your own words the meaning of the term *turning point.*

_____

_____

_____

❾ What do you think might have happened if the Americans had lost the Battle of Saratoga?

_____

_____

_____

The Americans had gone to war against one of the most powerful armies in the world. Most soldiers in the Continental Army had little training, and many had no guns or uniforms. Early on, the British won many battles and captured several important colonial cities.

By December 1776, many American soldiers were ready to give up. Then, on Christmas night, the Americans made a sneak attack on enemy soldiers near Trenton, New Jersey. In a short fight, the Americans defeated the enemy. This victory gave the Americans new hope for winning the war.

Earlier that year, Congress had sent Benjamin Franklin to France to try to gain its support. At first, the French refused to help. Then, in October 1777, the Continental Army won the Battle of Saratoga in New York. This was a turning point in the war. A **turning point** is an event that causes an important change. After the victory at Saratoga, Franklin convinced France to help the Americans. The French provided guns, ships, and soldiers.

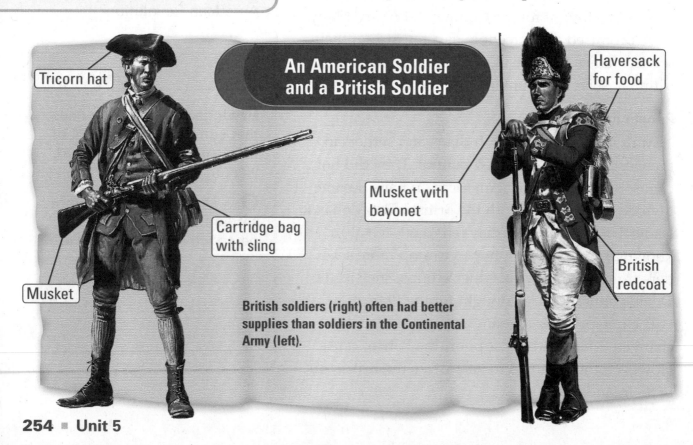

An American Soldier and a British Soldier

Tricorn hat

Musket

Cartridge bag with sling

Musket with bayonet

Haversack for food

British redcoat

British soldiers (right) often had better supplies than soldiers in the Continental Army (left).

George Washington and his army marched through snow to Valley Forge in 1777.

Winter at Valley Forge

The Americans were encouraged by their victories. However, they still struggled. In the winter of 1777 they needed a safe place to camp. In December 1777, General Washington set up headquarters at Valley Forge, Pennsylvania. He chose the site because it was high and flat. From there, soldiers could easily watch for enemies.

The weather at Valley Forge was bitterly cold that winter. The army did not have enough supplies, and diseases spread quickly. By Washington's own count, 2,898 of his men had no boots. The Continental Army was almost destroyed.

However, the Patriots got help from some European friends. Marquis de Lafayette, from France, spent his own money to buy warm clothes for the soldiers. Friedrich Wilhelm von Steuben, from Germany, taught the American troops better ways to march and fight. He showed them how to work better together and gave them confidence. By 1778, the Continental Army was much stronger.

TextWork

10 Study the painting and text. What hardships did Washington's army face at Valley Forge?

_____

_____

_____

11 🟊 **Focus Skill** Write an effect of this cause:

Cause: European allies helped train the Continental Army at Valley Forge.

Effect: _____

_____

_____

1. **SUMMARY** What hardships did the Americans face during the American Revolution?

_____

_____

_____

2. What were the different perspectives of **Patriots**, **Loyalists**, and people who were **neutral**?

_____

_____

_____

Circle the letter of the correct answer.

3. The most important effect of the Battle of Saratoga was—

   A France's decision to help the Americans

   B France's decision to help Great Britain

   C the Continental Army's decision to surrender

   D the British army's decision to surrender

4. Why was the Continental Army stronger after spending the winter at Valley Forge?

   F It was larger.

   G It was rested.

   H It had learned to march and fight better.

   J It had trained with American Indians.

Match the person to his or her role in the American Revolution.

5. Friedrich Wilhelm von Steuben   warned Patriots about a British attack

6. Sybil Ludington   tried to stop settlers from moving west

7. Thayendanegea   taught American troops better ways of fighting

writing

✎ **Write a Report** Choose one person you read about in this lesson. Then write a report for your class, describing who the person was and what role he or she played in the American Revolution.

George Washington's military camp chest

Winning Independence

The Patriots had declared their independence from Great Britain, but would their army be strong enough to win it? Although the Americans faced difficulties in their war against the British, they continued to fight hard for freedom. **Think about how a strong belief in a cause can help the people fighting for it.**

General George Washington

ESSENTIAL QUESTIONS

✔ Who were some of the key individuals in the Revolutionary War?
✔ What role did key individuals play in the Revolutionary War?
✔ What were some of the key events that occurred during the Revolutionary War?
✔ What advantages helped the American colonists win the Revolutionary War?

HISTORY AND SOCIAL SCIENCE SOL
USI.1d, USI.1f, USI.6c, USI.6d

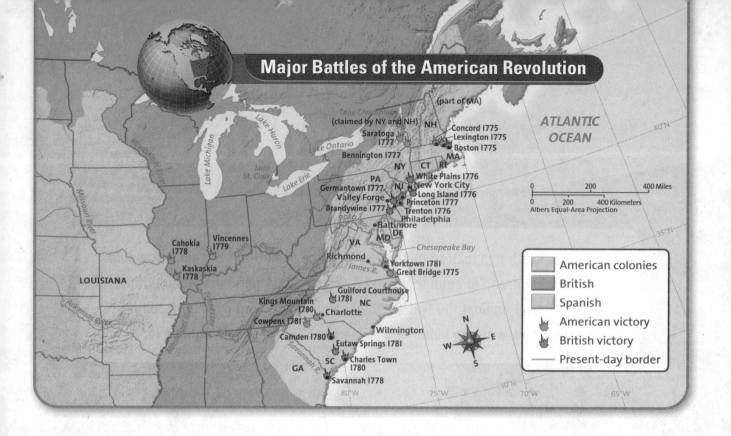

Major Battles of the American Revolution

ATLANTIC OCEAN

American colonies
British
Spanish
American victory
British victory
Present-day border

① (Focus Skill) **What effect did France's decision to help the Americans have on the British?**

_____

_____

_____

② **Why did the British decide to move the fighting to the South?**

_____

_____

③ **Study the map. Place an X on the battle that took place in Georgia.**

The War Moves South

When the British learned that the French were helping the Americans, the British planned a new campaign in the South. A **campaign** is a series of military actions carried out for a certain goal. The British had captured many important cities in the North. Now they wanted to defeat the Americans in the South before French help could arrive.

The British hoped to get help from the many Loyalists who lived in the South. They also hoped to capture ports in the South. That would make it easier for the British army to receive supplies from British ships. Savannah, Georgia, was Great Britain's first target in the South. On November 25, 1778, about 3,500 British soldiers captured the city. In 1780, the British took Charles Town, later known as Charleston, in South Carolina.

Early in 1781, Benedict Arnold, a former Continental Army officer, led British attacks on Virginia towns. Arnold had become a traitor, or someone who acts against his or her country.

Americans Fight Back

The Americans eventually received help from Spain, too. Spain had declared war on Great Britain in 1779. Bernardo de Gálvez, the governor of Spanish Louisiana, gave guns, food, and money to the Americans and captured many British forts. Spanish-born sailor Jorge Farragut also helped.

Although the Americans lost several battles, they did not give up. General Nathanael Greene, who led the Continental Army in the South, wrote "We fight, get beat, rise, and fight again."

The Americans won a major victory at Cowpens, South Carolina, in January 1781. The Battle of Cowpens proved that American forces could defeat the British in the South.

The British army then pushed into North Carolina, where it battled American troops at Guilford Courthouse in March 1781. The British held the battlefield. However, victory came at a high price. The British army lost many soldiers, and it never fully recovered.

TextWork

4 Scan the text on pages 258 and 259. Circle the names of the battles that the Americans won. Underline the names of the battles that the British won.

5 (Focus Skill) What effect did the Battle of Cowpens have on American forces?

_____

_____

_____

_____

_____

Biography

Loyalty

Bernardo de Gálvez

During the American Revolution, Bernardo de Gálvez protected New Orleans against British attack and gained control of the Mississippi River. He let the Americans move weapons, food, and soldiers on the river. After the war, the new United States Congress thanked Bernardo de Gálvez for his help during the American Revolution.

Time

1746 Born — **1786** Died

1777 Gálvez becomes governor of Spanish Louisiana

1781 Gálvez captures the town of Pensacola, Florida

Yorktown

❻ Scan the page. Underline the sentences that explain how the Americans and the French were able to trap General Cornwallis at Yorktown.

❼ Study the graph. What was the combined number of American and French soldiers at the Battle of Yorktown?

It is bigger.

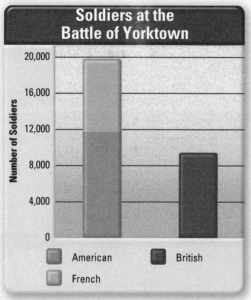

Soldiers at the Battle of Yorktown

Number of Soldiers

20,000
16,000
12,000
8,000
4,000
0

■ American   ■ British
■ French

Because America combine with french sodiers.

By the summer of 1781, British General Lord Charles Cornwallis had set up his headquarters at Yorktown, Virginia. Yorktown was a small town located on Chesapeake Bay. The bay made it easy for British ships to bring in supplies. However, Yorktown's location also meant that the town could be surrounded easily. Knowing this, the Americans and their French allies made a plan to defeat Cornwallis at Yorktown.

Victory for the Americans

Both French and American soldiers marched south to surround Yorktown. At the same time, the French navy took control of Chesapeake Bay. Cornwallis was trapped. The French fleet blocked supplies from reaching the British troops, and the Americans shelled the city for weeks.

In late September, Cornwallis sent word to his commander in the North. "If you cannot relieve me very soon," he said, "you must be prepared to hear the worst." The worst happened. The 5,000 extra soldiers that were sent to help Cornwallis did not get to Yorktown in time. After being surrounded for weeks, Cornwallis finally gave up on October 19, 1781. It was a huge victory for the Americans, and it helped end the war.

"The World Turned Upside Down"

More than 7,000 British soldiers marched out of Yorktown and laid down their weapons in a grassy field. The British soldiers marched out between long lines of French and American soldiers. During the surrender ceremony, a British military band reportedly played a popular tune called "The World Turned Upside Down." After hearing about the victory, some Patriot soldiers threw their hats in the air and yelled cheers. When news of the surrender at Yorktown reached Philadelphia, the Liberty Bell rang out the news of the American victory.

The Battle of Yorktown

Naval strategies were important in fighting the Battle of Yorktown. The French navy (right) prevented British ships from getting supplies to the British soldiers.

French soldiers

French ship

York River

British soldiers

French ship

British soldiers

British earthworks

Field where the British surrendered

French soldiers

American soldiers

French soldiers

American officers' headquarters

Cornwallis ordered his troops to scuttle, or sink, his own ships (left) to block the French navy from attacking Yorktown. This drum was carried by an American soldier at Yorktown (right).

9 List what the Americans wanted in the peace treaty and what the British wanted.

Americans: The America want freedoom from britan so they can be free,

British: The want the 13 conines to Pay towont for freedum

The War Ends

The American victory over the forces of Lord Cornwallis marked the end of the Revolutionary War. News of Great Britain's surrender at Yorktown quickly spread throughout the colonies. The long fight was over. The Patriots had finally won their independence. The United States of America was an independent country, free from British rule.

The war had clearly been decided by the victory at Yorktown in 1781. However, the fighting dragged on in some places for more than two years. It was not until April 1782 that the two sides met in Paris, France, to write a peace treaty. A **treaty** is an agreement between countries that satisfies people on different sides.

The Americans, represented by John Jay, Benjamin Franklin, and John Adams, wanted Great Britain to recognize American independence. They also wanted all British soldiers to leave American lands. The British wanted Loyalists who remained in the United States to be treated fairly.

The American Revolution EIP

George Washington is named commander in chief of the Continental Army

George Washington leads American soldiers to Trenton

June 1775   **July 1776**   **December 1776**

The Treaty of Paris

On September 3, 1783, the British and the Americans signed the Treaty of Paris. In the treaty, Great Britain recognized the United States of America as a nation. The treaty also set the borders for the United States. The new nation reached from Georgia in the south to the Great Lakes in the north. The Mississippi River formed the western border.

After the War

After British troops left the country, George Washington stopped in Annapolis, Maryland, where Congress was meeting at the time. Washington told Congress that since the nation was now at peace, his work was done. He retired as leader of the Continental Army. Congress thanked Washington for his loyal service and wished him well.

As a new nation, the United States faced many challenges as it prepared to take its place in the world. The writer Mercy Otis Warren called the new nation "a child just learning to walk."

TextWork

10 Use the events listed below to complete the time line. Add the letter of the event to the correct box in the time line.

A. British General Cornwallis surrenders to the Americans after the Battle of Yorktown

B. The Declaration of Independence is signed

11 What challenges do you think the United States faced after becoming an independent country?

_____

_____

_____

_____

The Battle of Cowpens

The Treaty of Paris is signed

January 1781

October 1781

September 1783

⓬ List three factors that helped the Americans defeat the British army.

_____

_____

_____

⓭ (Focus Skill) How did fighting on their own land affect the Americans in the war?

_____

_____

_____

Why the Colonists Won

With independence achieved, the Americans had done what had seemed impossible. Their small, poorly trained army had defeated one of the most powerful armies in the world. How did they do it?

Perhaps the biggest advantage for the Americans was the fact that they were defending their principles and beliefs on their own land. In the colonies, the Patriots had much support for their cause. Many colonists wanted to help them. As the Americans made progress in their struggle against the British, other nations, such as France and Spain, offered help.

The Americans also had very strong leadership. General George Washington made good decisions that helped the Continental Army win important battles. John Adams said that Washington had "great talents and universal character."

It was hard for the British to fight a war more than 3,000 miles from home. Loyalists offered some aid. However, the British had to wait a long time for supplies and more soldiers to arrive. Also, unlike the Continental Army, British soldiers were not familiar with the land on which they were fighting.

American Advantages

Foreign support

Strong leadership

Patriotism

1. **SUMMARIZE** How did the Americans defeat the British?

_____

_____

_____

_____

2. Use the word **campaign** in a sentence about the Revolutionary War.

_____

_____

_____

3. How did Yorktown's location put the British at a disadvantage?

_____

_____

_____

Circle the letter of the correct answer.

4. The British hoped to capture important cities in the South with help from—

   A Loyalists who lived in the region

   B American Indians who lived in the region

   C the French navy

   D other European nations

5. What country helped the Americans win the Battle of Yorktown?

   F France

   G Germany

   H Spain

   J The Netherlands

6. In what way was General Washington a strong leader?

   A He treated Loyalists fairly.

   B He helped the Americans win at Savannah and Charles Town.

   C He negotiated peace.

   D He made good decisions.

7. The Treaty of Paris set the western boundary of the United States at the—

   F Pacific Ocean

   G Rocky Mountains

   H Mississippi River

   J Appalachian Mountains

writing

Write a Letter Imagine you are an American in 1782. Write a letter to Benjamin Franklin in Paris, telling what you think the American representatives should agree to in the Treaty of Paris. Share your letter with a classmate.

The Treaty of Paris

Fun With Social Studies

Writers, Spies, and Commanders

Circle the writers in red, the commanders in blue, and the spy in green.

George Washington

Mercy Otis Warren

James Armistead

Joseph Brant

Phillis Wheatley

Thomas Jefferson

Rebus Revolution

VOCABULARY

Fill in the blanks, and then circle the rebus word that doesn't belong.

 + = _____

 + = _____

 re + = _____

au + + = _____

Vacation Station

What vacation spot does each poster advertise? Write your answers in the blanks below the posters.

VICTORY!

Visit the site of the battle that decided the war!

Today, everyone is welcome!

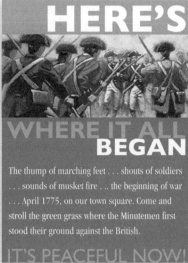

HERE'S WHERE IT ALL BEGAN

The thump of marching feet . . . shouts of soldiers . . . sounds of musket fire . . . the beginning of war . . . April 1775, on our town square. Come and stroll the green grass where the Minutemen first stood their ground against the British.

IT'S PEACEFUL NOW!

It's a party!

Like no other!

Come on board a replica of an East India Company ship. Imagine you're one of the Sons of Liberty, turning this vacation spot into a giant teapot! Come see where history was made.

You'll have a TEA-riffic time!

_____

_____

Confusion in Cyberspace

These e-mails did not land in the right mailboxes. Who should have received each one?

From: guest@America.com

To: _____

Subject: Freedom Writer

Love your poems and stories about Americans fighting for freedom. You are an amazing woman.

From: gwashington@ca.com

To: _____

Subject: Welcome

I'm proud that you've traveled to the American colonies all the way from France to join the Continental Army.

Review and Test Prep

The Big Idea

People are willing to face many dangers to win their freedom.

Summarize the Unit

(Focus Skill) **Cause and Effect** Complete the organizer to show that you understand the causes and effects of some key events during the American Revolution.

Cause	Effect
Great Britain needs money to pay for the French and Indian War.	_____ _____
_____ _____	**Congress approves the Declaration of Independence.**

Use Vocabulary

Fill in the missing term in each sentence, using the correct vocabulary term from the Word Bank.

1. _____ is the freedom of people to govern themselves.

2. The Battle of Saratoga was a _____ in the war.

3. The colonists had no _____ in the British Parliament.

4. The Daughters of Liberty chose to _____ British goods.

5. A _____ is a sudden, complete change of government.

Word Bank

representation p. 235

boycott p. 236

revolution p. 242

independence p. 245

Patriot p. 251

turning point p. 254

Think About It

Circle the letter of the correct answer.

6. Great Britain increased its control over the colonies because it wanted to—

  A give land to settlers

  B trade with American Indians

  C restore French rule

  D remain a world power

7. King George III issued the Proclamation of 1763 because he wanted to—

  F take land from American Indians

  G stop a war with American Indians

  H give land back to France

  J stop colonists from settling lands west of the Appalachians

8. The colonists were angered by the new British tax laws because the colonists—

  A did not have to follow British laws

  B supplied Great Britain with raw materials

  C had no representation in Parliament

  D did not have money to pay the taxes

9. How did colonists show their dissatisfaction with British taxes?

  F They left the colonies.

  G They elected new tax collectors.

  H They boycotted British goods.

  J They bought goods from other countries.

10.

> 1. The Stamp Act
> 2. The French and Indian War
> 3. The Proclamation of 1763
> 4. The Boston Massacre

  What is the correct order for this list?

  A 1, 2, 3, 4

  B 3, 1, 4, 2

  C 2, 3, 1, 4

  D 4, 3, 2, 1

11.

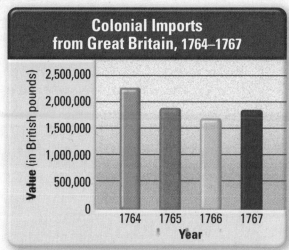

Colonial Imports from Great Britain, 1764–1767

The value of colonial imports from Great Britain fell between 1764 and 1766 because many colonists—

  F boycotted British goods

  G started manufacturing products

  H began buying goods from France

  J produced more crops

12.

Which 1770 event is shown in this picture by Paul Revere?

  A Stamp Act

  B Battle of Lexington

  C Boston Massacre

  D Boston Tea Party

13.

"We hold these truths to be self-evi-dent, that all men are created equal, that they are endowed [provided] by their Creator with certain unalienable rights ... "

What are the "unalienable rights" described in this excerpt from the Declaration of Independence?

F Freedoms of speech and religion

G Life, liberty, and the pursuit of happiness

H The power to vote and assemble

J Representation in Parliament and Congress

14. Which best explains the meaning of Patrick Henry's "Give me liberty or give me death" slogan?

A The colonists had to choose right away between liberty or death.

B The colonists should fight for their freedom.

C The colonists should support the king and Parliament.

D The colonists should not have to fight for their freedom.

15. The first MAJOR battle of the American Revolution was the—

F Battle of Lexington

G Battle of Bunker Hill

H Battle of Concord

J Battle of Yorktown

16. Who was chosen to be the commander of the Continental Army?

A Samuel Adams

B Thomas Gage

C George Mason

D George Washington

17.

Cause		Effect
British soldiers lost the Battle of Saratoga	→	?

Which effect replaces the question mark?

F France decided to help the Americans.

G France decided to help the British.

H The British army surrendered.

J Parliament declared war.

18.

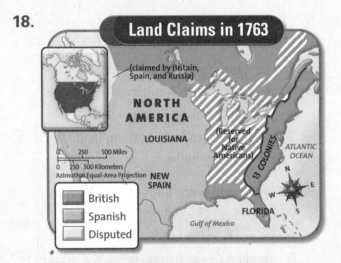

Land Claims in 1763

Land Claims in 1783

What areas shown on the maps changed very little between 1763 and 1783?

A The areas claimed by Great Britain

B The disputed lands

C The areas claimed by Spain

D Florida

19.

The American Revolution

1770   1780   1790

1775 The Battle of Bunker Hill is fought

1777 The Americans win the Battle of Saratoga

1781 The last major battle of the war is fought at Yorktown

What battle shown in the time line above was fought in 1781?

F   The Battle of Lexington

G   The Battle of Bunker Hill

H   The Battle of Yorktown

J   The Battle of Saratoga

20. Which European country helped the Americans win the Battle of Yorktown?

A   Portugal

B   Spain

C   France

D   Germany

21. As a result of the American Revolution and the Treaty of Paris—

F   the United States became an independent country

G   France became part of Great Britain

H   Spain took control of the southern colonies

J   Canada fell under the control of the United States

Answer these questions.

22. What effect did new ideas about government and independence have on people in the colonies?

_____

_____

_____

_____

23. How do you think that the ideas in the Declaration of Independence affect people's lives today?

_____

_____

_____

_____

24. How were the perspectives of Patriots different from those of Loyalists?

_____

_____

_____

_____

There's a party going on over here.

HMH

The American Revolution has begun, and you and Eco are right in the middle of the action. Join the cause as spies working on the side of the Patriots. You're not the only spies in town, though! Let's hope the two of you aren't betrayed and captured by Great Britain's army! Play the game now online.

Show What You Know

Writing Write a Speech

Imagine that you are a soldier at Valley Forge. Write a speech to lift the spirits of the other soldiers. Tell why being a soldier in the Continental Army is important. Describe the actions of Great Britain that caused you to join the fight for independence. Tell why you are fighting and what you hope to accomplish.

Activity Create a Newspaper

Publish a colonial newspaper that tells about the events leading up to the American Revolution and how the colonists won their freedom. Decide which people and events you will report on in your newspaper. Use articles, editorials, letters to the editor, and cartoons to tell the story of the revolution.

The New Nation

Independence Day fireworks over the United States Capitol, in Washington, D.C.

Spotlight on Standards

THE BIG IDEA Government leaders often have to overcome differences to work for the common good of the country.

SOL **HISTORY AND SOCIAL SCIENCE SOL**

USI.1a, USI.1b, USI.1c, USI.1d, USI.1f, USI.1h, USI.7a, USI.7b, USI.7c

Set the Stage

Study the map. Circle the landform that formed the western boundary of the Louisiana Purchase.

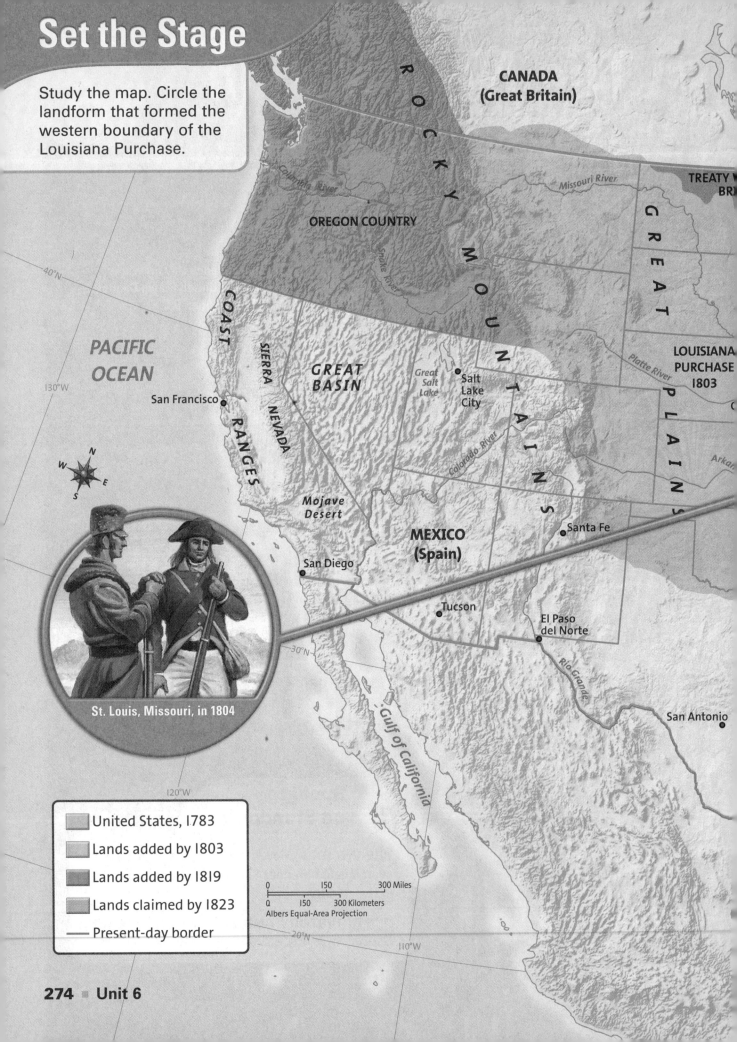

CANADA
(Great Britain)

ROCKY MOUNTAINS

Columbia River

Missouri River

TREATY W
BR

OREGON COUNTRY

Snake River

GREAT PLAINS

PACIFIC
OCEAN

COAST RANGES

SIERRA NEVADA

GREAT BASIN

Great Salt Lake

Salt Lake City

LOUISIANA PURCHASE 1803

Platte River

San Francisco

Colorado River

Arkan

Mojave Desert

MEXICO
(Spain)

Santa Fe

San Diego

Tucson

El Paso del Norte

Rio Grande

San Antonio

Gulf of California

St. Louis, Missouri, in 1804

United States, 1783

Lands added by 1803

Lands added by 1819

Lands claimed by 1823

Present-day border

0   150   300 Miles
0   150   300 Kilometers
Albers Equal-Area Projection

40°N
130°W
120°W
30°N
20°N
110°W

274 ■ Unit 6

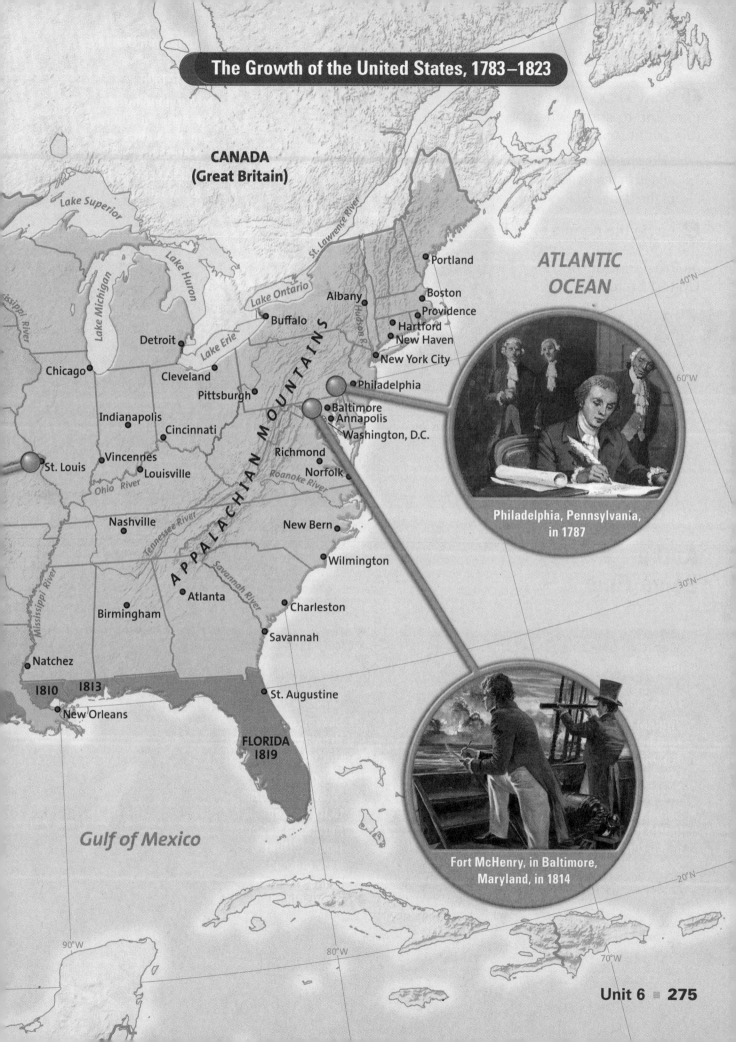

The Growth of the United States, 1783–1823

CANADA
(Great Britain)

Lake Superior

Lake Michigan

Lake Huron

St. Lawrence River

Lake Ontario

Lake Erie

Mississippi River

Portland

Boston

Albany

Providence

Buffalo

Hartford
New Haven

Detroit

Hudson R.

New York City

Chicago

Cleveland

Philadelphia

Pittsburgh

Baltimore
Annapolis

Indianapolis

Washington, D.C.

Cincinnati

Richmond

St. Louis

Vincennes

Roanoke River

Louisville

Norfolk

Ohio River

Nashville

New Bern

Tennessee River

Wilmington

Savannah River

Birmingham

Atlanta

Charleston

Mississippi River

Savannah

Natchez

St. Augustine

1810   1813

New Orleans

FLORIDA
1819

Gulf of Mexico

ATLANTIC
OCEAN

40°N

60°W

30°N

20°N

Philadelphia, Pennsylvania,
in 1787

Fort McHenry, in Baltimore,
Maryland, in 1814

90°W   80°W   70°W

Set the Stage

1 Draw an *X* on the time line to show where this event would appear:

1791 The Bill of Rights is added to the Constitution of the United States

2 Circle the names of the people who served as President of the United States.

1731–1806
- Maryland farmer who taught himself mathematics and astronomy
- Helped survey the land for Washington, D.C.

The New Nation

1777 The Articles of Confederation are written, p. 282

1788 The United States Constitution is ratified, p. 292

1800 The Federal government moves to the District of Columbia, p. 297

1775

1795

At the Same Time

1789 The French Revolution begins

1804 Haiti gains independence from France

James Madison

1751–1836
- Virginia leader who helped organize the Constitutional Convention
- Served as the fourth President of the United States

James Monroe

1758–1831
- Served as the fifth President of the United States
- Announced the Monroe Doctrine, to try to stop European nations from starting new colonies in the Western Hemisphere

John Adams

1735–1826
- Served as the second President of the United States
- Prevented a war between the United States and France in 1798

Abigail Adams

1744–1818
- Wife of President John Adams
- Wanted the Constitution of the United States to include more rights for women

1803 The United States makes the Louisiana Purchase, p. 302

1812 The United States goes to war against Great Britain, p. 303

1823 The Monroe Doctrine is issued, p. 304

1815

1835

1810 The Mexican Revolution begins

1822 Freed African Americans start the colony of Liberia in Africa

1834 Slavery is abolished in Great Britain

Meriwether Lewis

1774–1809
- Captain in the United States Army
- Explored the lands of the Louisiana Purchase with William Clark

Francis Scott Key

1779–1843
- Worked as a lawyer in Washington, D.C.
- Wrote "The Star-Spangled Banner" after the Battle of Fort McHenry

Preview Vocabulary

constitution

The nation's founders wrote a **constitution**, or plan of government, for the United States. p. 282

convention

Leaders attended a **convention**. At this important meeting, they discussed many issues. p. 285

ratify

Delaware was the first state to **ratify** the Constitution. Rhode Island was the last to vote in favor of it. p. 292

Cabinet

The members of George Washington's **Cabinet** were his most important advisors. p. 296

political party

The two major **political parties** in the United States want to elect people who support their policies. p. 298

nationalism

After the War of 1812, Americans felt a new sense of **nationalism**. They had great pride in their country. p. 303

Reading Social Studies

Generalize

LEARN

When you **generalize**, you make a statement that shows how different facts in a piece of writing are related. Being able to generalize can help you better understand and remember what you read. Words such as *most, many, some, generally,* and *usually* can help you make generalizations and identify them.

Facts

Information in passage	Information in passage	Information in passage

Generalization

General statement about the information

PRACTICE

Write a generalization about each paragraph. The first generalization has been written for you.

> After the American Revolution, each state had its own laws and money. Most people thought of themselves as citizens of a state first and as citizens of the United States second. Some Americans doubted that the states could ever agree to be part of the same country.   **Facts**

Generalization: In general, the United States was not a strongly united nation.   **Generalization**

Two leaders argued about what was best for the United States. Alexander Hamilton wanted a stronger central government. Thomas Jefferson wanted a central government with less power. They had to work together to solve their differences to create a plan of government for the United States.

Generalization: _____

Read the article. Then complete the activities below.

The First Political Parties

People in the new United States had different ideas about what kind of government the nation should have. These differences led to the creation of the first political parties in the United States. A political party is a group of people who share ideas about how the government should work.

People who wanted a strong federal government formed the Federalist party. They pictured a country with large, bustling cities full of trade. Wealthy merchants, business owners, and some shopkeepers supported the Federalist party. So did some rich plantation owners in the South.

People who wanted to keep the government small and simple formed the Democratic-Republican party. They were mostly farmers or people from small communities. The Democratic-Republicans pictured a country where most people lived in small towns. They wanted government to stay close to the people it served.

Over time, the names and ideas of political parties in the United States have changed. However, there have usually been only two major political parties. Today, most government leaders belong to either the Democratic party or the Republican party.

1. **Circle the sentence that supports the generalization that many Federalists were wealthy business owners.**

2. **From the third paragraph, what generalization can you make about the Democratic-Republicans?**

   _____

   _____

   _____

3. **Underline the sentence that supports the generalization that political parties change as the United States grows and changes.**

The Articles of Confederation

The Americans had fought hard to win independence from Great Britain. However, the work of making a new country had just begun. The first order of business was to strengthen the national government. **Think about why people would want a stronger national government.**

Nassau Hall, in Princeton, New Jersey, served as the United States capitol for five months in 1783.

ESSENTIAL QUESTIONS

✔ What were the basic weaknesses of the Articles of Confederation?
✔ What events led to the development of the Constitution of the United States?
✔ What people helped develop the Constitution of the United States?

HISTORY AND SOCIAL SCIENCE SOL
USI.1a, USI.1d, USI.1f, USI.7a, USI.7b

TextWork

1 Scan the text. Underline the name of the first plan of government for the United States.

2 Why were the states afraid of a strong national government?

Because they don't want to Losse their goverment because than they have to listen to the King George III.

3 (Focus Skill) Write a sentence that makes a generalization about the powers of Congress under the Articles of Confederation.

The Articles of confederation is the Main socre of the goverment

4 Study the flag on page 283. How is it different from today's United States flag?

Because it has a Eagle on the flag and toady it doesn't have a Eagle on it.

The Articles of Confederation

In 1777, while the American Revolution was being fought, the Continental Congress drafted a **constitution** for the United States. That plan of government was called the Articles of Confederation. It established the powers of the new national, or central, government.

The Articles of Confederation were approved by all 13 states and went into effect in 1781. Under the Articles, the 13 states would work together to settle national issues. However, the national government was weak, and it could not work effectively.

Weaknesses of the Articles

Americans did not want to give one person too much authority. That person might become too much like the British king. For that reason, the Articles of Confederation did not provide for an executive or a judicial branch. There was no single national leader, such as a president, and there was no national court system.

Under the Articles of Confederation, the states selected representatives to meet in a Congress. Each state, whether large or small, had one vote. Representatives from at least 9 of the 13 states had to approve any law before Congress could pass it. However, the representatives rarely agreed. No state wanted to be controlled by the other states. Even if representatives in the Congress approved a law, they did not have the power to enforce it.

The Congress could not raise an army without the states' permission. The Congress could declare war, make treaties, and borrow money. However, it could not collect taxes or regulate commerce, or trade. To cover the government's expenses, the Congress could only ask the states for money. It could not force them to pay. Many states printed money. However, this money was not always accepted in other states. There was no common currency that could be used throughout the nation.

The Articles of EIP CONFEDERATION

The Articles of Confederation

STRENGTHS	WEAKNESSES
• Helped keep the states united during the American Revolution • Made laws for the new nation	• Provided for a weak national government • Gave Congress no power to tax or regulate commerce among the states • Provided for no common currency • Each state had one vote in Congress, regardless of population • Provided for no executive or judicial branch

Congress issued money, called Continentals, that had little value.

United States flag, 1781

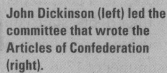

John Dickinson (left) led the committee that wrote the Articles of Confederation (right).

ARTICLES
OF
Confederation
AND
Perpetual Union
BETWEEN THE
STATES

The national government could not stop angry farmers from taking over an arsenal in Massachusetts.

Shays's Rebellion

While the Congress struggled to pay its debts from the American Revolution, people grew frustrated. Although many Americans were poor, they had to pay high state taxes. People often had to borrow money and go into debt. When they could not repay their debts, state courts took away their farms or businesses and sent people to prison.

In the summer of 1786, poor farmers in Massachusetts protested by preventing the courts from meeting. Armed with pitchforks and guns, they shut down courthouses and destroyed debt records.

In January 1787, another mob of farmers, led by Daniel Shays, tried to take over a Massachusetts **arsenal**, or weapons storehouse. Because there was no national army to defend the arsenal, the state government had to send the militia to stop Shays. During the attack on the arsenal, four of Shays's followers were killed. Shays's Rebellion made some people think that the national government could not keep order.

TextWork

5 Why did Daniel Shays and other farmers rebel against the government?

Because when the People are Poor they have to Pay the high taxes.

6 Use the word *arsenal* in a sentence about Shays's Rebellion.

When Daniel Shays was arsenal because the bristh King was taxeing on them.

Ideas for Change

Weaknesses in the Articles of Confederation convinced James Madison of Virginia and other leaders that the country needed a stronger national government and a new constitution. Others did not want a stronger government. Patrick Henry of Virginia was among those who wanted to keep the Articles of Confederation as they were. Henry argued that Americans had fought the British because they did not want a powerful government ruling their lives.

In May 1787, delegates from 12 states assembled in a **convention**, or an important meeting, at the Pennsylvania State House. They chose George Washington to be president of the Constitutional Convention, as this meeting later was known.

When the Constitutional Convention began, the delegates agreed to keep their discussions secret. They felt that talking in private would allow them to speak freely and make good decisions. Windows in the State House were covered, and guards stood at the doors. After four months of discussion, the delegates had written the new Constitution of the United States.

7 How was James Madison's view of the Articles of Confederation different than Patrick Henry's view?

James madison's View was that he wanted others form a goverment. patick Henry view is that he had a spech of Give me Death or give liba,

8 Travel was slower in the 1780s than it is today, and there were often not enough representatives present for either Congress or the Constitutional Convention to meet. Study the map and the graph. About how long would it take a delegate to travel in a horse-drawn carriage from Richmond to the Constitutional Convention?

2 1/2 Hours

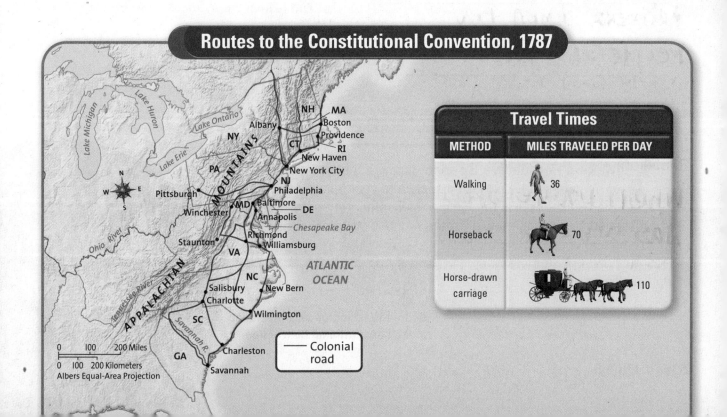

Routes to the Constitutional Convention, 1787

Travel Times	
METHOD	**MILES TRAVELED PER DAY**
Walking	36
Horseback	70
Horse-drawn carriage	110

Colonial road

0 100 200 Miles
0 100 200 Kilometers
Albers Equal-Area Projection

1. **SUMMARIZE** What were the main weaknesses of the Articles of Confederation?

_____

_____

_____

_____

2. Use the word **convention** in a sentence about improving the Articles of Confederation.

_____

_____

_____

3. How did Shays's rebellion make people think that the national government was weak?

_____

_____

_____

Circle the letter of the correct answer.

4. Which of the following was NOT a part of the Articles of Confederation?

   A Voters in each state elected leaders to serve in Congress.

   B The Congress served as the government of the United States.

   C The size of the states determined the number of votes in Congress.

   D State leaders kept a lot of power.

5. Under the Articles of Confederation, which of these powers did Congress have?

   F To collect taxes

   G To declare war

   H To create an army

   J To enforce the laws

6. Who supported a strong national government?

   A James Madison

   B Patrick Henry

   C Daniel Shays

   D The British king

writing

Make a Persuasive Speech Imagine that you are a member of Congress in 1787. Make a speech to your fellow delegates about the weaknesses of the Articles of Confederation. In your speech, present some ideas for how to fix the Articles or propose the idea of writing a new constitution.

George Washington was president of the Constitutional Convention.

The Constitution of the United States

The delegates at the Constitutional Convention had different ideas about government. The delegates often had to **compromise**, or give up some of what they wanted, in order to create the Constitution of the United States. The Preamble, or first part of the Constitution, gives its main purposes, including securing peace and freedom. **Think about how compromising is an important skill for resolving disagreements.**

The National Constitution Center, in Philadelphia

ESSENTIAL QUESTIONS

✓ What events led to the development of the Constitution of the United States?

✓ What people helped develop the Constitution of the United States?

 HISTORY AND SOCIAL SCIENCE SOL
USI.1a, USI.1b, USI.1c, USI.1d, USI.7b

Federal System of Government

POWERS OF THE NATIONAL GOVERNMENT

- Control trade between states and with foreign countries
- Create and maintain an army and a navy
- Conduct a census, or population count
- Print and coin money
- Admit new states
- Declare war and make peace
- Make laws for immigration and citizenship

SHARED POWERS

- Collect taxes
- Set up court systems
- Establish banks
- Borrow money
- Make laws to provide for public health and welfare

Washington, D.C. ★

POWERS OF THE STATE GOVERNMENTS

- Set up public schools
- Set up local governments
- Conduct elections
- Control trade within the state
- Make laws for marriage and divorce
- Set qualifications for voting

 **TextWork**

❶ Underline the sentence that describes the first goal of the delegates at the Constitutional Convention. How did that goal change?

Write a completely
new plan of goverment
completely new plan of goverment

❷ Write a sentence describing how power is shared in a federal system.

Federal system
in which the national
state goverment share
power.

❸ Study the chart. Circle two powers shared by the states and the federal government.

The Work Begins

When the Constitutional Convention began, the delegates' only goal was to improve the Articles of Confederation. However, they soon decided to write a completely new plan of government.

A Federal System

First, the delegates debated how much power should be given to the new federal, or national, government. Some delegates thought there should be a strong federal government. Others believed that the states should have more power.

The delegates agreed to create a **federal system** in which the national and state governments would share power. The states would keep some powers. However, the federal government would have the power over matters that affected the nation as a whole. The Constitution of the United States would become the supreme law of the land. It would serve as the foundation of the American republic. In a **republic**, the people choose representatives to run the government.

A Major Debate

During the convention, the delegates often disagreed with one another. One major disagreement was about how large and small states should be represented in the new government.

Edmund Randolph and the other Virginia delegates introduced a proposal called the Virginia Plan. Under this plan, Congress would have two parts, or houses. The number of representatives that a state would have in each house would be based on the state's population.

William Paterson of New Jersey accused the Virginia Plan of "striking at the existence of the lesser states." Delegates from small states worried that the plan would give large states control of Congress.

Paterson offered a different proposal, called the New Jersey Plan. Under this plan, Congress would have one house, in which all states would be equally represented. This plan would give small states the same number of representatives as large states.

TextWork

4 How did Edmund Randolph's view of representation in Congress differ from that of William Paterson?

Edmund Randolph want two house and William Paterson wanted 1 house

5 Why do you think the Virginia delegates wanted a state's population to determine how many representatives it had in Congress?

Because virginia want more reprensatres because alot of people that live in virginia.

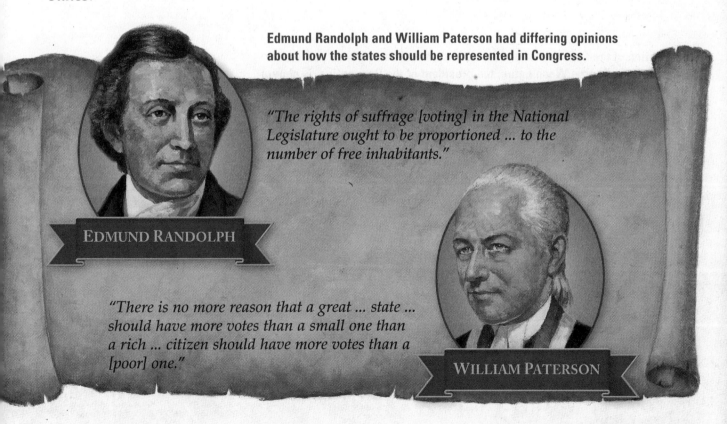

Edmund Randolph and William Paterson had differing opinions about how the states should be represented in Congress.

"The rights of suffrage [voting] in the National Legislature ought to be proportioned ... to the number of free inhabitants."

EDMUND RANDOLPH

"There is no more reason that a great ... state ... should have more votes than a small one than a rich ... citizen should have more votes than a [poor] one."

WILLIAM PATERSON

TextWork

6 How did the delegates settle the issue of representation in Congress?

Each state had 2
Sentoners and have
Represenfaves Based
on the population.

7 Study the painting. Why do you think George Washington is shown seated on a stage?

The president of
the Convention.

The Great Compromise

For weeks, the delegates argued about how the states would be represented in Congress. Finally, a committee, led by Roger Sherman of Connecticut and other delegates, presented a new plan. It is known as the Great Compromise.

The Great Compromise was based on having a two-house Congress, made up of a House of Representatives and a Senate. The Great Compromise also decided how many votes each state had in the Senate and the House of Representatives. In the House of Representatives, the number of representatives for each state would vary. It would be based on the state's population. In the Senate, all states would be equally represented, with two senators each. This plan was adopted.

At first, delegates from the large states thought the compromise gave too much power to the small states. Congress decided that only the House of Representatives would be able to propose tax bills. A **bill** is an idea for a new law.

This painting of the Constitutional Convention was made nearly 80 years after the convention. George Washington, the president of the Convention, is shown seated on the stage.

BRANCHES OF GOVERNMENT

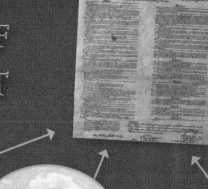

The Constitution divides the federal government into three branches.

The legislative branch writes the laws that are used by the entire nation.

The executive branch enforces, or carries out, national laws.

The judicial branch makes sure that laws follow the Constitution.

Three Branches

The delegates divided the national government into three separate branches—legislative, executive, and judicial. Each branch has different government powers. This **separation of powers** helps prevent any one branch from controlling the government. The legislative branch is Congress, which makes laws, raises an army and a navy, declares wars, and coins and prints money. The executive branch is led by the President. The President oversees the day-to-day business of the national government, deals with other countries, and leads the military. The judicial branch is made up of all the federal courts. This branch sees that laws are carried out fairly. The Supreme Court is the nation's highest court.

Each branch of government has a way to check, or limit, the power of the other two. For example, the President can **veto**, or reject, a law that Congress proposes. Congress can cancel a President's veto by a two-thirds majority vote.

TextWork

8 What generalization can you make about the role of the three branches of the national government?

There Eqaul and they Share power.

9 Circle the description of the main powers of the legislative branch. How can the President check the powers of Congress?

With the veto.

10 Study the quote from Franklin. What do you think he meant?

There good things comeing for the contary.

11 Study the table. Circle the state that was the ninth to ratify the Constitution. Why was this state's vote important to the Constitution?

The last vote put into effect.

Constitution Ratification Vote

STATE	DATE	VOTES FOR	VOTES AGAINST
Delaware	Dec. 7, 1787	30	0
Pennsylvania	Dec. 12, 1787	46	23
New Jersey	Dec. 18, 1787	30	0
Georgia	Jan. 2, 1788	26	0
Connecticut	Jan. 9, 1788	128	40
Massachusetts	Feb. 6, 1788	187	168
Maryland	Apr. 28, 1788	63	11
South Carolina	May 23, 1788	149	73
New Hampshire	June 21, 1788	57	47
Virginia	June 25, 1788	89	79
New York	July 26, 1788	30	27
North Carolina	Nov. 21, 1788	194	77
Rhode Island	May 29, 1790	34	32

Ratification

At the end of the convention, delegates approved the Constitution and signed it on September 17, 1787. In 2004, Congress declared every September 17 as Constitution Day. On this day, students across the country learn about the Constitution.

During the convention, Benjamin Franklin often looked at the sun design on the back of the chair used by George Washington. Afterward, he said, "I have the happiness to know that it is a rising and not a setting sun."

Nine of the thirteen states still had to **ratify**, or vote in favor of, the Constitution before it could become law. In each state, there was much debate over the new Constitution. Some delegates thought it gave too much power to the federal government. Other delegates said they would approve the Constitution only if a bill of rights were added to it. Supporters of the Constitution promised to propose a bill of rights after the document was ratified. On June 21, 1788, New Hampshire became the ninth state to ratify the Constitution—the last vote needed to put it into effect.

The Constitution of the United States is kept at the National Archives in Washington, D.C.

Freedom of assembly

Freedom of worship

Freedom of speech

The Bill of Rights gives people in the United States freedom of religion and freedom of speech. It also says that people can hold meetings to discuss problems and share information.

The Bill of Rights

In 1791, as promised, ten **amendments**, or changes, were added to the Constitution. These 10 amendments, called the Bill of Rights, provide a written guarantee of individual rights. The Bill of Rights is based in part on the Virginia Declaration of Rights by George Mason and the Virginia Statute for Religious Freedom by Thomas Jefferson.

The First Amendment protects freedom of speech, freedom of the press, freedom of religion, freedom to petition the government, and the right to assemble, or gather. The Second Amendment protects the right to have weapons. The Third Amendment says the government cannot make people house soldiers in peacetime. The Fourth Amendment protects against unfair searches.

The Fifth through Eighth Amendments deal with **due process of law**, or the right to a fair trial. The Ninth Amendment says people have rights not listed in the Constitution. The Tenth Amendment says the government can do only what is listed in the Constitution. All other authority belongs to the states or to the people.

 TextWork

12 Which came first, the Constitution or the Bill of Rights?

Bill of rights

13 Why is the Bill of Rights important?

Guarantee of Individual Rights.

14 Why do you think it is important for citizens today to know what their rights are?

People get fair treated

1. **SUMMARIZE** How was the new Constitution developed at the Constitutional Convention?

   Thorgh compromise

2. Explain the meaning of the word **ratify**.

   To sign to law.

3. Why is separation of powers among the branches of government important?

   It is styems of checks and baluces

Circle the letter of the correct answer.

4. Why did United States leaders want to write a new constitution?

   A They wanted to make the national government stronger.

   B They wanted to give the national government less power.

   C They wanted to form a monarchy.

   D They wanted to give the states more power.

5. Some people wanted a bill of rights in order to—

   F protect the federal government's power

   G explain the Constitution

   H give more power to the states

   J protect people's rights

Match the delegate's name on the left with his plan's name on the right.

6. Roger Sherman   the Virginia Plan

7. William Paterson   the Great Compromise

8. Edmund Randolph   the New Jersey Plan

writing

Write a Newspaper Article Imagine that you are a newspaper reporter at the Constitutional Convention. Write an article describing the debate over representation in Congress. Tell how the issue was settled.

Reading news of the Constitution's ratification

Presidents Washington and Adams

The first two Presidents were George Washington and John Adams. Each of them worked with Congress to help establish a strong national government. **Think about some of the challenges involved in setting up a new government.**

George Washington was sworn in as President on April 30, 1789.

ESSENTIAL QUESTION

✓ What were the major national issues and events faced by the first five Presidents?

HISTORY AND SOCIAL SCIENCE SOL
USI.1a, USI.1d, USI.7c

The President's House and Capitol Building still stand where they are shown on this original plan of Washington D.C.

EIP

President Washington

TextWork

1 Study the plan of Washington, D.C. How can you tell where the important government buildings are located in the city?

_____

_____

_____

2 Use the word *Cabinet* in a sentence about Washington's presidency.

_____

_____

3 Circle the sentences that identify some of the early accomplishments of Washington's Cabinet departments.

Washington's Presidency

In 1789, George Washington became the first President of the United States, and John Adams became the first Vice President. Washington helped organize the new government. He also set examples that all future Presidents would follow.

Setting up the Federal Courts and the Cabinet

One of Congress's first actions was to pass the Judiciary Act. This law set up the federal court system and decided the number of Supreme Court justices. Washington named John Jay of New York to be the Supreme Court's first chief justice.

Washington set up a State Department, Treasury Department, and War Department. Together, the heads of these departments became known as the **Cabinet**. Cabinet members advise the President.

During Washington's presidency, the State Department helped form relationships with other countries. The Treasury Department helped set up a new banking system, new tax laws, and the printing and coining of money. The War Department began to build the nation's military.

Planning a New National Capital

In 1790, members of Congress agreed to build a new national capital on land beside the Potomac River. George Washington chose the location for the city that bears his name—Washington, D.C. Washington hired Pierre Charles L'Enfant to design the capital. Later, a surveyor named Andrew Ellicott and his assistant, Benjamin Banneker, took over the job. Banneker, a free African American, helped complete the designs for the city.

A Second Term for Washington

In 1791, while Washington was President, the Bill of Rights was added to the Constitution. The next year, Washington was elected to a second term. Four years later, many people wanted him to run for a third term, but he refused. Washington did not think that a President should hold power for life. His decision set an example for future Presidents.

TextWork

4 (Focus Skill) Write a generalization about the presidency of George Washington, based on the following facts.

A. The Judiciary Act was passed during Washington's presidency.

B. Washington chose a Cabinet to advise him.

C. Washington chose the location for the new national capital.

Generalization: _____

_____

_____

Biography

Responsibility

Benjamin Banneker

At a time when African Americans had few rights, Benjamin Banneker became a respected scientist, inventor, and author. He taught himself mathematics and science and was a skilled astronomer and surveyor. He also wrote almanacs. However, Banneker is best remembered for helping plan Washington, D.C. Today, the nation's capital stands as a monument to the hard work of planners such as Banneker.

Time

1731		1806
Born		Died

1791 Banneker helps plan Washington, D.C.

1792 Banneker publishes an almanac

TextWork

5 What was important about the way that John Adams became President?

_____

_____

6 How did John Adams's perspective on the power of the central government differ from that of Thomas Jefferson?

_____

_____

_____

_____

Adams's Presidency

On March 4, 1797, John Adams became the second President of the United States, and Thomas Jefferson became the Vice President. The day Adams took office was an important one—it marked the first time the United States changed leaders. The change was peaceful.

A Two-Party System

In the election of 1796, Adams had run against Jefferson for President. Adams and Jefferson belonged to different political parties. A **political party** is a group that tries to elect officials who will support its policies. The two-party system emerged during the Adams presidency. That system continues today. The President belongs to one of two major political parties.

John Adams belonged to the Federalist party. He favored a stronger national government. Thomas Jefferson belonged to the Democratic-Republican party. He wanted to limit the national government's power.

PRESIDENT JOHN ADAMS

This pitcher celebrates the election of John Adams (left) as President in 1796.

Relations with France and Great Britain

During the presidencies of Washington and Adams, Great Britain was often at war with France. Some people thought that the United States should support Great Britain because it was the United States' closest trading partner. Others wanted the United States to favor the French because France had supported the American Revolution.

President Washington thought the United States should remain neutral, or not take sides, in the conflict. When Adams became President, he also tried to follow Washington's policy. In 1798, Adams was able to prevent the United States from going to war with France. However, he urged Congress to develop a stronger navy to protect American merchants from French attacks at sea.

During Adams's presidency, the national capital moved to Washington, D.C. John and Abigail Adams were the first couple to live in the White House. Many Americans were unhappy with Adams. When Adams ran for reelection in 1800, he lost to Thomas Jefferson.

 **TextWork**

7 How did people's views on the United States' relations with France and Great Britain differ?

_____

_____

_____

8 Underline the sentences that explain how the policies of Presidents Washington and Adams were similar.

9 What action did Adams take to protect United States merchants at sea?

_____

_____

The White House was still under construction when John and Abigail Adams moved in. Abigail Adams supported equal rights for women. In 1776, she had wanted Congress to "Remember the Ladies" in planning a new constitution.

Lesson 3 Review

1. **SUMMARIZE** Name one accomplishment of President Washington and one of President Adams.

   _____

   _____

   _____

   _____

2. Write a sentence explaining the differences in the first two **political parties**.

   _____

   _____

   _____

   _____

   _____

Circle the letter of the correct answer.

3. Why was the Judiciary Act important?

   A It allowed petitioning the government to change laws.

   B It ratified the Bill of Rights.

   C It set up the federal court system.

   D It protected freedom of speech.

4. John Adams believed in—

   F a stronger central government

   G a weaker central government

   H developing stronger ties with France

   J starting a war with Great Britain

5. During John Adams's presidency, the national capital moved to—

   A New York City

   B Washington, D.C.

   C Philadelphia

   D Baltimore

Match the Cabinet department named on the left with an accomplishment described on the right.

6. State Department   began to build the nation's military

7. Treasury Department   established ties with other countries

8. War Department   set up a national bank system

activity

Design a Campaign Poster Choose one of the two political parties in the presidential campaign of 1800. Design a campaign poster that tells how that party differs from the other. Illustrate the poster with drawings.

A campaign banner from the 1800 election

Presidents Jefferson, Madison, and Monroe

Presidents Thomas Jefferson, James Madison, and James Monroe were all from Virginia. In fact, four of the first five Presidents of the United States were Virginians. Only President Adams was not. During their presidencies, these five Presidents made decisions that strengthened the national government and helped the nation grow in size and power. **Think about why leaders would want to increase the size of the country.**

The Jefferson Memorial, in Washington, D.C.

ESSENTIAL QUESTION

✓ What were the major national issues and events faced by the first five Presidents?

HISTORY AND SOCIAL SCIENCE SOL
USI.1c, USI.1h, USI.7c

Daniel Drake

Daniel Drake and his family moved to Kentucky when it was still part of the United States' western frontier. Daniel was a small child, but he worked very hard. He got up before sunrise to feed his family's horses, cows, and pigs.

Daniel did not go to school, but he studied his lessons at home. When he was fifteen, he became an apprentice to a doctor. In time, he became a doctor himself. Later, he moved to Cincinnati, Ohio, where he started a medical school.

Make It Relevant How were Daniel's chores different from the chores you do today?

 **TextWork**

❶ Scan the text. Underline the sentence that gives the effect of the Louisiana Purchase.

❷ Whom did Jefferson send to explore the lands of the Louisiana Purchase?

_____

_____

Thomas Jefferson

President Jefferson

In 1801, Thomas Jefferson became the third President of the United States. He hoped to expand the nation's borders. The United States had no port on the Gulf of Mexico. Farmers in Ohio, Kentucky, and other western areas had to ship crops down the Ohio and Mississippi Rivers to the port of New Orleans, which was controlled by Spain.

The Louisiana Purchase

In 1801, Spain gave New Orleans and the rest of Louisiana back to France. At the time, France was preparing for war with Great Britain and needed money. The United States bought Louisiana from France for $15 million. The sale, which came to be known as the Louisiana Purchase, more than doubled the size of the country. Little was known about the lands of the Louisiana Purchase, so Jefferson sent Meriwether Lewis and William Clark to explore the new lands west of the Mississippi River.

Madison's Presidency

In 1809, James Madison became the fourth President of the United States. Great Britain was again at war with France. To stop Americans from trading with its enemies, the British navy captured American trading ships. It also forced American sailors to work on British navy ships. This action, called **impressment**, angered many Americans.

In June 1812, Madison asked Congress to declare war on Great Britain. The war became known as the War of 1812. During the war, the British attacked Washington, D.C., and burned much of the city. When the British attacked Fort McHenry, in Baltimore, Francis Scott Key wrote the poem "The Star-Spangled Banner." It later became the national anthem, or national song, of the United States.

There was no clear winner of the War of 1812. However, the war caused European nations to gain respect for the United States. Americans felt a new sense of **nationalism**, or pride in their country.

James Madison

 TextWork

❸ Underline the sentence that gives the meaning of the word *impressment*.

❹ Study the excerpt from "The Star-Spangled Banner." What inspired Key to write it?

_____

_____

_____

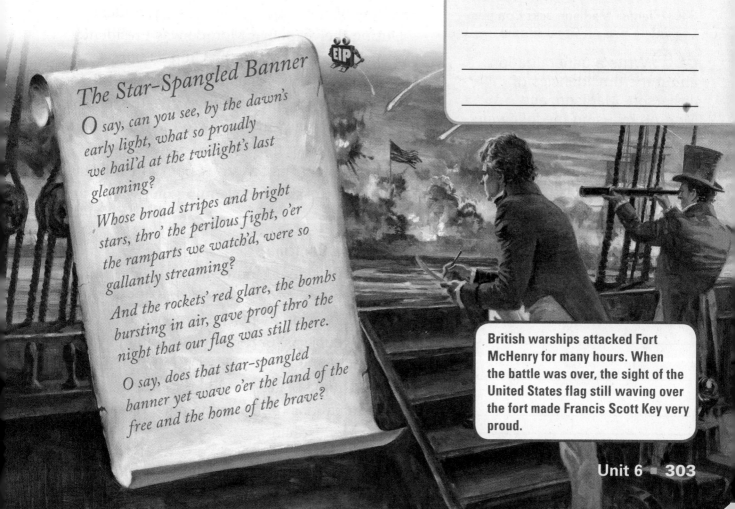

The Star-Spangled Banner

O say, can you see, by the dawn's early light, what so proudly we hail'd at the twilight's last gleaming?

Whose broad stripes and bright stars, thro' the perilous fight, o'er the ramparts we watch'd, were so gallantly streaming?

And the rockets' red glare, the bombs bursting in air, gave proof thro' the night that our flag was still there.

O say, does that star-spangled banner yet wave o'er the land of the free and the home of the brave?

British warships attacked Fort McHenry for many hours. When the battle was over, the sight of the United States flag still waving over the fort made Francis Scott Key very proud.

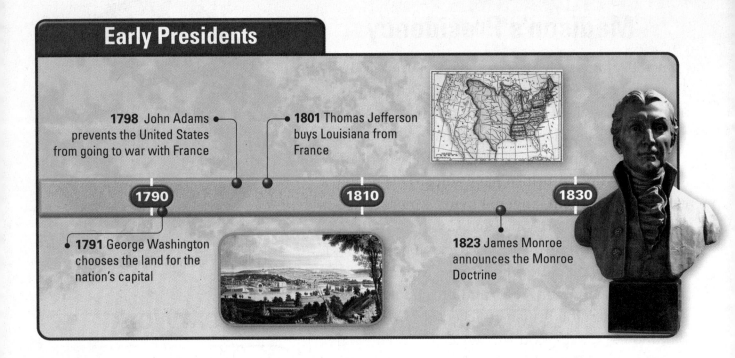

Early Presidents

1798 John Adams prevents the United States from going to war with France

1801 Thomas Jefferson buys Louisiana from France

1790

1810

1830

1791 George Washington chooses the land for the nation's capital

1823 James Monroe announces the Monroe Doctrine

TextWork

⑤ Place an *X* on the time line where this event would appear:

1812 James Madison asks Congress to delare war on Great Britain

⑥ 🌟 (Focus Skill) Write a generalization about the presidencies of Jefferson, Madison, and Monroe by using the following facts.

The Louisiana Purchase more than doubled the size of the United States.

During James Monroe's presidency, five states were added to the United States.

Generalization: _____

_____

_____

_____

Monroe's Presidency

In 1817, James Monroe became the fifth President of the United States. Monroe was a tobacco planter from Virginia. He had served as the country's Secretary of State during Madison's presidency.

During the years that Monroe was President, five states were added to the United States—Mississippi, Illinois, Alabama, Maine, and Missouri. Monroe also persuaded Spain to give the remaining lands it claimed in Florida to the United States. Monroe knew that if the United States was to keep growing, he had to stop Spain, Great Britain, France, and Russia from claiming more lands in the Americas.

The Monroe Doctrine

In 1823, President Monroe announced a policy now known as the Monroe Doctrine. It said that "the American continents . . . [are] not to be considered as subjects for future colonization by any European powers. . . ." This meant that, if necessary, the United States would go to war to stop European nations from starting new colonies in the Western Hemisphere.

1. **SUMMARIZE** What were the main accomplishments of Presidents Jefferson, Madison, and Monroe?

_____

_____

_____

_____

_____

2. Give some examples of how people can show feelings of **nationalism** today.

_____

_____

_____

_____

_____

Circle the letter of the correct answer.

3. Why did Jefferson purchase the Louisiana Territory from France?

   A To keep Louisiana out of Spanish control

   B To set up military headquarters

   C To establish a port for farmers

   D To improve relationships with Spain

4. The practice of forcing American sailors to work on British ships was known as—

   F nationalism

   G impressment

   H mutinies

   J a siege

5. Which President issued a doctrine stating that European nations must stop colonizing lands in the Americas?

   A John Adams

   B Thomas Jefferson

   C James Madison

   D James Monroe

Match the President on the left with an event on the right.

6. Thomas Jefferson   statehood for Illinois

7. James Madison   War of 1812

8. James Monroe   Louisiana Purchase

James Monroe

activity

Make a Poster Make a poster that highlights the accomplishments of Presidents Jefferson, Madison, and Monroe. Illustrate your poster with pictures and a time line.

Fun with Social Studies

Just the Facts

Trace a trail along the path that shows correct information about the Constitution. Circle the letters of the statements that are true. The circled letters will spell the answer to the question below.

START

The plan of government for the United States today

R

E Sets up a federal system

T Written by Daniel Shays

P Replaced the Articles of Confederation

U Three branches of government

U No guarantee of individual rights

C The President is head of the executive branch

I Each state has two senators

B Has a Bill of Rights

S People have rights not listed in the Constitution.

B

L Sets up a two-house Congress

A Ratified by all 13 states in 1788

We the People

S Each state has two representatives

FINISH

What are governments in which people elect their leaders?

_____

Under Construction

VOCABULARY

Finish building the terms on the left by adding the word blocks on the right.

FE_ _ _ _AL

AM_ _ _ _ _MENT

REPU _ _ _ _ _ C

_ _ _ _INET

CON _ _ _ _TION

_ _ _ _IFY

COM _ _ _ _MISE

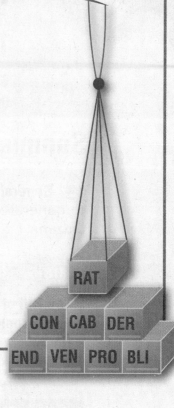

RAT

CON | CAB | DER

END | VEN | PRO | BLI

Whose Views?

Match each person with the bumper sticker he or she might own.

Francis Scott Key

Benjamin Banneker

Abigail Adams

James Monroe

Remember the **LADIES**

EUROPE KEEP OUT!

A **MAN**
A **PLAN**
A **CAPITAL**

Follow me to **FORT McHENRY**

Review and Test Prep

The Big Idea

Government leaders often have to overcome differences to work for the common good of the country.

Summarize the Unit

Generalize Complete the graphic organizer to show how to generalize information about the rights of United States citizens.

Facts

| The Bill of Rights lists people's basic rights. | The national government can only do what the Constitution allows. | People have many other rights not specifically listed in the Constitution. |

Generalization

_____

_____

Use Vocabulary

Fill in the missing terms, using vocabulary terms from the Word Bank.

1. A _____ tries to elect people who will support its policies.

2. The form of government in the United States is a _____.

3. Americans felt a sense of _____ after the War of 1812.

4. Nine of the thirteen states had to _____ the Constitution.

5. The Constitution can be changed through _____.

Word Bank

constitution p. 282

republic p. 288

ratify p. 292

amendments p. 293

political party p. 298

nationalism p. 303

Think About It

Circle the letter of the correct answer.

6. Which was NOT a weakness of the Articles of Confederation?

   A Congress had no power to collect taxes.

   B It gave each state one vote in Congress.

   C It provided for no common currency.

   D The executive branch was too powerful.

7. Which made Americans think that the central government was not strong enough?

   F Shays's Rebellion

   G The War of 1812

   H The Louisiana Purchase

   J The Monroe Doctrine

8. Who was elected president of the Constitutional Convention?

   A Benjamin Franklin

   B Patrick Henry

   C Edmund Randolph

   D George Washington

9.
   > • Control trade between states and with foreign countries
   > • Create and maintain an army and a navy
   > • Print and coin money
   > • Declare war and make peace

   Under the federal system of government, these are some of the powers that belong to—

   F city governments

   G state governments

   H the national government

   J a town government

10. Which settled the debate about how states should be represented in Congress?

    A The New Jersey Plan

    B The Great Compromise

    C The Three-Fifths Compromise

    D The Virginia Plan

11. In which part of government is the number of representatives based on the population of each state?

    F The Senate

    G The House of Representatives

    H The Cabinet

    J The Supreme Court

12.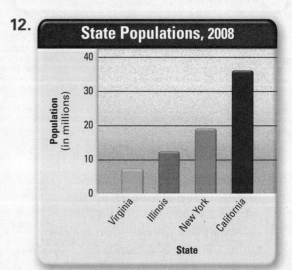

State Populations, 2008

Based on the graph, which state has the most representatives in the House of Representatives today?

    A Virginia

    B California

    C Illinois

    D New York

13. One generalization that can be made about the separation of powers is that it—

    F guarantees the individual rights of United States citizens

    G gives large and small states equal power

    H makes the President like a king

    J prevents the President from being like a king

14. The President can check the power of Congress by—

A proposing annual budgets

B choosing members of the Cabinet

C vetoing proposed laws

D appointing justices of the Supreme Court

15.

1. Delegates agree on the Great Compromise.
2. The Bill of Rights is added to the Constitution.
3. The Constitution is ratified.
4. George Washington becomes president of the Constitutional Convention.

What is the correct order of these events?

F 1, 2, 3, 4

G 4, 3, 2, 1

H 2, 4, 3, 1

J 4, 1, 3, 2

16.

"We the people of the United States, in order to form a more perfect Union ...do ordain and establish this Constitution for the United States of America."
-- Constitution of the United States

Which idea do these words illustrate?

A All people have certain rights.

B People form a government to help make their country a better place.

C All people are born free.

D Government should not tax without representation.

17. People wanted a bill of rights to—

F protect the government's power

G explain how bills became a law

H give more power to the states

J protect people's rights

18.

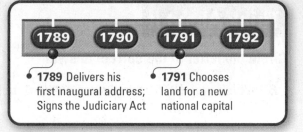

1789 Delivers his first inaugural address; Signs the Judiciary Act

1791 Chooses land for a new national capital

Who was President when these events occurred?

A George Washington

B John Adams

C Thomas Jefferson

D James Madison

19.

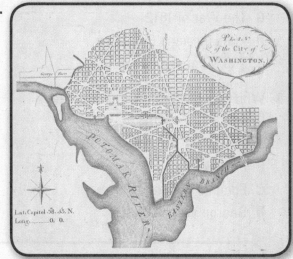

Who helped complete the design for this city?

F Francis Scott Key

G Benjamin Banneker

H Edmund Randolph

J William Paterson

20. Which of these was accomplished during the presidency of John Adams?

A The two-party system emerged.

B The Federal courts were established.

C Louisiana was purchased from France.

D The War of 1812 ended.

21.

The United States

United States, 1783

Louisiana Purchase, 1803

CANADA

ROCKY MOUNTAINS

Missouri

Platte R.

Mississippi R.

Colorado R.

Arkansas R.

Ohio R.

APPALACHIAN MOUNTAINS

MEXICO

PACIFIC OCEAN

ATLANTIC OCEAN

0   200   800 Miles
0   200   800 Kilometers
Albers Equal-Area Projection

Rio Grande

Gulf of Mexico

What was the western boundary of the United States before the Louisiana Purchase?

F Appalachian Mountains

G Mississippi River

H Rocky Mountains

J Pacific Ocean

22. The United States went to war with Great Britain in 1812 because the British—

A attacked American Indians

B tried to start more colonies in the Western Hemisphere

C tried to take control of Louisiana

D forced American sailors to work on British ships

Answer these questions.

23. How did the Great Compromise settle differences about representation in Congress?

_____

_____

_____

_____

24. Why is the Bill of Rights important today?

_____

_____

_____

25. How did Americans view the Monroe Doctrine? How do you think that Europeans viewed it?

_____

_____

_____

Keep that canoe from going over the falls!

A thief has stolen the Constitution of the United States. If you can't get it back, history as we know it may change. You and Eco will need to explore Philadelphia, Washington, D.C., and even the new lands of the Louisiana Purchase. Americans are counting on you to save our history! Play the game now online.

Show What You Know

✎ Writing Write a Letter

Imagine that you are writing to a student in another country. In your letter, convince your pen pal that the Constitution of the United States is an important document. Tell why the Constitution is the foundation of the American republic and how it protects people's rights.

🖍 Activity Make a Constitutional Hall of Fame

Plan a Hall of Fame to honor the Constitution of the United States. Choose important people, events, and ideas related to the Constitution to highlight in your Hall of Fame. Then show these different topics through posters, displays, poems, and narratives.

Expansion and Reform

A wagon train reenactment, in North Dakota

Spotlight on Standards

THE BIG IDEA Nations grow larger as more people arrive and new lands are added.

HISTORY AND SOCIAL SCIENCE SOL

USI.1b, USI.1c, USI.1d, USI.1f, USI.1h, USI.1i, USI.8a, USI.8b, USI.8c, USI.8d

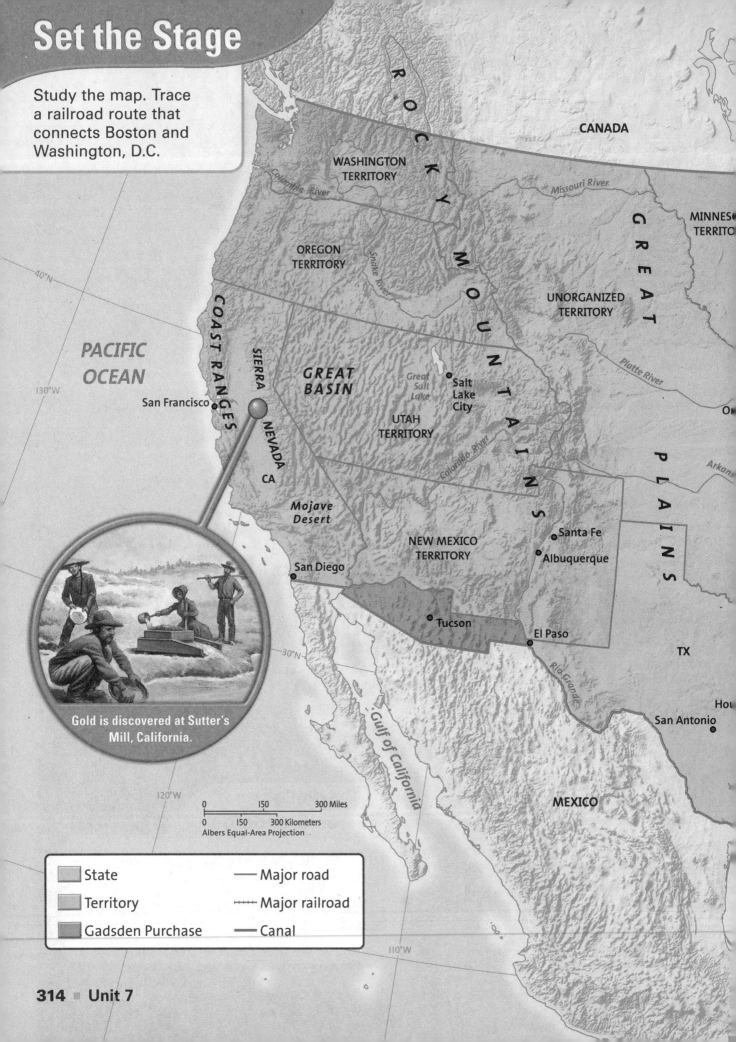

Set the Stage

Study the map. Trace a railroad route that connects Boston and Washington, D.C.

CANADA

ROCKY

WASHINGTON
TERRITORY

Columbia River

Missouri River

MINNES
TERRITO

OREGON
TERRITORY

Snake River

M
O
U
N
T
A
I
N
S

UNORGANIZED
TERRITORY

G
R
E
A
T

40°N

130°W

PACIFIC
OCEAN

COAST RANGES

SIERRA NEVADA

GREAT
BASIN

Great
Salt
Lake

Salt
Lake
City

UTAH
TERRITORY

Platte River

O

San Francisco

CA

Colorado River

Arkans

P
L
A
I
N
S

Mojave
Desert

NEW MEXICO
TERRITORY

Santa Fe

Albuquerque

San Diego

Tucson

El Paso

TX

30°N

Rio Grande

Gold is discovered at Sutter's Mill, California.

Hou

San Antonio

Gulf of California

120°W

0   150   300 Miles

0   150   300 Kilometers

Albers Equal-Area Projection

MEXICO

110°W

State

Major road

Territory

Major railroad

Gadsden Purchase

Canal

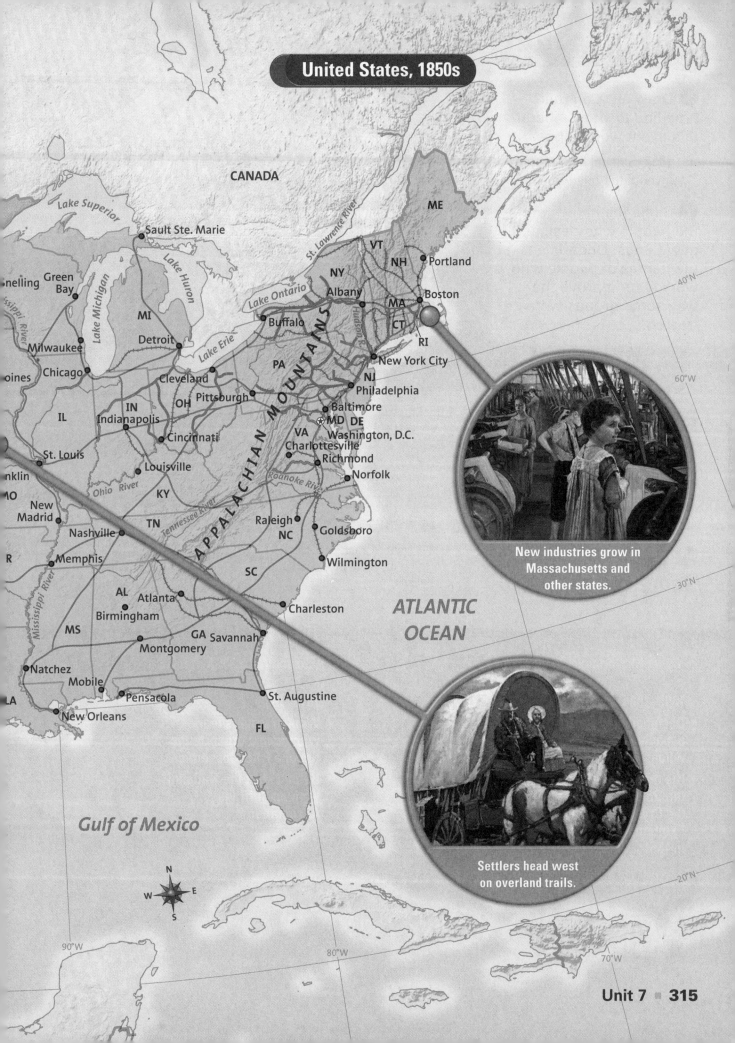

United States, 1850s

CANADA

Lake Superior

Sault Ste. Marie

Snelling
Green Bay

Lake Michigan

Lake Huron

St. Lawrence River

ME

VT

NH

Portland

Mississippi River

MI

Milwaukee

Detroit

Lake Erie

Lake Ontario

NY

Albany

Buffalo

MA

Boston

CT

RI

Des Moines

Chicago

Cleveland

Pittsburgh

PA

Hudson R.

New York City

NJ

Philadelphia

IL

IN

Indianapolis

OH

Baltimore

MD DE

Washington, D.C.

St. Louis

Cincinnati

VA

Charlottesville

Franklin

MO

New Madrid

Louisville

Ohio River

KY

APPALACHIAN MOUNTAINS

Richmond

Norfolk

Roanoke River

Nashville

Tennessee River

TN

Raleigh

NC

Goldsboro

AR

Memphis

Mississippi River

Wilmington

SC

AL

Atlanta

Birmingham

Charleston

MS

GA

Savannah

Montgomery

Natchez

Mobile

Pensacola

St. Augustine

LA

New Orleans

FL

ATLANTIC OCEAN

Gulf of Mexico

N
W E
S

New industries grow in Massachusetts and other states.

Settlers head west on overland trails.

40°N

60°W

30°N

20°N

90°W

80°W

70°W

Set the Stage

① Draw an *X* on the time line to show where this event would appear:

1832 Samuel F. B. Morse invents the telegraph

② Circle the names of the people who designed new things. Underline the names of people who worked to improve the way some groups were treated.

Robert Fulton

1765–1815

- Created the first successful commercial steamboat
- Designed an early submarine for France in 1800

Expansion and Reform

1804 The Corps of Discovery sets out from St. Louis, p. 322

1825 The Erie Canal opens, p. 328

1845 T[...] becom[...] state, [...]

1800

1825

At the Same Time

1806 Noah Webster publishes his first dictionary of American English

1825 British inventors build the first steam locomotive

Cyrus McCormick

1809–1884

- Designed the reaper, a machine to harvest wheat
- His reaper won the Gold Medal at the Crystal Palace Exhibition in London in 1851

Elizabeth Cady Stanton

1815–1902

- Women's rights leader who helped organize the Seneca Falls Convention
- Helped start the National Woman Suffrage Association

Eli Whitney

1765–1825
- Designed the cotton gin, a machine to remove seeds from cotton
- Developed a new system for manufacturing

S

1786?–
- Daughter a Shoshone Indian chief
- Served as an interpreter and guide for the Lewis and Clark expedition

1848 Gold is discovered in California, p. 331

1853 The United States makes the Gadsden Purchase, p. 324

1864 Oregon becomes a territory of the United States, p. 324

1850

1875

1837 Victoria becomes queen of Great Britain

1869 The Transcontinental Railroad is completed

Frederick Douglass

1818–1895
- Escaped from slavery when he was 20 years old
- Became a well-known writer and speaker

Harriet Tubman

1820?–1913
- Led hundreds of enslaved people to freedom along the Underground Railroad
- Leader in the movement to abolish slavery

territory

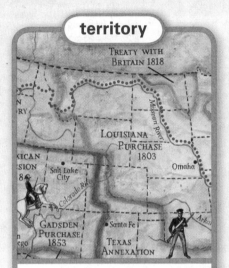

A **territory** belongs to the nation but is not a state and is not represented in the national government. p. 321

migration

Opportunities for a better life started a **migration**, or movement of people, to new western lands. p. 324

annex

In 1845, the United States **annexed** Texas. It was added to the country. p. 324

pioneer

Many **pioneers** settled in the West. They were among the first Americans to live there. p. 330

manufacturing

People who work in **manufacturing** make goods in factories. p. 335

suffrage

Women marched in support of **suffrage**. They wanted to win the right to vote. p. 344

Reading Social Studies

Categorize and Classify

LEARN

Information is often easier to find and to understand if facts are classified. To **classify** is to sort information into categories. A **category** is a group of items that have something in common. To help you classify, you can use graphic organizers such as tables, charts, and webs to show categories of information about people, places, objects, events, or ideas.

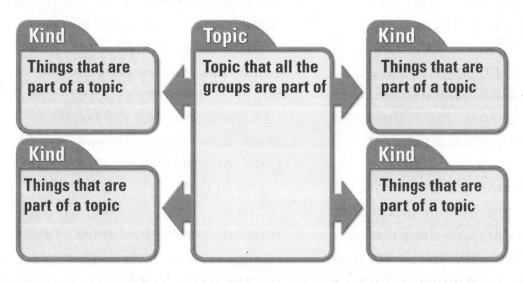

Kind
Things that are part of a topic

Topic
Topic that all the groups are part of

Kind
Things that are part of a topic

Kind
Things that are part of a topic

Kind
Things that are part of a topic

PRACTICE

Underline two categories of information that could be classified as needs of gold miners. One category has been underlined for you.

Thousands of people rushed to California when gold was discovered there. Most of the people arrived in California with only what they could carry. They had many needs. They needed goods, such as tents, food, clothes, and mining tools. Merchants often sold these goods at very high prices.

People also needed services. Towns had to provide more police officers, bankers, grocers, doctors, blacksmiths, barbers, and other workers. Some women opened hotels, restaurants, and laundries.

Topic

Kind

Read the article. Then complete the activities below.

Bound for California

The discovery of gold in California in 1848 set off one of the largest movements of people in history. During the next year, about 90,000 people rushed to California hoping to find gold. They were called forty-niners because most arrived in 1849.

Most forty-niners who traveled to California from the eastern United States took one of three main routes. Even the shortest of these routes took two to three months. On one route, the travelers went by ship to the narrowest part of Central America—the Isthmus of Panama. Then they traveled across the isthmus by riverboat, on mules, and by foot. Once they reached the Pacific Ocean, they waited to board ships to California.

On another route, travelers went by ship around the tip of South America. This route was the longest, and it could take from three to eight months to complete.

Forty-niners were lucky if they could make the journey around South America on a clipper ship. Clipper ships were the fastest ships at the time and could sail to California from the eastern United States in three to four months.

The third route to California took travelers across the United States along overland trails. This route usually took three to five months to complete.

1. **Into what three categories can the ways of traveling to California be classified?**

   _____

   _____

   _____

2. **Underline the description of the route to California that could take less than three months.**

3. **Circle the descriptions of routes that could take more than three months.**

Lesson

From Ocean to Ocean

Between 1801 and 1861, the United States expanded its borders westward. New territories were acquired, opening up large areas of land for exploration and settlement. A **territory** is a land that belongs to a nation but is not a state and is not represented in the national government. **Think about what the United States would be like if it did not include all the land between the Atlantic and Pacific coasts.**

Explorers Lewis and Clark, in the western territories

ESSENTIAL QUESTIONS

✓ What new territories became part of the United States between 1801 and 1861?

✓ What factors influenced westward migration?

 HISTORY AND SOCIAL SCIENCE SOL
USI.1c, USI.1f, USI.8a, USI.8b

TextWork

1 Scan the text. Underline the sentence that describes how the Louisiana Purchase changed the United States.

2 Why do you think controlling the Mississippi River was so important?

_____

_____

3 Study the time line. Circle the date that Sacagawea joined the Corps of Discovery. How did Sacagawea help the expedition?

_____

_____

The Louisiana Purchase

In 1803, the United States bought Louisiana from France. The Louisiana Purchase, which stretched from the Mississippi River to the Rocky Mountains, more than doubled the size of the United States. It gave the nation control of the Mississippi River and the port of New Orleans.

Little was known about the land in the Louisiana Purchase. President Jefferson wanted to learn about the area's resources, so he chose Meriwether Lewis to lead an expedition. Lewis asked William Clark to help. They put together a team of about 40 people. This group was known as the Corps of Discovery.

The Corps of Discovery set out in May 1804. From St. Louis, the group traveled by boat up the Missouri River. In what is now North Dakota, an American Indian woman named Sacagawea (sak•uh•juh•WEE•uh) joined the group. She guided the group through American Indian lands.

THE JOURNEY OF
LEWIS & CLARK

Meriwether Lewis

MAY 1804

The Corps of Discovery departs from Missouri

William Clark

NOVEMBER 1804

Sacagawea joins the expedition

Meriwether Lewis keeps an expedition journal (above)

Reaching the Pacific

In November 1805, the Corps of Discovery finally reached the Pacific Ocean. The group returned to St. Louis in September 1806. The work done by the Corps of Discovery added to the knowledge Americans had about the United States' new lands. They brought back seeds, plants, and even animals. They also drew maps of the major rivers and mountains of the West.

Adding Florida

As a result of the Louisiana Purchase, the United States claimed that it owned the western part of Spanish Florida. The Spanish disagreed. The issue would not be resolved until 1819, when the two countries signed the Adams-Onís Treaty.

In the treaty, Spain gave western Florida to the United States. In return, the United States promised not to collect $5 million that the Spanish government owed it.

TextWork

❹ Study the map on page 325. Circle the place where Lewis and Clark began their expedition. Place an X at the place where it ended.

❺ Study the time line. How long did it take the Corps of Discovery to travel from Missouri to the Pacific Ocean?

_____

_____

❻ Why did Spain give up Florida?

_____

_____

The expedition reaches the Pacific Ocean

SEPTEMBER 1805

The expedition reaches present-day Montana

NOVEMBER 1805

The Corps of Discovery expedition returns to St. Louis

SEPTEMBER 1806

Many American Indian leaders later travel to Washington, D.C., to meet with President Jefferson, who presents this peace medal to them

Expanding Borders

Many Americans believed that western expansion was good for the country. This idea was called **Manifest Destiny**. Those who believed in Manifest Destiny thought the United States was meant to stretch from the Atlantic Ocean to the Pacific Ocean. This belief encouraged a **migration**, or large movement, of people to the West.

Annexing Texas

By the 1830s many Americans were living in Texas, which was controlled by Mexico. When the Mexican General Antonio López de Santa Anna sent troops to Texas to enforce Mexican laws, fighting broke out. On March 6, 1836, Santa Anna's army defeated the Texas army at the Alamo mission in San Antonio.

The Texas army did not give up. Santa Anna was captured on April 21. In return for his freedom, he gave Texas its independence. Texas remained an independent republic until it was **annexed**, or added on, by the United States in 1845.

The Oregon Territory

In the 1840s, both the United States and Great Britain claimed the Oregon Country, in the Pacific Northwest. However, in 1846, the two nations agreed to divide this land. The southern part of the Oregon Country became a United States territory.

The Mexican Cession

In 1848, the United States gained lands as a result of a war with Mexico. As part of the peace settlement, Mexico sold the United States a large area known as the Mexican Cession. A **cession**, or concession, is something that is given up. The Mexican Cession included California and most of what is now the southwestern United States. In 1853, the United States bought the rest of New Mexico and Arizona from Mexico in what is called the Gadsden Purchase.

---

7 In your own words, explain the term *Manifest Destiny*.

_____

_____

_____

8 (Focus Skill) Underline a detail that can be classified under the category of territories claimed by the United States and Great Britain.

9 Study the map. Circle the lands gained by the United States in the Mexican Cession. In what year did the United States gain these lands?

_____

_____

10 How might the United States be different today if Manifest Destiny had not been a popular idea during the 1800s?

_____

_____

_____

_____

The Alamo, in San Antonio, Texas

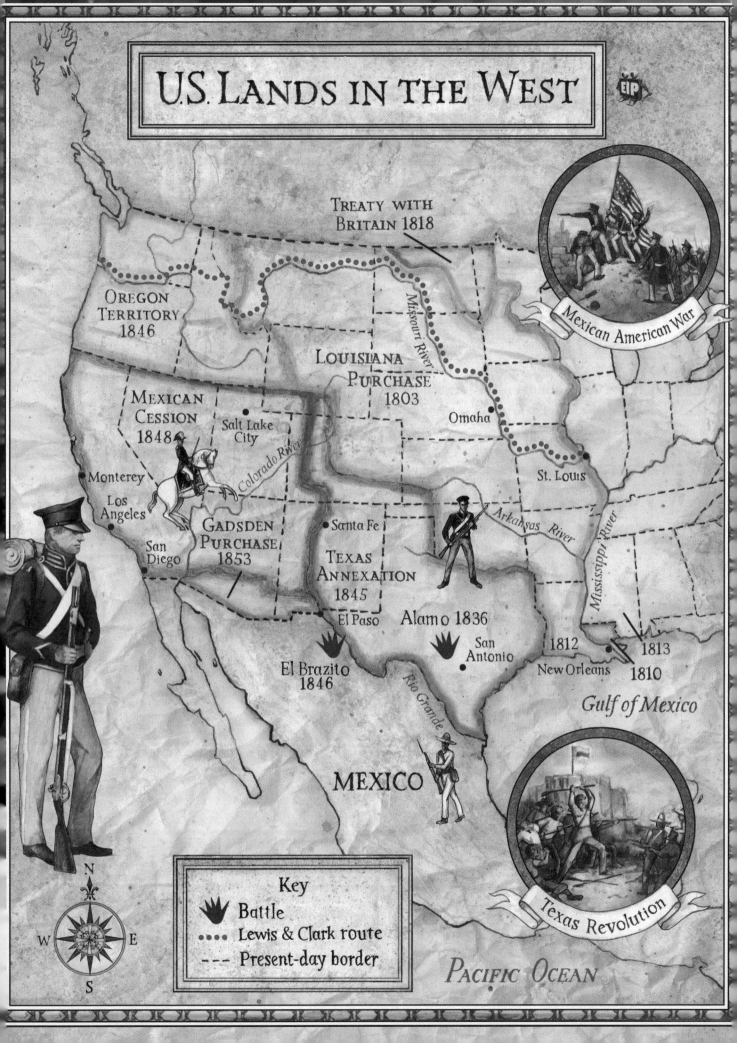

U.S. LANDS IN THE WEST

EIP

Mexican American War

TREATY WITH BRITAIN 1818

OREGON TERRITORY 1846

LOUISIANA PURCHASE 1803

Missouri River

Omaha

MEXICAN CESSION 1848

Salt Lake City

Colorado River

Monterey

Los Angeles

San Diego

GADSDEN PURCHASE 1853

Santa Fe

St. Louis

Arkansas River

Mississippi River

TEXAS ANNEXATION 1845

El Paso

Alamo 1836

San Antonio

1812

New Orleans

1813

1810

El Brazito 1846

Rio Grande

Gulf of Mexico

MEXICO

Texas Revolution

Key

✹ Battle

•••• Lewis & Clark route

- - - Present-day border

PACIFIC OCEAN

N W E S

1. SUMMARIZE List the territories that became part of the United States between 1801 and 1861.

_____

_____

_____

_____

_____

2. How are the terms **annexed** and **cession** related?

_____

_____

_____

3. How did Texas become part of the United States?

_____

_____

_____

_____

Circle the letter of the correct answer.

4. Which area stretched from the Mississippi River to the Rocky Mountains?

A The Louisiana Purchase

B The Gadsden Purchase

C The Mexican Cession

D The Oregon Country

5. What was a goal of the Corps of Discovery?

F To buy Louisiana from France

G To learn about the resources of Louisiana

H To help Santa Anna enforce Mexican laws in Texas

J To claim the western part of Spanish Florida

6. The United States acquired most of what is now the southwestern United States as a result of the—

A Louisiana Purchase

B Gadsden Purchase

C Mexican Cession

D Adams-Onís Treaty

7. What was the main goal expressed by the idea of Manifest Destiny?

F Gaining religious freedom

G Abolishing slavery

H Increasing immigration

J Extending land claims

writing

Write a Persuasive Letter Imagine that you are an American in the 1840s. Write a letter to a friend explaining whether you are for or against Manifest Destiny and why.

A compass from the Lewis and Clark expedition

Westward Movement

In the first half of the 1800s, thousands of settlers moved into western lands. This migration was influenced by both geography and economic factors. It changed life in the United States. **Think about the reasons that people might want to move to a new place.**

Settlers often traveled in wagon trains as they moved west on overland trails.

ESSENTIAL QUESTIONS

✔ What factors influenced westward migration?
✔ How did inventions and entrepreneurs affect the lives of Americans?

 HISTORY AND SOCIAL SCIENCE SOL
USI.1b, USI.1d, USI.1f, USI.8b, USI.8c

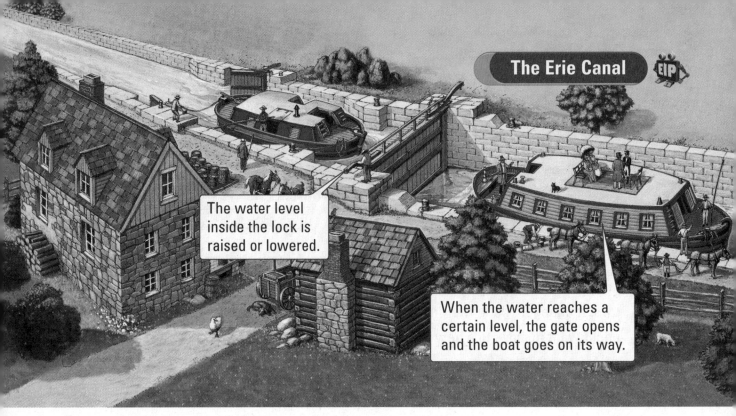

The water level inside the lock is raised or lowered.

When the water reaches a certain level, the gate opens and the boat goes on its way.

The Erie Canal

The locks on the Erie Canal raised and lowered the water level so that boats could safely travel through different elevations.

TextWork

1 Scan the text. Underline the reasons why settlers moved west.

2 How did the Erie Canal help open up western lands to people in the East?

_____

_____

_____

3 Study the illustration. Does the water in the upper lock need to be raised or lowered? Explain.

_____

_____

_____

Growth and Transportation

The United States grew rapidly in the early 1800s. As the population of the eastern states increased and land there became more costly, settlers began to move west across the Appalachian Mountains. Later, they moved even farther west.

Many early settlers traveled west by boat. Most roads were rough dirt paths. Traveling on them by horse and wagon was slow and costly. New forms of transportation, such as canals and steam-powered boats, allowed people to travel and transport goods more quickly and at a lower cost.

The Erie Canal

In 1817, leaders in New York planned the Erie Canal. When the canal was completed in 1825, it connected the Great Lakes to the Hudson River and the Atlantic Ocean. Before the Erie Canal was built, it took 20 days to ship a ton of goods from Buffalo to New York City. After the canal opened, it took just 8 days. Soon, many states were building canals.

Steamboats and Railroads

The invention of the steam engine also made it easier to travel inland. In 1807, an entrepreneur named Robert Fulton used a steam engine to power his boat, the *Clermont*. An **entrepreneur** (ahn•truh•pruh•NER) is someone who organizes resources to bring a new or better good or service to market in hopes of earning a profit. Until this time, boats had not been able to easily travel upstream against the current.

Before long, steamboats were making journeys up and down major rivers, such as the Ohio and Mississippi Rivers. Steamboats provided faster and cheaper transportation that connected Southern plantations and farms to Northern industries and Western territories. Steamboats also affected the growth of cities in the West. Many western cities, such as Cincinnati and St. Louis, grew around river ports.

Steam power was also used in locomotives, or railroad engines. Rail travel was faster and less expensive than steamboats. By 1850, more than 9,000 miles of railroad track crossed the nation. Many new cities and towns grew near railroad stations.

The *DeWitt Clinton* was one of the first passenger trains in the United States.

Robert Fulton

TextWork

❹ Put these events in the correct sequence:

_____ The United States has more than 9,000 miles of railroad track.

_____ The Erie Canal is completed.

_____ A steam engine is first used to power a boat.

❺ (Focus Skill) Underline two details that can be classified under the category of new methods of transportation during the 1800s.

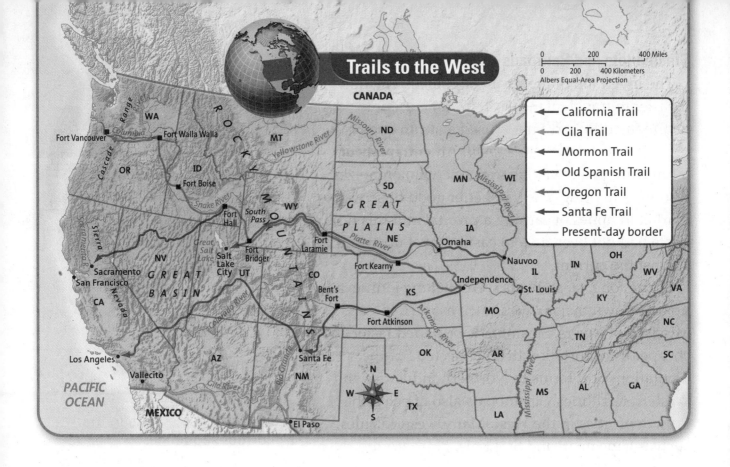

Trails to the West

Legend:
- California Trail
- Gila Trail
- Mormon Trail
- Old Spanish Trail
- Oregon Trail
- Santa Fe Trail
- Present-day border

0   200   400 Miles
0   200   400 Kilometers
Albers Equal-Area Projection

TextWork

6 Give an example of a present-day pioneer.

_____

7 Study the map. On the map legend, circle the names of the trails that followed the Platte River and trace those trails.

8 Draw an *X* at the end of the Mormon Trail. How was the Mormons' view of westward movement different from that of other pioneers in the West?

_____

_____

_____

Opportunities Farther West

As the frontier was pushed farther west, more and more people decided to start new lives there. The West was also seen as a land of economic opportunity. Land was cheap and good for farming. In the forests, loggers found plenty of timber. Soon, many pioneers were heading west. A **pioneer** is a person who is one of the first to settle in a place.

Overland Trails

Knowledge of overland trails was another factor that encouraged westward movement. As the frontier was pushed farther west, pioneers traveled on overland trails. Many pioneers followed the Oregon Trail to Oregon and the Santa Fe Trail to New Mexico.

In 1846, Brigham Young, a Mormon leader, led a group from Illinois to Utah on what became known as the Mormon Trail. The Mormons, or members of the Church of Jesus Christ of Latter-day Saints, traveled west to find greater religious freedom.

The Gold Rush

In 1848, workers near San Francisco, California, found a few gold nuggets. The discovery of gold caused a **gold rush**, or a sudden rush of people to an area where gold has been found. In the year following the discovery, about 90,000 people traveled to California to seek their fortunes. They were called **forty-niners** because most arrived in 1849.

Most of the forty-niners came from other parts of the United States. Some made their way west along the overland trails. Others reached California by sailing around the tip of South America or by crossing the Isthmus of Panama and then sailing up the Pacific coast.

Among the forty-niners were women and as many as 1,000 African Americans, both free and enslaved. Some African Americans had gained their freedom by running away from slavery. They made their way to California in the hopes of starting their own businesses. Others were brought as enslaved workers to mine gold.

TextWork

9 (Focus Skill) List three reasons people migrated to California after 1848.

_____

_____

_____

10 Study the text on page 332. What do you think is the effect of the gold rush of 1849 on the present-day population of California?

_____

_____

_____

Gold Mining

Water was poured into a cradle, which was rocked back and forth to separate the heavier gold from soil.

Water and soil were sent through long ramps called sluices.

Moving from Other Countries

Many of the forty-niners came from other parts of the world, including Mexico, South America, Europe, and Asia. In fact, about one in four of the newcomers was Chinese. Lu Ng (LOO ING), from China, explained his decision to come to California this way: "Crops had failed and floods had ruined our fields … What else could I do?"

Most people did not find gold in California. However, many people had opportunities that were not available to them in other places. Those who did not find gold often stayed and turned to ranching or farming. Others started businesses. In 1850, California became a state.

A Chinese immigrant to California

Lesson 2 Review

1. **SUMMARIZE** Why did so many Americans move to the West during the 1800s?

   _____

   _____

   _____

2. Use the word **pioneer** in a sentence about westward movement.

   _____

   _____

   _____

3. Why did the forty-niners migrate to California?

   _____

   _____

Circle the letter of the correct answer.

4. What opened the middle of the country to people in the East in 1825?

   A The Erie Canal

   B The Oregon Trail

   C The Mormon Trail

   D The California gold rush

Gold-mining tools

writing

✎ **Write an Advertisement** Imagine that you are a writer during the early 1800s. Write an advertisement encouraging people to settle on the frontier.

New Inventions Bring Changes

During the 1800s and early 1900s, new inventions changed the way Americans lived and worked. People began to use machines to make large quantities of goods. This period came to be called the **Industrial Revolution**. Americans quickly went from walking and riding horses to traveling in steam-powered boats and trains. They went from weaving fabric by hand to using machines that could weave cloth in a fraction of the time. **Think about how new technology might change a person's life today.**

An inventor demonstrates a reaper, a machine used to harvest wheat.

ESSENTIAL QUESTION

✔ How did inventions and entrepreneurs affect the lives of Americans?

HISTORY AND SOCIAL SCIENCE SOL
USI.1b, USI.1c, USI.1i, USI.8c

Farming and Industry

In 1793, the inventor Eli Whitney visited a cotton plantation. An **inventor** is someone who is the first to think of or make something. Whitney saw how difficult it was for workers to remove seeds from cotton by hand. He invented the cotton gin, a machine that could remove the seeds.

The cotton gin provided important benefits for planters. A **benefit** is something gained. The cotton gin made it easier to remove seeds from cotton. As a result, cotton could be prepared for market in less time and for less money.

However, the cotton gin also had costs. A **cost** is the effort made to achieve or gain something. It took time to invent the cotton gin and money to manufacture and purchase it.

Like many inventions, the cotton gin caused certain **consequences**, or what happens because of some action. Some of the consequences were intended, or expected. For example, the cotton gin helped planters earn more money. It let them produce more cotton, which meant more cotton could be shipped to **textile**, or cloth, mills in the Northern states and in Europe. As a result, worldwide demand for cotton increased.

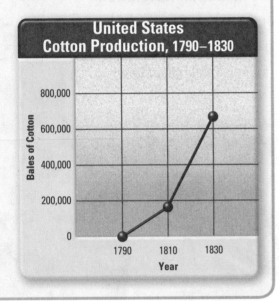

United States Cotton Production, 1790–1830

Bales of Cotton

800,000
600,000
400,000
200,000
0

1790   1810   1830

Year

Eli Whitney (left) invented the cotton gin (below), a machine that helped speed up the process of turning raw cotton into cloth.

Children IN HISTORY

Lowell Mill Girls

Many textile mills were started on the Charles River in Lowell, Massachusetts. Many of the workers in the mills in Lowell were young girls. Harriet Hanson was ten years old when she began working as a "doffer." From five o'clock in the morning until seven in the evening, Harriet changed spools of thread on the spinning machines. Harriet lived in a boardinghouse where rooms and meals were provided for the workers. Not all factory owners had boardinghouses for their workers, however.

Make It Relevant Why do you think children in the United States today are expected to go to school rather than work?

Growth of the Textile Industry

The cotton gin also had unintended, or unexpected, consequences. Because more cotton could be grown, more enslaved workers were needed on plantations. The number of enslaved workers in the South increased sharply. In turn, disagreements over the issue of slavery grew.

Other factors also increased the demand for cotton. Getting cotton from plantations in the South to factories in the North and the western parts of the country was easier, too. On steamboats, cotton could be moved quickly on important river routes, such as the Mississippi and Ohio Rivers.

At the same time, inventors in Britain developed new machines to spin thread and weave textiles. Because of these machines, cloth became much cheaper to make and buy. Samuel Slater, a British mill worker who knew how the machines worked, moved to the United States. In 1793, he started the first American textile mill, in Rhode Island. It marked the beginning of large-scale **manufacturing**, or the making of goods, in the United States.

 TextWork

❸ What was one unintended consequence of the cotton gin?

_____

_____

_____

❹ How do you think spinning and weaving machines made cloth cheaper to make and buy?

_____

_____

_____

Mass Production

In 1800, Eli Whitney had another good idea. He thought of a way to manufacture large amounts of goods at one time. His idea came to be known as **mass production**.

Before mass production, one craftworker made each product from start to finish. Muskets, for example, were made by hand, one at a time. To produce more muskets, Whitney built machines that made many interchangeable, or identical, copies of each part. Such parts could be used to make or repair many muskets in a short time.

Interchangeable parts made mass production possible. As a result, cheaper machine-made goods began to replace many expensive handmade goods.

Mass production also made it possible to use untrained workers in factories. No longer were craftworkers needed to make most products. Anyone could put together machine-made parts.

5 Use the term *mass production* in a sentence about manufacturing in the 1800s.

_____

_____

_____

_____

6 Scan the text. Underline the sentences that explain how interchangeable parts made mass production possible.

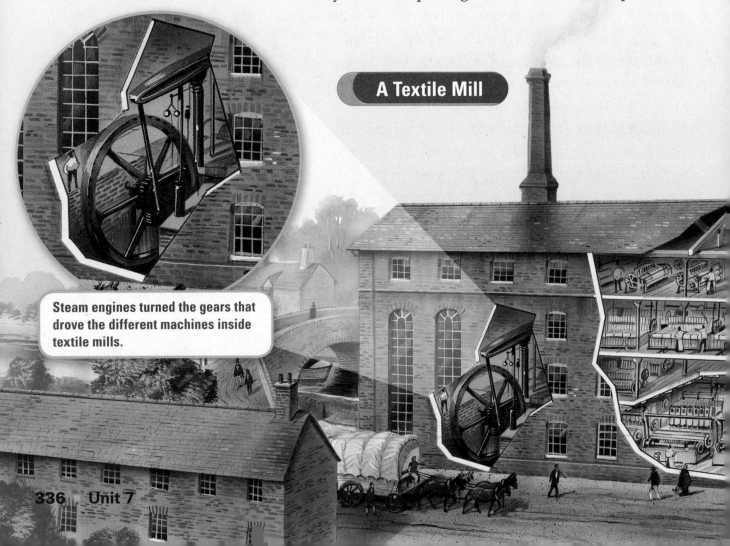

A Textile Mill

Steam engines turned the gears that drove the different machines inside textile mills.

The Growth of Factories

Soon, everything from guns to clocks was being mass-produced in factories. Like the textile mills, most factories were in the North.

As more factories were built, more workers were needed to run them. Many workers, both young and old, soon were working long hours in the factories. Their work was often boring, dangerous, and not well paid. Immigrants and many farmers moved to cities in the North to find factory jobs. The populations of manufacturing cities such as New York, Boston, Philadelphia, and Baltimore grew quickly.

Steam Power

During the Industrial Revolution, many factories began to use steam-powered machines. Before that, most factories were built next to rivers. The rushing water in rivers was used to turn waterwheels connected to machines inside the factories. That system changed when steam engines that could power machines were built. The steam engines were more reliable than waterpower, and factories no longer had to be next to rivers.

TextWork

7 Study the graph. How many more factories were there in 1869 than in 1849?

_____

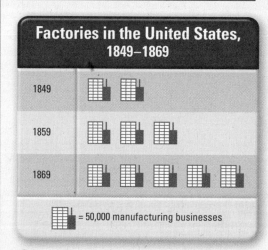

Factories in the United States, 1849–1869

1849	
1859	
1869	

= 50,000 manufacturing businesses

8 Scan the text. Circle the sentences that describe working conditions in factories.

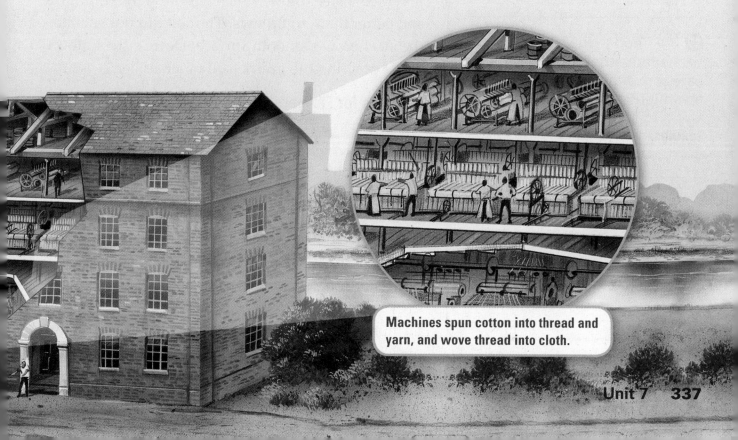

Machines spun cotton into thread and yarn, and wove thread into cloth.

New Farm Machinery

New farm machinery also made work faster and easier. As a result, farmers were soon planting more land and getting bigger harvests.

Reapers and Threshers

Using hand tools, farmers could harvest no more than 2 to 3 acres of wheat each day. Cyrus McCormick and Jo Anderson, an enslaved African American, changed that. In 1831, they invented a mechanical reaper to cut down the plants. With this invention, farmers could cut as much wheat in one day as they had been able to cut in two weeks with hand tools.

Once the wheat plants had been cut down, farmers had to thresh, or separate, the grain from the stems. In 1834, two brothers, Hiram and John Pitts, built a machine to do that. Threshing machines saved farmers many days of hard work.

Steel Plows

Iron plows were not very good at turning over the thick grass on the prairies of the Midwest. The soil stuck to the rough iron. In 1837, John Deere invented a steel plow, which cut through the prairie soil better than iron plows. The soil did not stick to the steel plow's smooth surface. Deere's steel plows made plowing the prairie soil much easier.

Changes for Farmers

New farm machinery meant that fewer farmworkers were needed. Many of those workers moved to cities to take jobs in factories.

Another problem for farmers was that the price of farm goods had dropped sharply. Larger harvests had created a huge surplus of crops. To make the same amount of money, farmers had to produce even more crops. In turn, these larger harvests drove farm prices down even more. Today most farming is done with large machines similar to the ones invented during the Industrial Revolution.

9 Look at the advertisement for McCormick reapers on page 339. How did McCormick try to persuade farmers to buy his machine?

_____

_____

_____

_____

_____

10 How did the mechanical reaper and the steel plow help farmers produce larger crops in less time?

_____

_____

_____

_____

_____

11 (Focus Skill) Choose four inventions of the Industrial Revolution and categorize them as either textile inventions or farming inventions.

Textiles: _____

_____

_____

Farming: _____

_____

_____

New Farming Machines

John Deere invented a strong steel plow.

Hiram A. and John A. Pitts patented a threshing machine in 1837.

Cyrus McCormick used advertising to sell his reapers to farmers.

1. **SUMMARIZE** How did inventions change Americans' lives during the Industrial Revolution?

_____

_____

_____

2. What was a **consequence** of the invention of the steam engine on **manufacturing**?

_____

_____

_____

3. What do you think was the most important invention of the Industrial Revolution? Why?

_____

_____

_____

4. What is something that was invented during the Industrial Revolution that we still use today? How do you think the inventions of the Industrial Revolution affect your life today?

_____

_____

_____

Circle the letter of the correct answer.

5. What marked the beginning of large-scale manufacturing in the United States?

   A The first textile mill in Pawtucket, Rhode Island

   B The cotton gin

   C The steam engine

   D New farm machinery

6. The steel plow made tilling prairie soil easier because—

   F it was heavier than iron plows

   G it was lighter than iron plows

   H soil stuck to the rough surface

   J soil did not stick to the smooth surface

7. What was a cost of new farm machinery?

   A More farm workers were needed.

   B Fewer farm workers were needed.

   C Farms became smaller.

   D Farms became larger.

A cotton gin

activity

🖋 **Make an Illustrated Time Line** Create a time line of some important events and inventions of the Industrial Revolution. Illustrate your time line.

As the United States continued to grow, people saw the need to reform, or change things for the better. Some groups worked to end slavery. Others worked to make sure women would have basic rights. **Think about how people might have worked to make things better for others.**

A monument to women's rights, in Seneca Falls, New York

ESSENTIAL QUESTIONS

✓ What were the main ideas expressed by the abolitionists?

✓ What were the main ideas expressed during the suffrage movement?

 HISTORY AND SOCIAL SCIENCE SOL
USI.1b, USI.1c, USI.1d, USI.1h, USI.8d

 **TextWork**

The Abolitionist Movement

❶ What is the base word of the term *abolitionist?* What does it mean?

_____

_____

_____

❷ Reread the quote by Frederick Douglass. In your own words, tell what he meant.

_____

_____

_____

Many people wanted to abolish, or end, slavery in the United States. Such people were called **abolitionists** (a•buh•LIH•shuhn•ists). Most abolitionists demanded the immediate freeing of all enslaved people. They believed that slavery was morally wrong. They thought it was cruel and inhumane and against the ideals of democracy.

William Lloyd Garrison, a white Northerner, published a newspaper called the *Liberator.* In it, Garrison called for the complete end to slavery.

Frederick Douglass escaped slavery and became well-known for speaking out against slavery and working for the rights of African Americans and women. He told audiences, "I appear this evening as a thief and a robber. I stole this head, these limbs, this body from my master [slave owner] and ran off with them." Douglass also began an abolitionist newspaper. It was called the *North Star.*

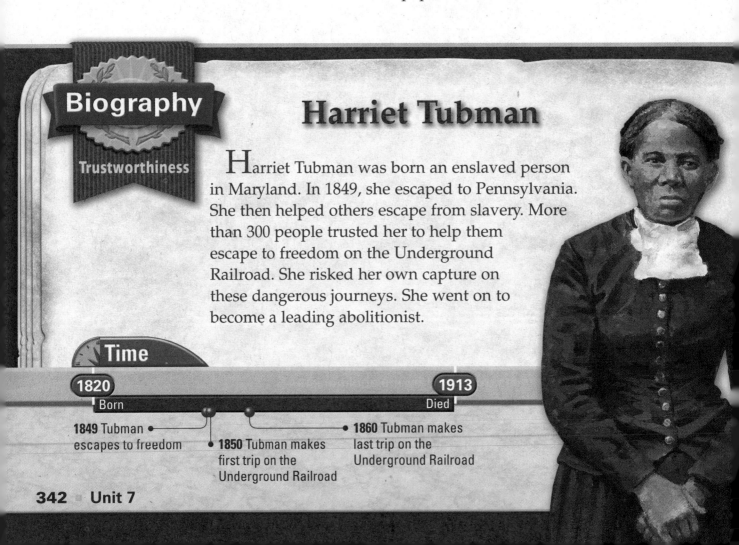

Biography

Trustworthiness

Harriet Tubman

Harriet Tubman was born an enslaved person in Maryland. In 1849, she escaped to Pennsylvania. She then helped others escape from slavery. More than 300 people trusted her to help them escape to freedom on the Underground Railroad. She risked her own capture on these dangerous journeys. She went on to become a leading abolitionist.

Time

1820 Born | **1913** Died

1849 Tubman escapes to freedom

1850 Tubman makes first trip on the Underground Railroad

1860 Tubman makes last trip on the Underground Railroad

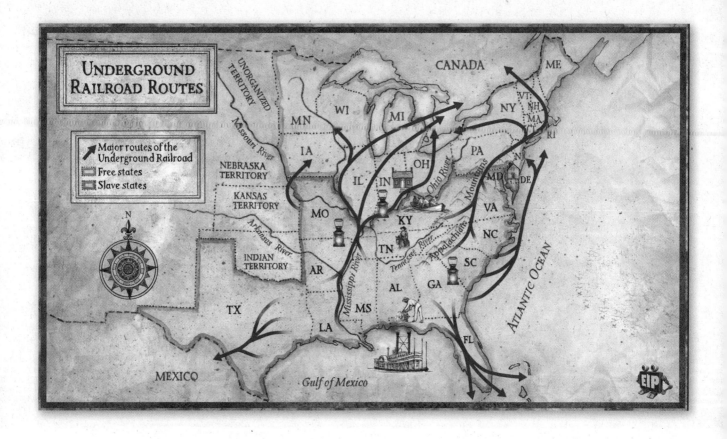

The Underground Railroad

Another abolitionist, Harriet Tubman, led hundreds of enslaved African Americans to their freedom along the Underground Railroad. The **Underground Railroad** was not a railroad, and it was not underground. It was a system of secret escape routes that led to free lands. Most routes led to free states in the North or to Canada.

Harriet Tubman, who had escaped from slavery herself, was one of the best-known conductors, or helpers, on the Underground Railroad. Working mostly at night, conductors led runaway enslaved people from one hiding place to the next along those routes. The hiding places—which included barns, attics, storage rooms, and churches—were called stations. There, runaways could rest and eat, preparing for the journey to the next station.

Escaping slavery was dangerous, both for the people escaping and for anyone who helped them. If enslaved people were captured, they were beaten and sometimes killed. Still, many escaped.

TextWork

❸ Scan the text on pages 342 and 343. Circle the names of three abolitionists.

❹ Study the map. Trace the Underground Railroad routes that ended in Canada. Then circle the areas on the map where these routes began.

❺ Study the map. Why do you think the Ohio River was important to people escaping slavery?

_____

_____

_____

THE SUFFRAGE MOVEMENT

Sojourner Truth gives a famous speech at the Ohio Woman's Rights Convention

Susan B. Anthony speaks before Congress in favor of voting rights for women

Seneca Falls Convention

The Nineteenth Amendment gives suffrage to all women in the United States

1848   1854   1884   1920

The Suffrage Movement

Some abolitionists also spoke out in support of women's rights. Many people believed that women were being denied their basic rights. At that time, women did not have the same educational opportunities as men. Many colleges did not allow women to attend. Women did not have equal opportunity in business and could not work in certain jobs. In most states, they had limited rights to own or control property.

Women also did not have **suffrage** (SUH•frij), or the right to vote. Some women organized to change these conditions. In 1848, Elizabeth Cady Stanton and Lucretia Mott organized a women's rights convention at Seneca Falls, New York. The delegates at the convention approved the Declaration of Sentiments. It began by saying, "We hold these truths to be self-evident; that all men *and* women are created equal." The Declaration of Sentiments was based on the Declaration of Independence.

TextWork

6 (Focus Skill) In the chart, categorize people who were abolitionists or suffragists. Write the names of three people in each category.

Abolitionists	Suffragists

Other Reformers

Isabella Van Wagener, a former enslaved African American, also spoke out against slavery and in support of equality and justice. She believed that God had called her to "travel up and down the land" to preach. She changed her name to Sojourner Truth. *Sojourner* means "traveler."

Another leading **suffragist**, or supporter of women's suffrage, was Susan B. Anthony. In 1884, she spoke before Congress in favor of a constitutional amendment granting suffrage to women.

Women won a few rights during this time. However, they continued to work for suffrage and other basic rights. It would not be until 1920 that the Nineteenth Amendment gave all women the right to vote in all elections in the United States.

TextWork

7 How is the wording of the Declaration of Independence different from that of the Declaration of Sentiments?

_____

8 Some people were against woman's suffrage during the 1800s. Why do you think this was so?

_____

_____

Lesson 4 Review

1. **SUMMARIZE** What were the purposes of the abolitionist and women's rights movements?

   _____

   _____

2. Describe the **Underground Railroad** in a sentence.

   _____

   _____

3. How is life in the United States today affected by the efforts of abolitionists and suffragists in the 1800s and 1900s?

   _____

   _____

Circle the letter of the correct answer.

4. Women gained suffrage because of the—

   A Fifteenth Amendment

   B Seventeenth Amendment

   C Nineteenth Amendment

   D Twenty-First Amendment

activity

Make Protest Signs Imagine that you are either an abolitionist or a suffragist in the 1800s. Create signs with slogans to explain why you are marching for your cause.

Working for women's rights

VOTES FOR WOMEN

Fun with Social Studies

Which Movies Don't Belong?

Some of these DVDs don't belong on these shelves. Circle the two titles that do not belong.

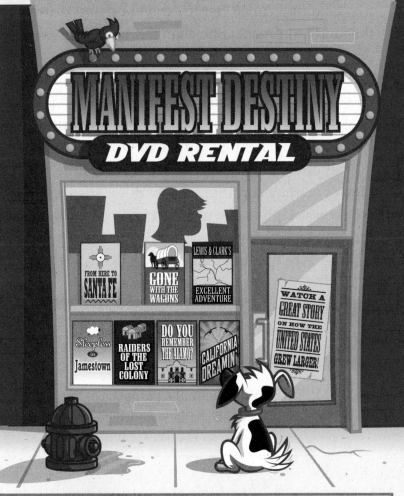

Got a Consonant?

abc VOCABULARY

Borrow some consonants and vowels from the words *consonant* and *vowel* to complete the vocabulary words that fit the clues.

I _ _ _ _ _ _ _ R

_ _ _ _ X

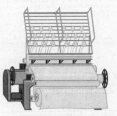

_ _ X _ I _ _

PI _ _ _ _ R

_ B _ _ I _ _ I _ _

Best Sellers?

Draw lines to match each person to the book he or she might have written.

 Harriet Tubman

 Sacagawea

 Forty-niner

 Elizabeth Cady Stanton

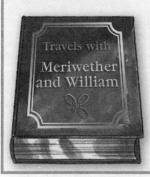 Travels with Meriwether and William

 Suffering for Suffrage

 SECRETS OF A CONDUCTOR

 GOLD FEVER

If They Had the Internet

Write the names of the people who might have used these e-mail addresses.

From: merilew@corpsofdiscovery.net

_____

To: theprez@USA.gov

_____

Subject: Destination reached!

Today the expedition reached the Pacific Ocean. When we return to the East, I'll give you a full report on all the plants and animals we saw in this part of the continent.

From: ecstant@seneca.org

_____

To: abolitionist1@NorthStar.com

_____

Subject: Speech at convention

Lucretia Mott and I are organizing a women's rights convention. Can you give one of your speeches about working to better the lives of African Americans and women?

Review and Test Prep

The Big Idea

Nations grow larger as more people arrive and new lands are added.

Summarize the Unit

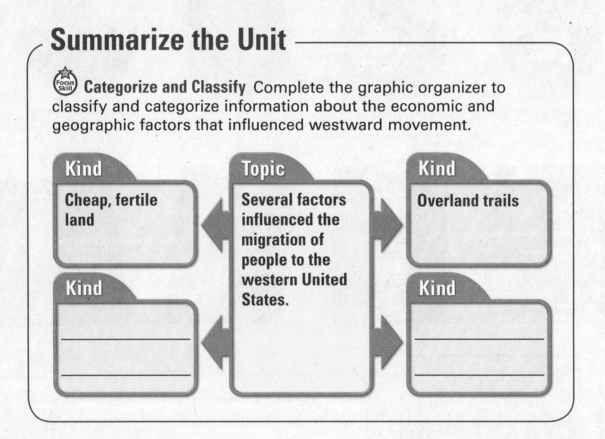

Focus Skill Categorize and Classify Complete the graphic organizer to classify and categorize information about the economic and geographic factors that influenced westward movement.

Kind
Cheap, fertile land

Topic
Several factors influenced the migration of people to the western United States.

Kind
Overland trails

Kind

_____
_____

Kind

_____
_____

Use Vocabulary

Fill in the missing terms, using the correct vocabulary term from the Word Bank.

1. Texas was _____ by the United States in 1845.

2. In the 1800s, women did not have _____.

3. An _____ considers the costs of starting a new business.

4. A _____ is one of the first people to settle in a place.

5. _____ allows large amounts of goods to be made at one time.

Word Bank

territory p. 321

annexed p. 324

entrepreneur p. 329

pioneer p. 330

mass production p. 336

suffrage p. 344

Think About It

Circle the letter of the correct answer.

6. The United States bought Louisiana from France to—

A build the Mormon Trail

B stop Great Britain from buying it

C have a port on the Gulf of Mexico

D control the Oregon Country

7.

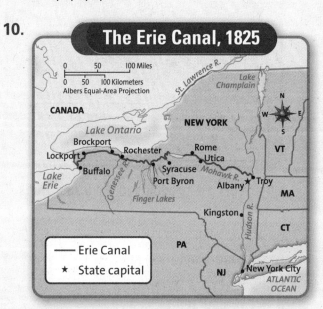

Growth of the United States

0   250   1,000 Miles
0   250   1,000 Kilometers
Albers Equal-Area Projection

CANADA

1842
1842
1846
1803
1848
1783
1853
1845
PACIFIC OCEAN
MEXICO
ATLANTIC OCEAN
1812 1810 1813 1819
Gulf of Mexico

— Present-day border

The area colored in orange was called the—

F Louisiana Purchase

G Gadsden Purchase

H Texas Annexation

J Mexican Cession

8. What made California a part of the United States?

A The California gold rush

B The Battle of the Alamo

C The Mexican Cession

D The Adams-Onís Treaty

9.

> 1. California
> 2. Texas
> 3. Louisiana
> 4. Oregon
> 5. Florida

In which order were these lands acquired by the United States?

F 1, 2, 3, 4, 5

G 5, 4, 3, 2, 1

H 1, 5, 4, 2, 3

J 3, 5, 2, 4, 1

10.

The Erie Canal, 1825

0   50   100 Miles
0   50   100 Kilometers
Albers Equal-Area Projection

CANADA

NEW YORK

Lake Ontario
Brockport   Rome
Lockport   Rochester   Utica
Buffalo   Syracuse
Lake Erie   Port Byron   Albany ★ Troy
Finger Lakes
Kingston
PA
VT
MA
CT
NJ   New York City
ATLANTIC OCEAN

— Erie Canal
★ State capital

What town on the Erie Canal was between Rochester and Syracuse?

A Brockport

B Port Byron

C Rome

D Utica

11. What was an effect of the Erie Canal?

F Cities developed along the Mississippi and Ohio Rivers.

G Americans gained greater knowledge of the Louisiana Purchase.

H Thousands of people rushed to California.

J New York City became a center of trade.

12. Which form of transportation became widely used in the 1800s and is still common today?

A Railroads

B Automobiles

C Airplanes

D Submarines

13.

Trails to California

California Trail ← Santa Fe Trail
Old Spanish Trail ← Present-day border
Oregon Trail

Where did the Oregon and California Trails meet?

F At Fort Hall

G At South Pass

H In the Sierra Nevada

J Near the Pacific Ocean

14. The discovery of which resource caused many people to go to California in 1849?

A Gold

B Oil

C Silver

D Coal

15. What was one cost of the increased cotton production that resulted from the cotton gin?

F Fewer acres of land were needed to grow cotton.

G More enslaved workers were needed to grow cotton.

H Steam was needed to grow more cotton.

J Cotton cloth was more expensive to produce.

16. What was a consequence of using steam-powered machines in factories?

A Factories needed fewer workers.

B Factories no longer had to be built only along rivers.

C Factories were moved to warmer climates.

D Factories started using interchangeable parts.

17.

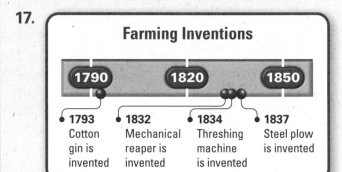

Farming Inventions

1790   1820   1850

1793 Cotton gin is invented   1832 Mechanical reaper is invented   1834 Threshing machine is invented   1837 Steel plow is invented

How many years after the invention of the cotton gin was the mechanical reaper invented?

F 3 years

G 5 years

H 39 years

J 41 years

18. Cyrus McCormick helped American farmers by—

A inventing a mechanical reaper

B developing the steel plow

C inventing the cotton gin

D designing threshing machines

19.

Kind: John Deere

Topic: ?

Kind: Jo Anderson

Kind: Hiram and John Pitts

Which is the best name for a topic that includes this information?

F Transportation inventors

G Farming inventors

H Communication inventors

J Textile manufacturing inventors

20. Abolitionists wanted to end—

A annexation

B revolution

C slavery

D suffrage

21. Which patriotic quote is from the Declaration of Sentiments and is similar to an important idea in the Declaration of Independence?

F "All men and women are created equal."

G "We the people of the United States, in order to form a more perfect union . . ."

H "I pledge allegiance to the flag of the United States of America . . ."

J "No taxation without representation."

Answer these questions.

22. How did population growth in the East influence westward migration in the United States?

_____

_____

_____

23. What were some of the benefits of industrialization? What were some of the costs?

_____

_____

_____

24. How might a factory owner have viewed the abolition movement? Why might a plantation owner have viewed it differently?

_____

_____

_____

Go Digital

Virginia Adventures

Hitch up the wagons! You and Eco are joining a wagon train heading west. The leaders of the group have asked you for your help with the many dangers they will face along the way. Can you manage to defend the wagon train from wild animals, cross flooded rivers, and survive mountain blizzards? Play the game now online.

Show What You Know

Writing Write a Summary

Imagine you are a student in the early 1800s and that your class is preparing a time capsule. Write a report to explain to people in the future how the United States has changed since the late 1700s. Summarize the changes in the United States' boundaries, population, economy, and society.

Activity Make an Illustrated Time Line

Complete a time line that shows the nation's growth during the late 1700s and early 1800s. Choose events that resulted in geographic, economic, and population growth. Illustrate these events with pictures. Write captions that explain cause-and-effect relationships between some of the events.

-1787-
The United States Constitution is written

-1791-
The Bill of Rights

-1804-
The Corps of Discovery

-1836-
The Battle of the Alamo

-1846-
The Mexican American War

1801

1815

The Civil War

The Battle of Gettysburg,
in Pennsylvania

Spotlight on Standards

THE BIG IDEA Regional differences can divide a
nation and its people.

HISTORY AND SOCIAL SCIENCE SOL

USI.1a, USI.1b, USI.1c, USI.1d, USI.1f, USI.1h, USI.9a, USI.9b, USI.9c,
USI.9d, USI.9e, USI.9f

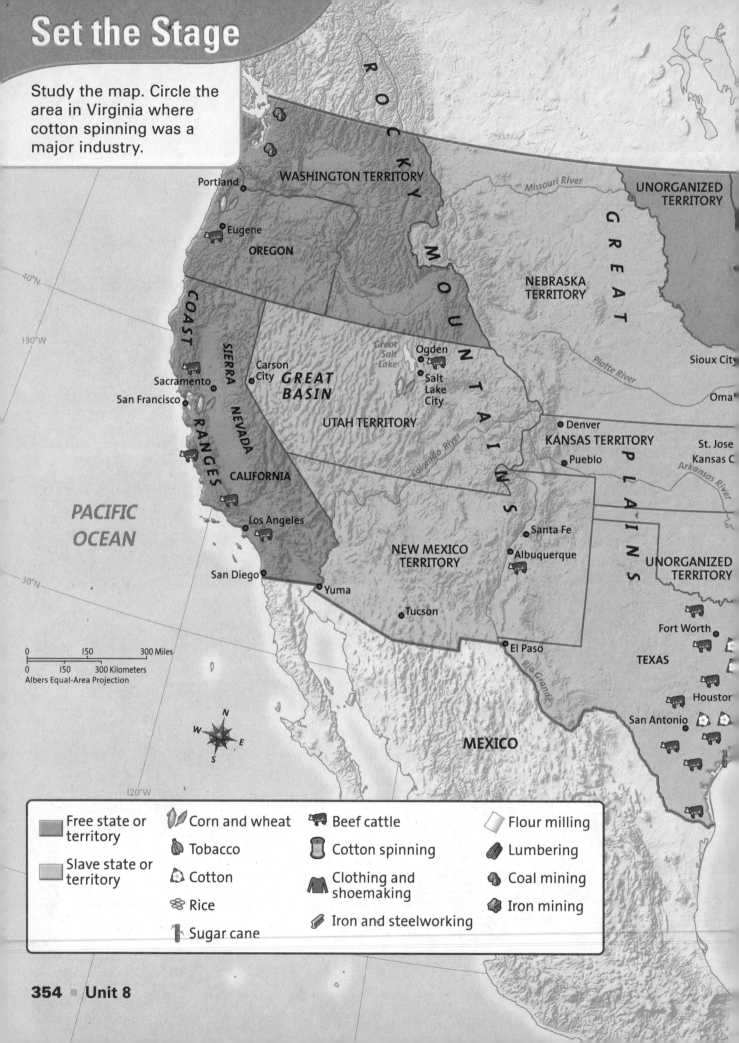

Set the Stage

Study the map. Circle the area in Virginia where cotton spinning was a major industry.

WASHINGTON TERRITORY

Portland

ROCKY

Missouri River

UNORGANIZED TERRITORY

Eugene

OREGON

40°N

130°W

NEBRASKA TERRITORY

GREAT

COAST

SIERRA

Great Salt Lake

Ogden

Platte River

Sioux City

Carson City

GREAT BASIN

Salt Lake City

Oma'

Sacramento

NEVADA

UTAH TERRITORY

Denver

KANSAS TERRITORY

St. Jose

San Francisco

M
O
U
N
T
A
I
N
S

Colorado River

Pueblo

Kansas C

Arkansas River

PACIFIC OCEAN

RANGES

CALIFORNIA

Santa Fe

P
L
A
I
N
S

Los Angeles

NEW MEXICO TERRITORY

Albuquerque

UNORGANIZED TERRITORY

San Diego

30°N

Yuma

Tucson

Fort Worth

TEXAS

El Paso

Houstor

0   150   300 Miles
0   150   300 Kilometers
Albers Equal-Area Projection

N
W   E
S

Rio Grande

San Antonio

MEXICO

120°W

Legend			
Free state or territory	Corn and wheat	Beef cattle	Flour milling
Slave state or territory	Tobacco	Cotton spinning	Lumbering
	Cotton	Clothing and shoemaking	Coal mining
	Rice		Iron mining
	Sugar cane	Iron and steelworking	

United States, 1860

CANADA

MAINE
Bangor

Burlington
VT
Portland
NH

Albany
Syracuse
MA Boston

Buffalo
NEW YORK
Hartford
CT
RI
Providence

MICHIGAN
Detroit
Lake Erie
PA
New York City
Trenton
NJ

WISCONSIN
Lake Superior
Lake Michigan
Lake Huron

NNESOTA

Milwaukee

loines
Chicago
Fort
Wayne
Cleveland
Pittsburgh
Philadelphia

ILLINOIS
INDIANA
OHIO
MD Baltimore
DE

OURI
St. Louis
Cincinnati
Richmond

ingfield
Louisville
VIRGINIA
Portsmouth

KENTUCKY

Nashville
TN
**NORTH
CAROLINA**

RKANSAS
Memphis
Wilmington

Smith
**SOUTH
CAROLINA**
Atlanta
Charleston

ALABAMA
GEORGIA
Savannah

MISSISSIPPI
Montgomery
Natchez

LOUISIANA
FLORIDA

New Orleans

St. Lawrence River
Lake Ontario
Ohio River
Tennessee River
Mississippi River
APPALACHIAN MOUNTAINS

**ATLANTIC
OCEAN**

Gulf of Mexico

A cotton mill,
in Massachusetts

The port of Charleston,
in South Carolina

A cotton plantation,
in Georgia

90°W 80°W 70°W
20°N

Set the Stage

1 How many years passed between the attack on Fort Sumter and Lee's surrender at Appomattox Court House?

_____

2 Circle the names of Union leaders. Underline the names of Confederate leaders.

Robert E. Lee

1807–1870
- Born in Virginia and attended West Point
- Commanded Confederate forces in the Civil War

The Civil War

1820 The Missouri Compromise is passed, p. 369

1828 Congress passes a high tax on imports, p. 364

|1820| |1830| |1840|

At the Same Time

1834 Slavery is abolished in the British empire

1839 The first photographic syste developed in Franc

Clara Barton

1821–1912
- Worked as a Union army nurse during the Civil War
- Founded the American Red Cross in 1881

Ulysses S. Grant

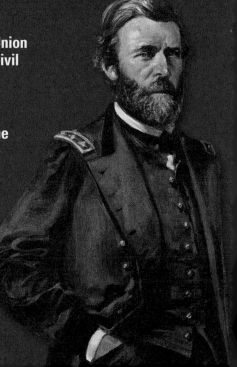

1822–1885
- Commanded Union forces in the Civil War
- Served as the eighteenth President of the United States

Jefferson Davis

1808–1889

- President of the Confederate States of America
- Represented Mississippi in the United States Senate before the Civil War

Abraham Lincoln

1809–1865

- President of the United States during the Civil War
- Signed the Emancipation Proclamation

1850 The Compromise of 1850 is passed, p. 370

1860 Abraham Lincoln is elected President, p. 372

1861 Confederate troops attack Fort Sumter, South Carolina, p. 373

1865 General Lee surrenders at Appomattox Court House, p. 393

1850

1860

1870

53 Napoleon Bonaparte points himself emperor France

1858 Great Britain takes control of India

1860 The Pony Express begins

Robert Smalls

1839–1915

- Freed African American who served in the Union navy during the Civil War
- Became a member of Congress from South Carolina after the war

Belle Boyd

1844–1900

- Spied for the Confederates
- Gave information that helped the Confederates capture Front Royal, Virginia

Preview Vocabulary

states' rights

Many people believed in **states' rights**. They thought the states should have the final say on laws that affected them. p. 364

secede

Several Southern states voted to **secede** from, or leave, the United States. They left to form their own government. p. 372

emancipate

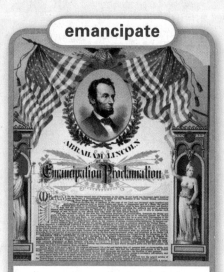

President Lincoln issued an order to **emancipate**, or free, enslaved people in areas of the South that were still fighting. p. 379

segregated

Civil War soldiers were **segregated**. They were kept in separate groups based on their race or culture. p. 385

siege

Vicksburg was under a **siege** for weeks. During this long-lasting attack, soldiers and townspeople ran out of food. p. 388

address

A crowd listened to President Lincoln's **address**. In this short speech, he talked about liberty and equality. p. 391

Reading Social Studies

 Draw Conclusions

LEARN

A **conclusion** is a broad statement about an idea or event. You draw a conclusion by using what you learn from reading, along with what you already know. Keep in mind the new facts you learn and the facts you already know about the subject. Look for hints, and try to figure out what they mean. Being able to draw a conclusion can help you better understand what you read.

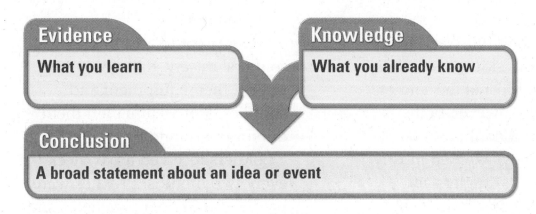

Evidence

What you learn

Knowledge

What you already know

Conclusion

A broad statement about an idea or event

PRACTICE

Draw a conclusion from each paragraph. The first one has been done.

The cotton gin set the Industrial Revolution in the United States in motion. Factory workers in the North turned out textiles, while plantation workers in the South planted more cotton to keep up with the growing demand for it.

Evidence

Knowledge

Conclusion: Many workers were needed to produce textiles and grow cotton.

Conclusion

Most Northerners were against slavery, but most Southerners believed the economy of the South depended upon the labor of enslaved people. A struggle between people against slavery and those in favor of it slowly began to grow.

Conclusion: _____

_____

Read the article. Then complete the activities below.

A Soldier's Life

Tensions rose between the North and the South, mostly because of different opinions about slavery. In time, there was talk of a war. Talk became reality when the first shots of the Civil War were fired on April 12, 1861.

During the Civil War, life was hard on both sides for soldiers of all ages. Most of the soldiers were men. However, both armies included thousands of boys. The boys worked mostly as musicians—buglers and drummers. Some boys were messengers or flag carriers. Historians believe that about 100,000 soldiers in the Union army were less than 15 years old.

Soldiers awoke before dawn. On peaceful days, they spent the morning and the evening practicing drills. For dinner, soldiers sometimes ate pork, beans, rice, and cornbread. However, food often ran out.

Weather could add to the soldiers' misery. Rainy weather soaked their equipment and supplies. Hot weather left them thirsty, dusty, and dirty.

Soldiers received a paycheck every two months. Privates were paid about $11 per paycheck, and generals were paid about $300. Pay was often late. One soldier complained that he was paid only three times in four years.

1. **From the second paragraph, what conclusion can you draw about the number of men who fought during the Civil War?**

_____

_____

_____

2. **Underline the evidence from the article that supports the conclusion that a soldier's life in the Civil War was not easy.**

In the early 1800s, the North and the South became very different regions. It was difficult for Northerners and Southerners to agree on many issues. **Think about the kinds of issues that might divide people in different regions of a country.**

A plantation mansion, in Natchez, Mississippi

ESSENTIAL QUESTIONS
✓ How did cultural, economic, and constitutional issues create bitter divisions between the North and the South?

✓ How did the issues of states' rights and slavery increase sectional tension between the North and South?

HISTORY AND SOCIAL SCIENCE SOL
USI.1b, USI.1c, USI.1d, USI.1h, USI.9a, USI.9b

As in Great Britain, factories were a growing part of the North's economy.

![TextWork](pencil icon) **TextWork**

1 (Focus Skill) Study the graphs. What conclusion can you draw about the North?

_____

_____

_____

Resources of the North and South, 1860

71% / 29% **Population**	86% / 14% **Factories**
67% / 32% **Farms**	71% / 29% **Railroad Mileage**

North   South

Economic Differences

By the mid-1800s, the North and the South had developed very different economies. The Southern economy continued to depend mostly on agriculture, and many plantation owners became wealthy growing cash crops such as cotton and tobacco. On large plantations, enslaved African Americans did most of the work.

In the Northern states, most farms were small and did not require many workers. The North was becoming a manufacturing region, where a growing number of people worked in factories. Trade became a growing part of the Northern economy.

People in the North generally favored high **tariffs**, or taxes on some imports. Tariffs made goods from Europe cost more than goods made in the United States. They helped protect Northern factory owners and workers from European competition. However, tariffs hurt people in the South, who imported more manufactured goods from Europe. Southern planters were also concerned that Great Britain might stop buying cotton from the South if tariffs were added.

Cultural Differences

Cultural differences also separated the North and the South. The North had more large urban centers in which people held many different kinds of jobs. Many people, including immigrants, moved from farms to cities to find work in the new factories that were being built in the North's growing cities.

Life in the South was not changing as quickly. Factories were being built, but not nearly as many as in the North. The South remained primarily agricultural. Most people lived in small villages and on farms and plantations. Although large planters held great power, most Southerners owned small farms. They did not own slaves.

Because of their economic and cultural differences, people of the North and the South disagreed on many social and political issues. National leaders often made decisions based on what was best for their own sections, or regions, instead of what was best for the country as a whole. This regional loyalty is called **sectionalism** (SEK•shuhn•uh•lih•zuhm).

TextWork

2 Which region had more large urban centers?

_____

3 Where did most people in the South live?

_____

_____

4 Use the word *sectionalism* in a sentence about the North and the South.

_____

_____

_____

Many people in the North moved to cities such as New York City (right) to find work. The South continued to rely on cash crops grown on plantations (below).

TextWork

5 (Focus Skill) What did many Southerners conclude would be an effect of the tariff on imported goods?

_____

_____

_____

_____

6 Scan the text. Circle John C. Calhoun's view of the power of the federal government. Underline Andrew Jackson's view.

Constitutional Differences

In 1828, Congress passed a high tariff on some imports. Many Southerners were against the tariff. They feared that the tariff would increase the prices of the goods that they imported from Europe. Planters were also worried that Great Britain might stop buying cotton from the South if a tariff were added on imports from Great Britain.

President Andrew Jackson and Vice President John C. Calhoun had different ideas about the tariff. Like most other Southerners, Calhoun believed in **states' rights**. He thought that the states, not the federal government, should have the final say on laws that affected them. He also believed that the South could declare any national law illegal.

Most Northerners believed that the federal government's power was supreme over that of the states. President Jackson supported states' rights. However, he still believed in a strong central government. Jackson believed that the federal government had the right to collect the tariff.

ANDREW JACKSON

"Our Federal Union—It must and shall be preserved!"

People in the North and the South disagreed about the powers of the federal government.

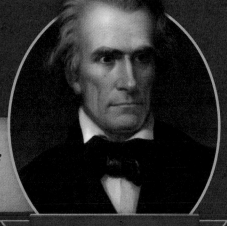

JOHN C. CALHOUN

"The Union, next to our liberty most dear. May we all remember that it can be preserved only by respecting the rights of the states."

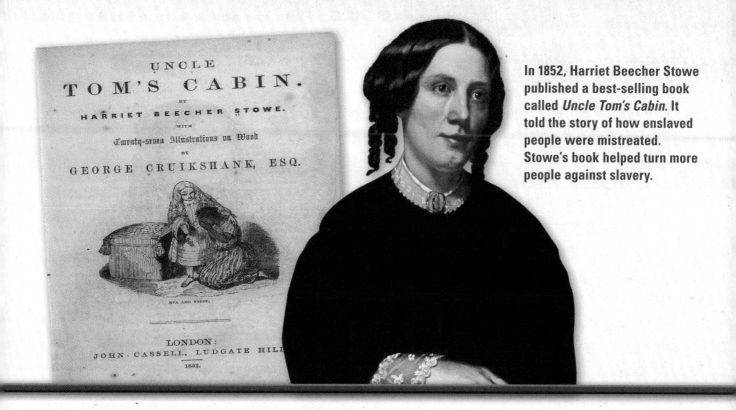

In 1852, Harriet Beecher Stowe published a best-selling book called *Uncle Tom's Cabin*. It told the story of how enslaved people were mistreated. Stowe's book helped turn more people against slavery.

Differences over Slavery

As the demand for cotton grew, so did the number of enslaved workers in the South. In 1800, there were about 900,000 enslaved people in the United States. By 1860, there were 4,000,000.

Many white Northerners and free African Americans thought that slavery was wrong and should be abolished for moral reasons. By 1804, all of the Northern states had abolished slavery.

Slavery continued in the South, however. Many Southerners felt that the abolition of slavery would destroy the region's economy.

Northerners and Southerners also disagreed about who should make decisions when questions about slavery arose. Many Northerners felt that the United States Congress should decide those questions for the whole nation. Many Southerners believed that the state governments should decide.

Slavery increasingly divided the nation. Eventually, it would lead to a civil war between the Northern and Southern states. A **civil war** is a war between people of the same country.

7 Study the graph. During which 20-year period did the number of enslaved people increase the most?

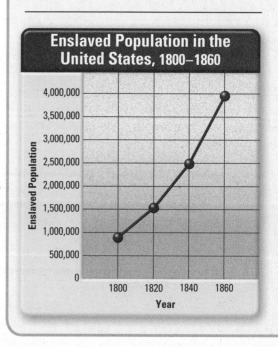

Enslaved Population in the United States, 1800–1860

1. **SUMMARIZE** What regional differences caused disagreements between the North and the South in the early 1800s?

_____

_____

_____

_____

2. How are **sectionalism** and **states' rights** related?

_____

_____

_____

3. Why did many Southerners oppose the tariffs on imported goods?

_____

_____

_____

_____

Circle the letter of the correct answer.

4. Andrew Jackson believed that—

   A sectional loyalty was more important than loyalty to the country

   B the federal government should have authority over the states

   C the federal government had no right to collect tariffs on imported goods

   D slavery should be abolished

5. What was a cause of the growth of slavery in the United States in the 1800s?

   F The growing demand for cotton

   G The demand for imported goods

   H The passing of high tariffs

   J The repeal of high tariffs

6. How did the issue of slavery divide the North and the South?

   A Many people in the North supported slavery, but many in the South did not.

   B Many people in the South supported slavery, but many in the North did not.

   C The North and the South wanted slavery to be abolished.

   D The South wanted more enslaved workers to move to the cities.

activity

Make a Chart Make a two-column chart that shows some of the differences between the Northern states and the Southern states in the early 1800s.

The economy of the South depended on the labor of enslaved workers.

$150 REWARD

RANAWAY from the subscri the night of the 2d instant, a neg who calls himself *Henry May*, ab years old, 5 feet 6 or 8 inches hi dinary color, rather chunky built, head, and has it divided mostly side, and keeps it very nicely cc has been raised in the house, and is rate dining-room servant, and w tavern in Louisville for 18 mon expect he is now in Louisville try make his escape to a free state, (in all probability to Cincinnati, Oh haps he may try to get employment on a steamboat. He is a good c is handy in any capacity as a house servant. Had on when he left cassinett coatee, and dark striped cassinett pantaloons, new—he ha clothing. I will give $50 reward if taken in Louisvill; 100 dollars a one hundred miles from Louisville in this State, and 150 dollars if ta of this State, and delivered to me, or secured in any jail so that I can again.
Bardstown, Ky., September 3d, 1838. WILLIAM BURE

Tensions Grow

In the early 1800s, the North and the South disagreed about the spread of slavery to western lands. Sectionalism grew stronger and threatened to tear the United States apart. **Think about how sectional differences can tear a nation apart.**

Representatives in Congress argued about slavery.

ESSENTIAL QUESTIONS

- ✔ How did the issues of states' rights and slavery increase sectional tension between the North and South?
- ✔ Which states seceded from the Union?
- ✔ Which four slave states stayed in the Union?
- ✔ Where were the other states that remained in the Union located?

HISTORY AND SOCIAL SCIENCE SOL
USI.1b, USI.1c, USI.1f, USI.1h, USI.1d, USI.9b, USI.9c

Enslaved African Americans were often sold at auctions.

① Why do you think it was important to keep a balance between free states and slave states?

_____

_____

_____

② (Focus Skill) Southerners wanted enslaved people to be included in a territory's population count. Northerners did not. Why do you think this was so?

_____

_____

_____

_____

Divisions Grow

As settlers moved into western territories, such as Arkansas, Illinois, Iowa, and Missouri, they took with them their own ways of life. For settlers from the North, this meant a way of life without slavery. For settlers from the South, this meant taking along their enslaved workers.

Once a territory had 60,000 people, it could apply to become a state. In each case, the same question arose. Would the new state become a free state or a slave state? A **free state** did not allow slavery. A **slave state** did.

Many Northerners thought slavery should go no farther that it had. Southern slave owners believed they had the right to take their enslaved workers wherever they wanted.

For a time, there was an equal number of free states and slave states in the nation. This kept a balance between the North and the South in the United States Senate, where each state had two senators. Then, in 1819, Missouri wanted to join the Union as a slave state. If this were allowed, there would be more slave states than free states.

The Missouri Compromise

The Missouri question was debated in Congress for months. Henry Clay, a member of Congress from Kentucky, owned enslaved workers, but he did not want to see the issue of slavery tear apart the nation. In 1820, Clay came up with the Missouri Compromise. A compromise is an agreement in which each side gives up something that it wants.

Under Clay's plan, Missouri was admitted to the Union, or the United States, as a slave state. Maine was admitted as a free state. This maintained the balance of free states and slave states.

Clay also advised that an imaginary line should be drawn on a map across all the lands gained in the Louisiana Purchase. Slavery would be allowed in the places south of the line. It would not be allowed in places north of the line.

Because of his work to settle the differences between the North and the South, Clay became known as the Great Compromiser. The Missouri Compromise kept peace between the North and the South for thirty years.

TextWork

❸ Scan the text. Circle the sentences that explain the details of the Missouri Compromise.

❹ How did the Missouri Compromise help keep the peace between the North and the South?

_____

_____

_____

_____

❺ Study the map. How are the slave states shown?

_____

_____

The Missouri Compromise, 1820

OREGON COUNTRY

UNORGANIZED TERR.

MICH. TERR.

ME.

VT.

N.H.

N.Y.

MASS.

R.I.

CONN.

PA.

N.J.

OHIO

MD.

DEL.

ILL.

IND.

VA.

MO.

KY.

Compromise Line 36° 30'

N.C.

TENN.

ARK. TERR.

S.C.

MEXICO

MISS.

ALA.

GA.

LA.

FLA. TERR.

Henry Clay

Free State   Slave State

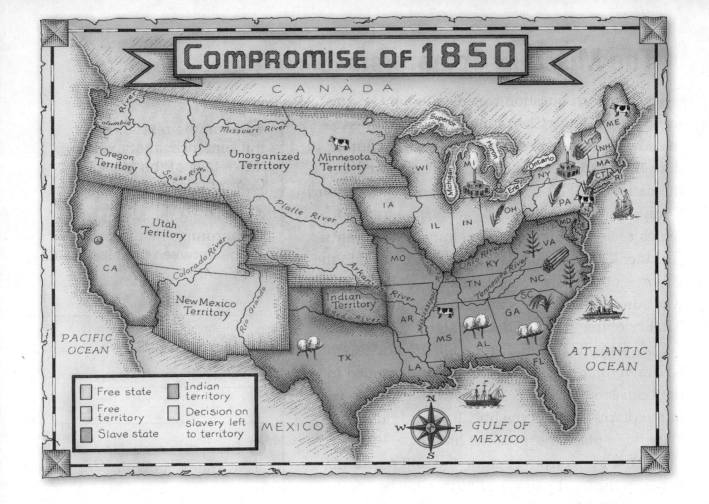

The Compromise of 1850

Until 1848, the number of free states and slave states remained equal. Then the United States gained lands in the Mexican Cession. The lands were not covered by the Missouri Compromise.

Settlers in California asked to join the Union as a free state. This would give the free states a majority in the United States Senate. Southern leaders feared that the North would take control of Congress and that Congress would outlaw slavery everywhere.

Once again, arguments about the spread of slavery broke out. Henry Clay again worked toward a compromise. Under the Compromise of 1850, California entered the Union as a free state. The other new lands from the Mexican Cession would be divided into two territories—New Mexico and Utah. The people in the Southwest territories would be able to decide for themselves whether to allow slavery.

TextWork

6 Scan the text. Underline the event that led to the Compromise of 1850.

7 Why did the Southern states not want California to join the Union as a free state?

_____

_____

8 Study the map. Circle the territories that could decide for themselves whether to be a slave territory or a free territory.

The Kansas-Nebraska Act

Henry Clay died in 1852. However, his work to keep the nation united would soon be challenged. In 1854, Congress passed the Kansas-Nebraska Act. It gave people living in those territories **popular sovereignty** (sahv•RUHN•tee), or the right to decide an issue by voting. Voters in the territories would decide whether to allow slavery there. This law went against the Missouri Compromise, which had outlawed slavery in those places.

The Kansas-Nebraska Act divided the nation even more. People for and against slavery moved into Kansas to influence the vote. Fighting often broke out between the two groups. The territory became known as "Bleeding Kansas."

Kansas would eventually be admitted as a free state. However, because of the fighting there, many people no longer saw a peaceful solution to the slavery issue. More people in the South began to say that states' rights was necessary for the region's self-protection. Some Southerners even began to talk about leaving the Union.

❾ Scan the text. Circle the effects of the Kansas-Nebraska Act.

❿ Study the poster below. Why do you think the slogan "United we stand, divided we fall" was used at the bottom of the poster?

_____

_____

_____

_____

_____

_____

The issue of slavery led to fighting in Kansas (right). People on both sides of the slavery issue held conventions in Kansas.

FREE STATE
ONVENTION!

rsons who are favorable to a union of effort, and a permanent organization of

...e elements of Kansas Territory, and who wish to secure upon the broadest platform the co-operation of all who agree upon this point, are re-
...al or a Delegate to Congress, will also come up before the General Convention.
...y are fully and effectually organized. No jars nor minor issues divide them. And so contend against them successfully, we also must be united.
...ce and harmony of action we are certain to fail. Let every man then do his duty and we are certain of victory.
...e men, without distinction, are earnestly requested to take immediate and effective steps to insure a full and correct representation for every
...tory. "United we stand; divided we fall."

Springs, Wednesday, Sept. 5th '55,

...M., for the purpose of adopting a Platform upon which all may act harmoniously who prefer Freedom to Slavery.

...he Executive Committee of the Free State Party of the Territory of Kansas, as per resolution of the Mass Convention in session at Law...
...6th, 1855.

GOODIN, Sec'y   C. ROBINSON, Chairman.

"United we stand; divided we fall."

TextWork

11 Use the word *secede* in a sentence about the election of 1860.

_____

_____

_____

_____

12 Study the map. Underline the names of the free states. Circle the names of the slave states.

13 Scan the text. Underline the sentence that explains why President Lincoln opposed secession.

Secession

Slavery was the main issue of the presidential election of 1860. The Republican party, which was against the spread of slavery, wanted Abraham Lincoln to be President. Some Southern states threatened to **secede** from, or leave, the Union if Lincoln was elected. Lincoln won the election, and seven Southern states soon seceded. South Carolina was the first. By the end of February 1861, Alabama, Florida, Georgia, Louisiana, Mississippi, and Texas had also seceded.

Like many Northerners, Lincoln believed that the United States was one nation that could not be separated. In 1858, he had said "A house divided against itself cannot stand." Most Southerners believed that states had freely created and joined the Union and could freely leave it. People in the border states—Delaware, Maryland, Kentucky, and Missouri—were torn between the two sides. These states, located between the North and the South, allowed slavery but had not seceded.

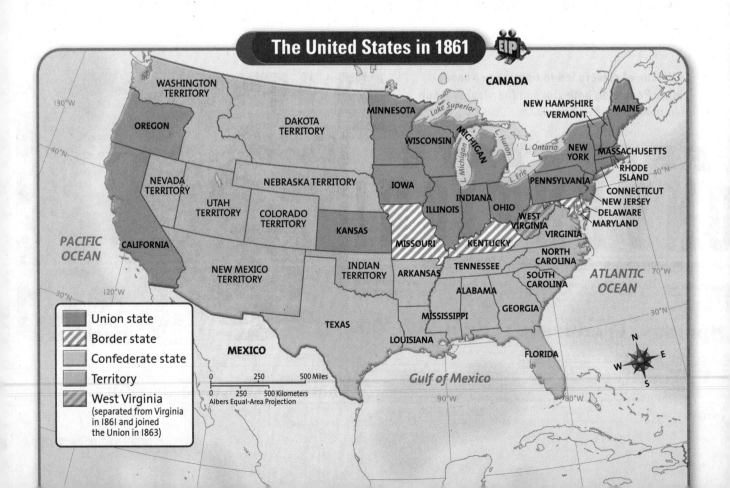

The United States in 1861

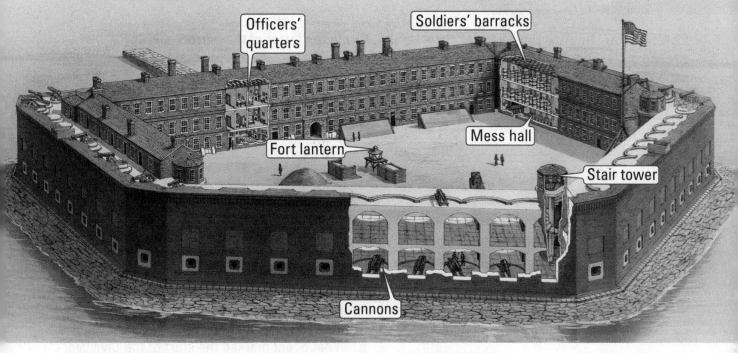

Fort Sumter

Officers' quarters

Soldiers' barracks

Mess hall

Fort lantern

Stair tower

Cannons

Confederate soldiers attacked Fort Sumter for more than 34 hours before Union soldiers surrendered.

Fort Sumter

The states that seceded formed their own country. It was called the Confederate States of America, or the Confederacy. Jefferson Davis, who had represented Mississippi in the United States Senate, was elected president of the Confederacy.

The Confederacy took control of federal property, including forts and post offices, in their states. However, Fort Sumter, on an island in South Carolina, still remained in Union hands.

In April 1861, Fort Sumter was running low on supplies. President Lincoln decided to send supply ships to the fort. On April 12, before the ships could arrive, Confederate troops attacked the fort. Union soldiers were forced to surrender.

After the attack on Fort Sumter, four more Southern states— Arkansas, North Carolina, Tennessee, and Virginia—seceded. The Civil War had begun.

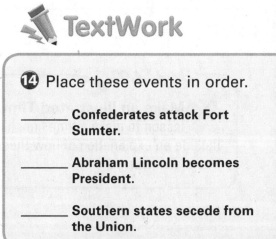

TextWork

14 Place these events in order.

_____ Confederates attack Fort Sumter.

_____ Abraham Lincoln becomes President.

_____ Southern states secede from the Union.

1. SUMMARIZE How did the issues of slavery and states' rights continue to divide the nation?

_____

_____

_____

2. Use the term **popular sovereignty** in a sentence about the Kansas-Nebraska Act.

_____

_____

_____

3. How did the Missouri Compromise differ from the Kansas-Nebraska Act?

_____

_____

_____

Circle the letter of the correct answer.

4. Which state was admitted as a free state as a result of the Missouri Compromise?

  A Missouri

  B Maine

  C California

  D Kansas

5. Which was a border state?

  F Kentucky

  G Virginia

  H Ohio

  J Kansas

6. What event marked the start of the Civil War?

  A The secession of the Southern states

  B The election of Abraham Lincoln

  C The attack on Fort Sumter

  D Fighting in "Bleeding Kansas"

writing

✎ **Make an Illustrated Time Line** Use events from the lesson to make a time line. Illustrate the time line with pictures. Include an explanation of how these events helped lead the nation into a civil war.

WAR BEGU

The South Strikes the Blow.

THE SOUTHERN CONFEDERACY AUT IZES HOSTILITIES.

Newspapers announced the start of the war in 1861.

The Civil War Begins

The Civil War divided the nation and the states. When Virginia seceded, the northwestern part of the state refused to secede. In 1863, this part of Virginia formed the Union state of West Virginia. Even families were divided. Sometimes members of the same family fought against one another. **Think about why it might be difficult to choose sides during a civil war.**

The Battle of Manassas, in Virginia

ESSENTIAL QUESTIONS

✓ Who are considered leaders of the Civil War?
✓ How did Lincoln's view of the nature of the Union differ from Lee's?
✓ Where did critical events of the Civil War take place?
✓ Where were the major battles fought?
✓ What are the ways location and topography influenced important developments in the war, including major battles?

 HISTORY AND SOCIAL SCIENCE SOL
USI.1a, USI.1c, USI.1d, USI.1f, USI.9d, USI.9e

TextWork

1 Scan the text. Underline President Lincoln's view of the nature of the Union. Circle Robert E. Lee's view.

2 Study the chart on page 377. Which side had more industry? How do you think this affected the Union's war plans?

_____

_____

_____

_____

3 Study the flags on page 377. Why do you think the first Confederate flag had seven stars?

_____

_____

_____

General Robert E. Lee

Preparing for War

After the Confederate attack on Fort Sumter President Lincoln was ready to go to war. He believed that the United States was one nation and not a collection of independent states. He was determined to save the Union—by force if necessary. Lincoln quickly asked for 75,000 volunteers to join the army.

Robert E. Lee, an Army general from Virginia, had a different view of the nature of the Union. Like President Lincoln, Lee was against secession. However, Lee did not believe that force should be used to hold the Union together.

Lincoln asked General Lee to lead the Union forces. However, when Virginia seceded, Lee resigned from the United States Army. He refused to fight against his home state. Lee became leader of the Army of Northern Virginia. By the end of the war, he was commander of the whole Confederate army.

War Plans

Location and **topography**, or the physical features of a place, were important to the Union's and Confederacy's war strategies. The Union's plan to win the war was to weaken the South and then to invade it. To weaken the Confederacy, Lincoln planned to blockade Southern ports. This would prevent the South from receiving weapons or supplies from European countries.

The Confederacy planned to protect its lands from Union attack. It also planned to make the war last a long time, hoping that Northerners would get tired of fighting. It also hoped Great Britain and France would provide supplies to the Confederacy, since those countries bought cotton from the South.

Each side planned to take over the other's capital. The North planned to attack the Confederate capital—Richmond, Virginia. The South planned to take Washington, D.C., on the Potomac River.

The North and the South

Union flag

Confederate flag

Weapons of War

The Confederates used hot air balloons for surveillance.

The Confederates also had large guns that were moved on railroads.

Union war technology included ironclad ships.

Advantages in the Civil War

NORTHERN ADVANTAGES
More industry
Advanced railroad system
Strong navy

SOUTHERN ADVANTAGES
Large number of military leaders
Troops experienced in outdoor living
Familiar with the environment of the South

President Abraham Lincoln (left) was the commander in chief of the Union army. Jefferson Davis (right) was the president of the Confederacy.

Thomas "Stonewall" Jackson (right) from Virginia became a hero at the Battle of Manassas.

EIP

TextWork

4 Scan the text. Underline the sentence that explains what influenced the location of many Civil War battles.

5 (Focus Skill) What conclusion can you draw about Thomas "Stonewall" Jackson's impact on his troops?

_____

_____

_____

6 List some of the effects of the Battle of Antietam.

_____

_____

_____

Early Battles

The locations of many Civil War battles were influenced by the struggle to capture the capital cities. Most of the war's early battles took place in the South. More than 100 battles were fought in Virginia alone, more than in any other state.

Manassas and Antietam

The first major battle of the Civil War was fought on July 21, 1861. The first Battle of Manassas, also called the Battle of Bull Run, was fought near Manassas Junction in Virginia. It was a long battle, but the Confederacy won. Confederate General Thomas Jackson kept his troops from falling back. Soldiers said he stood his ground like a stone wall. He became known as "Stonewall" Jackson.

In September 1862, the Confederates marched north. They were met by Union forces at Antietam (an•TEE•tuhm) Creek in Maryland. More soldiers died in the Battle of Antietam than on any other day during the war. The Confederates were forced back into Virginia.

The Emancipation Proclamation

After the Battle of Antietam, President Lincoln decided to issue an order to **emancipate**, or free, some enslaved people. When Lincoln took office, he opposed the spread of slavery to new lands. He was not against slavery in the South. He went to war to keep the nation united. However, as the fighting continued, Lincoln came to feel that the war should also be used to end slavery.

On January 1, 1863, Lincoln signed the Emancipation Proclamation. It said that all enslaved people in areas still fighting against the Union would be "then, thenceforward, and forever free." The signing of the Emancipation Proclamation made freeing enslaved people the new focus of the war.

After the Emancipation Proclamation was signed, Frederick Douglass urged freed African Americans to join the Union forces. Douglass, a formerly enslaved African American, had escaped slavery and had become a leading abolitionist.

TextWork

7 What is the meaning of *emancipate*?

_____

_____

_____

8 Use the letters to add these events to the time line:

A. Attack on Fort Sumter

B. Battle of Bull Run

C. President Lincoln signs the Emancipation Proclamation

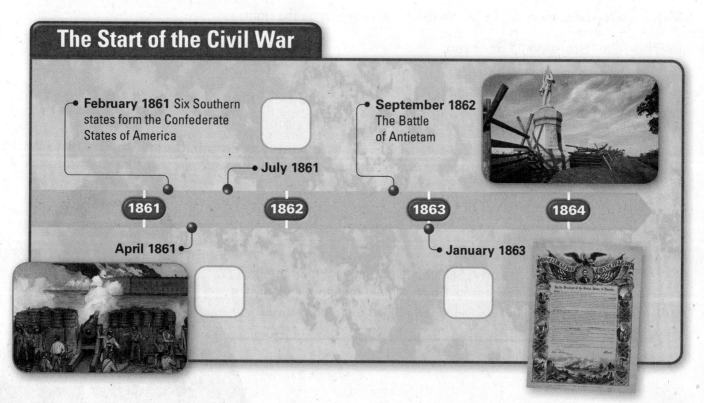

The Start of the Civil War

February 1861 Six Southern states form the Confederate States of America

July 1861

September 1862 The Battle of Antietam

1861　1862　1863　1864

April 1861

January 1863

1. **SUMMARIZE** How was President Lincoln's view of the Union different than Lee's view?

_____

_____

_____

_____

2. Use the term **topography** in a sentence about the Union's and Confederacy's strategies for winning the war.

_____

_____

_____

3. How did the Emancipation Proclamation change the goals of the Civil War?

_____

_____

_____

Circle the letter of the correct answer.

4. The South planned to win the war by—

    A invading the North

    B cutting off trade

    C defending its lands

    D attacking Northern factories

5. The first major battle of the Civil War was—

    F the Battle of Manassas

    G fought over West Virginia statehood

    H fought to blockade Southern ports

    J the Battle of Antietam

Match the leader's name on the left with his contribution on the right.

6. Thomas "Stonewall" Jackson   a leading abolitionist

7. Abraham Lincoln   led Confederate troops at Manassas

8. Frederick Douglass   issued the Emancipation Proclamation

writing

Write a Biography Select one of the leaders of the Civil War mentioned in this lesson. Do additional research and write a short biography that explains the person's role in the war.

Frederick Douglass

Americans at War

Many Americans on both sides suffered hardships during the Civil War. Life on the battlefield and at home was extremely harsh. The war changed the lives of soldiers, women, and enslaved African Americans. **Think about some of the challenges that people might face in wartime.**

African American soldiers, at Fort Corcoran, in Virginia

ESSENTIAL QUESTIONS

✔ What hardships were experienced during the Civil War?
✔ How did the Civil War change the lives of soldiers, women, and enslaved African Americans?

HISTORY AND SOCIAL SCIENCE SOL
USI.1c, USI.1d, USI.9f

❶ Scan the text on this page. Underline descriptions of the challenges and hardships soldiers faced.

❷ (Focus Skill) Why do you think Northern soldiers, in general, did not suffer as much as Southern soldiers?

_____

_____

_____

❸ Study the graph. In which years did the Confederacy have more soldiers, 1863 or 1864? How do you think this affected the average age of Confederate soldiers?

_____

_____

_____

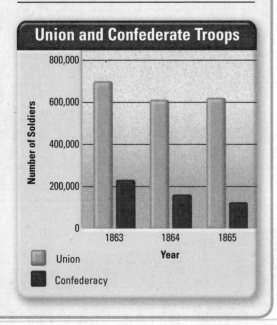

Union and Confederate Troops

The Effects of War

The Civil War brought many challenges to soldiers and their families. One challenge was the decision over which side to support. In the border states and the Southern states, family members and friends were sometimes divided. Some members of these families fought for the Confederacy, while others in the same families fought for the Union. Even President Lincoln's family was divided. His wife, Mary Todd Lincoln, was born in Kentucky. Four of her brothers fought for the South.

On the Battlefield and at Home

During the war, the South especially suffered because most of the battles were fought there. Many Southern cities, such as Atlanta and Richmond, were destroyed. The money that the Confederacy printed became nearly worthless. Prices rose, and food became very expensive.

Confederate troops and civilians often ran low on food and supplies. Many soldiers did not even have warm clothing. As the war went on, Southern troops became younger and younger. Thousands of boys went into battle.

Fighting was fierce and bloody. Often, combat was man-to-man. Many new weapons were used for the first time, such as machine guns and rifles that could shoot great distances. These weapons helped make the Civil War one of the deadliest in United States history.

Civil War Casualties

The Civil War had the most **casualties**, or losses of soldiers in battle, of any war in United States history. More than 600,000 Americans died during the war. In addition to the many who died in battle, thousands died from diseases, such as typhoid, pneumonia, and measles. Disease was a major killer. In fact, more Americans died of diseases than in battle during the Civil War.

A SOLDIER'S LIFE

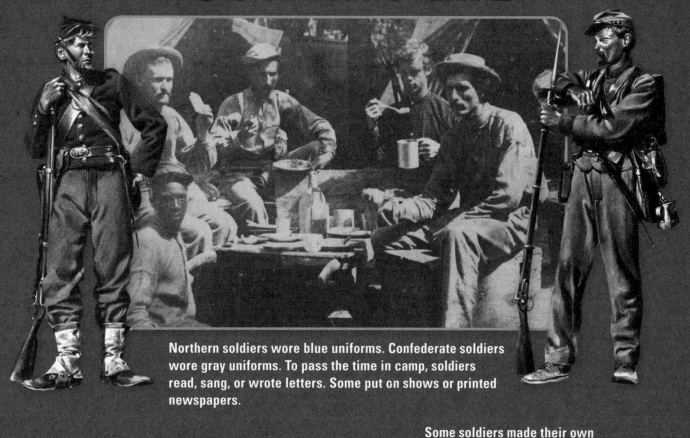

Northern soldiers wore blue uniforms. Confederate soldiers wore gray uniforms. To pass the time in camp, soldiers read, sang, or wrote letters. Some put on shows or printed newspapers.

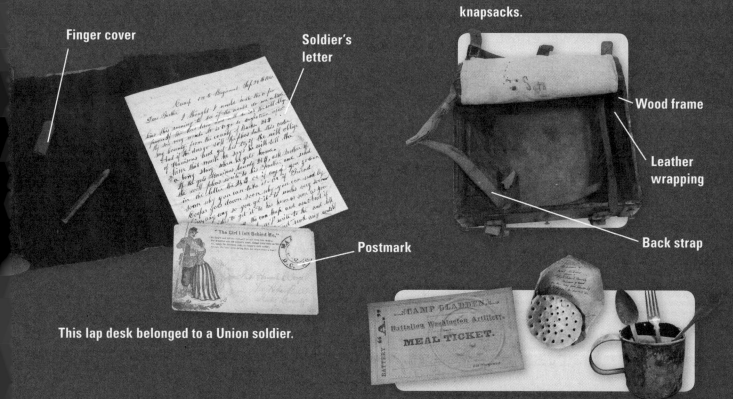

Finger cover

Soldier's letter

Postmark

This lap desk belonged to a Union soldier.

Some soldiers made their own knapsacks.

Wood frame

Leather wrapping

Back strap

Army food was usually poor. Soldiers sometimes had only hard biscuits, called hardtack, to eat.

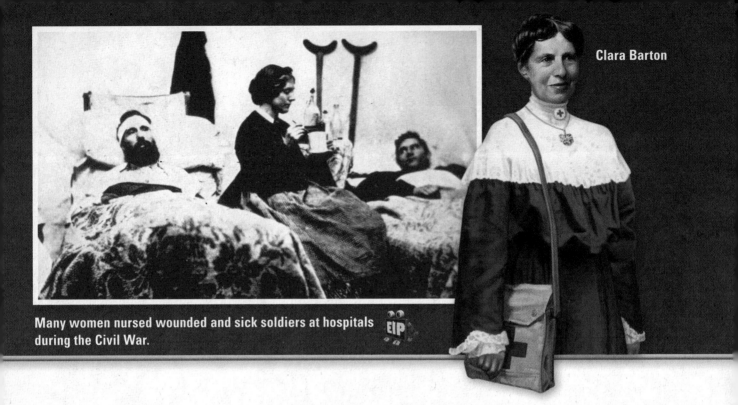

Clara Barton

Many women nursed wounded and sick soldiers at hospitals during the Civil War.

TextWork

4 Scan the text. Circle descriptions of how women in the North and women in the South helped the war effort.

5 In what ways were the contributions of Clara Barton and Sally Tompkins alike? How were they different?

Alike: _____

_____

_____

Different: _____

_____

_____

Women Help the War Effort

In both the North and the South, only men were allowed to join the army. However, when the men left home to fight, women took over many of their jobs. Women worked in factories, in businesses, and on farms and plantations. They also sent food to the troops and collected supplies.

Many women worked as nurses. Dorothea Dix and Clara Barton both worked as nurses for the Union army. Barton's kindness earned her the nickname "Angel of the Battlefield." Barton traveled from battle to battle to care for sick and wounded Union soldiers. After the war, Barton wanted to continue to help those in need. In 1881, she founded the American Red Cross.

Sally Tompkins started a hospital in Virginia for Confederate soldiers. This hospital was located in the home of Judge John Robertson and became known as the Robertson Hospital. During the war, about 1,300 soldiers were cared for at the hospital.

Some women served as spies. Belle Boyd, from Virginia, spied for the Confederacy. A few women even dressed as men and fought in battles.

African American Soldiers

African Americans fought in the Union army. The Union enlisted African American sailors and soldiers early in the war. Some African Americans accompanied Confederate army units on the field of battle. Others worked aboard ships or in camps.

African American soldiers in the Union army were not paid as much as white soldiers. They were also given poor equipment. They served in segregated units that were commanded by white officers. In a **segregated** group, people of one race or culture are kept separate from other people.

Despite this discrimination, or unfair treatment, African American soldiers served heroically. They led raids behind enemy lines, served as scouts and spies, and fought in many battles. Among those who served was Robert Smalls, a freed slave from South Carolina who became a Union naval captain. After the war, Smalls served in the South Carolina legislature and the United States Congress.

 TextWork

6 What clues can you use to remember the meaning of *segregated*?

_____

_____

_____

7 Why do you think that some African Americans accompanied Confederate army units?

_____

_____

_____

_____

_____

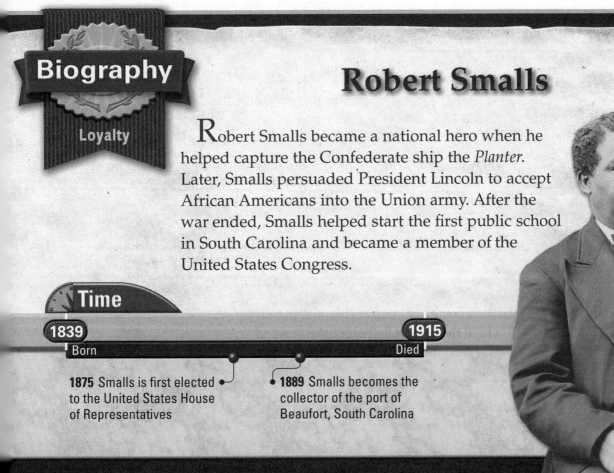

Biography

Loyalty

Robert Smalls

Robert Smalls became a national hero when he helped capture the Confederate ship the *Planter*. Later, Smalls persuaded President Lincoln to accept African Americans into the Union army. After the war ended, Smalls helped start the first public school in South Carolina and became a member of the United States Congress.

Time

1839 Born — **1915** Died

1875 Smalls is first elected to the United States House of Representatives

1889 Smalls becomes the collector of the port of Beaufort, South Carolina

385

Children IN HISTORY

Drummer Boys

During the Civil War, boys as young as 8 joined the army as drummer boys. Drummer boys traveled with the army and even marched into battles with them. Their job was to drum a beat for marching soldiers and to drum signals to the troops. Some drummer boys helped care for wounded soldiers. Clarence D. McKenzie of Brooklyn, New York, was 11 years old when he went off to war. He was the first resident of Brooklyn to die in the Civil War.

Make It Relevant How would you feel if you had to leave your home at a very young age to fight in a war?

Lesson 4 Review

1. **SUMMARIZE** How did the Civil War affect African Americans and women?

   _____

   _____

   _____

2. Use **segregate** in a sentence about African American soldiers in the Civil War.

   _____

   _____

   _____

Circle the letter of the correct answer.

3. What caused the most casualties in the Civil War?

   A Lack of food

   B Battle wounds

   C Disease

   D Poor equipment

4. Who was known for his bravery in the Union navy?

   F Judge John Robertson

   G Robert Smalls

   H Jefferson Davis

   J Abraham Lincoln

activity

Make a Poster Draw a poster entitled "Effects of the Civil War." Show the effects of the war from the perspectives of Union and Confederate soldiers, women, and African Americans.

This African American soldier fought in the Union army.

Toward Union Victory

By May 1863, the Union army finally had a leader as effective as Confederate General Robert E. Lee. His name was Ulysses S. Grant. Grant's leadership helped the Union army win many important battles. **Think about how changes in leadership might affect the outcome of a war.**

General Ulysses S. Grant (left) with other Union officers

ESSENTIAL QUESTIONS

- ✓ Who are considered leaders of the Civil War?
- ✓ Where did critical events of the Civil War take place?
- ✓ Where were the major battles fought?
- ✓ Which are the ways location and topography influenced important developments in the war, including major battles?
- ✓ What hardships were experienced during the Civil War?

HISTORY AND SOCIAL SCIENCE SOL

USI.1c, USI.1d, USI.1f, USI.1h, USI.9d, USI.9e, USI.9f

TextWork

1 How did the siege of Vicksburg affect the people living there?

_____

_____

_____

2 Scan the text. Circle the sentences that explain the importance of the location of the Battle of Vicksburg.

3 Focus Skill Based on the outcome of the Battle of Vicksburg, what conclusions can you draw about Ulysses S. Grant?

_____

_____

Battle of Vicksburg

One of Ulysses S. Grant's most important battles began in May 1863 at Vicksburg, Mississippi. Vicksburg was the Confederate headquarters on the Mississippi River.

Grant laid siege to the city of Vicksburg. A **siege** is a long-lasting attack. For weeks, Union cannons pounded the city, and the Union army cut off Confederate supply lines. The soldiers and townspeople of Vicksburg soon ran out of food. However, they refused to surrender.

Some Confederates ate mules, horses, and dogs to survive. They tore down houses for firewood and dug large caves in the hillsides for shelter.

Two months after the siege began, on July 4, 1863, the Confederate soldiers at Vicksburg surrendered. Vicksburg was a key victory for the Union. By taking Vicksburg, the Union forces gained control of the Mississippi River. This cut the Confederacy into two parts. Its western states could no longer communicate easily with its eastern states.

General Grant claimed victory at Vicksburg on July 4, 1863.

Major Battles of the Civil War

IA

IL

IN

OH

PA

NJ

MD

DE

Gettysburg 1863

Antietam (Sharpsburg) 1862

Bull Run (Manassas) 1861, 1862

Washington, D.C.

Chancellorsville 1863

Fredericksburg 1862

Cold Harbor 1864

ATLANTIC OCEAN

KS

MO

WV (1863)

VA

Richmond

Hampton Roads 1862

Perryville 1862

Petersburg 1864–1865

Seven Days 1862

0   100   200 Miles

0   100   200 Kilometers

Albers Equal-Area Projection

Fort Donelson 1862

KY

Fort Henry 1862

Nashville 1864

Bentonville 1865

Indian Territory

AR

Franklin 1864

Stones River 1862–1863

TN

NC

Chattanooga 1863

Shiloh (Pittsburg Landing) 1862

Chickamauga 1863

Kennesaw Mountain 1864

SC

Fort Fisher 1865

MS

Atlanta 1864

Charleston

Fort Sumter 1861

Fort Wagner 1863

Vicksburg 1863

AL

GA

Savannah

TX

LA

Mobile Bay 1864

FL

Gulf of Mexico

Legend

- Union victory
- Confederate victory
- March to the Sea
- Capital city
- Union state or territory
- Confederate state
- Border state
- West Virginia (separated from Virginia in 1861 and joined the Union in 1863)

Battle of Chancellorsville

Shortly before Grant's army attacked Vicksburg, Lee's army battled Union troops at Chancellorsville, Virginia. Even though the Confederate army at Chancellorsville was half the size of the Union army, Lee defeated the Union forces.

The victory was costly, however. The Confederacy lost one of its best generals. In the confusion of battle, General Thomas "Stonewall" Jackson was accidentally shot by one of his own soldiers and later died.

The victory at Chancellorsville gave the Confederacy the confidence to try again to invade the North. Southern leaders thought that a major victory there would cause Northerners to demand an end to the war.

In June 1863, General Lee's troops headed north. They reached the town of Gettysburg, Pennsylvania, on July 1.

 **TextWork**

4 Study the map. Circle the site of the Battle of Vicksburg and draw a box around the site of the Battle of Chancellorsville. Which side won the Battle of Chickamauga, also fought in 1863?

_____

5 Why was the Battle of Chancellorsville an important battle for the Confederacy?

_____

_____

_____

_____

6 Study the map and the text. How did topography help Union forces in the Battle of Gettysburg?

_____

_____

_____

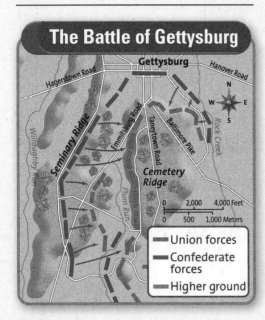

The Battle of Gettysburg

Gettysburg
Hanover Road
Hagerstown Road
Seminary Ridge
Emmitsburg Road
Taneytown Road
Baltimore Pike
Rock Creek
Willoughby Run
Cemetery Ridge
Plum Run

N W E S

0   2,000   4,000 Feet
0   500   1,000 Meters

— Union forces
— Confederate forces
— Higher ground

7 Underline the sentences that explain why the Battle of Gettysburg was a turning point in the Civil War.

Battle of Gettysburg

When Lee's troops arrived in Gettysburg, they were met by a Union army led by George G. Meade. The fighting raged for three days. On July 3, Lee ordered General George Pickett and his entire division to lead a charge across open land toward the Union army's center.

Joined by thousands more soldiers, in what became known as Pickett's Charge, they marched shoulder to shoulder in a line half a mile wide. They were met by gunfire from Union troops, which controlled the higher ground on the battlefield. This gave the Union an advantage, and they repelled, or turned back, the Confederates.

The Battle at Gettysburg was one of the deadliest battles of the war. During those three days, more than 3,000 Union soldiers and nearly 4,000 Confederate soldiers were killed. More than 20,000 on each side were wounded or listed as missing.

The Union victory at Gettysburg marked a turning point in the war. After the battle, General Lee and his army retreated to Virginia. The Confederate army would never again be able to launch a major attack against the Union.

Lincoln delivered his famous Gettysburg Address (right) just four months after the deadly battle (below).

The Gettysburg Address

On November 19, 1863, President Lincoln traveled to Gettysburg to dedicate a Union cemetery there. Lincoln wanted to speak to honor those who had died in the battle and to encourage people to continue to support the Union cause. A crowd of nearly 6,000 people gathered for the ceremony.

Lincoln gave an **address**, or short speech, that day. He spoke for less than three minutes. In fact, his speech was so short that many people in the crowd were disappointed. Over time, however, this address became one of the most famous speeches in United States history.

Lincoln spoke about the ideals of liberty and equality on which the country had been founded. He honored the soldiers who had died defending those ideals. He also called on the people of the Union to try even harder to win the struggle those soldiers died for. Lincoln ended with these words,

> **"we here highly resolve that these dead shall not have died in vain . . . that government of the people, by the people, for the people, shall not perish [disappear] from the earth."**

TextWork

8 Scan the text. Underline the reasons that President Lincoln wanted to speak at Gettysburg.

9 Use the word *address* in a sentence about Lincoln.

_____

_____

10 Study the excerpt from the Gettysburg Address. Why do you think people today still find meaning in Lincoln's address?

_____

_____

_____

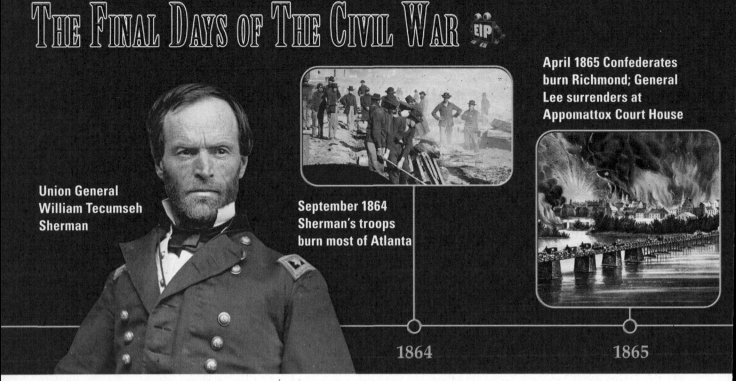

THE FINAL DAYS OF THE CIVIL WAR

Union General William Tecumseh Sherman

September 1864 Sherman's troops burn most of Atlanta

April 1865 Confederates burn Richmond; General Lee surrenders at Appomattox Court House

1864

1865

TextWork

11 Scan the text. Circle the sentences that describe the effects of the war on Atlanta and Richmond.

12 (Focus Skill) Why did the Confederates set fire to Richmond as they left?

_____

_____

_____

_____

13 Study the time line. How long after Sherman's troops burned most of Atlanta did Lee surrender?

_____

The Final Days of War

In 1864, President Lincoln appointed Ulysses S. Grant commander of all the Union forces. Grant planned to march to Richmond and capture the Confederate capital. He ordered Union General William Tecumseh Sherman to march from Chattanooga, Tennessee, to Atlanta, Georgia.

In September 1864, Sherman reached Atlanta. After burning most of the city, his army of 62,000 men set out for Savannah, Georgia. Their march has become known as Sherman's March to the Sea. The army cut a path of destruction 60 miles wide and 300 miles long. Union soldiers burned homes and stores, destroyed crops, and tore up railroad tracks.

In the North, Grant's army was defeating Lee's smaller army. Lee was running out of troops and supplies. In April 1865, Confederate troops evacuated Richmond, Virginia. As they left, they set parts of the city on fire. More than 900 buildings were destroyed, and hundreds more were badly damaged. Union soldiers soon took control of Richmond and chased Lee's army to the west. The Confederacy was collapsing.

The War Ends

On April 9, 1865, Lee met Grant in the Virginia village of Appomattox (a•puh•MA•tuhks) Court House. Grant wrote out the terms of surrender, and Lee signed his name. After four years of bloodshed, the war was over.

On April 14, 1865, just five days after Lee's surrender, President Lincoln was **assassinated**, or murdered. Andrew Johnson, the new President, made plans to rebuild the nation. In December 1865, Congress passed the Thirteenth Amendment, which ended slavery in the United States. In 1868, the Fourteenth Amendment gave all United States citizens equal treatment under the law.

This painting shows General Lee (right) surrendering to General Grant.

Lesson 5 Review

1. **SUMMARIZE** How did the Union defeat the Confederacy?

   _____

   _____

2. **VOCABULARY** Use the term **assassinate** in a sentence about the end of the Civil War.

   _____

   _____

3. How did the location of Vicksburg make the battle there an important victory for the Union?

   _____

   _____

4. How might the Battle of Gettysburg have turned out if the Confederates had controlled the higher ground?

   _____

   _____

writing

✎ **Write a Speech** Write a speech that either General Lee or President Lincoln might have given at the end of the war. The speech should clearly express the speaker's perspective.

President Lincoln

393

Heads and Tails

Draw a line to match the front of each coin with the correct reverse side.

Crack the Code

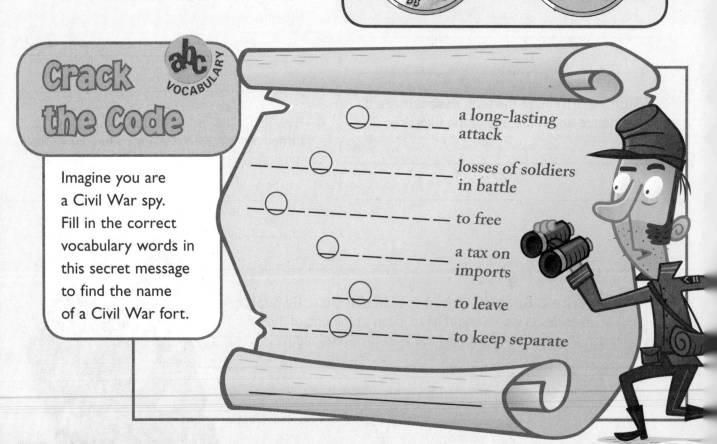

Imagine you are a Civil War spy. Fill in the correct vocabulary words in this secret message to find the name of a Civil War fort.

○ _ _ _ _ _ _ — a long-lasting attack

_ _ _ _ ○ _ _ _ _ _ _ — losses of soldiers in battle

_ _ ○ _ _ _ _ — to free

_ _ _ ○ _ _ _ — a tax on imports

_ _ _ ○ _ _ — to leave

_ _ _ ○ _ _ _ _ — to keep separate

Poster Perplexity

The second half of each title has been put on the wrong poster. Now help straighten out the confusion! In each box, place the number from the bottom half that matches the top half.

"NORTH AND SOUTH GO TO WAR ABOUT" ___

"LINCOLN ISSUES THE" ___

"LONG, BITTER WAR ENDS" ___

1 "WHEN GENERAL LEE SURRENDERS"

2 "States' Rights and Slavery"

3 "EMANCIPATION PROCLAMATION"

Review and Test Prep

The Big Idea

Regional differences can divide a nation and its people.

Summarize the Unit

⭐ **Focus Skill** **Draw Conclusions** Complete the graphic organizer to show that you know how to draw conclusions about the issues that divided the United States.

Evidence

The North and the South disagreed about the spread of slavery.

Knowledge

The North and South were located in different parts of the United States.

Conclusion

_____

_____

Use Vocabulary

Fill in the missing terms, using the correct vocabulary term from the Word Bank.

1. Some Southern states threatened to _____ from the Union.

2. _____ divided the country and led to a civil war.

3. In 1863, Lincoln issued an order to _____ some enslaved people.

4. The city of Vicksburg was under _____ for many weeks.

5. Those who supported _____ believed that the states, not the federal government, should have the final say in their own affairs.

Word Bank

sectionalism
p. 363

states' rights
p. 364

popular sovereignty
p. 371

secede p. 372

emancipate
p. 379

siege p. 388

Think About It

Circle the letter of the correct answer.

6. The South's economy depended mostly on—

   A manufacturing

   B farming

   C mining

   D shipping

7. Why did people in the North generally favor high tariffs?

   F Tariffs reduced the cost of transporting goods.

   G Tariffs provided salaries for factory workers.

   H Tariffs protected factory owners from foreign competition.

   J Tariffs increased the amount of technology used in production.

8. The Missouri Compromise kept peace between the North and the South by—

   A keeping the balance of free states and slave states

   B ending slavery in the newly acquired territories

   C ending high tariffs on imports

   D settling the issue of states' rights

9.
> "A house divided against itself cannot stand. I believe the government cannot endure {last} ... half slave and half free."
> — Abraham Lincoln

What was Lincoln explaining with this patriotic quotation?

   F His ideas about architecture

   G His position on slavery

   H His thoughts about the United States government

   J His life in the White House

10.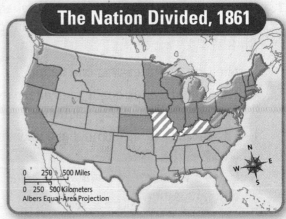

The Nation Divided, 1861

On the map, the states that seceded from the Union are shown in—

   A orange

   B orange and green stripes

   C green

   D orange and white stripes

11. The first Southern states seceded from the Union when—

   F Abraham Lincoln was elected President

   G California was admitted as a free state

   H Fort Sumter was attacked

   J the Battle of Manassas was won

12.

The poster best expresses the views of most people in the—

   A North

   B South

   C border states

   D western states

13. Which statement best describes Abraham Lincoln's view on the nature of the United States?

   F The United States was one nation.

   G The United States could be divided into Northern and Southern sections.

   H The United States did not have popular sovereignty.

   J Force should not be used to keep the Union together.

14.

The Union wanted to capture these Southern cities because they were located—

   A in the border states

   B near the capitals

   C at sources of raw materials

   D where supplies could be received

15. Who was the President of the Confederate States of America?

   F Jefferson Davis

   G Ulysses S. Grant

   H Thomas "Stonewall" Jackson

   J Robert E. Lee

16.

> "That ... all persons held as slaves within any State or designated part of a State, the people whereof shall then be in rebellion against the United States, ... shall be then, thenceforward, and forever free."
> — Abraham Lincoln

What was Lincoln explaining in this excerpt from the Emancipation Proclamation?

   A That all slaves should be freed immediately

   B That enslaved people should remain enslaved

   C That enslaved people in the parts of the South that were still fighting against the Union should be freed

   D That enslaved African Americans should be allowed to vote and hold office

17. Which battle gave the Union control of the Mississippi River and divided the Confederacy?

   F Vicksburg

   G Gettysburg

   H Chancellorsville

   J Manassas

18. How did topography affect the Battle of Gettysburg?

   A The South controlled the higher ground on the battlefield.

   B Gettysburg was located on a major waterway.

   C The North controlled the higher ground on the battlefield.

   D The South had to cross a major river before it met Northern forces.

19. Why is the Battle of Gettysburg considered a turning point in the Civil War?

F It gave the South confidence to try invading the North.

G The Southern army captured a major manufacturing city in the North.

H The South could no longer control the Mississippi River.

J The Southern army was weakened and could never again launch a major attack on the North.

20.

Abraham Lincoln and the Civil War

1861	1863	1865
?	Lincoln signs the Emancipation Proclamation.	Lincoln is assassinated.

What event is missing from the time line?

A Lincoln becomes President.

B Lincoln orders the attack on Fort Sumter.

C Lincoln gives the Gettysburg Address.

D Lincoln surrenders at Appomattox Court House.

21. The Civil War ended when—

F General Sherman's army burned Atlanta

G General Lee surrendered at Appomattox Court House

H President Lincoln was assassinated

J Andrew Johnson became President

22. Which of the following ended slavery in the United States?

A The Emancipation Proclamation

B The Thirteenth Amendment

C The Gettysburg Address

D The Missouri Compromise

Answer these questions.

23. How did the Emancipation Proclamation change the North's reasons for fighting the Civil War?

_____

_____

24. Why do you think people today still find meaning in the Gettysburg Address?

_____

_____

25. What effect did the siege of Vicksburg have on soldiers? What effect did it have on civilians?

_____

_____

The secret passage must be somewhere around here. Hurry!

It's not long before the start of the Civil War, and Harriet Tubman has come to you for help. Can you and Eco help her guide a group of enslaved people to freedom in the North? Your path will take you through dark swamps, secret stops, and underground tunnels. This might just be your toughest challenge yet! Play the game now online.

Show What You Know

✏ Writing Write Questions

Imagine you have the opportunity to interview a Southern leader and a Union leader at the time of the Civil War. Write a list of questions to ask about the differences between the North and South that are causing tension between the regions. Think about their different points of view, and write the responses to the questions that each leader might have given.

🖌 Activity Make a Civil War Scrapbook

Make a scrapbook about the Civil War. Write captions, stories, and poems about important people, places, and events in the war. Include maps to show where important events took place. Then use your scrapbook to explain to classmates some causes and effects of the Civil War.

For Your Reference

GLOSSARY

INDEX

STANDARDS OF LEARNING

Glossary

The Glossary contains important history and social science words and their definitions, listed in alphabetical order. Each word is respelled as it would be in a dictionary. When you see this mark ´ after a syllable, pronounce that syllable with more force. The page number at the end of the definition tells where the word is first used in this book. Guide words at the top of each page help you quickly locate the word you need to find.

add, āce, câre, pälm; end, ēqual; it, īce; odd, ōpen, ôrder; tŏŏk, pōōl; up, bûrn; yōō as *u* in *fuse*; oil; pout; ə as *a* in *above, e* in *sicken, i* in *possible, o* in *melon, u* in *circus*; check; ring; thin; this; zh as in *vision*

A

abolitionist (a•bə•li´shən•ist) A person who wanted to end slavery. p. 342

address (ə•dres´) A short speech. p. 391

adobe (ə•dō´bē) A brick made of sun-dried earth and straw. p. 81

alliance (ə•lī´ənts) A formal partnership. p. 144

ally (ə´lī) A partner. p. 157

amendment (ə•mend´mənt) A change. p. 293

annex (a´neks) To add on. p. 324

apprentice (ə•pren´təs) A person who lived and trained with a skilled worker for several years. p. 208

archaeology (ar•kē•ä´lə•jē)) The study of past cultures. p. 58

arsenal (ärs´nəl) A weapons storehouse. p. 284

artifact (är´tə•fakt) Any object made or used by people in the past. p. 58

artisan (är´tə•zən) A skilled craftworker. p. 208

assassinate (ə•sa´sən•āt) To murder. p. 393

B

barter (bär´tər) To exchange goods without using money. p. 90

basin (bā´sən) A low, bowl-shaped area with higher ground around it. pp. I1, 24

bay (bā) An inlet of the sea or some other body of water, usually smaller than a gulf. p. I1

benefit (be´nə•fit) Something gained. p. 334

bill (bil) An idea for a new law. p. 290

boycott (boi´kät) To refuse to buy or use goods and services. p. 236

C

Cabinet (kab´ə•nit) A group of the President's most trusted advisers. p. 296

campaign (kam•pān´) A series of military actions carried out for a certain goal. p. 258

canal (kə•nal´) A human-made waterway dug across the land. p. 10

canyon (kan´yən) A deep, narrow valley with steep sides. p. I1

cape (kāp) A point of land that extends into the water. p. I1

capital resources (ka´pə•təl rē´sôr•səz) Goods that are produced to make other goods or to provide services. p. 63

caravan (kar´ə•van) A group of travelers. p. 115

cardinal direction (kär´də•nəl də•rek´shən) One of the main directions: north, south, east, or west. p. I3

cash crop (kash kräp) A crop that people harvest to sell rather than to use themselves. p. 199

casualty (ka´zhəl•tē) Loss of a soldier in battle. p. 382

category (ka´tə•gōr•ē) A group of items that have something in common. p. 319

cause (kôz) An event or an action that makes something else happen. p. 231

cession (se´shən) Something that is given up. p. 324

channel (cha´nəl) The deepest part of a body of water. p. I1

civil war (si´vəl wôr) A war between people in the same country. p. 365

claim (klām) To declare ownership. p. 123

clan (klan) Extended family. p. 88

classify (kla´sə•fī) To sort information into categories. p. 319

coastal plain (kōs´təl plān) An area of flat land along a sea or ocean. p. I1

colony (kä´lə•nē) A land ruled by another country. p. 137

common (kä´mən) A grassy area at the center of a New England town shared by the town's people. p. 188

compare (kəm•par´) To tell how two or more things are alike, or similar. p. 55

compass rose (kəm´pəs rōz) A direction marker on a map. p. I3

compromise (käm´prə•mīz) An agreement in which each side gives up something that it wants. p. 287

conclusion (kən•kloo´zhən) A broad statement about an idea or event. p. 359

confederation (kən•fe•də•rā´shən) A loose group of governments working together. p. 70

congress (kän´grəs) A formal meeting of delegates, or representatives. p. 241

consequence (kän´sə•kwens) What happens because of some action. p. 334

constitution (kän•stə•too´shən) A written plan of government. p. 282

continent (kän´tə•nənt) A large landmass that is mostly surrounded by water. p. 7

contrast (kän´trast) To tell how two or more things are different. p. 55

convention (kən•ven´shən) An important meeting. p. 285

cost (kôst) The effort made to achieve or gain something. p. 334

county seat (koun´tē sēt) The city or town where the county government is located. p. 203

crossroads (krôs´ rōdz) A place that connects people, goods, and ideas. p. 40

cultural interaction (kəl´chə•rəl in•tə•rak´shən) The sharing or exchanging of ideas and ways of living. p. 153

culture (kul´chər) A way of life. p. 58

debtor (de´tərs) A person who was put into prison for owing money. p. 182

declaration (de•klə•rā´shən) An official statement. p. 246

delta (del´tə) A triangle-shaped area of land at the mouth of a river. p. I1

demand (di•mand´) A need or a desire for a good or service by people willing to pay for it. p. 144

detail (dē´tāl) A sentence that gives more information about the main idea. p. 5

diverse (di•vərs´) Different. p. 191

due process of law (doo prä´ses uv lô) The right to a fair trial and a lawyer. p. 293

economic interaction (e•kə•nä´mik in•tə•rak´shən) The sharing or exchanging of goods and resources to meet people's needs. p. 153

economy (i•kä´nə•mē) The way people use their resources to meet their needs. p. 90

effect (i•fekt´) What happens as a result of a cause. p. 231

elevation (e•lə•vā´shən) The height of the land above sea level. p. 16

emancipate (i•man´si•pāt) To free. p. 379

empire (em´pīr) Lands ruled by the nation that conquered them. p. 116

entrepreneur (än•trə•prə•nər´) Someone who organizes resources to bring a new or better good or service to market in hopes of earning a profit. p. 329

environment (in•vī´rən•mənt) Surroundings. p. 35

erosion (i•rō´zhən) The gradual wearing away of Earth's surface. p. 22

expedition (ek•spə•di´shən) A trip for the purpose of exploration. p. 130

export (ek´spôrt) A product that leaves a country. p. 215

fall line (fôl līn) The area along which rivers form waterfalls or rapids as the rivers drop to lower land. p. I1

federal system (fe´də•rəl sis´təm) A system of government in which the national and state governments share power. p. 288

fertile (fər´təl) Good for farming. p. 25

forty-niners (fôr´tē nī´nər) Gold seekers who arrived in California in 1849. p. 331

free state (frē stāt) A state that did not allow slavery before the Civil War. p. 368

frontier (frən•tir´) The land just beyond the areas already settled. p. 37

gateway (gāt´wā) A path that connects to distant lands. p. 31

generalize (jen´rə•līz) A statement that shows how different facts in a piece of writing are related. p. 279

glacier (glā´shər) A slow-moving sheet of ice. pp. I1, 25

gold rush (gōld rəsh) A sudden rush of people to an area where gold has been found. p. 331

grant (grant) A sum of money given for a particular purpose. p. 136

grid system (grid sis´təm) A set of lines the same distance apart that cross one another to form boxes. p. I4

gulf (gəlf) The part of a sea or ocean that extends into land, usually larger than a bay. p. I1

harbor (här´bər) A protected area of water where ships can dock safely. p. 20

historical map (hi•stôr´i•kəl map) A map that shows parts of the world as they were in the past. p. I3

historical perspective (hi•stôr´i•kəl pər•spek´tiv) How a person looks at the past. p. 59

human resources (hyoo´mən rē´sôr•səz) The workers who produce goods or provide services. p. 63

igloo (i´gloo) A dome-shaped temporary house made of ice blocks. p. 95

immigrant (i´mi•grənt) A person who comes into a country to make a new life. p. 28

import (im´pôrt) A product brought into a country to be sold. p. 215

impressment (im•pres´mənt) The taking of workers against their will. p. 303

indentured servant (in•den´chərd sûr´vənt) A person who agreed to work for a time without pay for a person who paid for the servant's trip to the colonies. p. 202

independence (in•də•pen´dəns) The freedom to govern on one's own. p. 245

Industrial Revolution (in•dəs´trē•əl rev•ə•loo´shən) The period during the 1800s when machines took the place of hand tools to manufacture goods. p. 333

industry (in´dəs•trē) All the businesses that make one kind of product or provide one kind of service. p. 38

inlet (in´let) An area of water extending into the land from a larger body of water. pp. I1, 29

inset map (in´set map) A smaller map within a larger one. p. I2

interact (in•tə•rakt´) To affect one another. p. 27

interdependence (in•tər•də•pen´dəns) Two or more people or places depending on each other for goods and services. p. 187

intermediate direction (in•tər•mē´dē•ət də•rek´shən) One of the in-between directions: northeast, northwest, southeast, or southwest. p. I3

inventor (in•ven´tər) Someone who is the first to think of or make something. p. 334

irrigation (ir•ə•gā´shən) The use of canals, ditches, or pipes to move water from one place to another. p. 81

isthmus (is´məs) A narrow strip of land connecting two larger areas of land. p. I1

kayak (kī´ak) A one-person canoe made of waterproof skins stretched over bone or wood. p. 94

land use (land yoos) The way most of the land in a place is used. p. 38

locator (lō´kā•tər) A small map or globe that shows where the place on the main map is located within a larger area. p. I2

Loyalist (loi´ə•list) A person who remained loyal to the British king. p. 251

main idea (mān ī•dē´ə) The most important idea in what you read. p. 5

majority rule (mə•jôr´ə•tē rool) The political idea that if more than half the people agree on a law or decision, everyone has to follow it. p. 189

Manifest Destiny (ma´nə•fest des´tə•nē) The idea that the United States was meant to stretch from the Atlantic Ocean to the Pacific Ocean. p. 324

manufacturing (man•yə•fak´chə•ring) The making of goods. p. 335

map legend (map le´jənd) A part of a map that explains the symbols used on the map. p. I2

map scale (map skāl) A part of a map that compares a distance on the map to a distance on Earth. p. I2

map title (map tī´təl) Words on a map that tell the subject of the map. p. I3

market (mär´kət) A place where goods are bought and sold. p. 194

marsh (marsh) Lowland with moist soil and tall grasses. p. I1

mass production (mas prə•dək´shən) The manufacturing of large amounts of goods at one time. p. 336

meridians of longitude (mə•rid´ē•ənz uv län´jə•tood) Lines on a map or globe that run north and south. p. 9

mesa (mā´sa) A flat-topped mountain with steep sides. p. I1

Middle Passage (mi´dəl pa´sij) The journey enslaved Africans were forced to travel across the Atlantic Ocean. p. 210

GLOSSARY

migration (mī•grā´shən) A large movement. p. 324

militia (mə•li´shə) An army of citizens. p. 241

mission (mi´shən) A small religious settlement. p. 157

missionary (mi´shə•ner•ē) A religious teacher. p. 123

monarch (mä´nərk) A king or queen. p. 122

motivate (mō´tə•vāt) To provide a reason for. p. 122

mountain pass (moun´tən pas) A gap between mountains. p. I1

mountain range (moun´tən rānj) A group of connected mountains. pp. I1, 22

mouth of river (mouth uv ri´vər) The place where a river empties into another body of water. p. I1

nationalism (nash´nə•lī•zəm) Pride in one's country. p. 303

natural resource (na´chə•rəl rē´sôrs) Something in nature that people can use to meet their needs. p. 36

naval stores (nā´vəl stōrz) Product or supplies, such as turpentine and tar, used to build ships. p. 186

navigation (na•və•gā´shən) The skill of planning and controlling the course of a ship. p. 128

neutral (nōō´trəl) Not choosing a side. p. 253

O

obstacle (äb´sti•kəl) Something that stands in the way. p. 124

ocean (ō´shən) A large body of salt water. p. 7

P

palisade (pa•lə•sād´) A wall made of tall wooden poles to protect a settlement from enemies. p. 68

parallels of latitude (pâr´ə•lelz uv la´tə•tōōd) Lines on a map or globe that run east and west. p. 9

Patriot (pā´trē•ət) A person who supported independence for the American colonies. p. 251

patriotic slogan (pā•trē•ä´tik slō´gən) A saying that people repeat to express their pride in their country. p. 241

peninsula (pə•nin´sə•lə) A piece of land bordered by water on three sides. pp. I1, 15

petition (pə•ti´shən) A signed request. p. 241

physical map (fi´zi•kəl map) A map that shows kinds of land and bodies of water. p. I3

pioneer (pī•ə•nir´) A person who is one of the first to settle in a place. p. 330

plain (plān) An area of mostly low, flat land. pp. I1, 15

plantation (plan•tā´shən) A large farm. p. 199

planter (plan´tər) A plantation owner. p. 202

plateau (pla•tō´) An area of high, flat land. pp. I1, 15

political map (pə•li´•ti•kəl map) A map that shows cities, states, and countries. p. I3

political party (pə•li´•ti•kəl pär´tē) A group that tries to elect officials who will support its policies. p. 298

popular sovereignty (pä´pyə•lər sä´vərn•tē) The right to decide by vote whether to allow slavery in a place. p. 371

port (pôrt) A place where ships are loaded and unloaded. p. 28

potlatch (pät´lach) A special gathering among American Indians that was meant to express the host's good fortune and to divide property among the people. p. 90

primary source (prī•mer´ē sôrs) A record with a direct link to the past. p. 149

profit (prä´fət) The money left after all costs have been paid. p. 150

proprietor (prə•prī´ə•tər) An owner. p. 181

protest (prō´test) To work against. p. 236

Q

quarter (kwôr´tər) To give food and housing. p. 240

R

ratify (ra´tə•fī) To vote in favor of. p. 292

raw material (rô mə•tir´ē•əl) Any resource that can be used to make a product. p. 151

reform (ri•fôrm´) Change. p. 123

region (rē´jən) An area of Earth with distinctive characteristics that make it different from other areas. p. 19

relief (ri•lēf´) Differences in elevation. p. 16

religious toleration (ri•li´jəs tä•lə•rā´shən) Acceptance of religious differences. p. 196

repeal (ri•pēl´) Cancel. p. 236

representation (re•pri´zen•tā•shən) The act of speaking or acting for someone else. p. 235

republic (ri•pub´lik) A form of government in which citizens choose representatives to run the government. p. 288

resolution (re•zə´lü•shən) A statement of a group's beliefs. p. 246

revenue (re´və•no͞o) Income. p. 235

revolution (rev•ə•lo͞o´shən) A sudden, complete change of government. p. 242

river system (ri´vər sis´təm) A river and its tributaries that drain, or carry water away from, the land around it. p. 30

rural (ro͞or´əl) Relating to the country. p. 36

S

savanna (sə•va´nə) An area of grassland and scattered trees. p. I1

scarce (skers) In short supply. p. 76

sea level (sē le´vəl) The level of the surface of an ocean or a sea. p. I1

secede (si•sēd´) To leave. p. 372

sectionalism (sek´shən•ə•li•zəm) Regional loyalty. p. 363

secondary source (se´kən•der•ē sôrs) A record made by someone who does not have a direct link to an event. p. 149

segregated (se•gri•gā´təd) Keeping people of one race or culture separate from other people. p. 385

separation of powers (se•pə•rā´shən əv pou´ərz) The division of powers among the three branches of government to prevent any one branch from controlling the government. p. 291

separatist (se´pə•rə•tist) A person who wanted to break away from the Church of England. p. 179

sequence (sēk´kwəns) The order in which events happen. p. 111

siege (sēj) A long-lasting attack. p. 388

slave state (slāv stāt) A state that allowed slavery before the Civil War. p. 368

slavery (slā´vər•ē) The practice of holding people against their will and making them work. p. 130

source of river (sôrs uv ri´vər) The place where a river begins. p. I1

specialization (spe•shə•lī•zā´shən) The focusing on making one or more products. p. 186

staple (stā´pəl) Something that is always needed and used. p. 86

GLOSSARY

states' rights (stāts rīts) The idea that the states, not the national government, should have the final say on laws that affect them. p. 364

stock (stäk) Shares of ownership in a company. p. 178

strait (strāt) A narrow channel of water that connects two larger bodies of water. p. I1

suffrage (su´frij) The right to vote. p. 344

suffragist (suf´ri•jist) A supporter of women's suffrage. p. 345

summarize (su´mə•rīz) To state in your own words a shortened version of what you have read. p. 175

supply (sə•plī´) The amount of a product that is offered for sale. p. 144

surplus (sûr´pləs) An extra amount. p. 81

swamp (swamp) An area of low, wet land with trees. p. I1

tariff (tar´əf) A tax on some imports. p. 362

tax (taks) Money collected by a government to pay for government services. p. 215

technology (tek•nä´lə•jē) The use of scientific knowledge or tools to make or do something. p. 127

territory (ter´ə•tôr•ē) A land that belongs to a nation but is not a state and is not represented in the national government. p. 321

textile (tek´stīl) Cloth. p. 334

topography (tə•pä´grə•fē) The physical features of a place. p. 376

town meeting (taûn mē´ting) In colonial New England, a meeting where citizens of a town voted on laws and elected town leaders. p. 189

tradition (trə•dish´ən) An idea, belief, or way of doing things that has been handed down from the past. p. 71

travois (trə•vôi´) A carrier made up of two poles tied together at one end and fastened to a harness on a dog or horse. p. 76

treaty (trē´tē) An agreement between countries that satisfies people on different sides. p. 262

triangular trade routes (trī•an´gyə•lər trād rōots) Ocean routes that connected England, the English colonies, and Africa. p. 187

tributary (tri´byə•ter•ē) A river that flows into a larger river. pp. I1, 14

tundra (tən´drə) A cold, dry treeless plain. p. 25

turning point (tər´ning point) An event that causes an important change. p. 254

Underground Railroad (un´dər•ground rāl´rōd) A system of secret escape routes that led enslaved African Americans to free lands. p. 343

urban (ûr´bən) Relating to the city. p. 36

veto (vē´tō) to reject. p. 291

volcano (vol•kā´nō) An opening in Earth, often raised, through which lava, rock, ashes, and gases are forced out. p. I1

wampum (wäm´pəm) Shell beads used by American Indians for recordkeeping and trade. p. 70

Index

The Index lets you know where information about important people, places, and events appear in the book. All key words, or entries, are listed in alphabetical order. For each entry, the page reference indicates where information about that entry can be found in the text. An italic *m* indicates a map. Page references set in boldface type indicate the pages on which vocabulary terms are defined. Related entries are cross-referenced with *See* or *See also*. Guide words at the top of the pages help you identify which words appear on which page.

INDEX

INDEX

INDEX

INDEX

VIRGINIA HISTORY AND SOCIAL SCIENCE STANDARDS OF LEARNING

Skills

USI.1 The student will demonstrate responsible citizenship and develop skills for historical and geographical analysis, including the ability to

a) identify and interpret primary and secondary source documents to increase understanding of events and life in United States history to 1865;

b) make connections between the past and the present;

c) sequence events in United States history from pre-Columbian times to 1865;

d) interpret ideas and events from different historical perspectives;

e) evaluate and discuss issues orally and in writing;

f) analyze and interpret maps to explain relationships among landforms, water features, climatic characteristics, and historical events;

g) distinguish between parallels of latitude and meridians of longitude;

h) interpret patriotic slogans and excerpts from notable speeches and documents;

i) identify the costs and benefits of specific choices made, including the intended and unintended consequences of the choices and how people and nations responded to positive and negative incentives.

Geography

USI.2 The student will use maps, globes, photographs, pictures, or tables to

a) locate the seven continents and five oceans;

b) locate and describe the location of the geographic regions of North America: Coastal Plain, Appalachian Mountains, Canadian Shield, Interior Lowlands, Great Plains, Rocky Mountains, Basin and Range, and Coastal Range;

c) locate and identify the water features important to the early history of the United States: Great Lakes, Mississippi River, Missouri River, Ohio River, Columbia River, Colorado River, Rio Grande, St. Lawrence River, Atlantic Ocean, Pacific Ocean, and Gulf of Mexico;

d) recognize key geographic features on maps, diagrams, and/or photographs.

Exploration to Revolution: Pre-Columbian Times to the 1770s

USI.3 The student will demonstrate knowledge of how early cultures developed in North America by

a) describing how archaeologists have recovered material evidence of early settlements including Cactus Hill;

b) locating where the American Indians lived, with emphasis on Arctic (Inuit), Northwest (Kwakiutl), Plains (Lakota); Southwest (Pueblo), and Eastern Woodland (Iroquois);

c) describing how the American Indians used the resources in their environment.

USI.4 The student will demonstrate knowledge of European exploration in North America and West Africa by

a) describing the motivations, obstacles, and accomplishments of the Spanish, French, Portuguese, and English explorations;

b) describing cultural and economic interactions between Europeans and American Indians that led to cooperation and conflict with emphasis on the American Indian concept of land;

c) identifying the location and describing the characteristics of West African societies (Ghana, Mali, and Songhai) and their interactions with traders.

USI.5 **The student will demonstrate knowledge of the factors that shaped colonial America by**

a) describing the religious and economic events and conditions that led to the colonization of America;

b) describing life in the New England, Mid-Atlantic, and Southern colonies, with emphasis on how people interacted with their environment to produce goods and services, including examples of specialization and interdependence;

c) describing colonial life in America from the perspectives of large landowners, farmers, artisans, women, free African Americans, indentured servants, and enslaved African Americans;

d) identifying the political and economic relationships between the colonies and Great Britain.

Revolution and the New Nation: 1770s to the Early 1800s

USI.6 **The student will demonstrate knowledge of the causes and results of the American Revolution by**

a) identifying the issues of dissatisfaction that led to the American Revolution.

b) identifying how political ideas shaped the revolutionary movement in America and led to the Declaration of Independence;

c) describing key events and the roles of key individuals in the American Revolution, with emphasis on George Washington, Benjamin Franklin, Thomas Jefferson, and Patrick Henry;

d) explaining reasons why the colonies were able to defeat Britain.

USI.7 **The student will demonstrate knowledge of the challenges faced by the new nation by**

a) identifying the weaknesses of the government established by the Articles of Confederation;

b) describing the historical developments of the Constitution of the United States;

c) describing the major accomplishments of the first five Presidents of the United States.

Expansion and Reform: 1801 to 1861

USI.8 **The student will demonstrate knowledge of westward expansion and reform in America from 1801 to 1861 by**

a) describing territorial expansion and how it affected the political map of the United States, with emphasis on the Louisiana Purchase, the Lewis and Clark expedition, and the acquisitions of Florida, Texas, Oregon, and California;

b) identifying the geographic and economic factors that influenced the westward movement of settlers;

c) describing the impact of inventions, including the cotton gin, the reaper, the steamboat, and the steam locomotive, on life in America;

d) identifying the main ideas of the abolitionist and suffrage movements.

Civil War: 1861–1865

USI.9 **The student will demonstrate knowledge of the causes, major events, and effects of the Civil War by**

a) describing the cultural, economic, and constitutional issues that divided the nation;

b) explaining how the issues of states' rights and slavery increased sectional tensions;

c) identifying on a map the states that seceded from the Union and those that remained in the Union;

d) describing the roles of Abraham Lincoln, Jefferson Davis, Ulysses S. Grant, Robert E. Lee, Thomas "Stonewall" Jackson, and Frederick Douglass in events leading to and during the war;

e) using maps to explain critical developments in the war, including major battles;

f) describing the effects of war from the perspectives of Union and Confederate soldiers (including black soldiers), women, and enslaved African Americans.

217, Courtesy of APVA Preservation Virginia. Page 225, Francis G. Mayer/Corbis; 228, ©Stock Montage; 228 (bl), ©The Granger Collection, New York; 228 (br), The Granger Collection, New York; 229, The Art Archive / Musée du Château de Versailles / Alfredo Dagli Orti; 230 (tr), MPI/Getty Images; 230 (br), North Wind Picture Archives / Alamy; 234, NTPL / Christopher Hurst/The Image Works; 235 (l), Colonial Williamsburg Foundation; 235 (r), SuperStock, Inc /SuperStock; 237 (b), Massachusetts Historical Society; Boston, MA; USA/Bridgeman Art Library; 237 (t), ©Stock Montage; 238, The Granger Collection, New York; 239, ©Eliot Cohen/Janelco; 243, (l), The Granger Collection, New York; 244 (b), The Granger Collection, New York; 245, Dennis Degnan/Corbis; 246(r), The Granger Collection, New York; 246 (c), The Granger Collection, New York; 246 (l), © Bildarchiv Monheim GmbH / Alamy; 249 (tl), Smithsonian Institiution; 249 (tr), Bettmann/Corbis; 249 (bl), Independence National Historical Park; 250, Réunion des Musées Nationaux / Art Resource, NY; 251, © North Wind / Nancy Carter\ North Wind Picture Archives -- All rights reserved.; 252 (r), Darlene Bordwell / Ambient Light Photography; 253 (tl), Independence National Historical Park; 254 (r), Painting by Don Troiani / Historical Art Prints; 254 (l), Painting by Don Troiani / Historical Art Prints; 255, ©SuperStock; 257, © The Corcoran Gallery of Art/ CORBIS; 261 (br), Yorktown Victory Center; 261 ROY ANDERSEN/National Geographic Stock; 262 (c), Library of Congress Prints & Photographs Division; 262, The Art Archive / Musée du Château de Versailles / Alfredo Dagli Orti; 262, Bettmann/CORBIS; 263 (l), Painting by Don Troiani / Historical Art Prints; 263 (r), The Granger Collection, New York; 264 (bc), Statue of George Washington in Trafalgar Square, London (bronze), Houdon, Jean-Antoine (1741-1828) (after) / Private Collection, / The Bridgeman Art Library; 264 (bl), North Wind Picture Archives / Alamy; 264 (r), Bettmann / Corbis; 265, © SuperStock, Inc. / SuperStock; 269, Massachusetts Historical Society; Boston, MA; USA/Bridgeman Art Library. Page 273, © Bill Ross/CORBIS; 276 (b), ©SuperStock; 277 (bl), ©SuperStock; 278 (bc), JupiterImages / Comstock Images / Alamy; 278 (tl), © Joseph Sohm/Visions of America/Corbis; 278 (tr), Künstler Enterprises; 281, Ellen Issacs / Alamy; 283 (bl), (br), The Granger Collection, New York; 283 (c), American flag, c.1781 (wool & cotton) American flag, c.1781 (wool & cotton), American School, (18th century) / © Collection of the New-York Historical Society, USA / The Bridgeman Art Library International; 283 (tl), The Granger Collection, New York; 283 (tr), © British Museum / Art Resource, NY; 286, Art Resource, NY; 287, Lee Foster / Alamy; 290 (b), Independence National Historical Park; 291 (l), Library of Congress Prints & Photographs Division; 291 (bc), Library of Congress Prints & Photographs Division; 291 (br), The Art Archive / Laurie Platt Winfrey; 292, Alex Wong/Getty Images; 293 (c), Joanna McCarthy / Getty Images; 293 (l), Ellen McKnight/Alamy; 294, Künstler Enterprises; 295, Mount Vernon Ladies' Association; 296 (l), The New York Public Library / Art Resource, NY; 296 (r), Portrait of George Washington, 1796 (oil on canvas), Stuart, Gilbert (1755-1828) / Brooklyn Museum of Art, New York, USA / The Bridgeman Art Library; 298 (l), John Adams (oil on canvas), Otis, Bass (1784-1861) (attr. to) / © Collection of the New-York Historical Society, USA, / The Bridgeman Art Library; 298 (r), © David J. & Janice L. Frent Collection/ CORBIS; 299 (l), Library of Congress Prints & Photographs Division; 299 (r), The Granger Collection, New York; 300, The Art Archive /

Laurie Platt Winfrey; 301, Karl Kost / Alamy; 302, Portrait of Thomas Jefferson, c.1835 (oil on canvas), Durand, Asher Brown (1796-1886) / © Collection of the New-York Historical Society, USA / The Bridgeman Art Library; 303, James Madison (oil on canvas), American School, (19th century) / Musee Franco-Americaine, Blerancourt, Chauny, France / Giraudon / The Bridgeman Art Library; 304 (l), The City of Washington from beyond the Navy Yard, engraved by William James Bennett, c.1824 (aquatint), Cooke, George (1793-1849) / Library of Congress, Washington D.C., USA / The Bridgeman Art Library International; 304, © North Wind Picture Archives / Alamy; 304 (r), © Heymo Vehse / Alamy; 305, Photos12/ Alamy. Page 313, Dave G. Houser/Corbis; 321, Sacagawea with Lewis and Clark during their expedition of 1804-06 (colour litho), Wyeth, Newell Convers (1882-1945) / Private Collection / Peter Newark American Pictures / The Bridgeman Art Library; 322 (c), ©The Granger Collection, New York; 322, Painting "Lewis and Clark: The Departure from St. Charles, May 21, 1804" by Gary R. Lucy. Courtesy of the Gary R. Lucy Gallery, Inc., Washington, MO - www.garylucy. com <http://www.garylucy.com> ; 322-323(bg), The Library of Congress Geography and Map Division; 323 (bl), Excerpt from "Lewis and Clark Meeting the Indians at Ross' Hole" by Charles M. Russell, Oil on Canvas 1912, Mural in State of Montana Capitol, Courtesy of the Montana Historical Society, Don Beatty photographer 10/1999; 323 (tl), ©Künstler Enterprises; 323 (tr), ©Stanley Meltzoff; 323, Breton Litllehales / National Geographic Stock; 323 (br), ©Henry Francis Dupont Winterthur Museum, Delaware, USA/Bridgeman Art Library; 324, © www. shinepicturesuk.com / Alamy; 326, © Smithsonian Institution/Corbis; 329, Henry Guttmann / Hulton Archive / Getty Images; 329 (t), Robert Fulton (1765-1815) (oil on canvas), American School / Private Collection / Peter Newark American Pictures / The Bridgeman Art Library; 332, Corel Stock Photo Library; 332, Getty Images Royalty Free; 333, N C Wyeth / WHS / Classicstock.com; 334, (bl), Detail from Morse, Samuel Finley Breese (1791-1872) Eli Whitney (1765-1825) B.A. 1792, M.A. 1795. 1822. Oil on canvas. 91.1 x 70.5 x 2.5 cm (35 7/8 x 27 3/4 x 1 in.). Gift of George Hoadley, B.A. 1801. 1827.1 Yale University Art Gallery / Art Resource, NY; 334 (r), © Bettmann/CORBIS; 339(tl), (tr), , The Granger Collection, New York; 339, © Bettmann/CORBIS; 339 (br), McCormick Harvesting Machine Company / WHS / ClassicStock; 339 (bl), © Bettmann/CORBIS; 340, © Bettmann/CORBIS; 341, Andre Jenny / Alamy; 344 (r), Hulton Archive/Getty Images; 344 (cr), Artville / Getty Images; 345, Hulton-Deutsch Collection/CORBIS; 347, © SuperStock, Inc. / SuperStock. Page 353, The Art Archive / Gettysburg National Military Park / Laurie Platt Winfrey; 356 (t), SEF / Art Resource, NY; 357 (tr), Library of Congress; 358, Library of Congress Prints and Photographs Division; 358, The Granger Collection, New York; 358 (bc), Library of Congress/AP Photo; 358 (br), Mort Künstler Enterprises / Künstler Enterprises Ltd.; 361, © Buddy Mays/CORBIS; 362, Power loom weaving, 1834 (engraving), Allom, Thomas (1804-72) (after) / Private Collection / The Bridgeman Art Library International; 363 (b), © CORBIS; 363 (inset), The Art Archive / Graham and Schweitzer Gallery New York / Laurie Platt Winfrey; 364 (l), Bettmann / CORBIS; 364 (r), John Caldwell Calhoun (1782-1850) c.1845 (oil on canvas), Lambdin, James Reid (1807-89) / © Chicago History Museum, USA / The Bridgeman Art Library; 365 (tr), The Granger Collection, New York; 365 (l), Library of Congress Prints & Photographs Division; 366, Runaway

slave poster from Kentucky, USA (print), American School, (19th century) / © Wilberforce House, Hull City Museums and Art Galleries, UK / The Bridgeman Art Library; 367, Art Resource, NY; 368, The Slave Market (oil on canvas), Schulz, Friedrich (1823-75) / Hirshhorn Museum, Washington D.C., USA / The Bridgeman Art Library; 371 (r), The Granger Collection, New York; 371 (l), Poster calling for a Free State Convention in Kansas, 1855 (litho), American School, (19th century) / Private Collection / Peter Newark American Pictures / The Bridgeman Art Library; 374, Headline from the 'Boston Evening Transcript' announcing the beginning of the Civil War, 13th April, 1861 (newsprint), American School, (19th century) / American Antiquarian Society, Worcester, Massachusetts, USA / The Bridgeman Art Library; 375, Mort Künstler, Künstler Enterprises Ltd.; 376, © The Corcoran Gallery of Art/CORBIS; 377 (bl), The Gettysburg Address, 1863 (oil), Ferris, Jean Leon Jerome (1863-1930) / Private Collection / The Bridgeman Art Library; 377 (c), © Bettmann/CORBIS; 377 (cl), © CORBIS; 378 (t) , Don Troiani / Historical Art Prints; 378, (inset), © The Corcoran Gallery of Art/ CORBIS; 379 (l), Richard Nowitz / Getty Images; 379 (r), Library of Congress Prints & Photographs Division; 380, Portrait of Frederick Douglass (1817-95) (oil on canvas), American School, (19th century) / Frederick Douglass National Historic Site, Washington, USA / The Bridgeman Art Library International; 383, (tl), (tr), Historical Image Bank; 383 (tc), Library of Congress Prints & Photographs Division; 383 (bl), (bc), (br), © Tria Giovan/CORBIS; 383 (cr), Military and Historical Image Bank; 383 (cl) , Dave King / DK Images; 384, A nurse attending the wounded at the Federal hospital in Nashville, Tennessee (b/w photo), American Photographer, (19th century) / Private Collection / Peter Newark American Pictures / The Bridgeman Art Library International; 385, Library of Congress Prints & Photographs Division; 386, Historical Image Bank; 387, Library of Congress Prints & Photographs Division; 388, Mort Künstler, Künstler Enterprises Ltd.; 390, Painting by Peter F. Rothermel, The State Museum of Pennsylvania, Pennsylvania Historical and Museum Commission; 391 (inset), Mort Künstler / Künstler Enterprises Ltd.; 392 (br), The Fall of Richmond, Virginia, 2nd April 1865 (colour litho), Currier, N. (1813-88) and Ives, J.M. (1824-95) / Private Collection / The Bridgeman Art Library International; 392, (l), (c), Library of Congress Prints & Photographs Division; 393 (r), The Granger Collection, New York; 393 (b), Portrait of Abraham Lincoln (oil on canvas), Healy, George Peter Alexander (1808-94) / National Portrait Gallery, Smithsonian Institution, USA / Photo © Boltin Picture Library / The Bridgeman Art Library.

All other photos from Houghton Mifflin Harcourt Photo Library and Photographers.